Graphic Classics:
RAFAEL SABATINI

Graphic Classics Volume Thirteen
2006

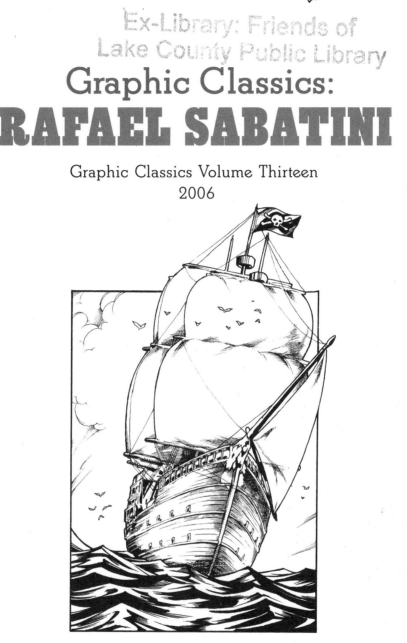

Edited by Tom Pomplun

EUREKA PRODUCTIONS
8778 Oak Grove Road, Mount Horeb, Wisconsin 53572
www.graphicclassics.com

ILLUSTRATION ©2006 CARLO VERGARA

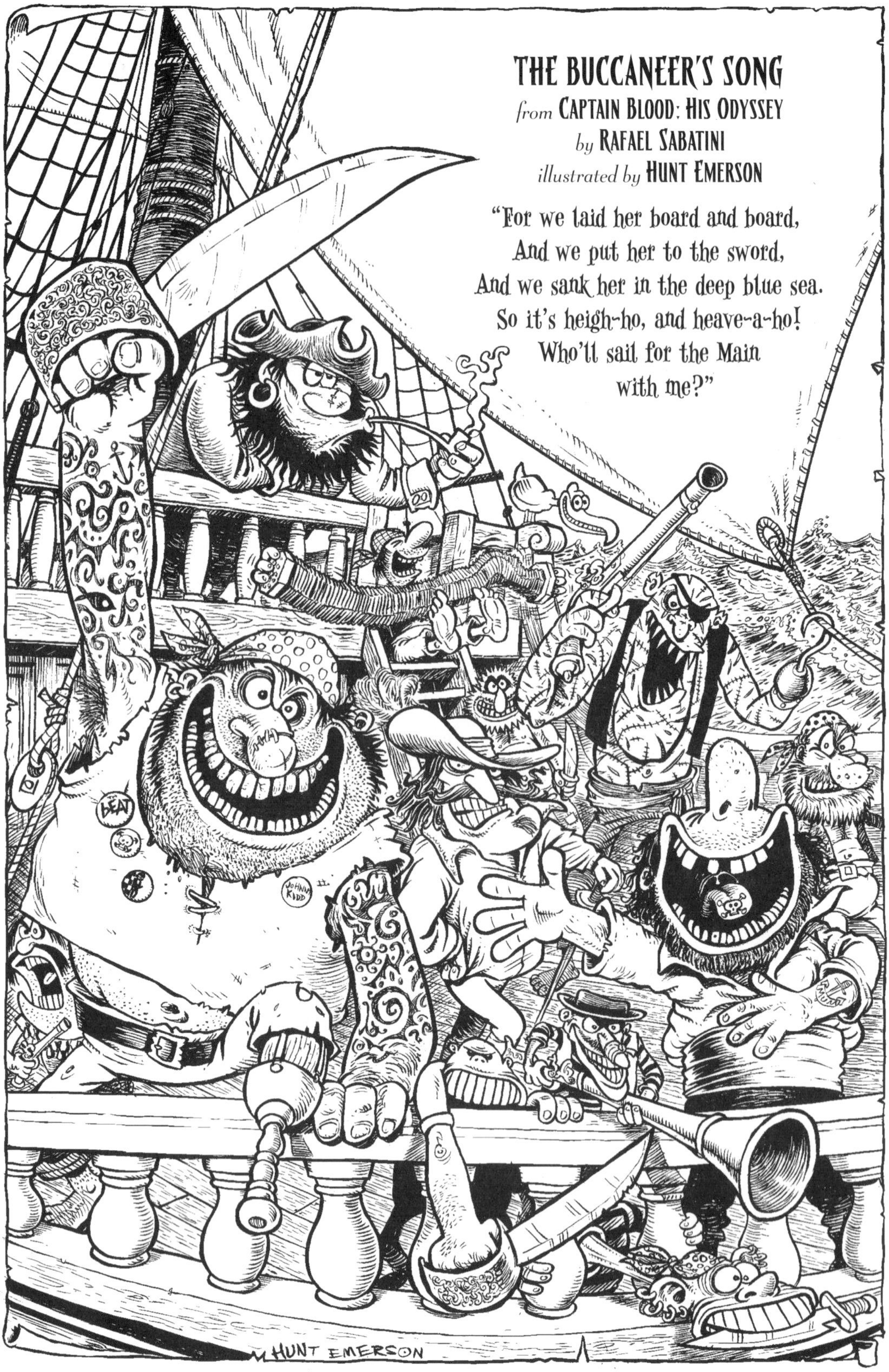
THE BUCCANEER'S SONG
from CAPTAIN BLOOD: HIS ODYSSEY
by RAFAEL SABATINI
illustrated by HUNT EMERSON
"For we laid her board and board,
And we put her to the sword,
And we sank her in the deep blue sea.
So it's heigh-ho, and heave-a-ho!
Who'll sail for the Main
with me?"
HUNT EMERSON

Graphic Classics:
RAFAEL SABATINI

©2006 ROGER LANGRIDGE

Cover illustration by Joel F. Naprstek / Back cover illustration by Milton Knight

Graphic Classics: Rafael Sabatini is published by Eureka Productions. ISBN:13 #978-0-9746648-6-6 / ISBN:10 #0-9746648-6-3. Price US $11.95. Available from Eureka Productions, 8778 Oak Grove Road, Mount Horeb, WI 53572. Tom Pomplun, designer and publisher, tom@graphicclassics.com. Eileen Fitzgerald, editorial assistant. Compilation and all original works ©2006 Eureka Productions. All rights revert to creators after publication. Graphic Classics is a trademark of Eureka Productions. For ordering information and previews of upcoming volumes visit the Graphic Classics website at http://www.graphicclassics.com. Printed in Canada.

Rafael Sabatini's Captain Blood

Adaptation by **Rod Lott** • Illustrated by **Carlo Vergara**

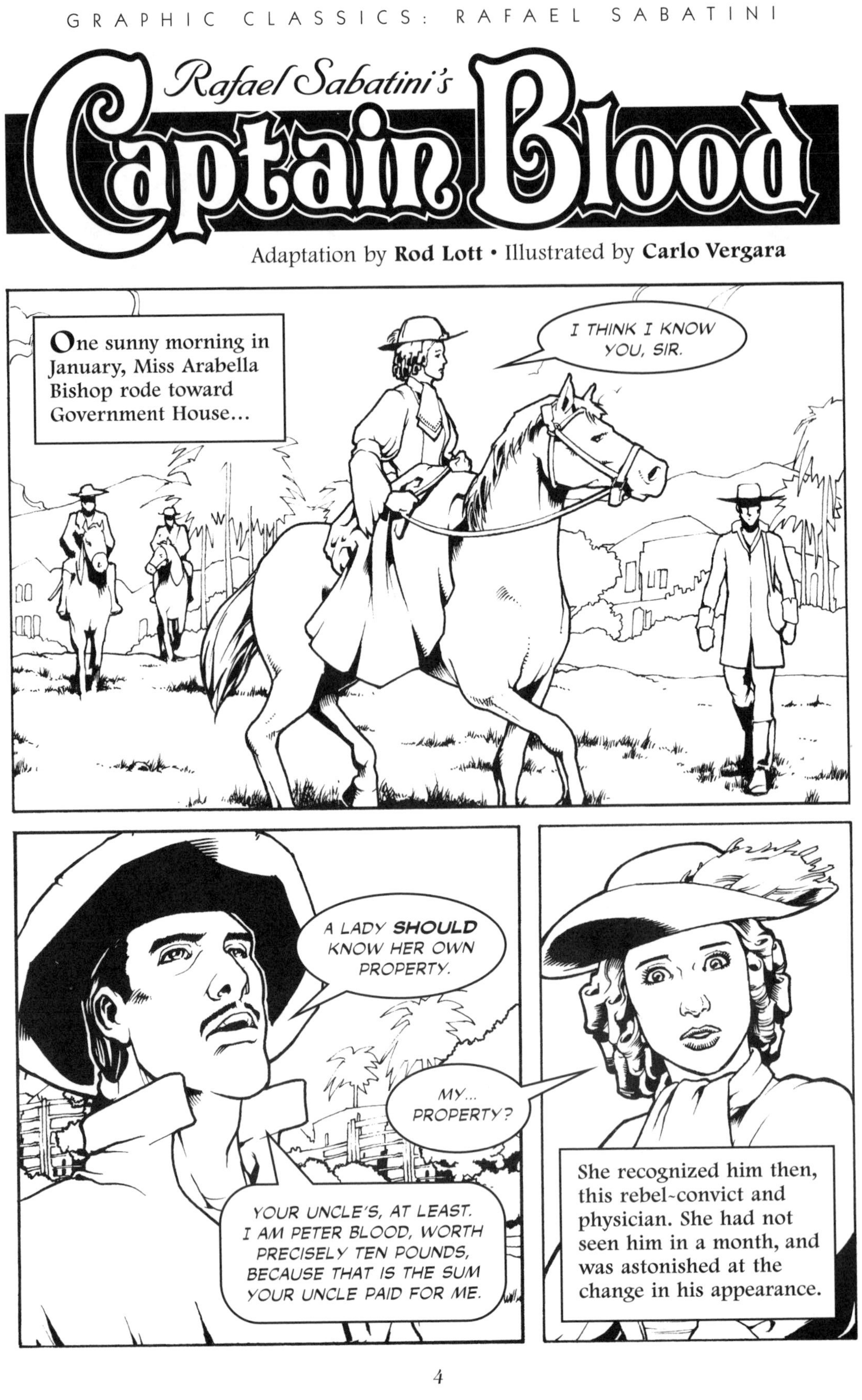
One sunny morning in January, Miss Arabella Bishop rode toward Government House...
I THINK I KNOW YOU, SIR.
A LADY **SHOULD** KNOW HER OWN PROPERTY.
MY... PROPERTY?
YOUR UNCLE'S, AT LEAST. I AM PETER BLOOD, WORTH PRECISELY TEN POUNDS, BECAUSE THAT IS THE SUM YOUR UNCLE PAID FOR ME.
She recognized him then, this rebel-convict and physician. She had not seen him in a month, and was astonished at the change in his appearance.

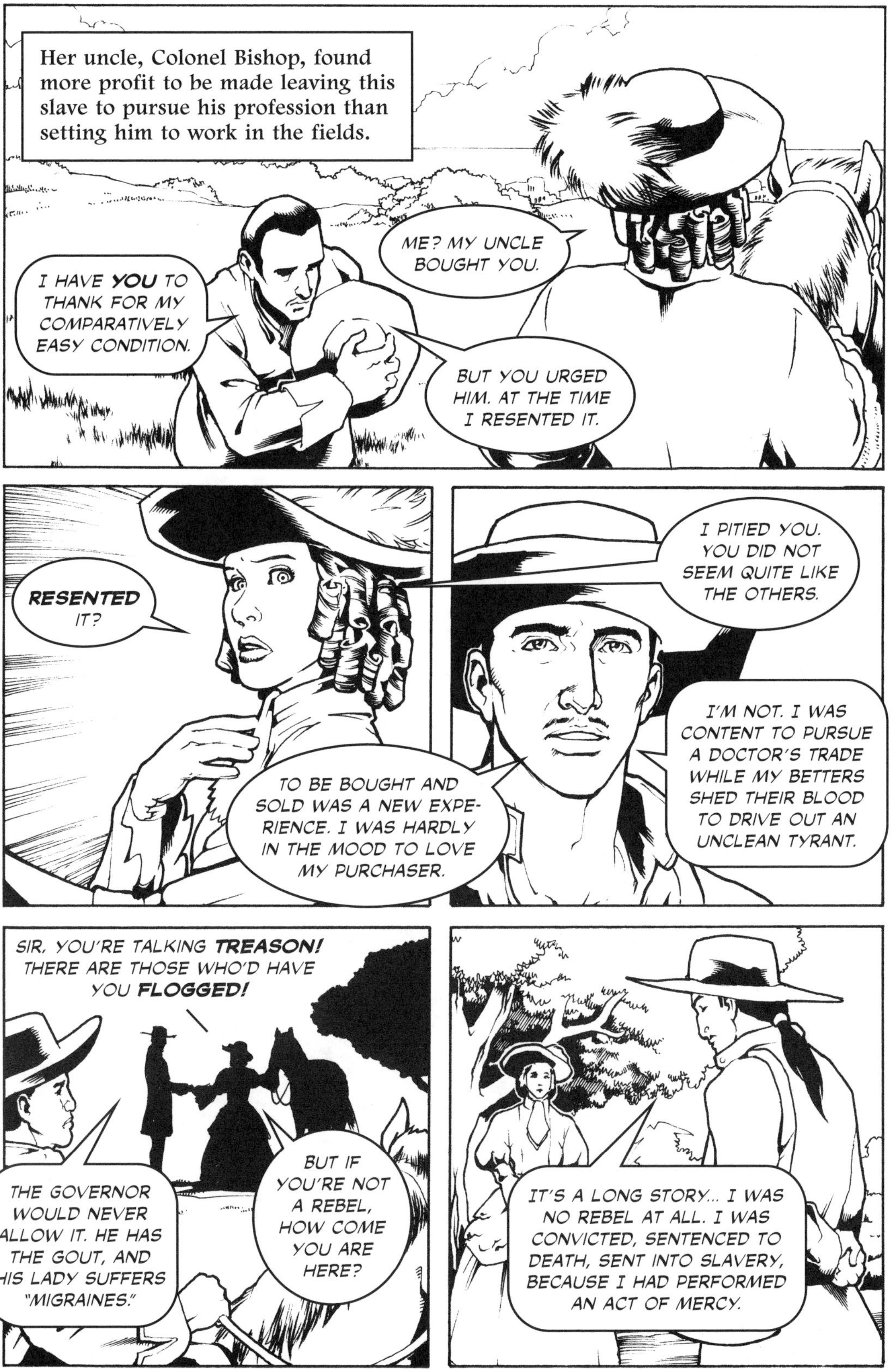
Her uncle, Colonel Bishop, found more profit to be made leaving this slave to pursue his profession than setting him to work in the fields.
I HAVE YOU TO THANK FOR MY COMPARATIVELY EASY CONDITION.
ME? MY UNCLE BOUGHT YOU.
BUT YOU URGED HIM. AT THE TIME I RESENTED IT.
RESENTED IT?
I PITIED YOU. YOU DID NOT SEEM QUITE LIKE THE OTHERS.
TO BE BOUGHT AND SOLD WAS A NEW EXPE-RIENCE. I WAS HARDLY IN THE MOOD TO LOVE MY PURCHASER.
I'M NOT. I WAS CONTENT TO PURSUE A DOCTOR'S TRADE WHILE MY BETTERS SHED THEIR BLOOD TO DRIVE OUT AN UNCLEAN TYRANT.
SIR, YOU'RE TALKING TREASON! THERE ARE THOSE WHO'D HAVE YOU FLOGGED!
THE GOVERNOR WOULD NEVER ALLOW IT. HE HAS THE GOUT, AND HIS LADY SUFFERS "MIGRAINES."
BUT IF YOU'RE NOT A REBEL, HOW COME YOU ARE HERE?
IT'S A LONG STORY... I WAS NO REBEL AT ALL. I WAS CONVICTED, SENTENCED TO DEATH, SENT INTO SLAVERY, BECAUSE I HAD PERFORMED AN ACT OF MERCY.

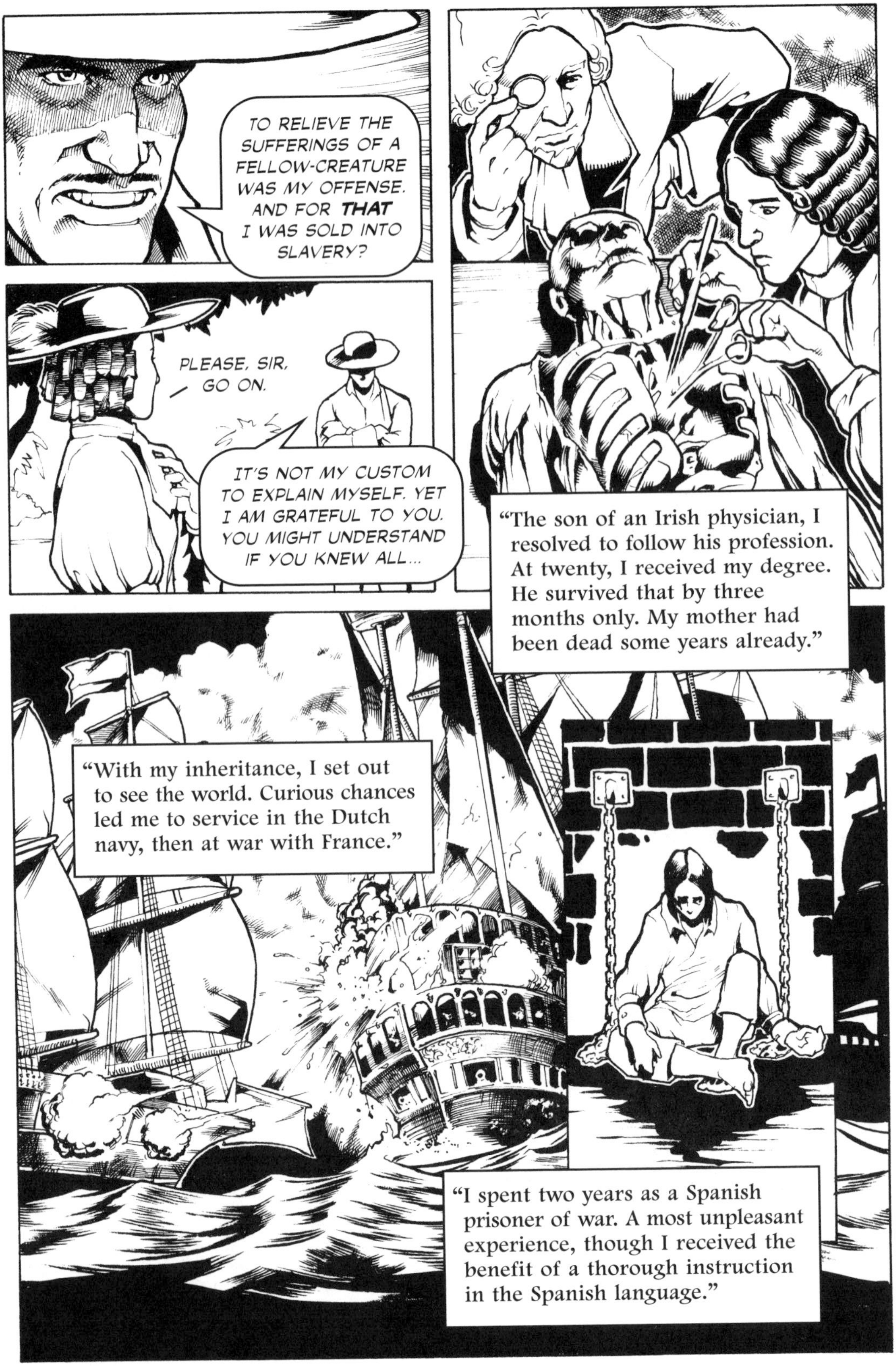
TO RELIEVE THE SUFFERINGS OF A FELLOW-CREATURE WAS MY OFFENSE. AND FOR **THAT** I WAS SOLD INTO SLAVERY?
PLEASE, SIR, GO ON.
IT'S NOT MY CUSTOM TO EXPLAIN MYSELF. YET I AM GRATEFUL TO YOU. YOU MIGHT UNDERSTAND IF YOU KNEW ALL...
"The son of an Irish physician, I resolved to follow his profession. At twenty, I received my degree. He survived that by three months only. My mother had been dead some years already."
"With my inheritance, I set out to see the world. Curious chances led me to service in the Dutch navy, then at war with France."
"I spent two years as a Spanish prisoner of war. A most unpleasant experience, though I received the benefit of a thorough instruction in the Spanish language."

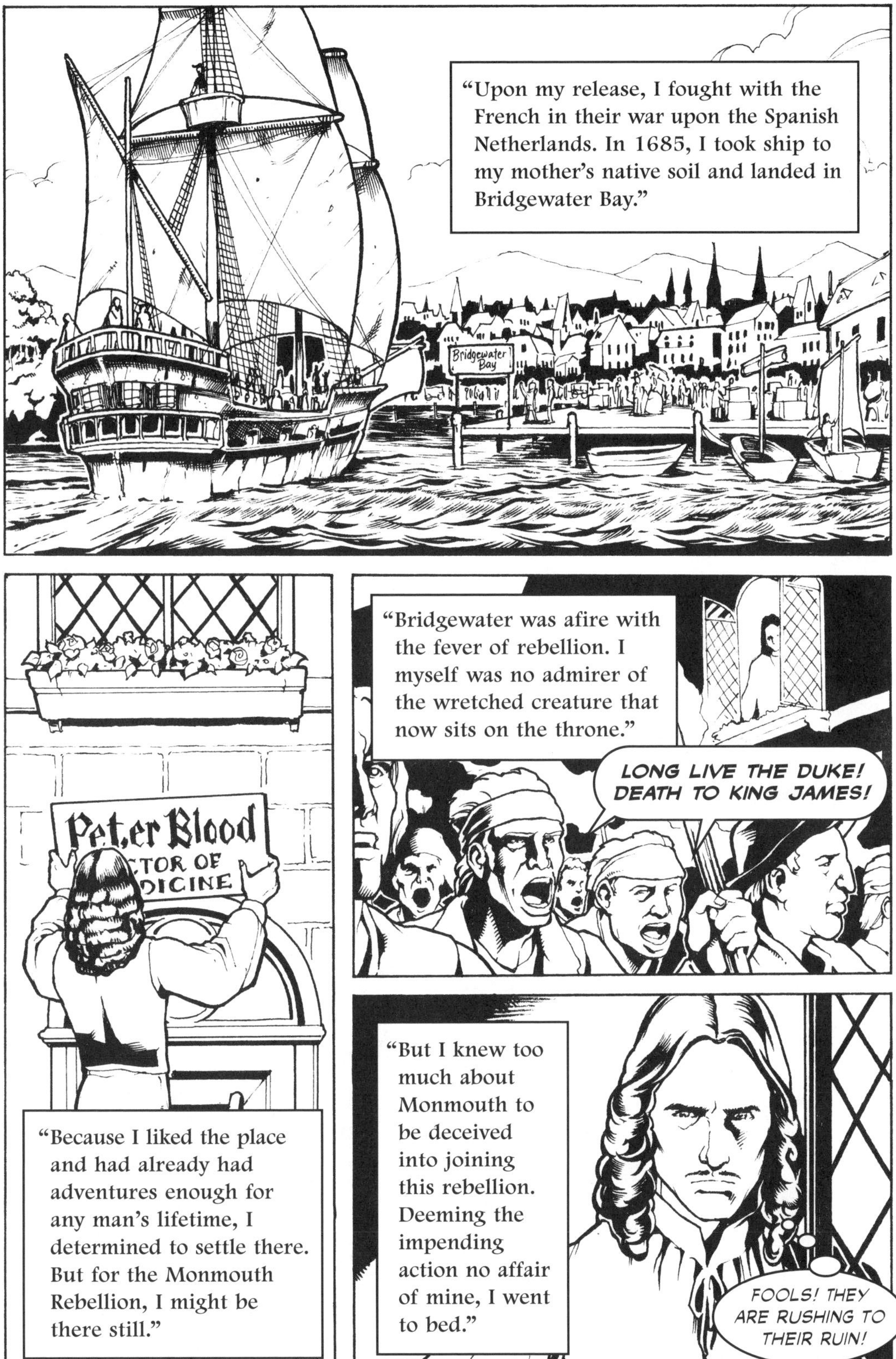
"Upon my release, I fought with the French in their war upon the Spanish Netherlands. In 1685, I took ship to my mother's native soil and landed in Bridgewater Bay."
Bridgewater Bay
Peter Blood
CTOR OF
DICINE
"Because I liked the place and had already had adventures enough for any man's lifetime, I determined to settle there. But for the Monmouth Rebellion, I might be there still."
"Bridgewater was afire with the fever of rebellion. I myself was no admirer of the wretched creature that now sits on the throne."
LONG LIVE THE DUKE! DEATH TO KING JAMES!
"But I knew too much about Monmouth to be deceived into joining this rebellion. Deeming the impending action no affair of mine, I went to bed."
FOOLS! THEY ARE RUSHING TO THEIR RUIN!

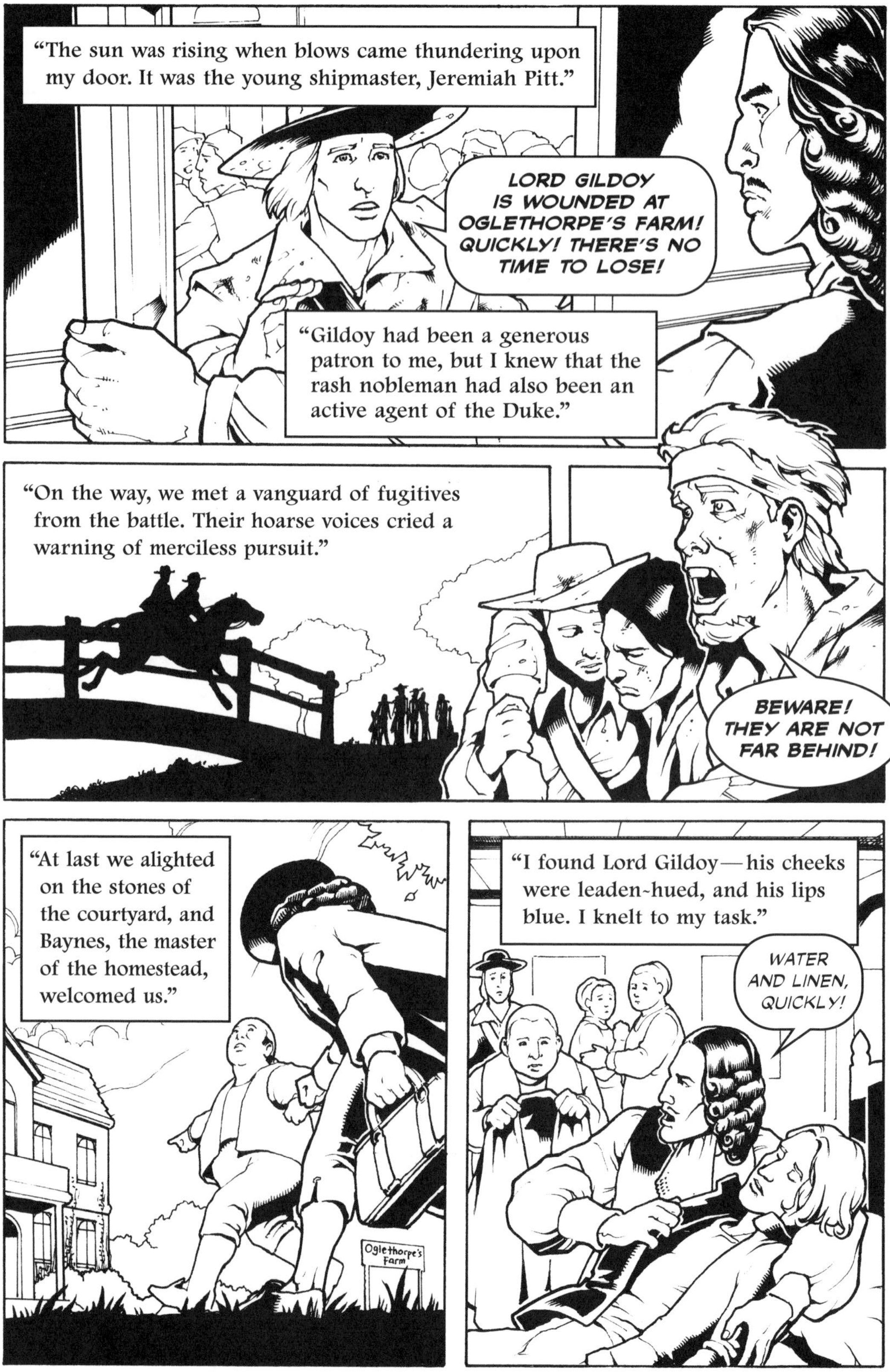
"The sun was rising when blows came thundering upon my door. It was the young shipmaster, Jeremiah Pitt."
LORD GILDOY IS WOUNDED AT OGLETHORPE'S FARM! QUICKLY! THERE'S NO TIME TO LOSE!
"Gildoy had been a generous patron to me, but I knew that the rash nobleman had also been an active agent of the Duke."
"On the way, we met a vanguard of fugitives from the battle. Their hoarse voices cried a warning of merciless pursuit."
BEWARE! THEY ARE NOT FAR BEHIND!
"At last we alighted on the stones of the courtyard, and Baynes, the master of the homestead, welcomed us."
Oglethorpe's Farm
"I found Lord Gildoy—his cheeks were leaden-hued, and his lips blue. I knelt to my task."
WATER AND LINEN, QUICKLY!

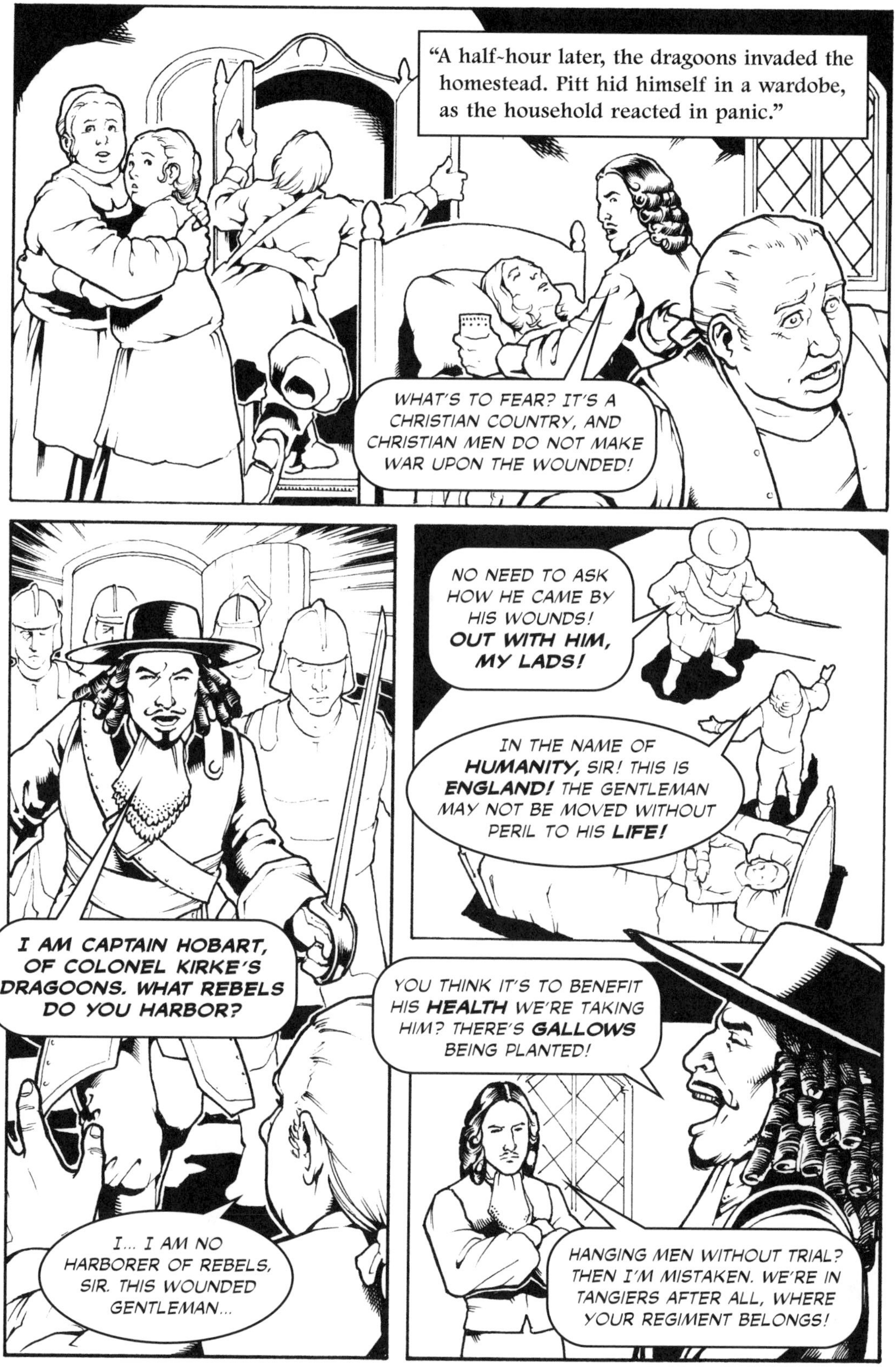
"A half-hour later, the dragoons invaded the homestead. Pitt hid himself in a wardobe, as the household reacted in panic."
WHAT'S TO FEAR? IT'S A CHRISTIAN COUNTRY, AND CHRISTIAN MEN DO NOT MAKE WAR UPON THE WOUNDED!
I AM CAPTAIN HOBART, OF COLONEL KIRKE'S DRAGOONS. WHAT REBELS DO YOU HARBOR?
I... I AM NO HARBORER OF REBELS, SIR. THIS WOUNDED GENTLEMAN...
NO NEED TO ASK HOW HE CAME BY HIS WOUNDS! OUT WITH HIM, MY LADS!
IN THE NAME OF HUMANITY, SIR! THIS IS ENGLAND! THE GENTLEMAN MAY NOT BE MOVED WITHOUT PERIL TO HIS LIFE!
YOU THINK IT'S TO BENEFIT HIS HEALTH WE'RE TAKING HIM? THERE'S GALLOWS BEING PLANTED!
HANGING MEN WITHOUT TRIAL? THEN I'M MISTAKEN. WE'RE IN TANGIERS AFTER ALL, WHERE YOUR REGIMENT BELONGS!

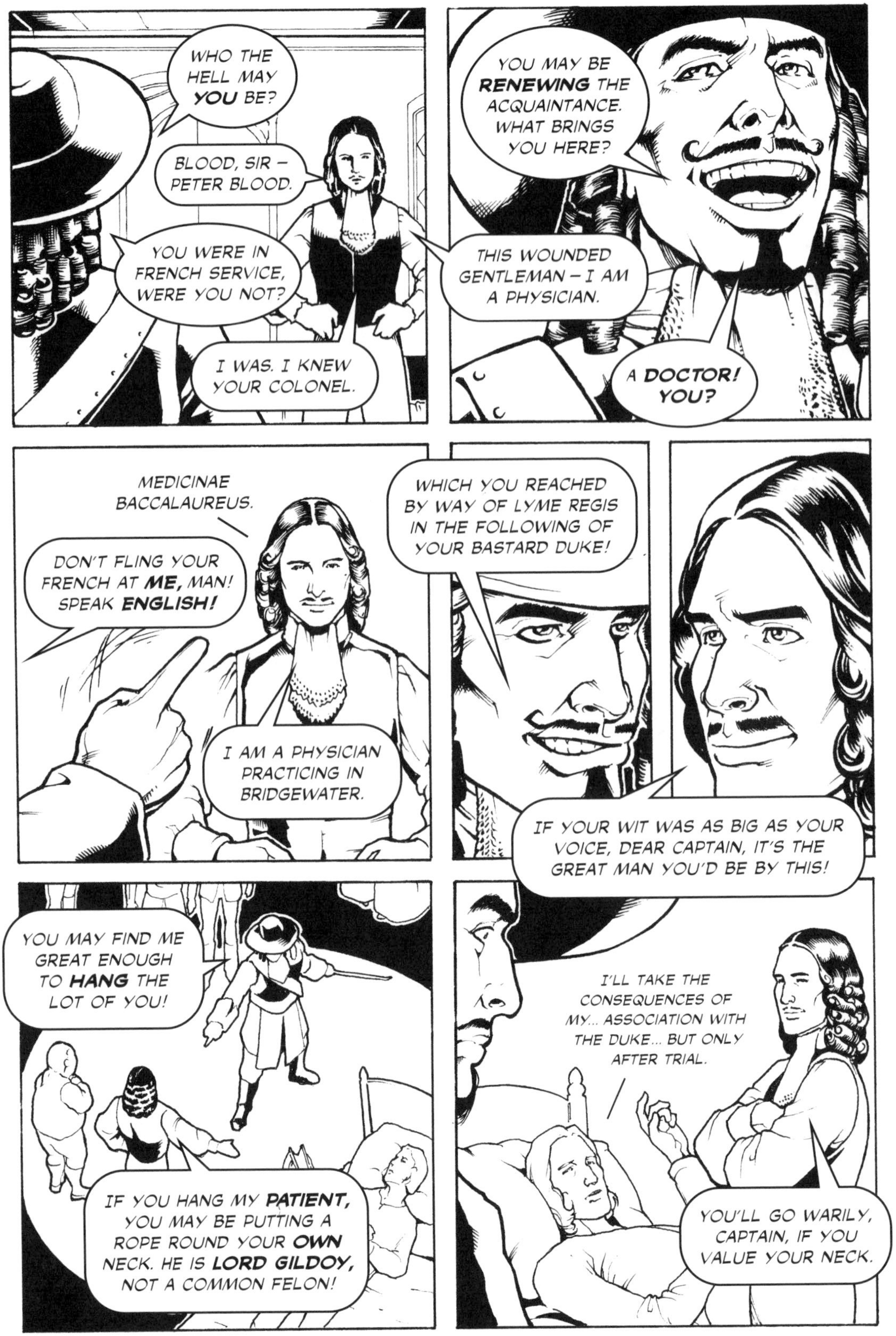
WHO THE HELL MAY YOU BE?
BLOOD, SIR – PETER BLOOD.
YOU WERE IN FRENCH SERVICE, WERE YOU NOT?
I WAS. I KNEW YOUR COLONEL.
YOU MAY BE RENEWING THE ACQUAINTANCE. WHAT BRINGS YOU HERE?
THIS WOUNDED GENTLEMAN – I AM A PHYSICIAN.
A DOCTOR! YOU?
MEDICINAE BACCALAUREUS.
DON'T FLING YOUR FRENCH AT ME, MAN! SPEAK ENGLISH!
I AM A PHYSICIAN PRACTICING IN BRIDGEWATER.
WHICH YOU REACHED BY WAY OF LYME REGIS IN THE FOLLOWING OF YOUR BASTARD DUKE!
IF YOUR WIT WAS AS BIG AS YOUR VOICE, DEAR CAPTAIN, IT'S THE GREAT MAN YOU'D BE BY THIS!
YOU MAY FIND ME GREAT ENOUGH TO HANG THE LOT OF YOU!
IF YOU HANG MY PATIENT, YOU MAY BE PUTTING A ROPE ROUND YOUR OWN NECK. HE IS LORD GILDOY, NOT A COMMON FELON!
I'LL TAKE THE CONSEQUENCES OF MY... ASSOCIATION WITH THE DUKE... BUT ONLY AFTER TRIAL.
YOU'LL GO WARILY, CAPTAIN, IF YOU VALUE YOUR NECK.

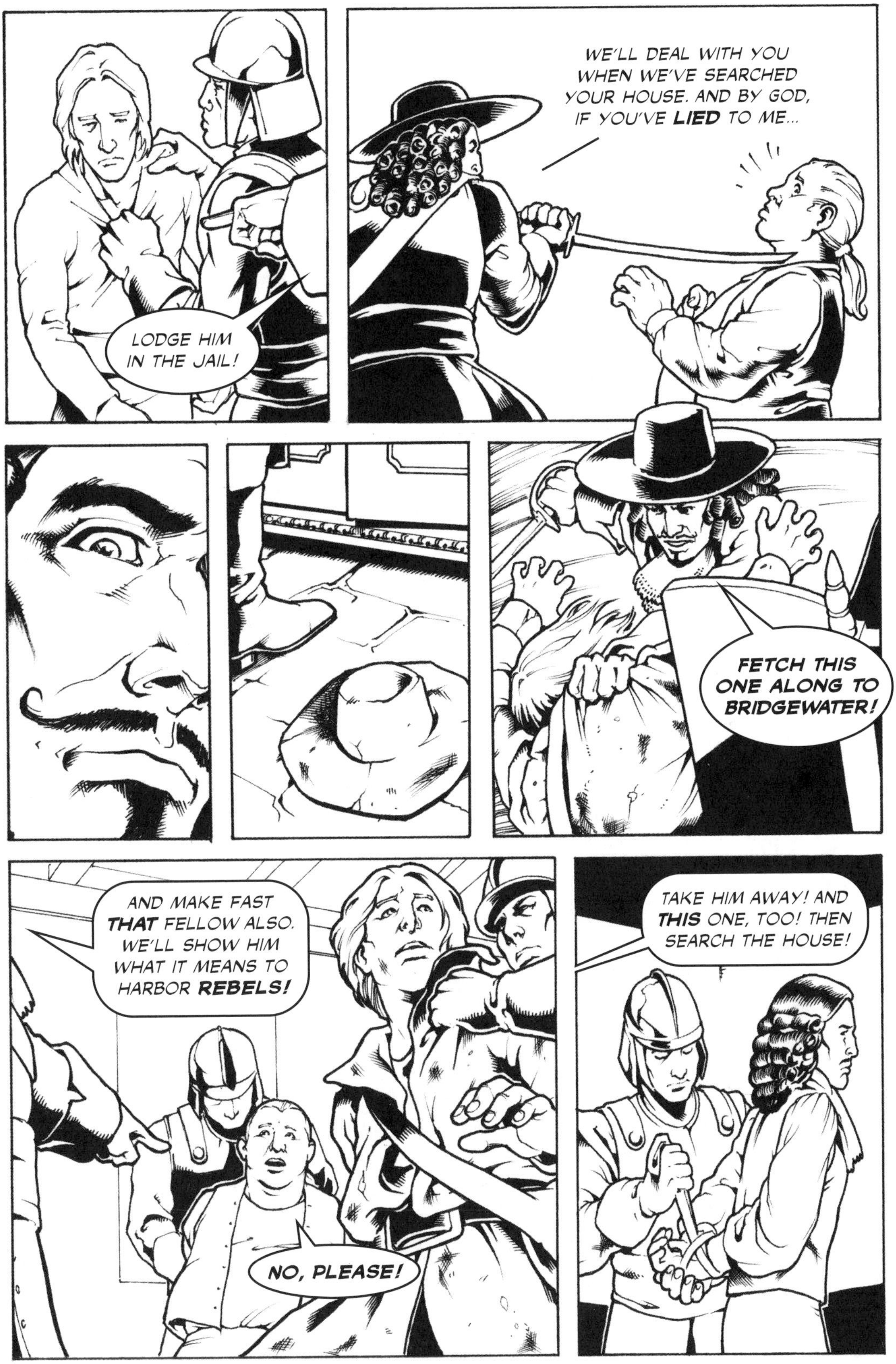
LODGE HIM IN THE JAIL!
WE'LL DEAL WITH YOU WHEN WE'VE SEARCHED YOUR HOUSE. AND BY GOD, IF YOU'VE **LIED** TO ME...
FETCH THIS ONE ALONG TO BRIDGEWATER!
AND MAKE FAST **THAT** FELLOW ALSO. WE'LL SHOW HIM WHAT IT MEANS TO HARBOR **REBELS!**
NO, PLEASE!
TAKE HIM AWAY! AND **THIS** ONE, TOO! THEN SEARCH THE HOUSE!

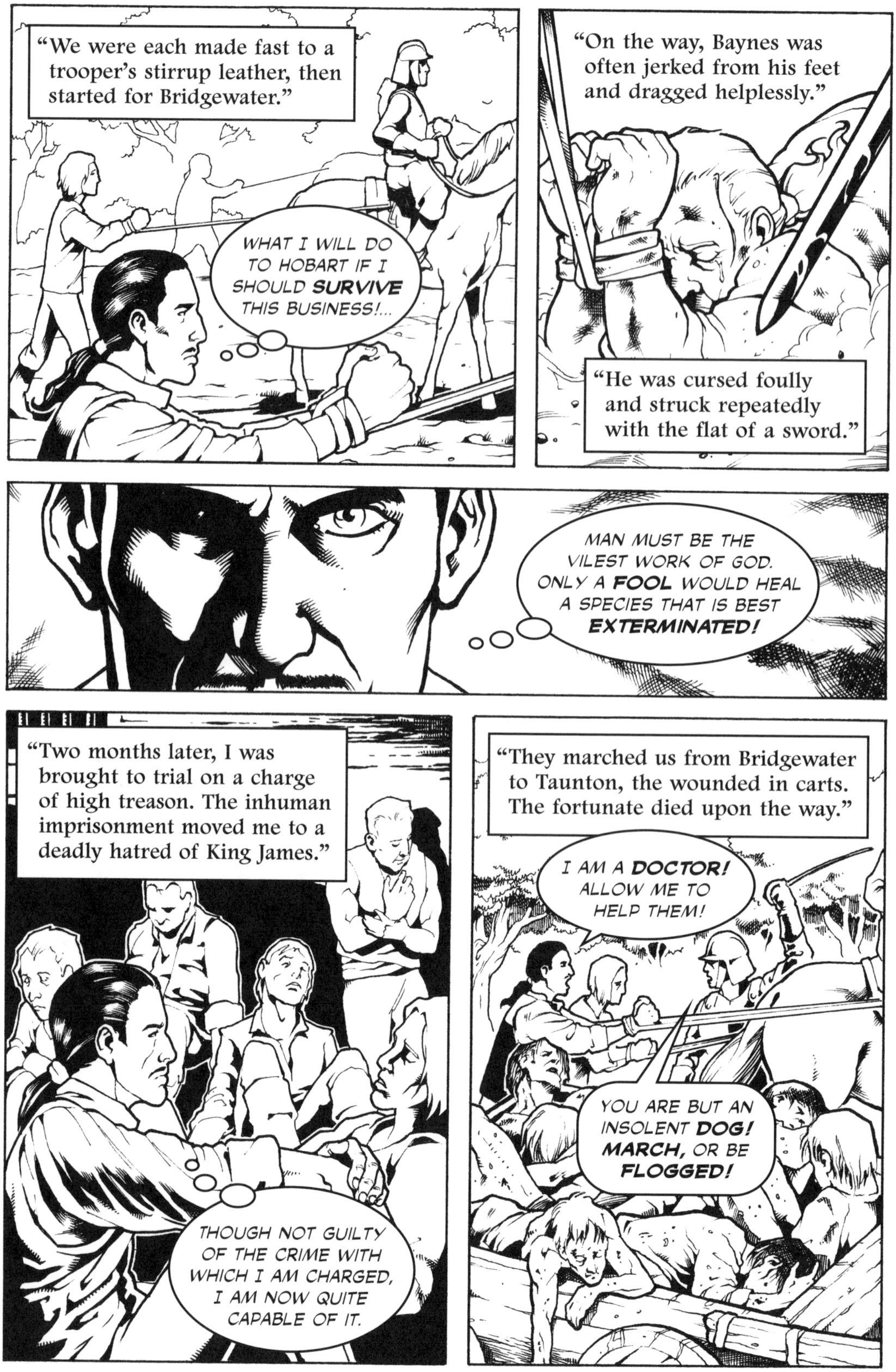
"We were each made fast to a trooper's stirrup leather, then started for Bridgewater."
WHAT I WILL DO TO HOBART IF I SHOULD SURVIVE THIS BUSINESS!...
"On the way, Baynes was often jerked from his feet and dragged helplessly."
"He was cursed foully and struck repeatedly with the flat of a sword."
MAN MUST BE THE VILEST WORK OF GOD. ONLY A FOOL WOULD HEAL A SPECIES THAT IS BEST EXTERMINATED!
"Two months later, I was brought to trial on a charge of high treason. The inhuman imprisonment moved me to a deadly hatred of King James."
THOUGH NOT GUILTY OF THE CRIME WITH WHICH I AM CHARGED, I AM NOW QUITE CAPABLE OF IT.
"They marched us from Bridgewater to Taunton, the wounded in carts. The fortunate died upon the way."
I AM A DOCTOR! ALLOW ME TO HELP THEM!
YOU ARE BUT AN INSOLENT DOG! MARCH, OR BE FLOGGED!

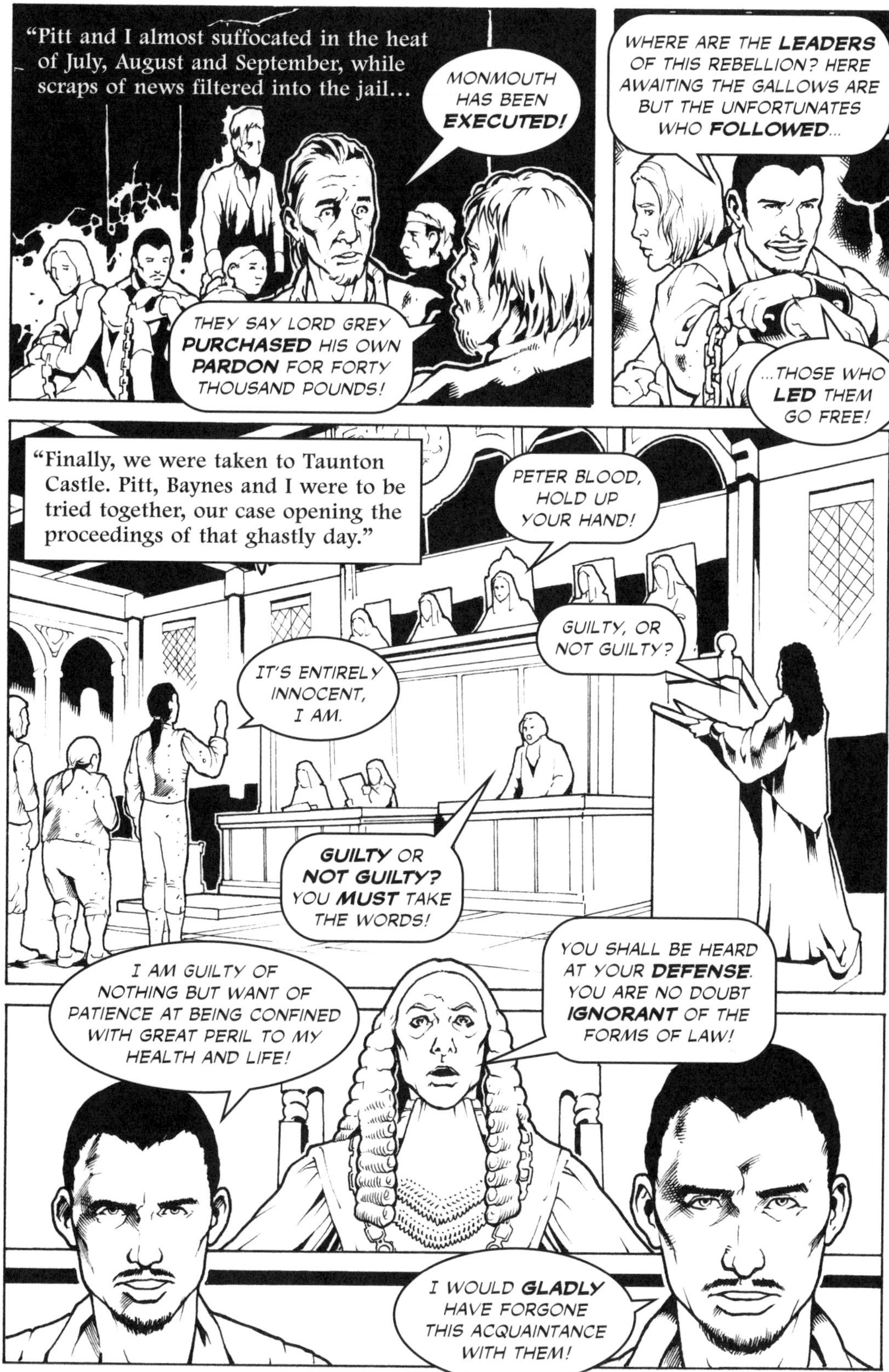
"Pitt and I almost suffocated in the heat of July, August and September, while scraps of news filtered into the jail...
MONMOUTH HAS BEEN EXECUTED!
THEY SAY LORD GREY PURCHASED HIS OWN PARDON FOR FORTY THOUSAND POUNDS!
WHERE ARE THE LEADERS OF THIS REBELLION? HERE AWAITING THE GALLOWS ARE BUT THE UNFORTUNATES WHO FOLLOWED...
...THOSE WHO LED THEM GO FREE!
"Finally, we were taken to Taunton Castle. Pitt, Baynes and I were to be tried together, our case opening the proceedings of that ghastly day."
PETER BLOOD, HOLD UP YOUR HAND!
GUILTY, OR NOT GUILTY?
IT'S ENTIRELY INNOCENT, I AM.
GUILTY OR NOT GUILTY? YOU MUST TAKE THE WORDS!
I AM GUILTY OF NOTHING BUT WANT OF PATIENCE AT BEING CONFINED WITH GREAT PERIL TO MY HEALTH AND LIFE!
YOU SHALL BE HEARD AT YOUR DEFENSE. YOU ARE NO DOUBT IGNORANT OF THE FORMS OF LAW!
I WOULD GLADLY HAVE FORGONE THIS ACQUAINTANCE WITH THEM!

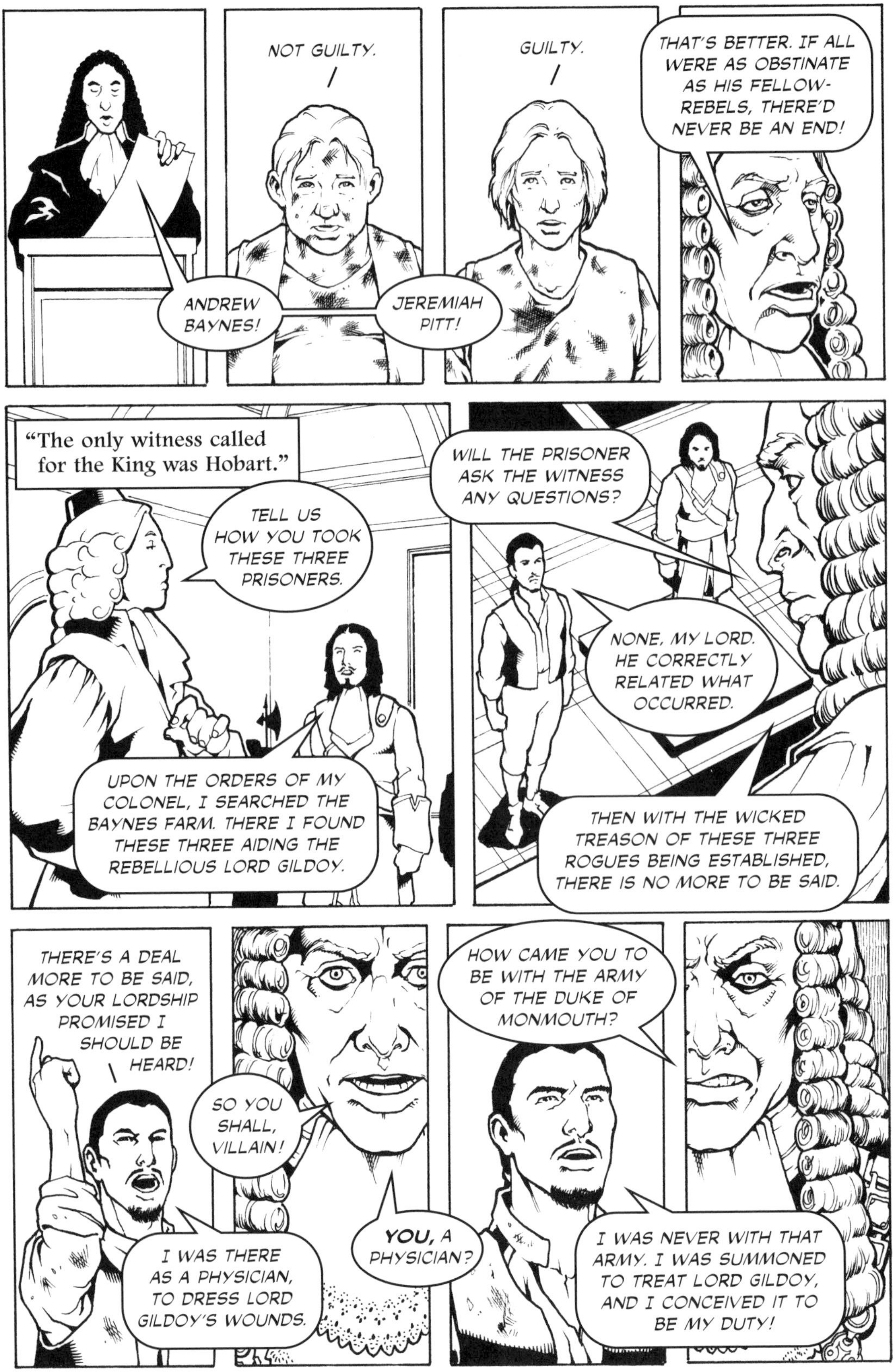
ANDREW BAYNES!
NOT GUILTY.
JEREMIAH PITT!
GUILTY.
THAT'S BETTER. IF ALL WERE AS OBSTINATE AS HIS FELLOW-REBELS, THERE'D NEVER BE AN END!
"The only witness called for the King was Hobart."
TELL US HOW YOU TOOK THESE THREE PRISONERS.
UPON THE ORDERS OF MY COLONEL, I SEARCHED THE BAYNES FARM. THERE I FOUND THESE THREE AIDING THE REBELLIOUS LORD GILDOY.
WILL THE PRISONER ASK THE WITNESS ANY QUESTIONS?
NONE, MY LORD. HE CORRECTLY RELATED WHAT OCCURRED.
THEN WITH THE WICKED TREASON OF THESE THREE ROGUES BEING ESTABLISHED, THERE IS NO MORE TO BE SAID.
THERE'S A DEAL MORE TO BE SAID, AS YOUR LORDSHIP PROMISED I SHOULD BE HEARD!
SO YOU SHALL, VILLAIN!
I WAS THERE AS A PHYSICIAN, TO DRESS LORD GILDOY'S WOUNDS.
YOU, A PHYSICIAN?
HOW CAME YOU TO BE WITH THE ARMY OF THE DUKE OF MONMOUTH?
I WAS NEVER WITH THAT ARMY. I WAS SUMMONED TO TREAT LORD GILDOY, AND I CONCEIVED IT TO BE MY DUTY!

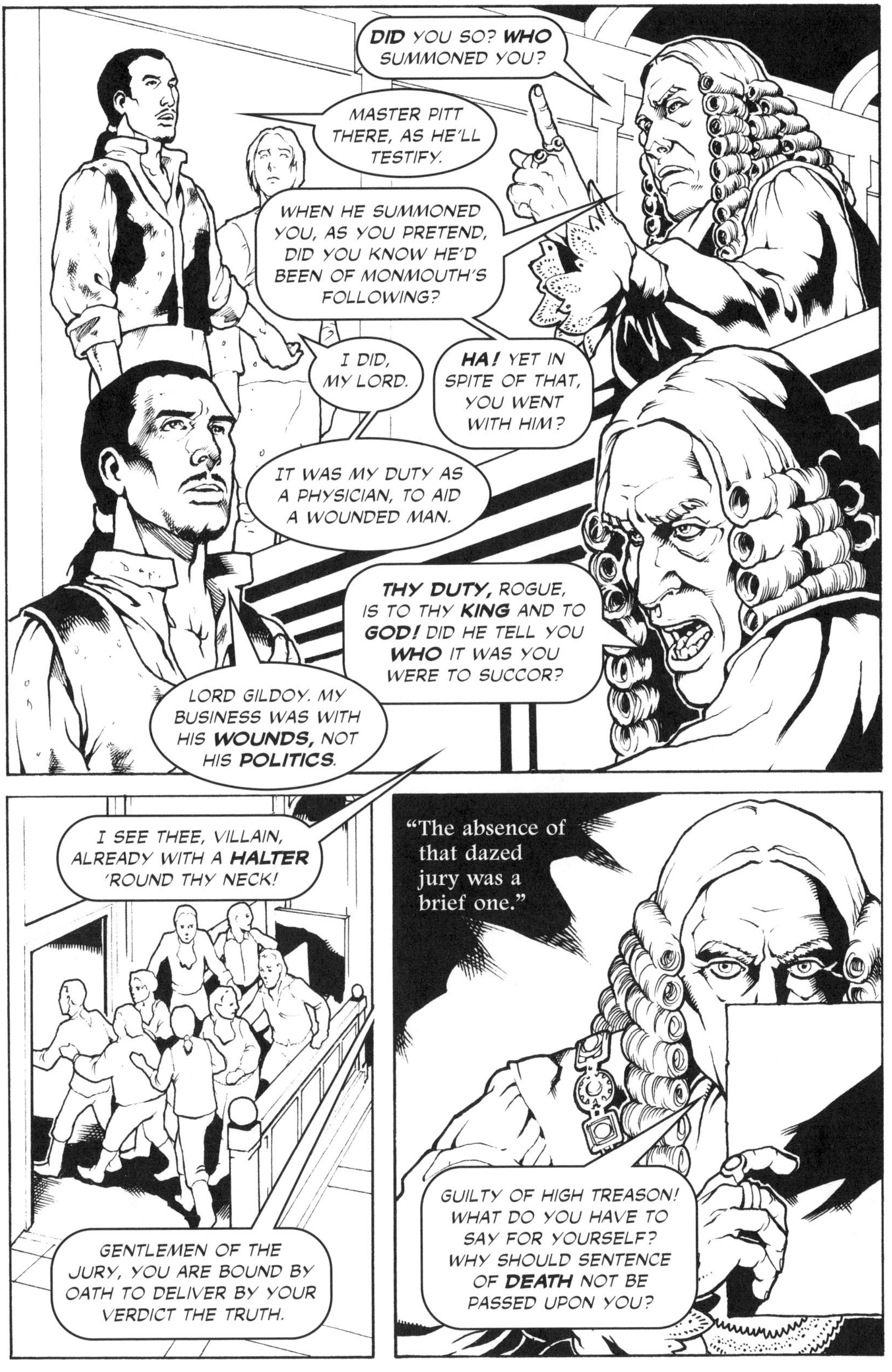
DID YOU SO? WHO SUMMONED YOU?
MASTER PITT THERE, AS HE'LL TESTIFY.
WHEN HE SUMMONED YOU, AS YOU PRETEND, DID YOU KNOW HE'D BEEN OF MONMOUTH'S FOLLOWING?
I DID, MY LORD.
HA! YET IN SPITE OF THAT, YOU WENT WITH HIM?
IT WAS MY DUTY AS A PHYSICIAN, TO AID A WOUNDED MAN.
THY DUTY, ROGUE, IS TO THY KING AND TO GOD! DID HE TELL YOU WHO IT WAS YOU WERE TO SUCCOR?
LORD GILDOY. MY BUSINESS WAS WITH HIS WOUNDS, NOT HIS POLITICS.
I SEE THEE, VILLAIN, ALREADY WITH A HALTER 'ROUND THY NECK!
GENTLEMEN OF THE JURY, YOU ARE BOUND BY OATH TO DELIVER BY YOUR VERDICT THE TRUTH.
"The absence of that dazed jury was a brief one."
GUILTY OF HIGH TREASON! WHAT DO YOU HAVE TO SAY FOR YOURSELF? WHY SHOULD SENTENCE OF DEATH NOT BE PASSED UPON YOU?

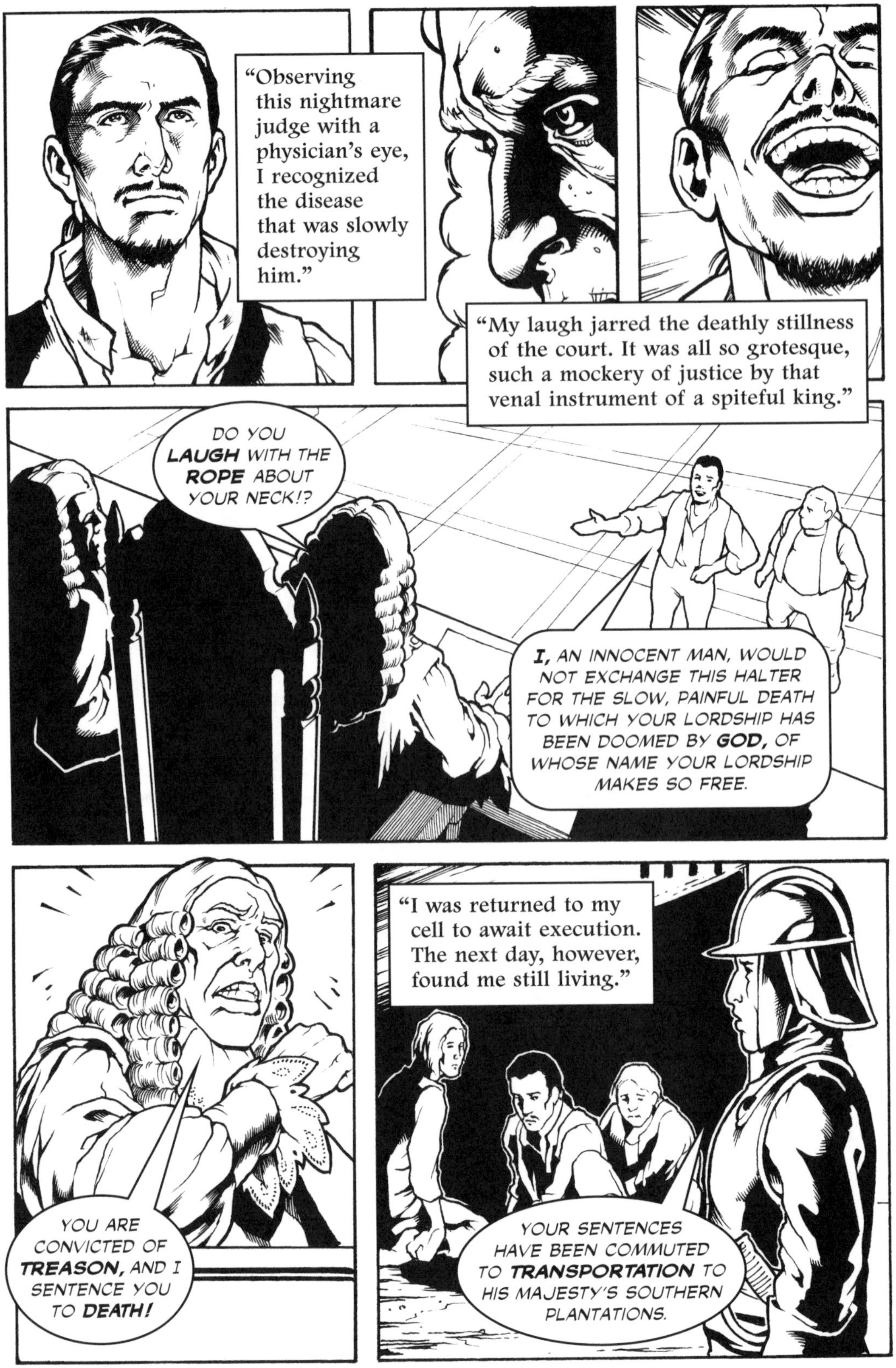
"Observing this nightmare judge with a physician's eye, I recognized the disease that was slowly destroying him."
"My laugh jarred the deathly stillness of the court. It was all so grotesque, such a mockery of justice by that venal instrument of a spiteful king."
DO YOU LAUGH WITH THE ROPE ABOUT YOUR NECK!?
I, AN INNOCENT MAN, WOULD NOT EXCHANGE THIS HALTER FOR THE SLOW, PAINFUL DEATH TO WHICH YOUR LORDSHIP HAS BEEN DOOMED BY GOD, OF WHOSE NAME YOUR LORDSHIP MAKES SO FREE.
YOU ARE CONVICTED OF TREASON, AND I SENTENCE YOU TO DEATH!
"I was returned to my cell to await execution. The next day, however, found me still living."
YOUR SENTENCES HAVE BEEN COMMUTED TO TRANSPORTATION TO HIS MAJESTY'S SOUTHERN PLANTATIONS.

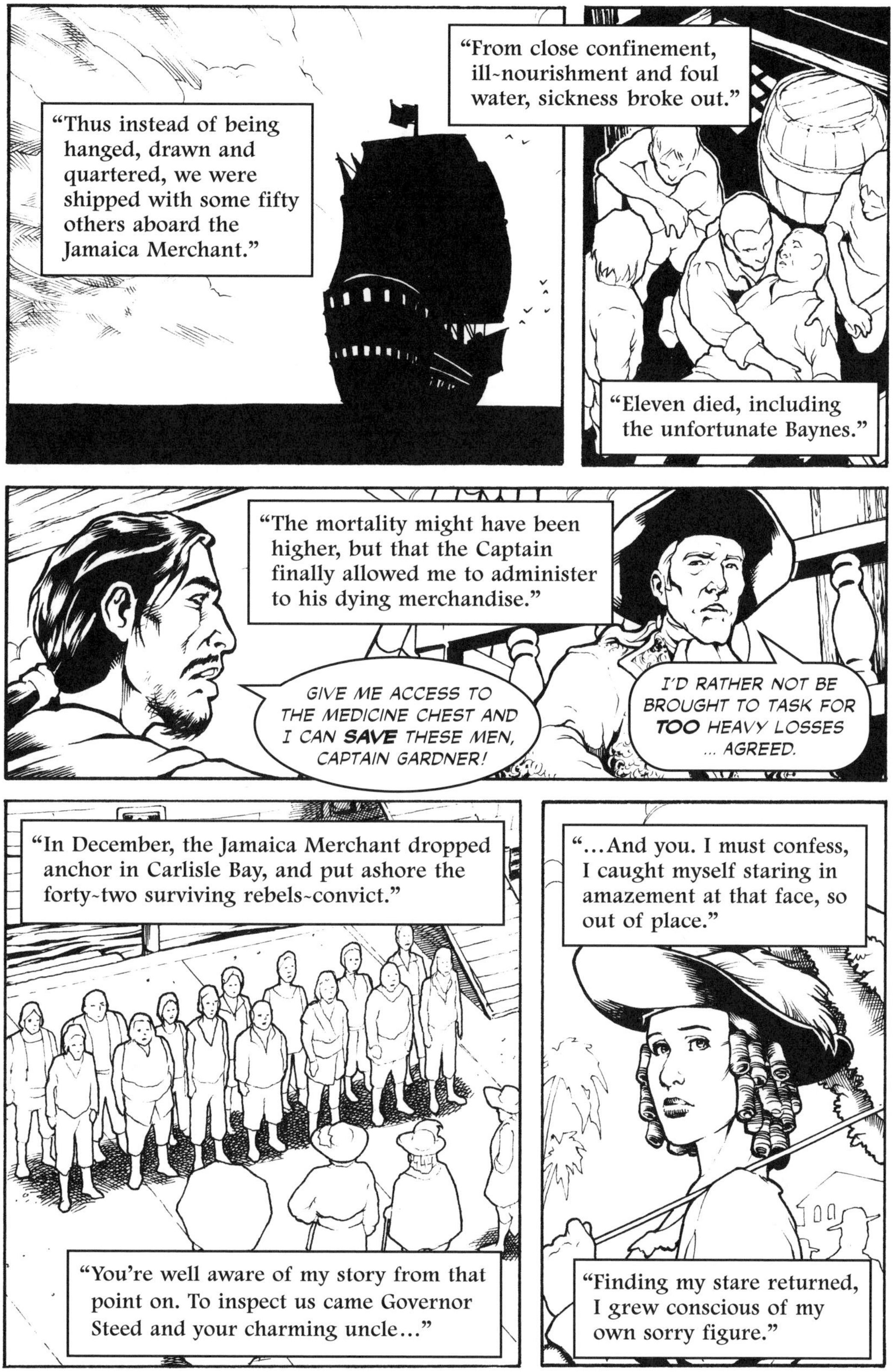
"Thus instead of being hanged, drawn and quartered, we were shipped with some fifty others aboard the Jamaica Merchant."
"From close confinement, ill-nourishment and foul water, sickness broke out."
"Eleven died, including the unfortunate Baynes."
"The mortality might have been higher, but that the Captain finally allowed me to administer to his dying merchandise."
GIVE ME ACCESS TO THE MEDICINE CHEST AND I CAN SAVE THESE MEN, CAPTAIN GARDNER!
I'D RATHER NOT BE BROUGHT TO TASK FOR TOO HEAVY LOSSES ... AGREED.
"In December, the Jamaica Merchant dropped anchor in Carlisle Bay, and put ashore the forty-two surviving rebels-convict."
"You're well aware of my story from that point on. To inspect us came Governor Steed and your charming uncle..."
"...And you. I must confess, I caught myself staring in amazement at that face, so out of place."
"Finding my stare returned, I grew conscious of my own sorry figure."

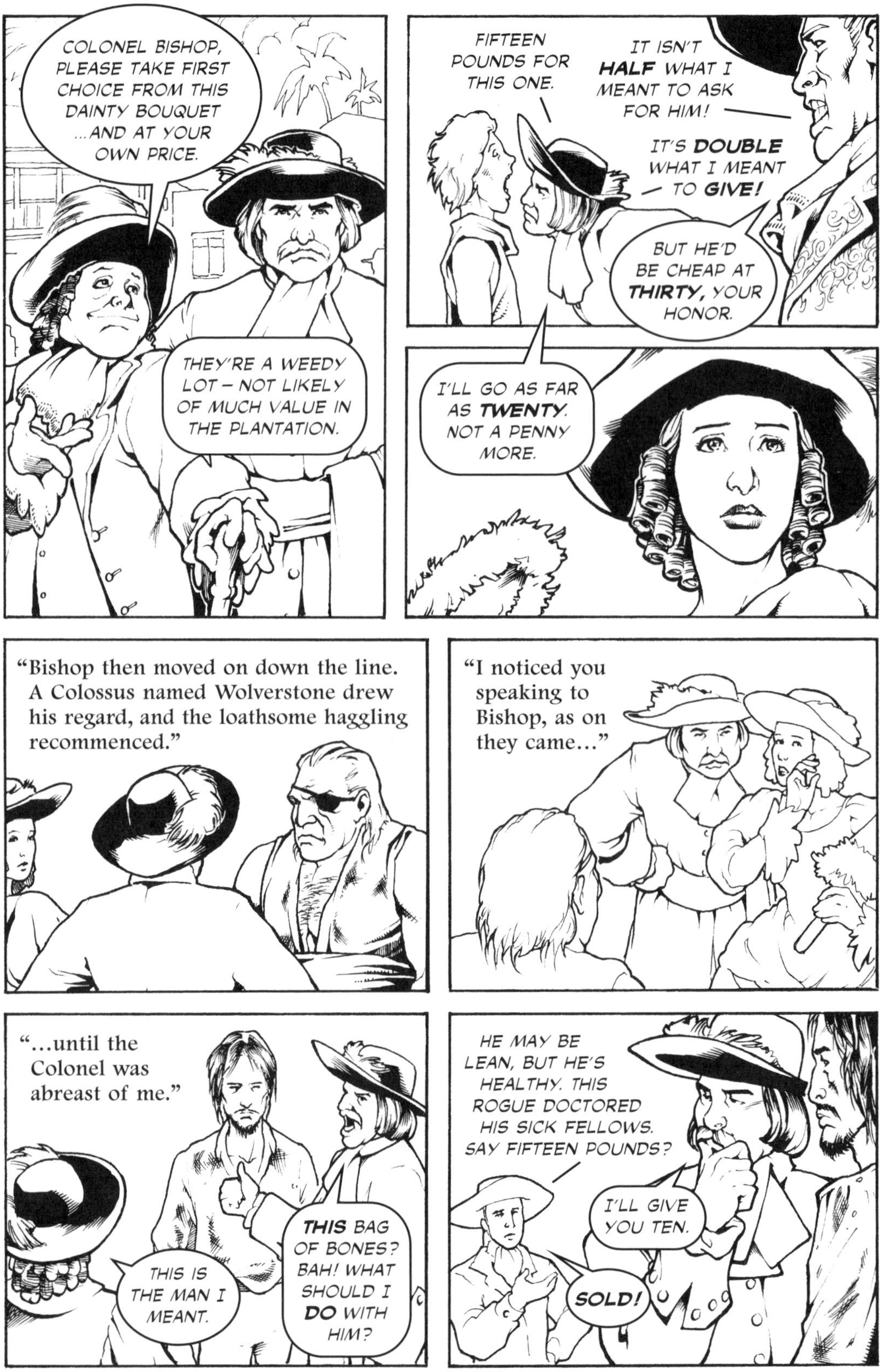
COLONEL BISHOP, PLEASE TAKE FIRST CHOICE FROM THIS DAINTY BOUQUET ...AND AT YOUR OWN PRICE.
THEY'RE A WEEDY LOT – NOT LIKELY OF MUCH VALUE IN THE PLANTATION.
FIFTEEN POUNDS FOR THIS ONE.
IT ISN'T **HALF** WHAT I MEANT TO ASK FOR HIM!
IT'S **DOUBLE** WHAT I MEANT TO **GIVE!**
BUT HE'D BE CHEAP AT **THIRTY,** YOUR HONOR.
I'LL GO AS FAR AS **TWENTY**. NOT A PENNY MORE.
"Bishop then moved on down the line. A Colossus named Wolverstone drew his regard, and the loathsome haggling recommenced."
"I noticed you speaking to Bishop, as on they came..."
"...until the Colonel was abreast of me."
THIS IS THE MAN I MEANT.
THIS BAG OF BONES? BAH! WHAT SHOULD I **DO** WITH HIM?
HE MAY BE LEAN, BUT HE'S HEALTHY. THIS ROGUE DOCTORED HIS SICK FELLOWS. SAY FIFTEEN POUNDS?
I'LL GIVE YOU TEN.
SOLD!

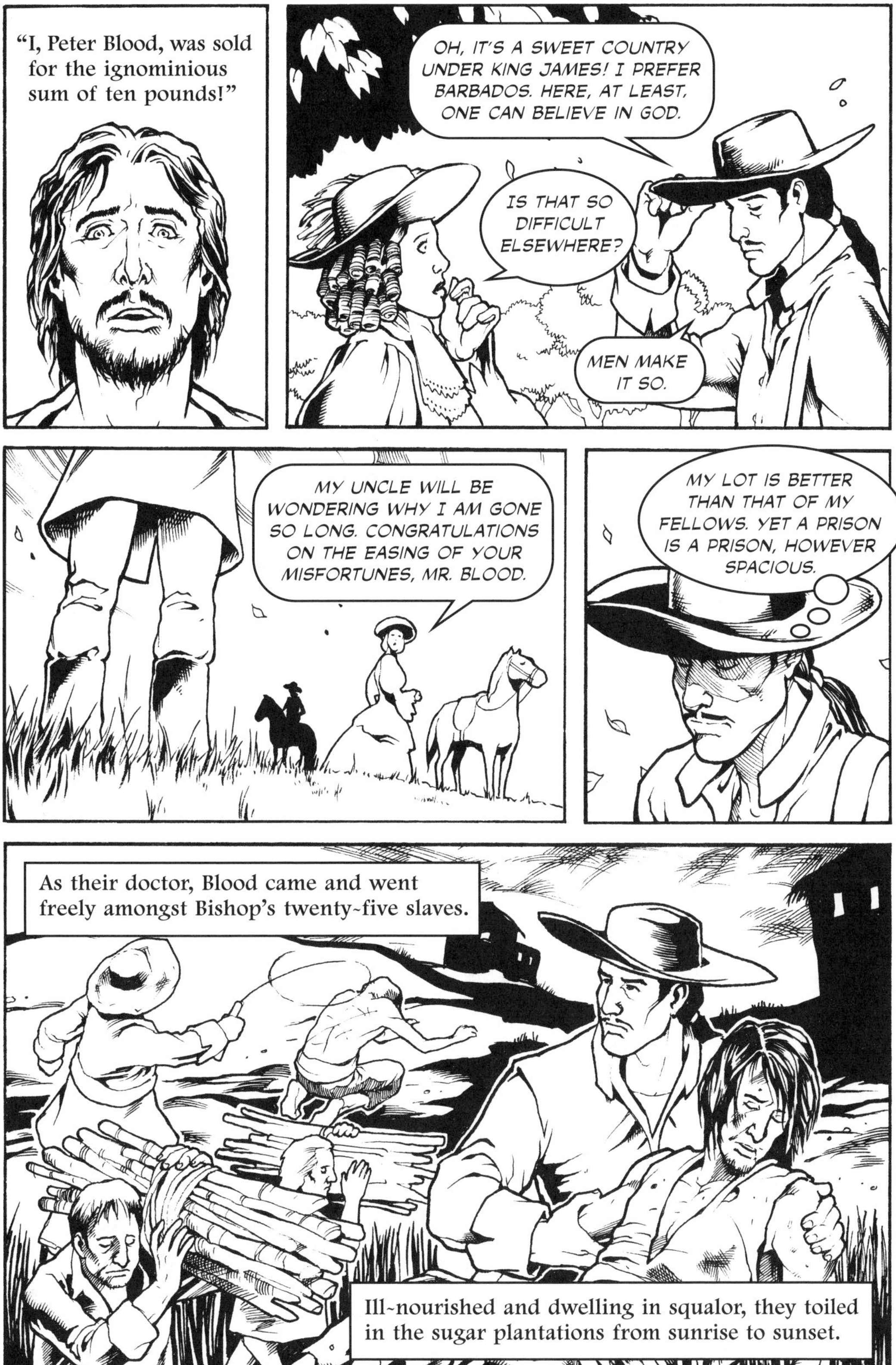
"I, Peter Blood, was sold for the ignominious sum of ten pounds!"
OH, IT'S A SWEET COUNTRY UNDER KING JAMES! I PREFER BARBADOS. HERE, AT LEAST, ONE CAN BELIEVE IN GOD.
IS THAT SO DIFFICULT ELSEWHERE?
MEN MAKE IT SO.
MY UNCLE WILL BE WONDERING WHY I AM GONE SO LONG. CONGRATULATIONS ON THE EASING OF YOUR MISFORTUNES, MR. BLOOD.
MY LOT IS BETTER THAN THAT OF MY FELLOWS. YET A PRISON IS A PRISON, HOWEVER SPACIOUS.
As their doctor, Blood came and went freely amongst Bishop's twenty-five slaves.
Ill-nourished and dwelling in squalor, they toiled in the sugar plantations from sunrise to sunset.

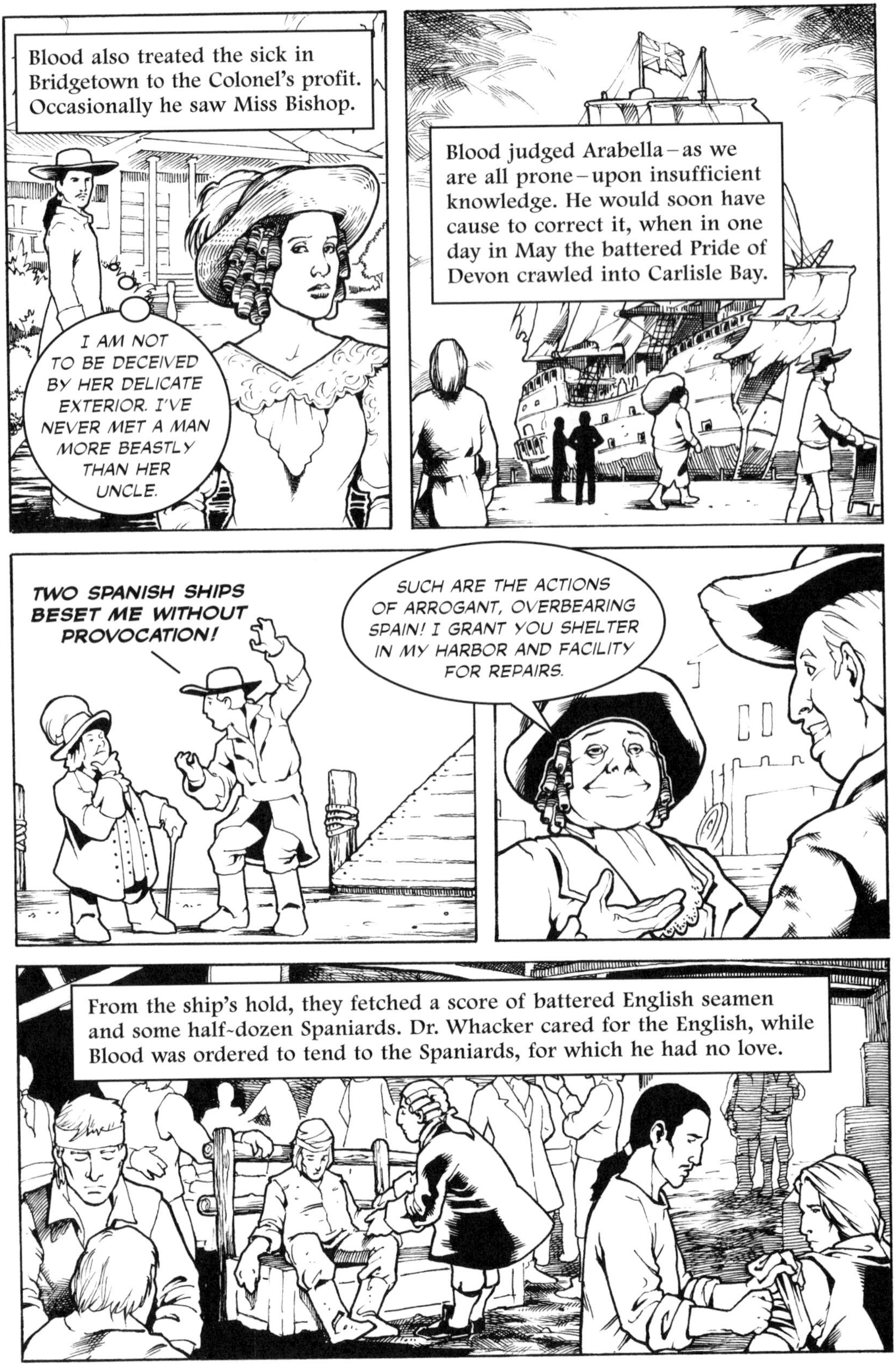
Blood also treated the sick in Bridgetown to the Colonel's profit. Occasionally he saw Miss Bishop.
I AM NOT TO BE DECEIVED BY HER DELICATE EXTERIOR. I'VE NEVER MET A MAN MORE BEASTLY THAN HER UNCLE.
Blood judged Arabella – as we are all prone – upon insufficient knowledge. He would soon have cause to correct it, when in one day in May the battered Pride of Devon crawled into Carlisle Bay.
TWO SPANISH SHIPS BESET ME WITHOUT PROVOCATION!
SUCH ARE THE ACTIONS OF ARROGANT, OVERBEARING SPAIN! I GRANT YOU SHELTER IN MY HARBOR AND FACILITY FOR REPAIRS.
From the ship's hold, they fetched a score of battered English seamen and some half-dozen Spaniards. Dr. Whacker cared for the English, while Blood was ordered to tend to the Spaniards, for which he had no love.

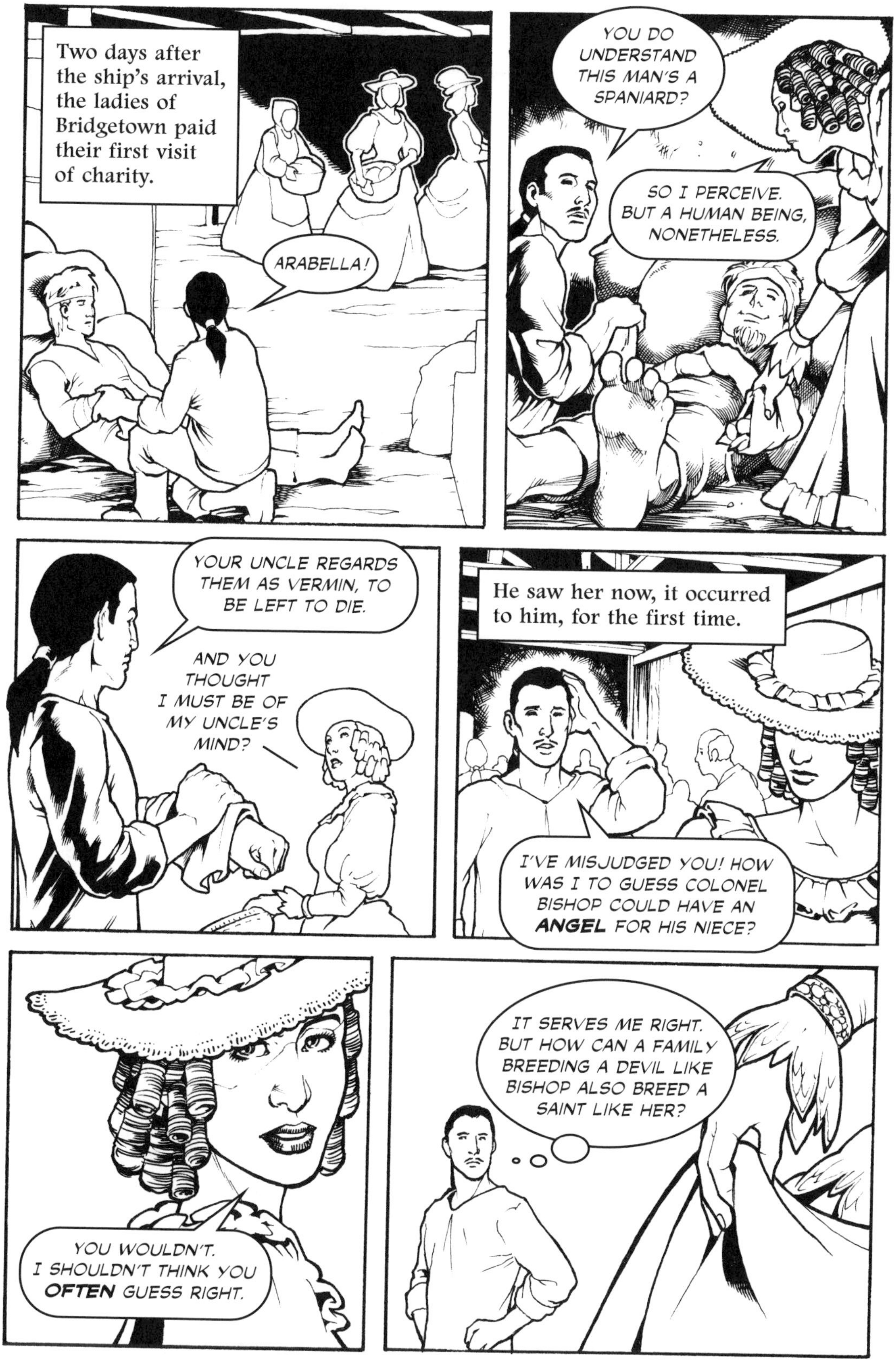
Two days after the ship's arrival, the ladies of Bridgetown paid their first visit of charity.
ARABELLA!
YOU DO UNDERSTAND THIS MAN'S A SPANIARD?
SO I PERCEIVE. BUT A HUMAN BEING, NONETHELESS.
YOUR UNCLE REGARDS THEM AS VERMIN, TO BE LEFT TO DIE.
AND YOU THOUGHT I MUST BE OF MY UNCLE'S MIND?
He saw her now, it occurred to him, for the first time.
I'VE MISJUDGED YOU! HOW WAS I TO GUESS COLONEL BISHOP COULD HAVE AN ANGEL FOR HIS NIECE?
YOU WOULDN'T. I SHOULDN'T THINK YOU OFTEN GUESS RIGHT.
IT SERVES ME RIGHT. BUT HOW CAN A FAMILY BREEDING A DEVIL LIKE BISHOP ALSO BREED A SAINT LIKE HER?

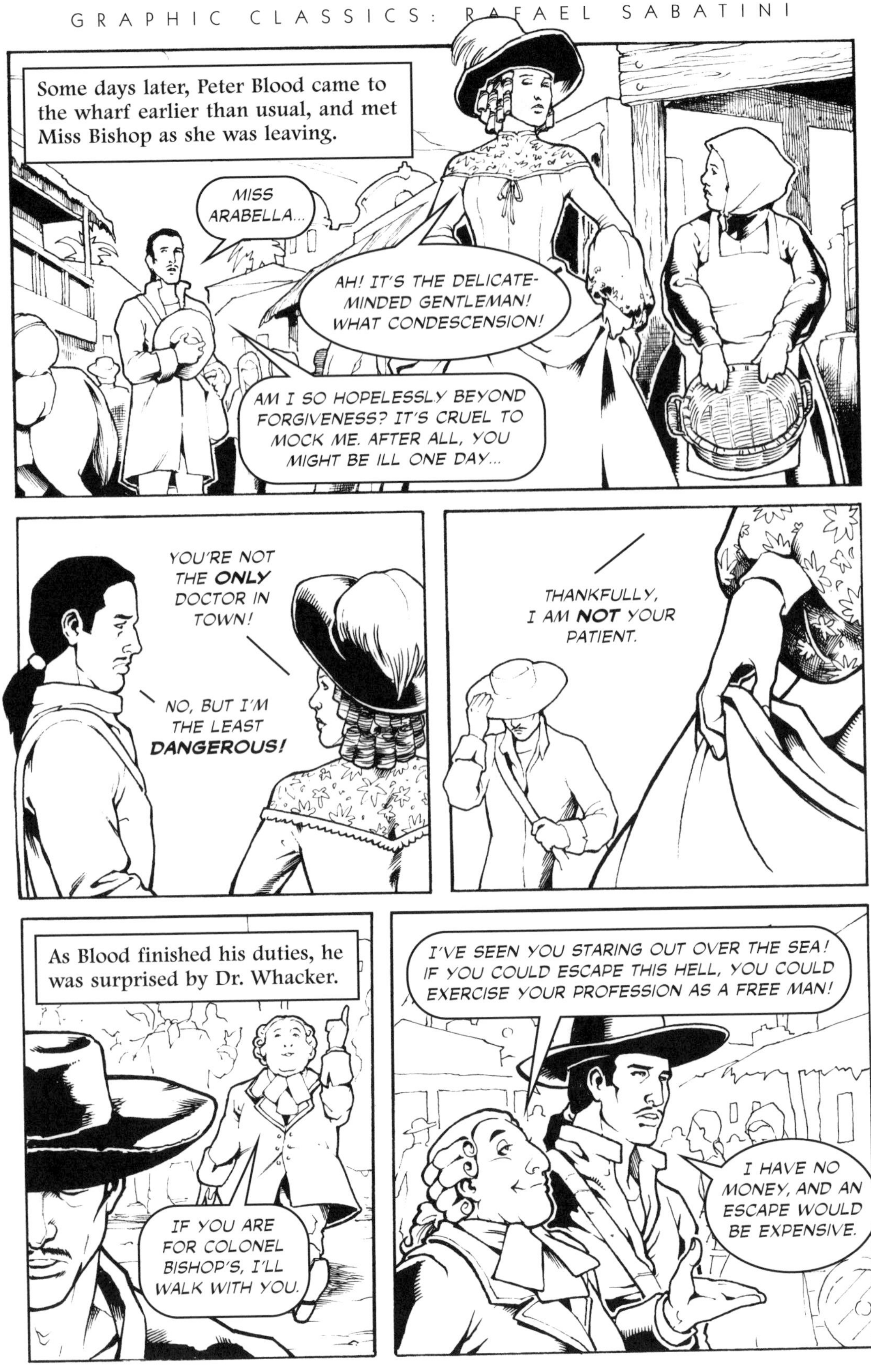
Some days later, Peter Blood came to the wharf earlier than usual, and met Miss Bishop as she was leaving.
MISS ARABELLA...
AH! IT'S THE DELICATE-MINDED GENTLEMAN! WHAT CONDESCENSION!
AM I SO HOPELESSLY BEYOND FORGIVENESS? IT'S CRUEL TO MOCK ME. AFTER ALL, YOU MIGHT BE ILL ONE DAY...
YOU'RE NOT THE ONLY DOCTOR IN TOWN!
NO, BUT I'M THE LEAST DANGEROUS!
THANKFULLY, I AM NOT YOUR PATIENT.
As Blood finished his duties, he was surprised by Dr. Whacker.
IF YOU ARE FOR COLONEL BISHOP'S, I'LL WALK WITH YOU.
I'VE SEEN YOU STARING OUT OVER THE SEA! IF YOU COULD ESCAPE THIS HELL, YOU COULD EXERCISE YOUR PROFESSION AS A FREE MAN!
I HAVE NO MONEY, AND AN ESCAPE WOULD BE EXPENSIVE.

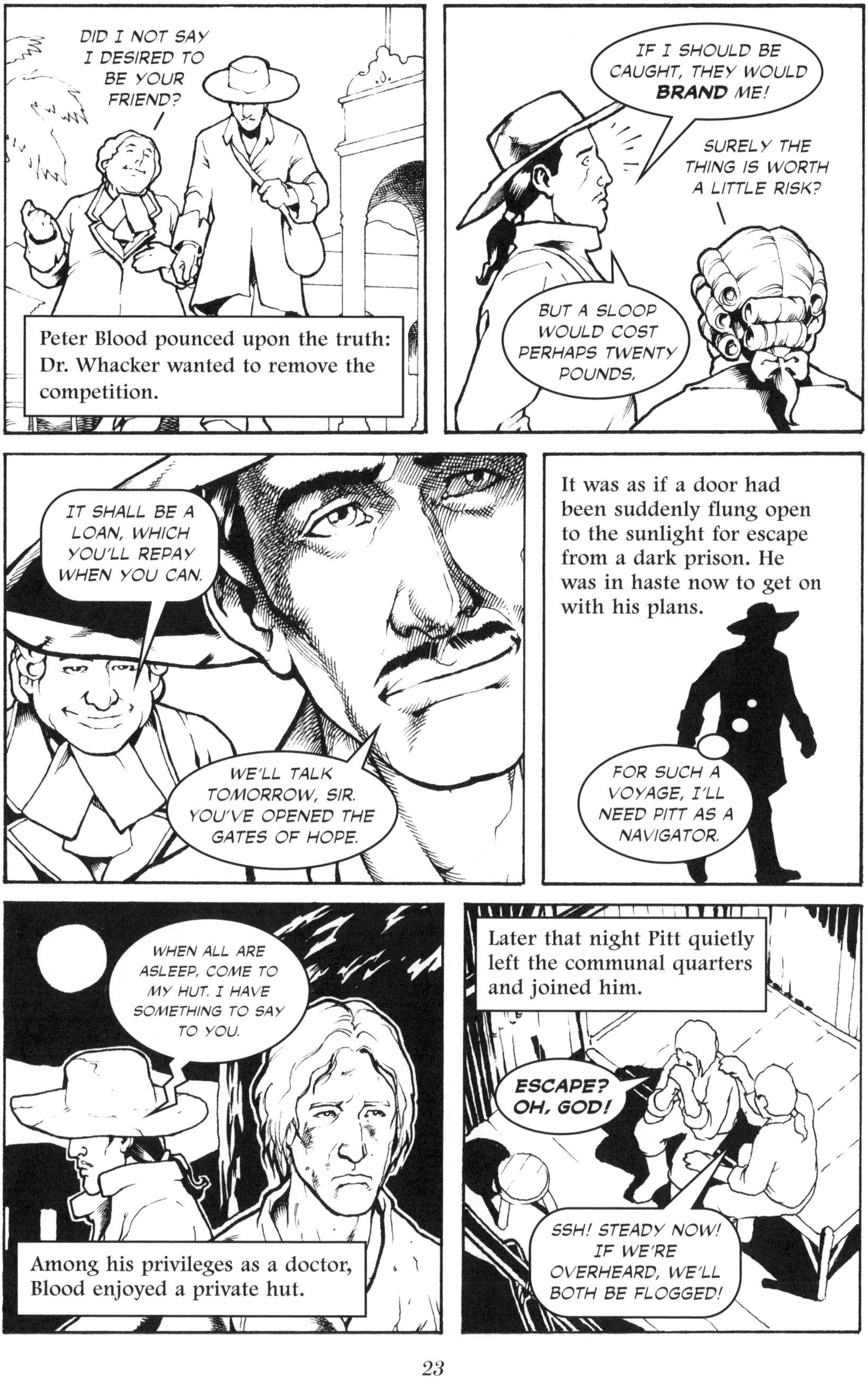
DID I NOT SAY I DESIRED TO BE YOUR FRIEND?
Peter Blood pounced upon the truth: Dr. Whacker wanted to remove the competition.
IF I SHOULD BE CAUGHT, THEY WOULD **BRAND** ME!
SURELY THE THING IS WORTH A LITTLE RISK?
BUT A SLOOP WOULD COST PERHAPS TWENTY POUNDS.
IT SHALL BE A LOAN, WHICH YOU'LL REPAY WHEN YOU CAN.
WE'LL TALK TOMORROW, SIR. YOU'VE OPENED THE GATES OF HOPE.
It was as if a door had been suddenly flung open to the sunlight for escape from a dark prison. He was in haste now to get on with his plans.
FOR SUCH A VOYAGE, I'LL NEED PITT AS A NAVIGATOR.
WHEN ALL ARE ASLEEP, COME TO MY HUT. I HAVE SOMETHING TO SAY TO YOU.
Among his privileges as a doctor, Blood enjoyed a private hut.
Later that night Pitt quietly left the communal quarters and joined him.
ESCAPE? OH, GOD!
SSH! STEADY NOW! IF WE'RE OVERHEARD, WE'LL BOTH BE FLOGGED!

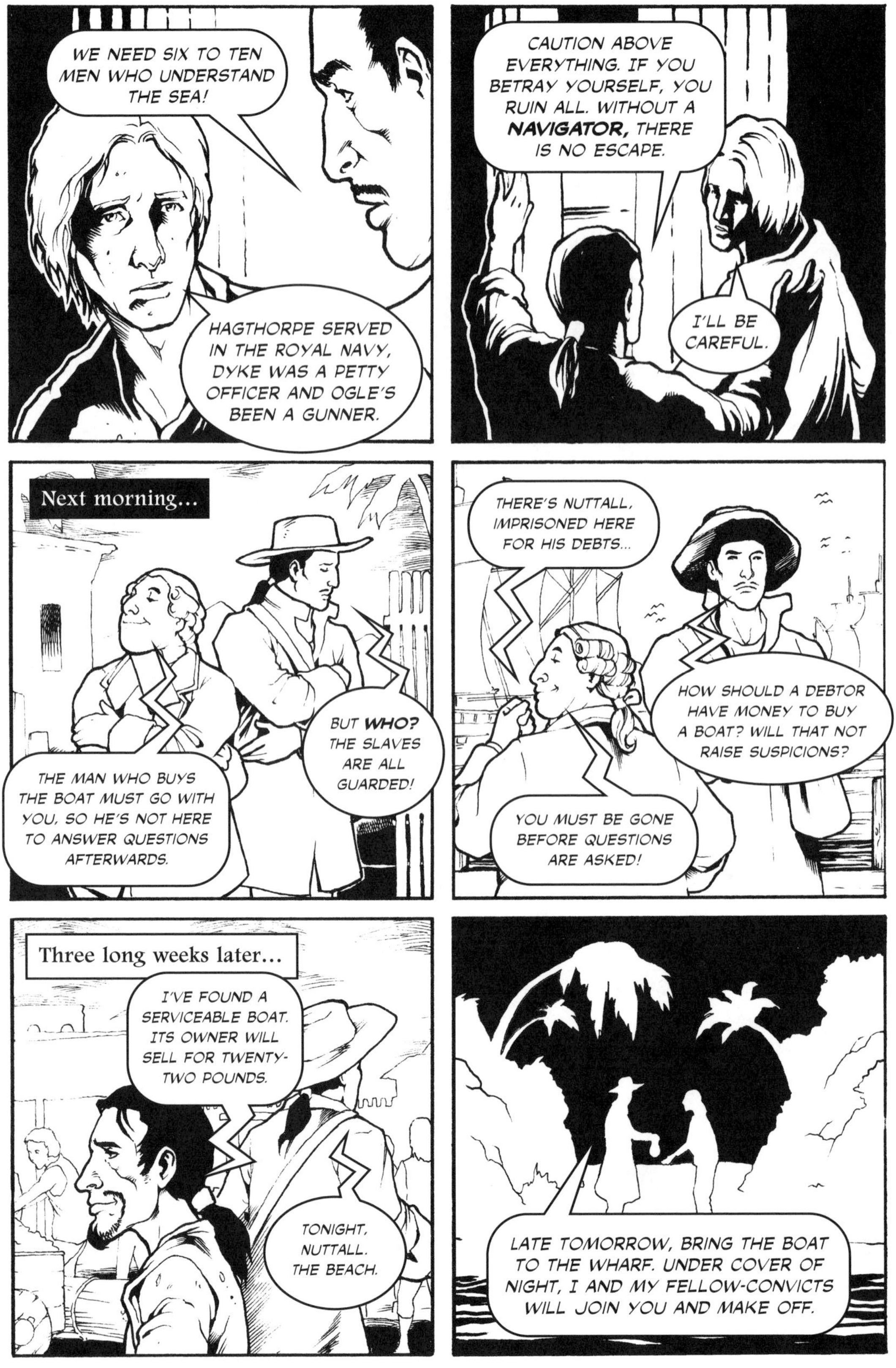
WE NEED SIX TO TEN MEN WHO UNDERSTAND THE SEA!
HAGTHORPE SERVED IN THE ROYAL NAVY, DYKE WAS A PETTY OFFICER AND OGLE'S BEEN A GUNNER.
CAUTION ABOVE EVERYTHING. IF YOU BETRAY YOURSELF, YOU RUIN ALL. WITHOUT A **NAVIGATOR,** THERE IS NO ESCAPE.
I'LL BE CAREFUL.
Next morning...
BUT **WHO?** THE SLAVES ARE ALL GUARDED!
THE MAN WHO BUYS THE BOAT MUST GO WITH YOU, SO HE'S NOT HERE TO ANSWER QUESTIONS AFTERWARDS.
THERE'S NUTTALL, IMPRISONED HERE FOR HIS DEBTS...
HOW SHOULD A DEBTOR HAVE MONEY TO BUY A BOAT? WILL THAT NOT RAISE SUSPICIONS?
YOU MUST BE GONE BEFORE QUESTIONS ARE ASKED!
Three long weeks later...
I'VE FOUND A SERVICEABLE BOAT. ITS OWNER WILL SELL FOR TWENTY-TWO POUNDS.
TONIGHT, NUTTALL. THE BEACH.
LATE TOMORROW, BRING THE BOAT TO THE WHARF. UNDER COVER OF NIGHT, I AND MY FELLOW-CONVICTS WILL JOIN YOU AND MAKE OFF.

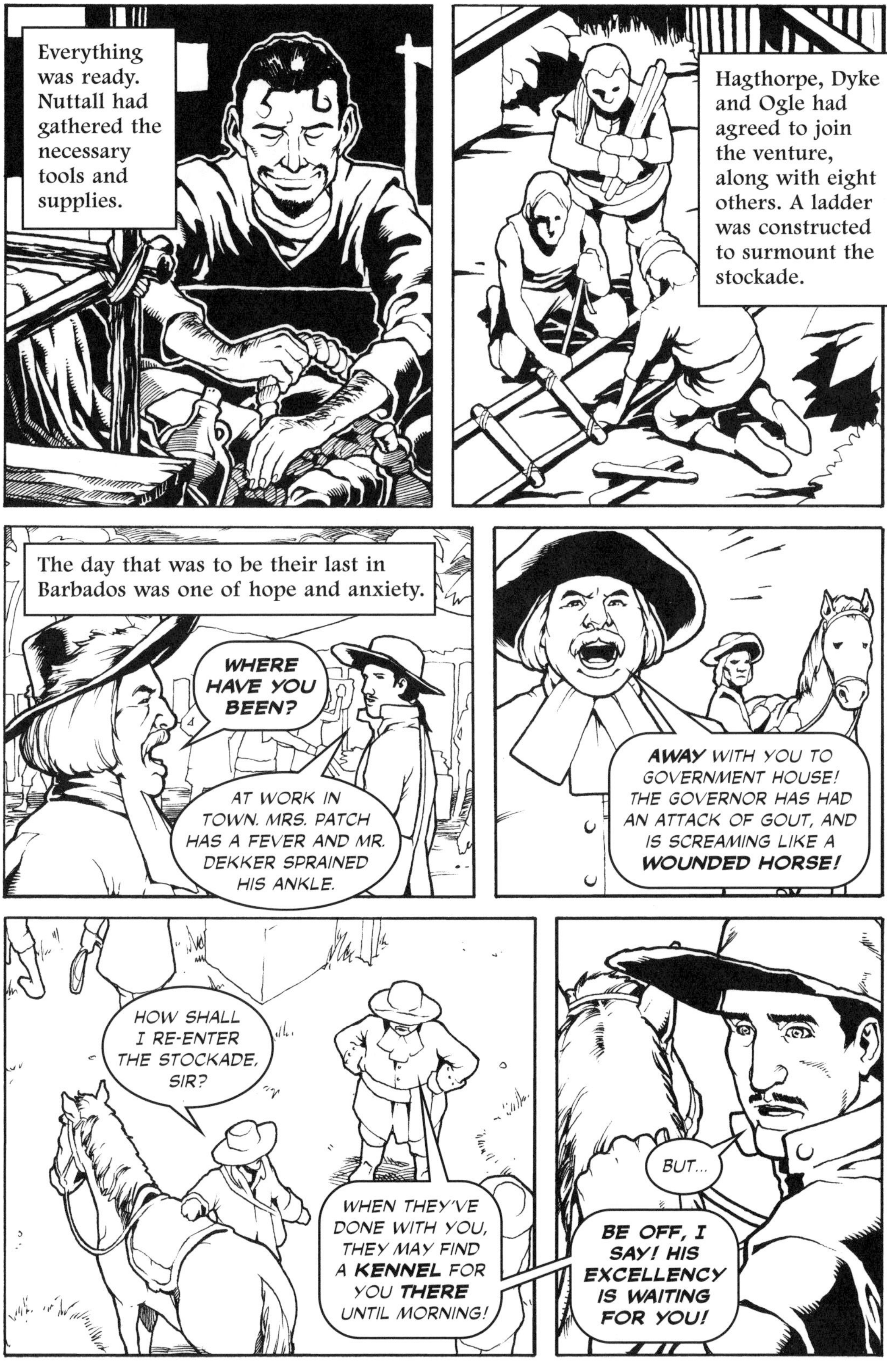
Everything was ready. Nuttall had gathered the necessary tools and supplies.
Hagthorpe, Dyke and Ogle had agreed to join the venture, along with eight others. A ladder was constructed to surmount the stockade.
The day that was to be their last in Barbados was one of hope and anxiety.
WHERE HAVE YOU BEEN?
AT WORK IN TOWN. MRS. PATCH HAS A FEVER AND MR. DEKKER SPRAINED HIS ANKLE.
AWAY WITH YOU TO GOVERNMENT HOUSE! THE GOVERNOR HAS HAD AN ATTACK OF GOUT, AND IS SCREAMING LIKE A WOUNDED HORSE!
HOW SHALL I RE-ENTER THE STOCKADE, SIR?
WHEN THEY'VE DONE WITH YOU, THEY MAY FIND A KENNEL FOR YOU THERE UNTIL MORNING!
BUT...
BE OFF, I SAY! HIS EXCELLENCY IS WAITING FOR YOU!

Peter rode off in despair.

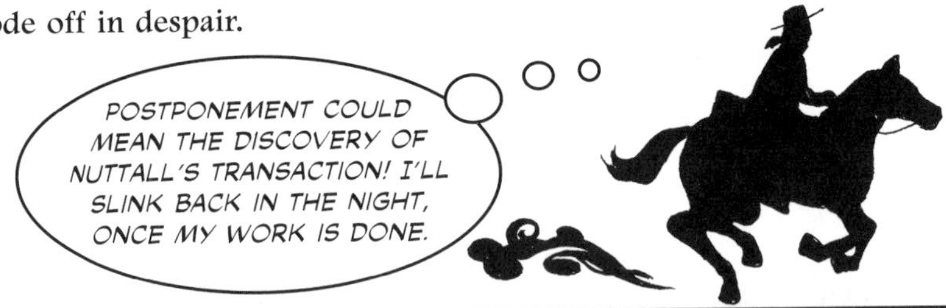
POSTPONEMENT COULD MEAN THE DISCOVERY OF NUTTALL'S TRANSACTION! I'LL SLINK BACK IN THE NIGHT, ONCE MY WORK IS DONE.

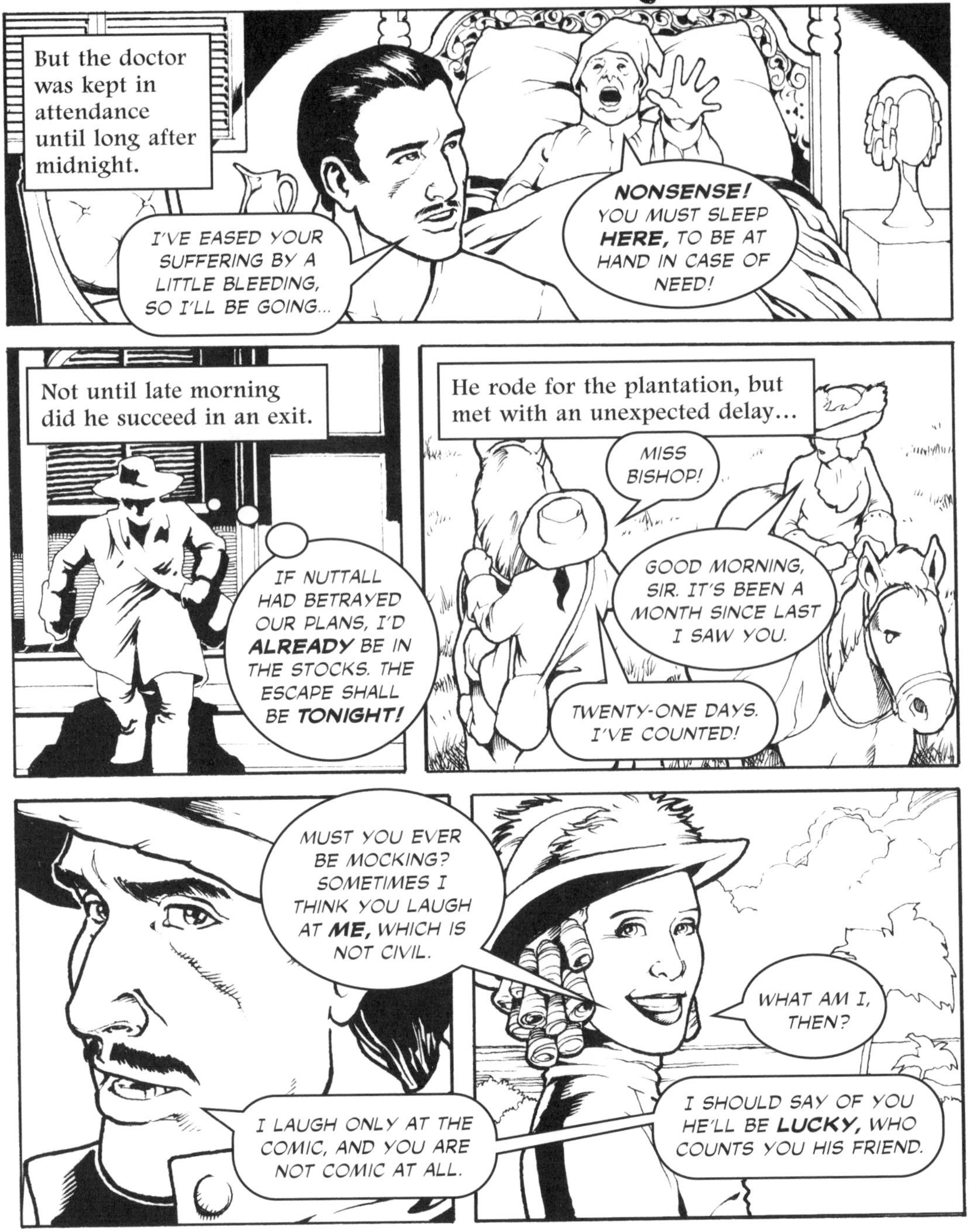
But the doctor was kept in attendance until long after midnight.
I'VE EASED YOUR SUFFERING BY A LITTLE BLEEDING, SO I'LL BE GOING...
NONSENSE! YOU MUST SLEEP **HERE,** TO BE AT HAND IN CASE OF NEED!
Not until late morning did he succeed in an exit.
IF NUTTALL HAD BETRAYED OUR PLANS, I'D **ALREADY** BE IN THE STOCKS. THE ESCAPE SHALL BE **TONIGHT!**
He rode for the plantation, but met with an unexpected delay...
MISS BISHOP!
GOOD MORNING, SIR. IT'S BEEN A MONTH SINCE LAST I SAW YOU.
TWENTY-ONE DAYS. I'VE COUNTED!
MUST YOU EVER BE MOCKING? SOMETIMES I THINK YOU LAUGH AT **ME,** WHICH IS NOT CIVIL.
I LAUGH ONLY AT THE COMIC, AND YOU ARE NOT COMIC AT ALL.
WHAT AM I, THEN?
I SHOULD SAY OF YOU HE'LL BE **LUCKY,** WHO COUNTS YOU HIS FRIEND.

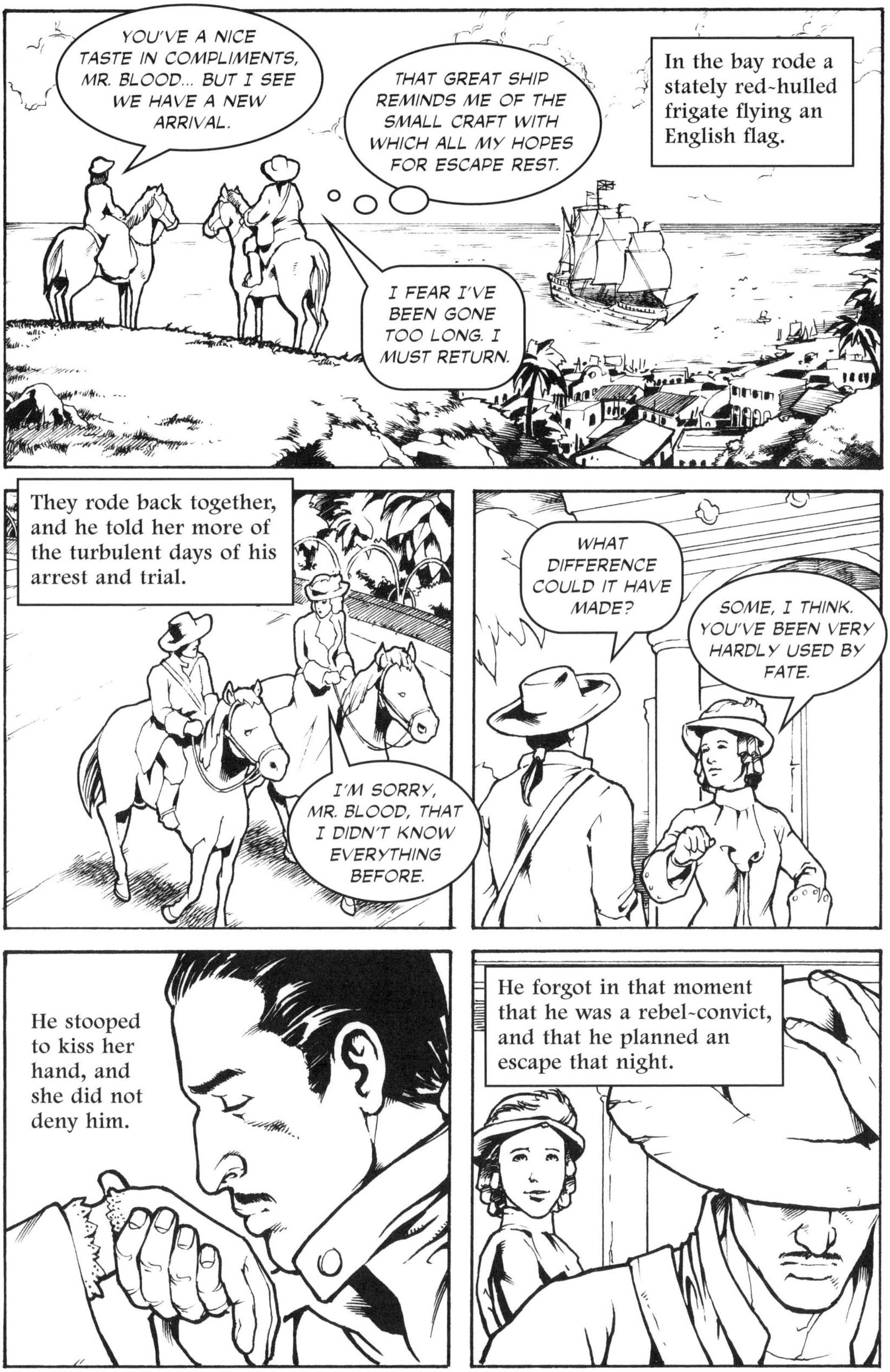
YOU'VE A NICE TASTE IN COMPLIMENTS, MR. BLOOD... BUT I SEE WE HAVE A NEW ARRIVAL.
THAT GREAT SHIP REMINDS ME OF THE SMALL CRAFT WITH WHICH ALL MY HOPES FOR ESCAPE REST.
In the bay rode a stately red-hulled frigate flying an English flag.
I FEAR I'VE BEEN GONE TOO LONG. I MUST RETURN.
They rode back together, and he told her more of the turbulent days of his arrest and trial.
I'M SORRY, MR. BLOOD, THAT I DIDN'T KNOW EVERYTHING BEFORE.
WHAT DIFFERENCE COULD IT HAVE MADE?
SOME, I THINK. YOU'VE BEEN VERY HARDLY USED BY FATE.
He stooped to kiss her hand, and she did not deny him.
He forgot in that moment that he was a rebel-convict, and that he planned an escape that night.

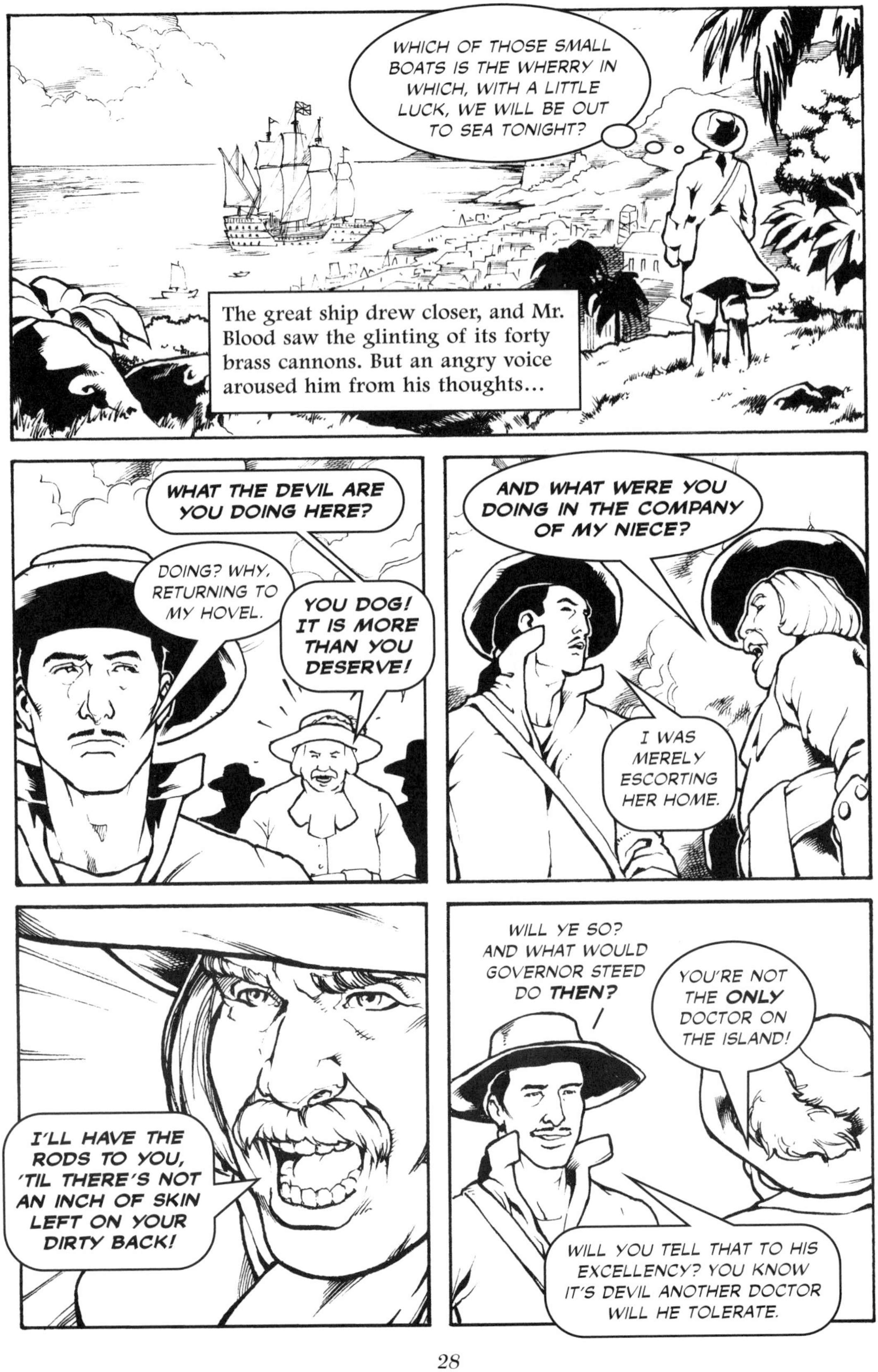
WHICH OF THOSE SMALL BOATS IS THE WHERRY IN WHICH, WITH A LITTLE LUCK, WE WILL BE OUT TO SEA TONIGHT?
The great ship drew closer, and Mr. Blood saw the glinting of its forty brass cannons. But an angry voice aroused him from his thoughts...
WHAT THE DEVIL ARE YOU DOING HERE?
DOING? WHY, RETURNING TO MY HOVEL.
YOU DOG! IT IS MORE THAN YOU DESERVE!
AND WHAT WERE YOU DOING IN THE COMPANY OF MY NIECE?
I WAS MERELY ESCORTING HER HOME.
I'LL HAVE THE RODS TO YOU, 'TIL THERE'S NOT AN INCH OF SKIN LEFT ON YOUR DIRTY BACK!
WILL YE SO? AND WHAT WOULD GOVERNOR STEED DO THEN?
YOU'RE NOT THE ONLY DOCTOR ON THE ISLAND!
WILL YOU TELL THAT TO HIS EXCELLENCY? YOU KNOW IT'S DEVIL ANOTHER DOCTOR WILL HE TOLERATE.

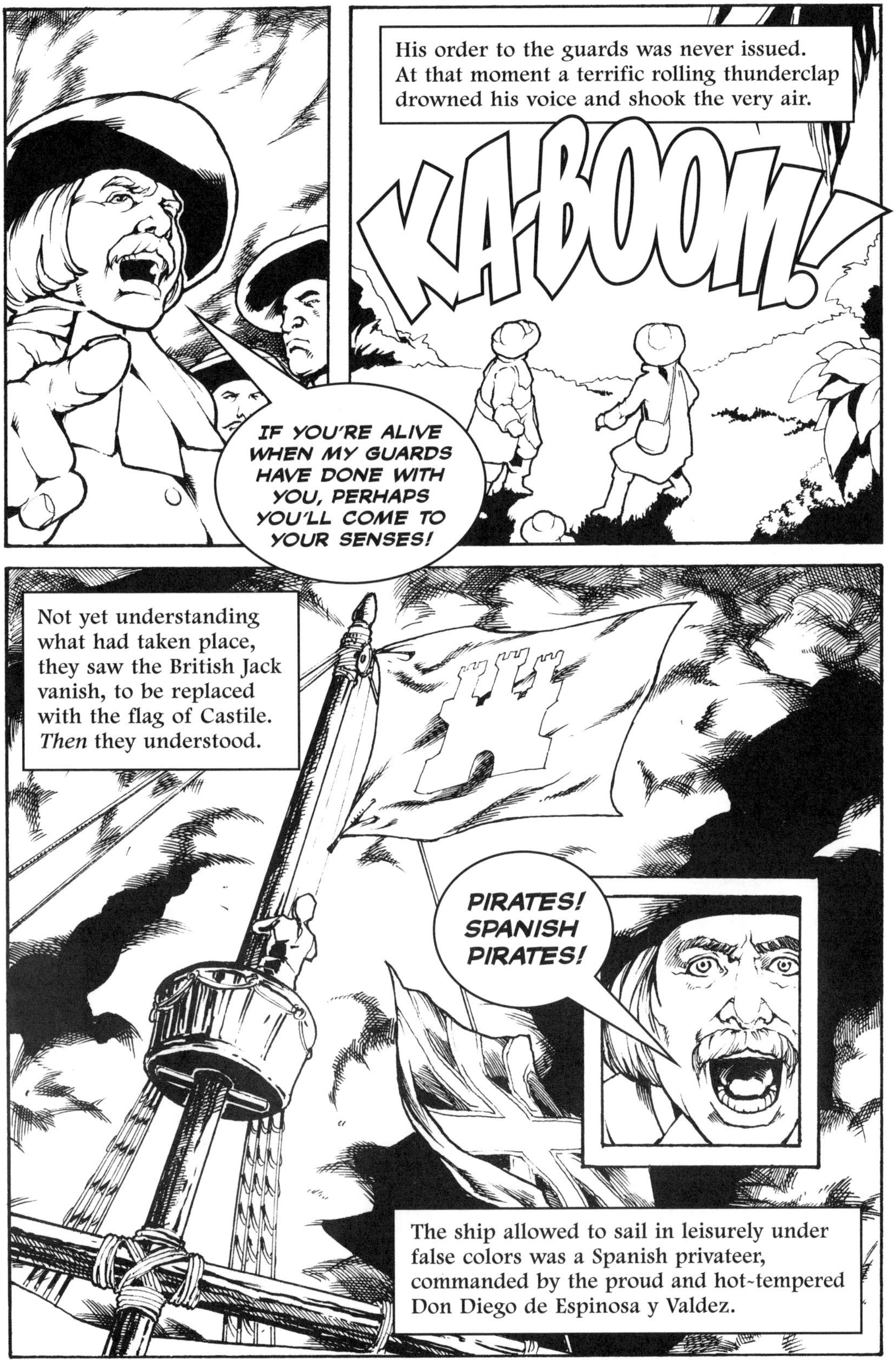
His order to the guards was never issued. At that moment a terrific rolling thunderclap drowned his voice and shook the very air.
IF YOU'RE ALIVE WHEN MY GUARDS HAVE DONE WITH YOU, PERHAPS YOU'LL COME TO YOUR SENSES!
KA-BOOM!
Not yet understanding what had taken place, they saw the British Jack vanish, to be replaced with the flag of Castile. *Then* they understood.
PIRATES! SPANISH PIRATES!
The ship allowed to sail in leisurely under false colors was a Spanish privateer, commanded by the proud and hot-tempered Don Diego de Espinosa y Valdez.

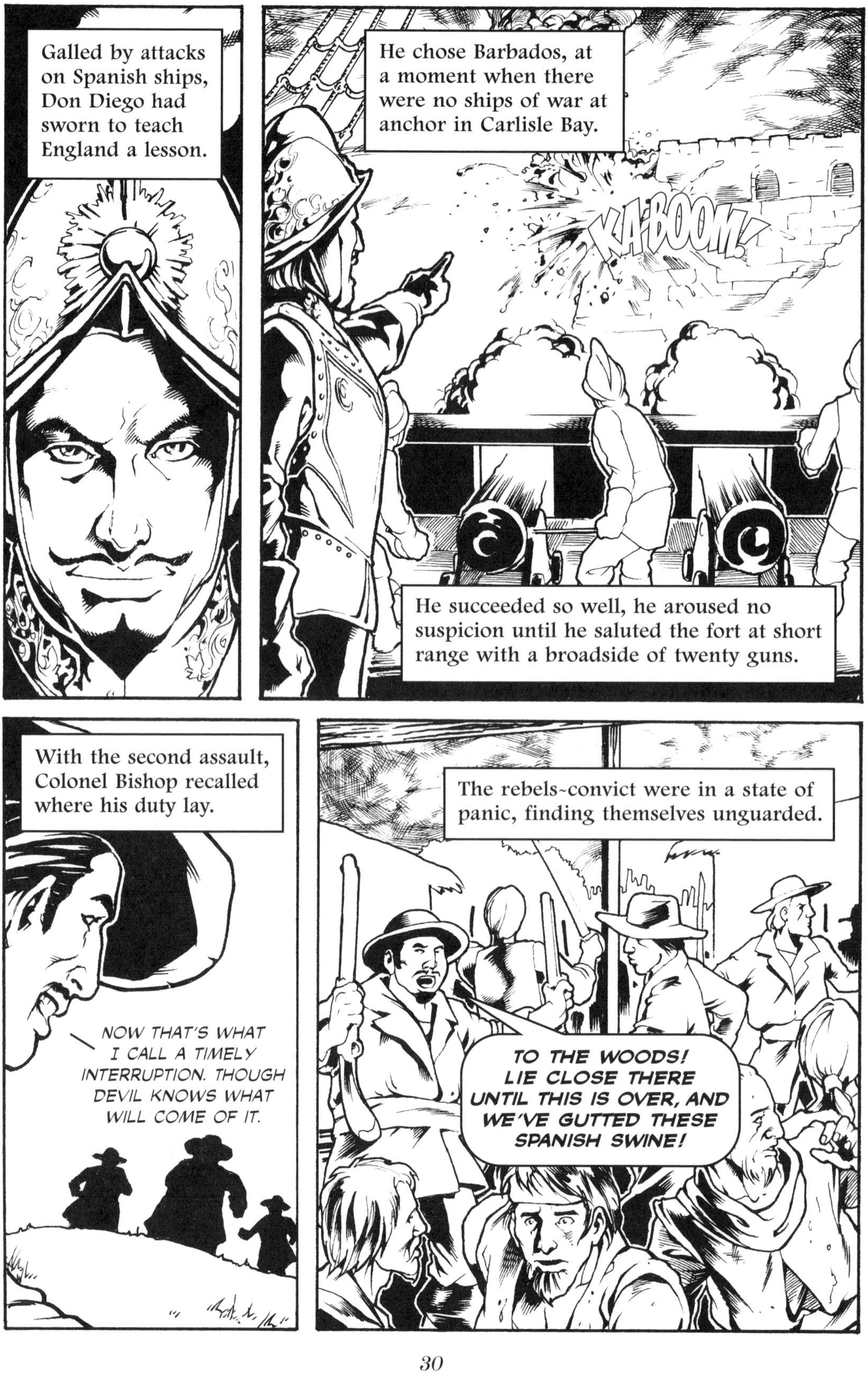
Galled by attacks on Spanish ships, Don Diego had sworn to teach England a lesson.
He chose Barbados, at a moment when there were no ships of war at anchor in Carlisle Bay.
KA-BOOM!
He succeeded so well, he aroused no suspicion until he saluted the fort at short range with a broadside of twenty guns.
With the second assault, Colonel Bishop recalled where his duty lay.
NOW THAT'S WHAT I CALL A TIMELY INTERRUPTION. THOUGH DEVIL KNOWS WHAT WILL COME OF IT.
The rebels-convict were in a state of panic, finding themselves unguarded.
TO THE WOODS! LIE CLOSE THERE UNTIL THIS IS OVER, AND WE'VE GUTTED THESE SPANISH SWINE!

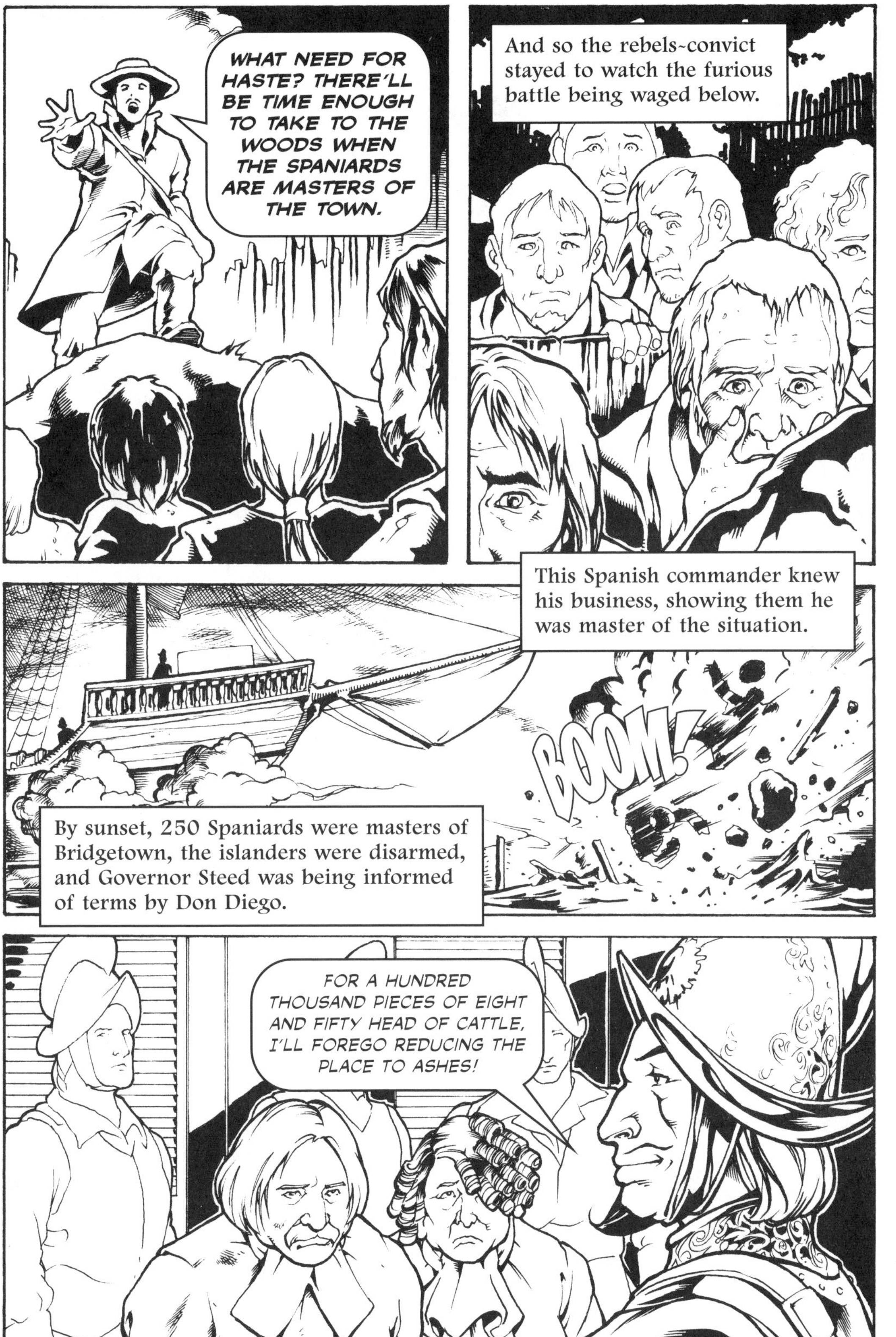
WHAT NEED FOR HASTE? THERE'LL BE TIME ENOUGH TO TAKE TO THE WOODS WHEN THE SPANIARDS ARE MASTERS OF THE TOWN.
And so the rebels-convict stayed to watch the furious battle being waged below.
This Spanish commander knew his business, showing them he was master of the situation.
BOOM!
By sunset, 250 Spaniards were masters of Bridgetown, the islanders were disarmed, and Governor Steed was being informed of terms by Don Diego.
FOR A HUNDRED THOUSAND PIECES OF EIGHT AND FIFTY HEAD OF CATTLE, I'LL FOREGO REDUCING THE PLACE TO ASHES!

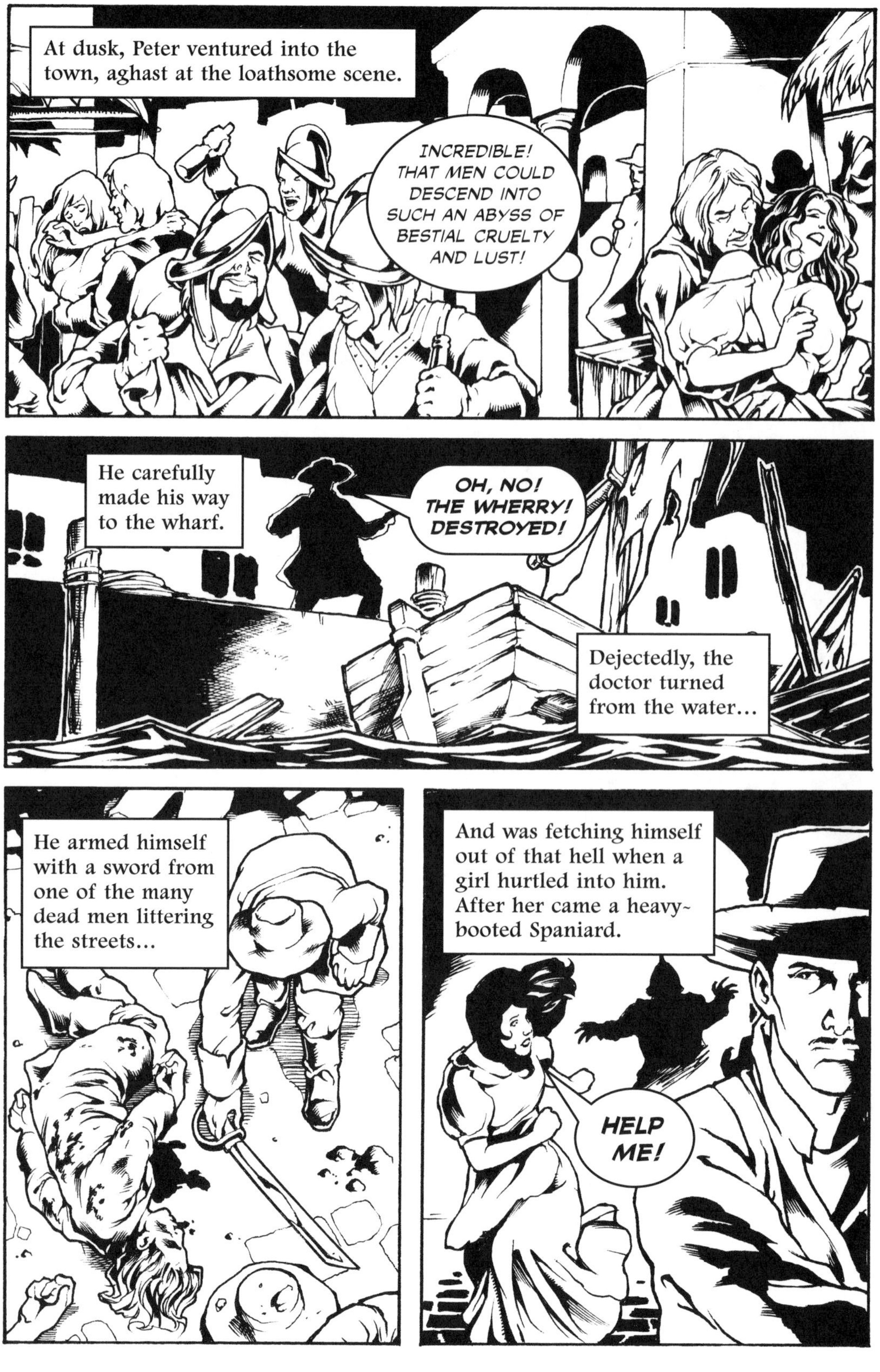
At dusk, Peter ventured into the town, aghast at the loathsome scene.
INCREDIBLE! THAT MEN COULD DESCEND INTO SUCH AN ABYSS OF BESTIAL CRUELTY AND LUST!
He carefully made his way to the wharf.
OH, NO! THE WHERRY! DESTROYED!
Dejectedly, the doctor turned from the water...
He armed himself with a sword from one of the many dead men littering the streets...
And was fetching himself out of that hell when a girl hurtled into him. After her came a heavy-booted Spaniard.
HELP ME!

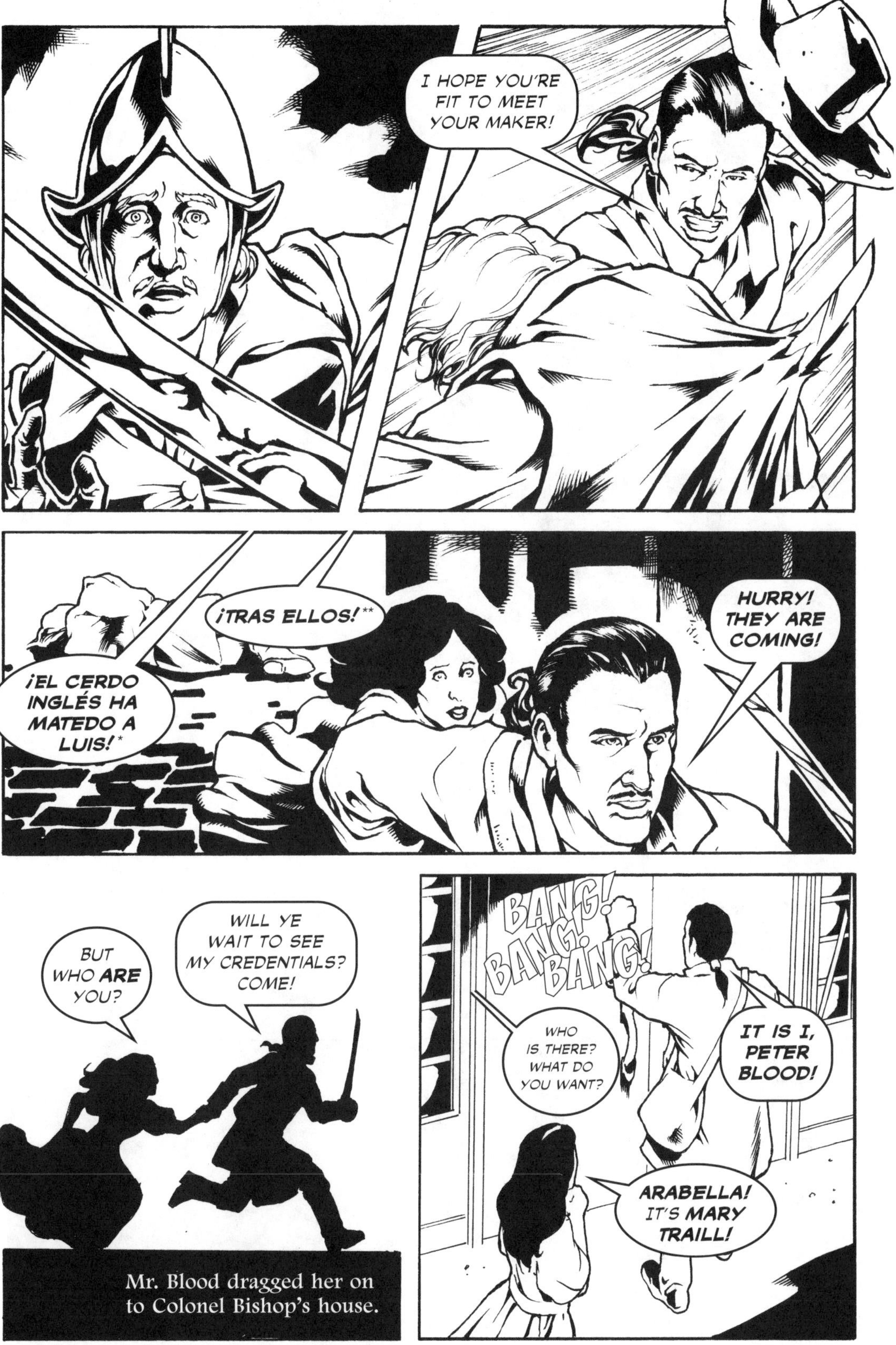
I HOPE YOU'RE FIT TO MEET YOUR MAKER!
¡EL CERDO INGLÉS HA MATEDO A LUIS!*
¡TRAS ELLOS!**
HURRY! THEY ARE COMING!
BUT WHO ARE YOU?
WILL YE WAIT TO SEE MY CREDENTIALS? COME!
Mr. Blood dragged her on to Colonel Bishop's house.
BANG! BANG! BANG!
WHO IS THERE? WHAT DO YOU WANT?
IT IS I, PETER BLOOD!
ARABELLA! IT'S MARY TRAILL!

** The English pig has killed Luis!*
*** After them!*

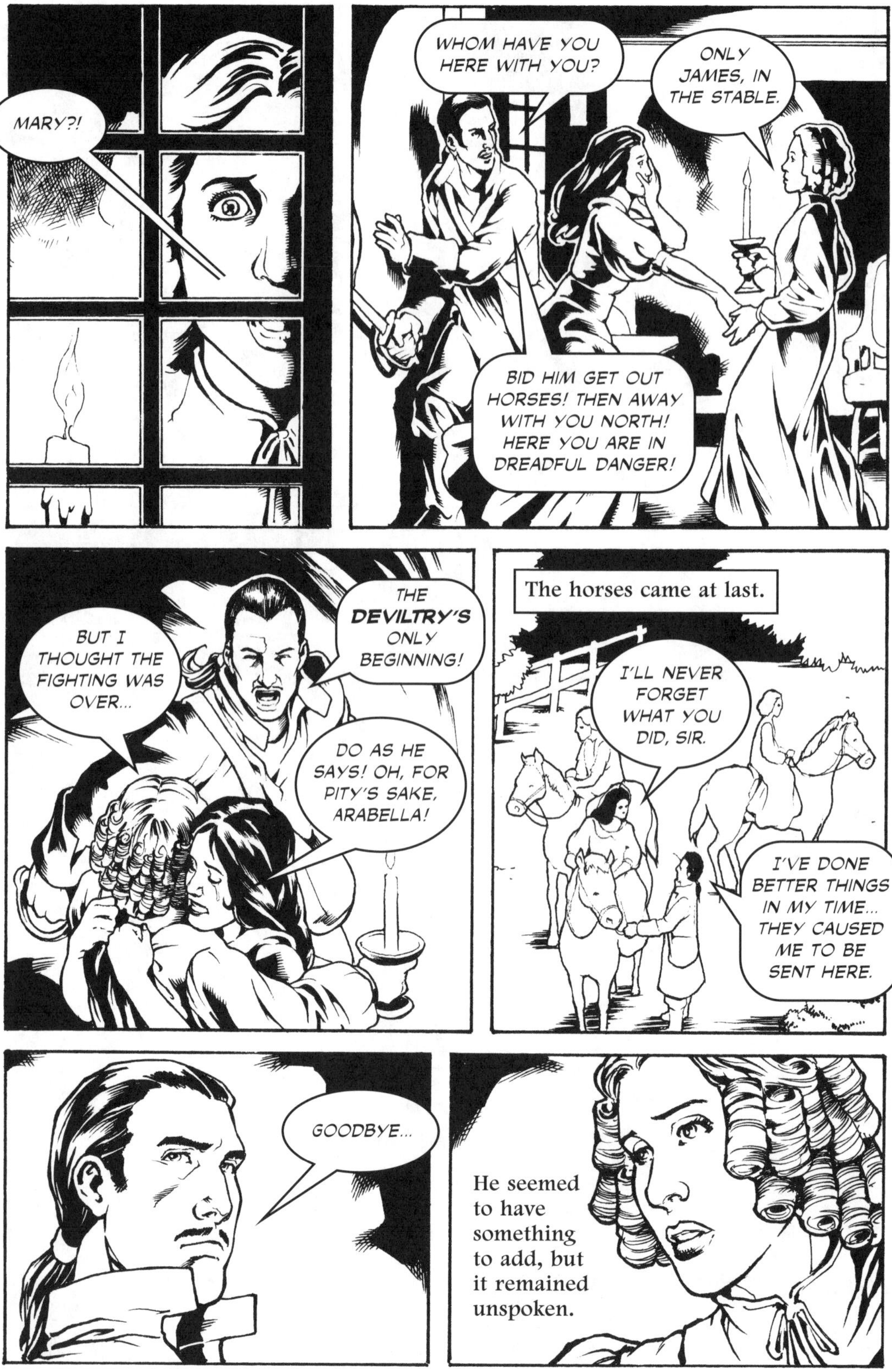
MARY?!
WHOM HAVE YOU HERE WITH YOU?
ONLY JAMES, IN THE STABLE.
BID HIM GET OUT HORSES! THEN AWAY WITH YOU NORTH! HERE YOU ARE IN DREADFUL DANGER!
BUT I THOUGHT THE FIGHTING WAS OVER...
THE DEVILTRY'S ONLY BEGINNING!
DO AS HE SAYS! OH, FOR PITY'S SAKE, ARABELLA!
The horses came at last.
I'LL NEVER FORGET WHAT YOU DID, SIR.
I'VE DONE BETTER THINGS IN MY TIME... THEY CAUSED ME TO BE SENT HERE.
GOODBYE...
He seemed to have something to add, but it remained unspoken.

The horses receded into starlit night. Peter Blood went off to the stockade, where his fellow~slaves waited in anxiety and hope.

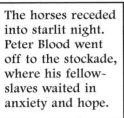

Later that night, while the Spanish gunner and crew feasted, only two sentinels kept vigil aboard the Cinco Llagas, at stem and stern.

Nor were they vigilant, or they must have observed the two boats gliding from the wharf under the great ship's quarter.

From the gallery aft hung the ladder which Don Diego had descended to the boat that had taken him ashore.

QUIEN ESTÁ ALLÍ?... PEDRO?...*

PETER IS MY NAME, BUT NOT THE PETER YOU'RE EXPECTING!

* Who's there?... Pedro?...

35

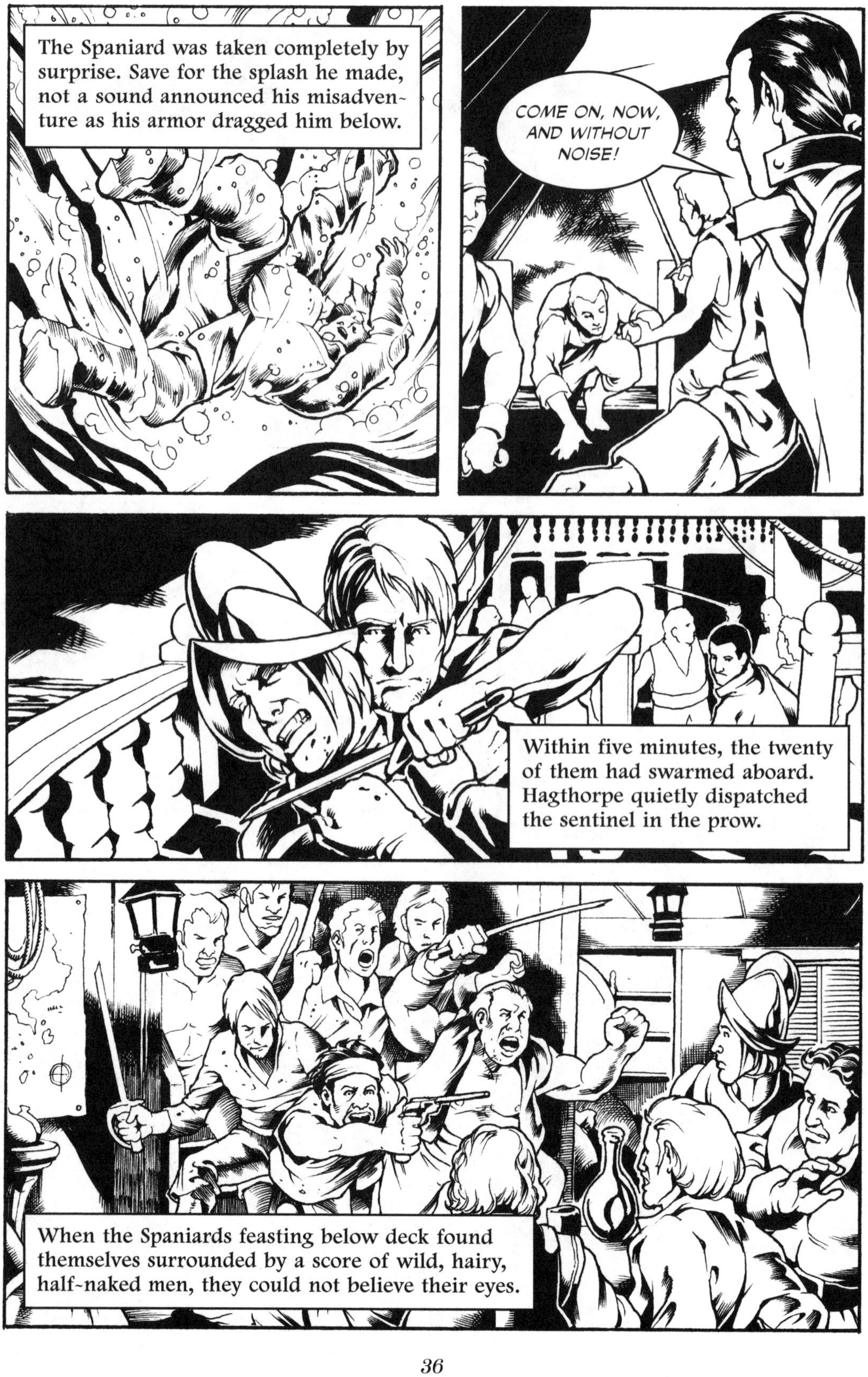
The Spaniard was taken completely by surprise. Save for the splash he made, not a sound announced his misadventure as his armor dragged him below.
COME ON, NOW, AND WITHOUT NOISE!
Within five minutes, the twenty of them had swarmed aboard. Hagthorpe quietly dispatched the sentinel in the prow.
When the Spaniards feasting below deck found themselves surrounded by a score of wild, hairy, half-naked men, they could not believe their eyes.

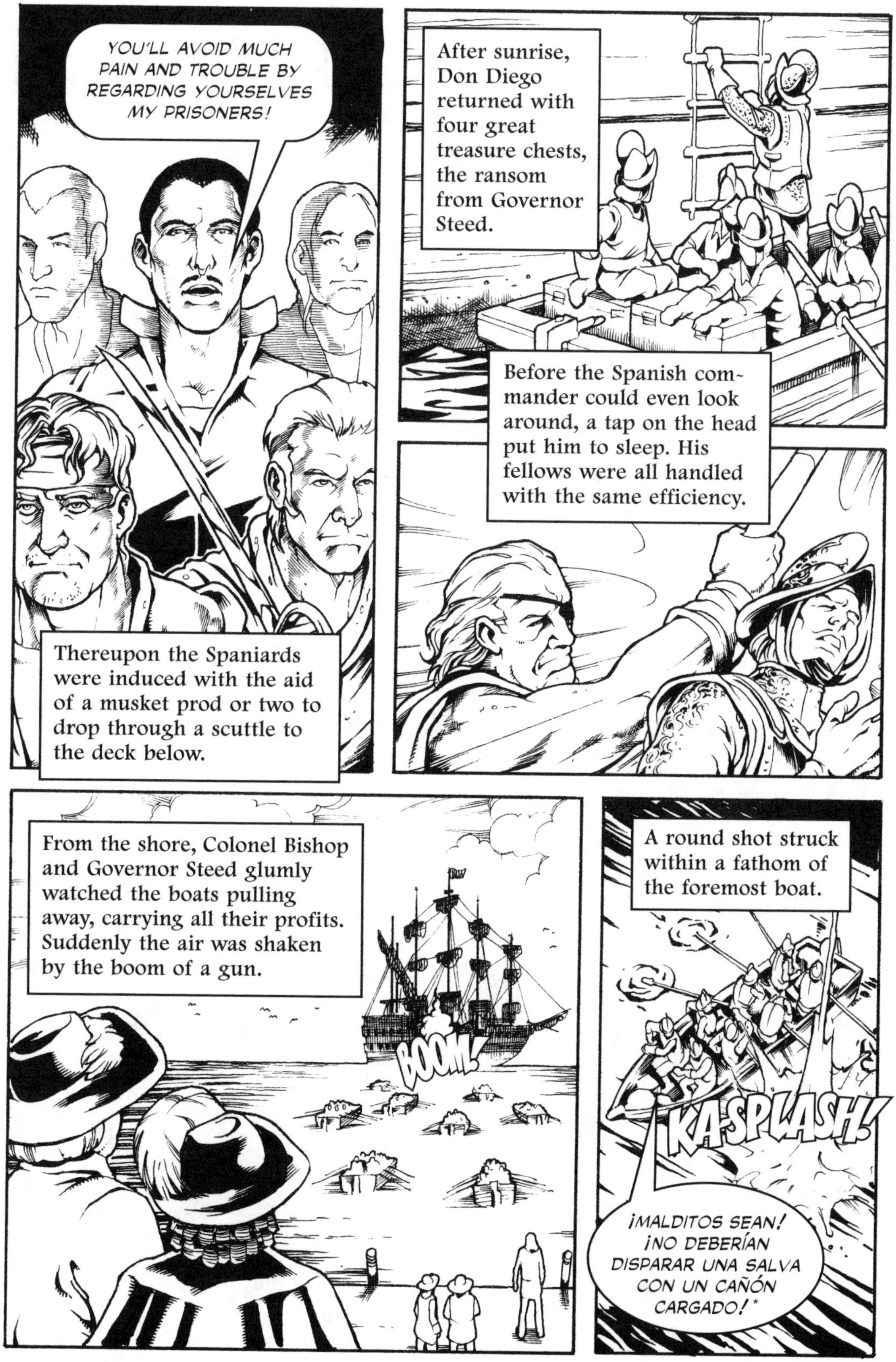
YOU'LL AVOID MUCH PAIN AND TROUBLE BY REGARDING YOURSELVES MY PRISONERS!
Thereupon the Spaniards were induced with the aid of a musket prod or two to drop through a scuttle to the deck below.
After sunrise, Don Diego returned with four great treasure chests, the ransom from Governor Steed.
Before the Spanish commander could even look around, a tap on the head put him to sleep. His fellows were all handled with the same efficiency.
From the shore, Colonel Bishop and Governor Steed glumly watched the boats pulling away, carrying all their profits. Suddenly the air was shaken by the boom of a gun.
BOOM!
A round shot struck within a fathom of the foremost boat.
KA-SPLASH!
¡MALDITOS SEAN! ¡NO DEBERÍAN DISPARAR UNA SALVA CON UN CAÑÓN CARGADO! *

* Damn them! They should know better than to fire a salute from a loaded cannon!

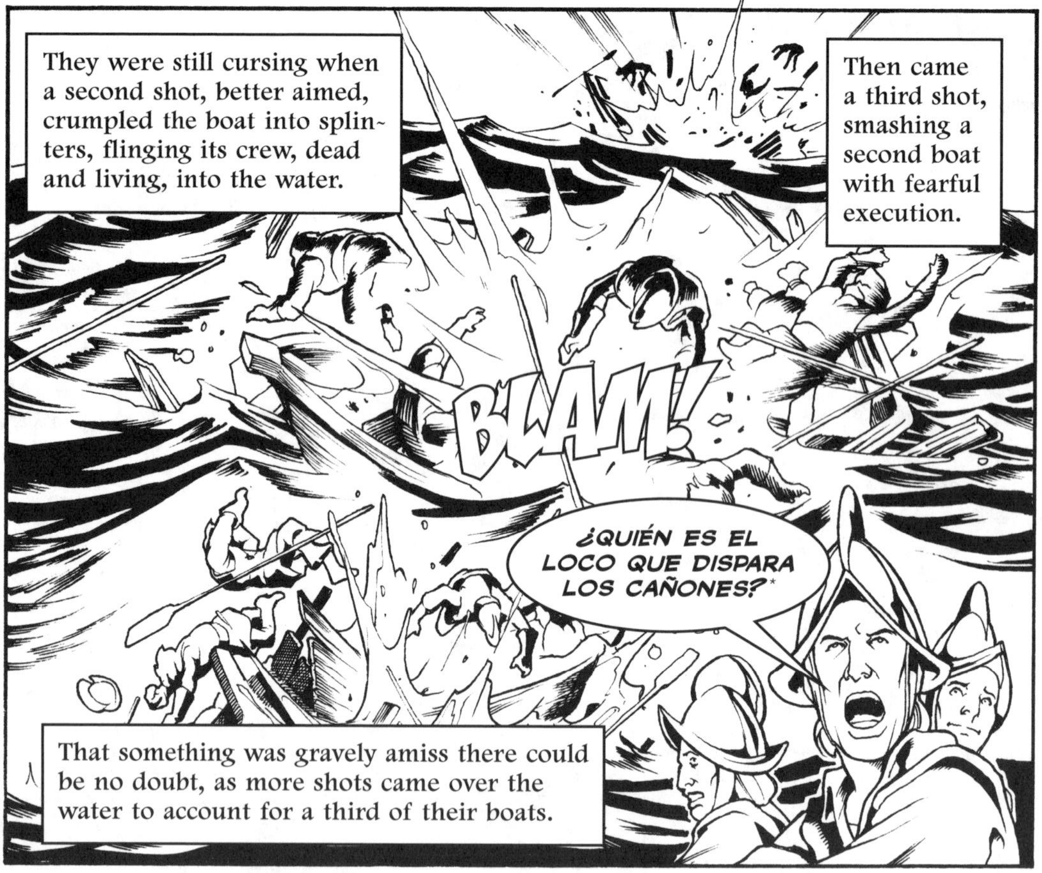
They were still cursing when a second shot, better aimed, crumpled the boat into splinters, flinging its crew, dead and living, into the water.
Then came a third shot, smashing a second boat with fearful execution.
BLAM!
¿QUIÉN ES EL LOCO QUE DISPARA LOS CAÑONES?*
That something was gravely amiss there could be no doubt, as more shots came over the water to account for a third of their boats.

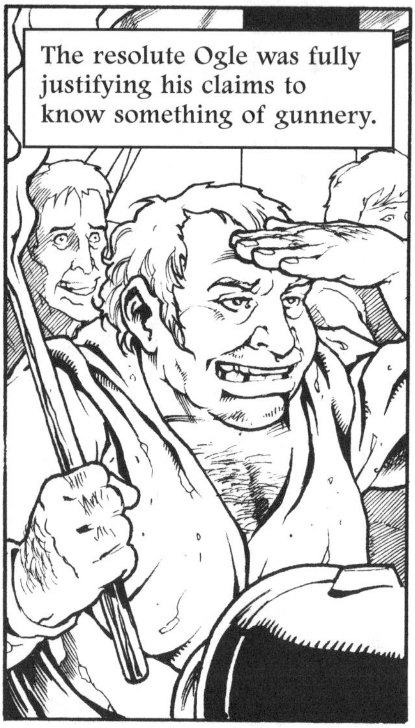
The resolute Ogle was fully justifying his claims to know something of gunnery.

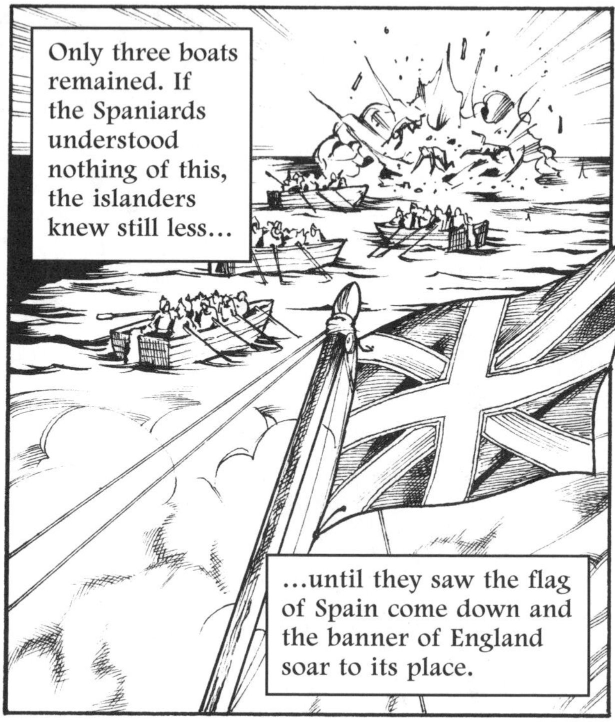
Only three boats remained. If the Spaniards understood nothing of this, the islanders knew still less…
…until they saw the flag of Spain come down and the banner of England soar to its place.

* *What madman has been let loose among the guns?*

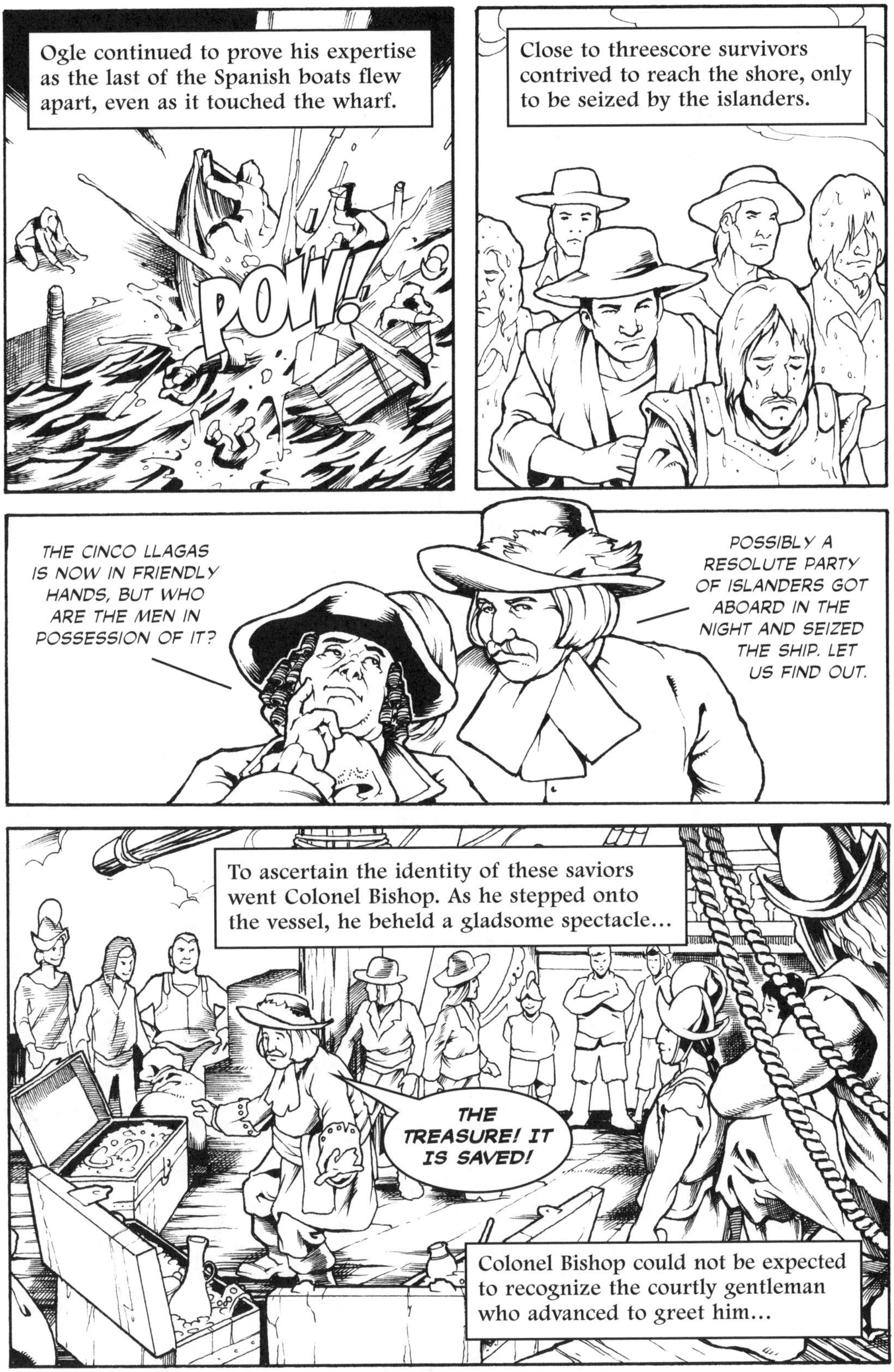
Ogle continued to prove his expertise as the last of the Spanish boats flew apart, even as it touched the wharf.
POW!
Close to threescore survivors contrived to reach the shore, only to be seized by the islanders.
THE CINCO LLAGAS IS NOW IN FRIENDLY HANDS, BUT WHO ARE THE MEN IN POSSESSION OF IT?
POSSIBLY A RESOLUTE PARTY OF ISLANDERS GOT ABOARD IN THE NIGHT AND SEIZED THE SHIP. LET US FIND OUT.
To ascertain the identity of these saviors went Colonel Bishop. As he stepped onto the vessel, he beheld a gladsome spectacle...
THE TREASURE! IT IS SAVED!
Colonel Bishop could not be expected to recognize the courtly gentleman who advanced to greet him...

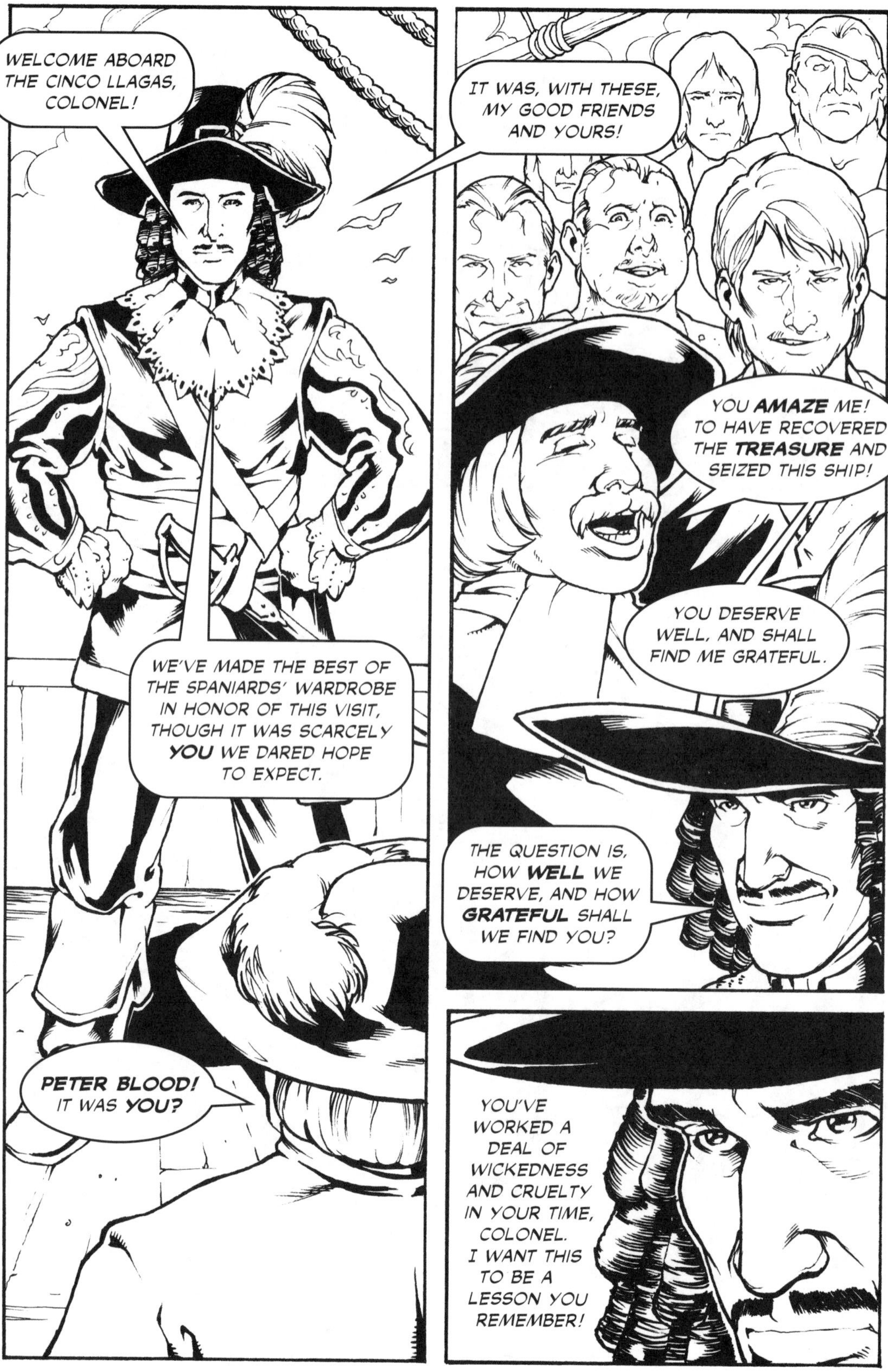
WELCOME ABOARD THE CINCO LLAGAS, COLONEL!
WE'VE MADE THE BEST OF THE SPANIARDS' WARDROBE IN HONOR OF THIS VISIT, THOUGH IT WAS SCARCELY **YOU** WE DARED HOPE TO EXPECT.
PETER BLOOD! IT WAS **YOU?**
IT WAS, WITH THESE, MY GOOD FRIENDS AND YOURS!
YOU **AMAZE** ME! TO HAVE RECOVERED THE **TREASURE** AND SEIZED THIS SHIP!
YOU DESERVE WELL, AND SHALL FIND ME GRATEFUL.
THE QUESTION IS, HOW **WELL** WE DESERVE, AND HOW **GRATEFUL** SHALL WE FIND YOU?
YOU'VE WORKED A DEAL OF WICKEDNESS AND CRUELTY IN YOUR TIME, COLONEL. I WANT THIS TO BE A LESSON YOU REMEMBER!

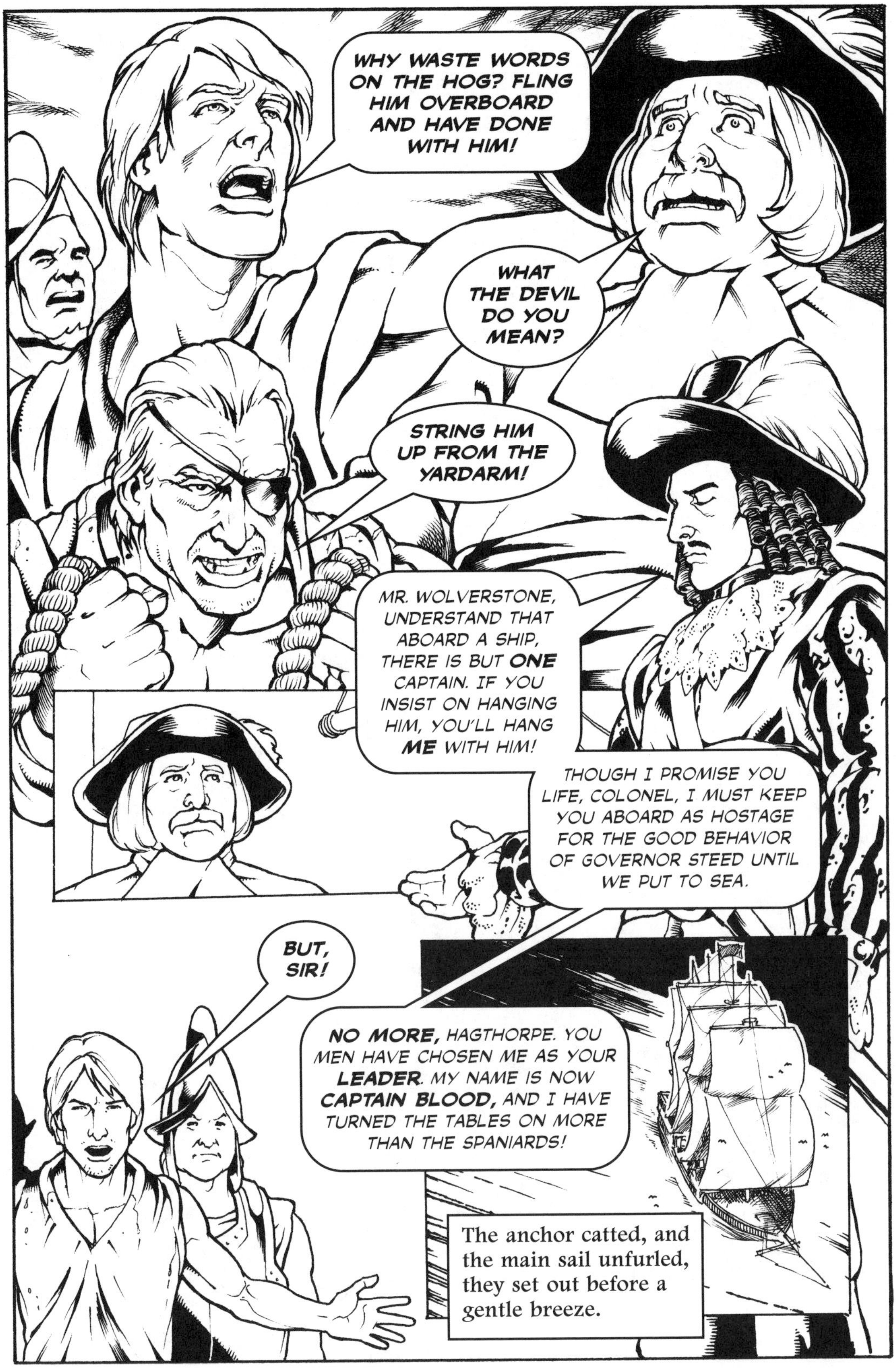
WHY WASTE WORDS ON THE HOG? FLING HIM OVERBOARD AND HAVE DONE WITH HIM!
WHAT THE DEVIL DO YOU MEAN?
STRING HIM UP FROM THE YARDARM!
MR. WOLVERSTONE, UNDERSTAND THAT ABOARD A SHIP, THERE IS BUT ONE CAPTAIN. IF YOU INSIST ON HANGING HIM, YOU'LL HANG ME WITH HIM!
THOUGH I PROMISE YOU LIFE, COLONEL, I MUST KEEP YOU ABOARD AS HOSTAGE FOR THE GOOD BEHAVIOR OF GOVERNOR STEED UNTIL WE PUT TO SEA.
BUT, SIR!
NO MORE, HAGTHORPE. YOU MEN HAVE CHOSEN ME AS YOUR LEADER. MY NAME IS NOW CAPTAIN BLOOD, AND I HAVE TURNED THE TABLES ON MORE THAN THE SPANIARDS!
The anchor catted, and the main sail unfurled, they set out before a gentle breeze.

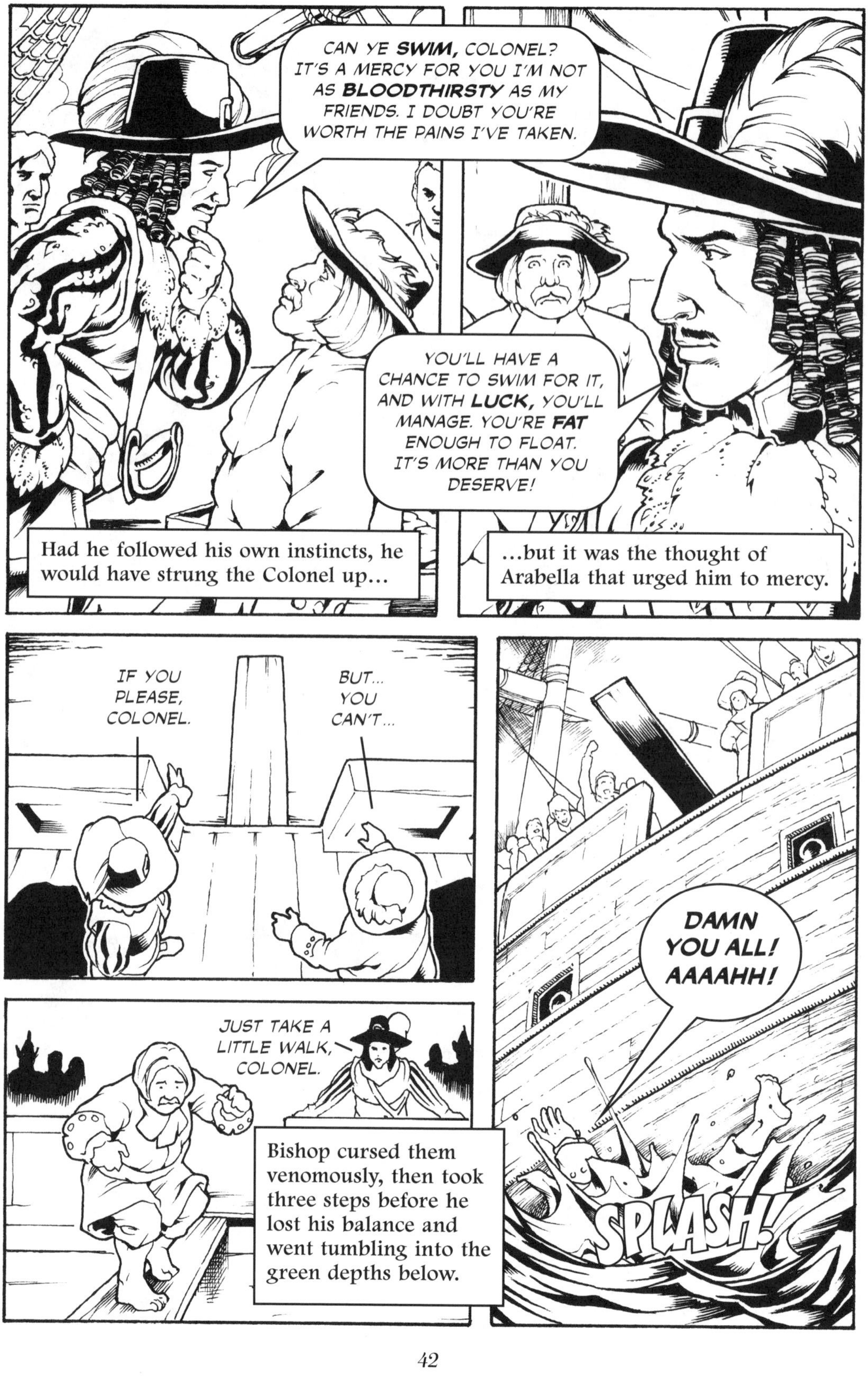
CAN YE SWIM, COLONEL? IT'S A MERCY FOR YOU I'M NOT AS BLOODTHIRSTY AS MY FRIENDS. I DOUBT YOU'RE WORTH THE PAINS I'VE TAKEN.
YOU'LL HAVE A CHANCE TO SWIM FOR IT, AND WITH LUCK, YOU'LL MANAGE. YOU'RE FAT ENOUGH TO FLOAT. IT'S MORE THAN YOU DESERVE!
Had he followed his own instincts, he would have strung the Colonel up...
...but it was the thought of Arabella that urged him to mercy.
IF YOU PLEASE, COLONEL.
BUT... YOU CAN'T...
JUST TAKE A LITTLE WALK, COLONEL.
Bishop cursed them venomously, then took three steps before he lost his balance and went tumbling into the green depths below.
DAMN YOU ALL! AAAAHH!
SPLASH!

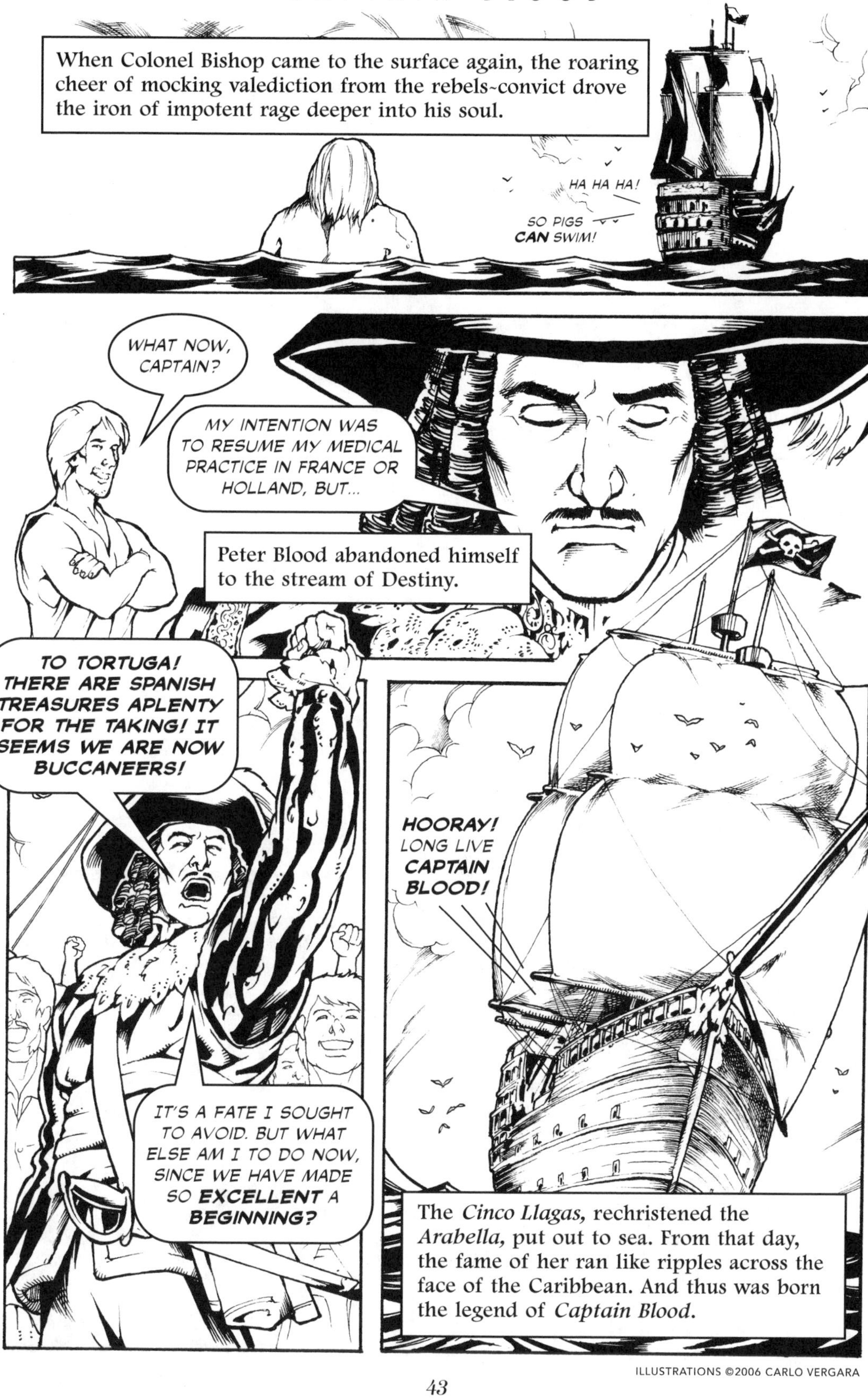
When Colonel Bishop came to the surface again, the roaring cheer of mocking valediction from the rebels-convict drove the iron of impotent rage deeper into his soul.
HA HA HA!
SO PIGS **CAN** SWIM!
WHAT NOW, CAPTAIN?
MY INTENTION WAS TO RESUME MY MEDICAL PRACTICE IN FRANCE OR HOLLAND, BUT...
Peter Blood abandoned himself to the stream of Destiny.
TO TORTUGA! THERE ARE SPANISH TREASURES APLENTY FOR THE TAKING! IT SEEMS WE ARE NOW BUCCANEERS!
IT'S A FATE I SOUGHT TO AVOID. BUT WHAT ELSE AM I TO DO NOW, SINCE WE HAVE MADE SO **EXCELLENT** A **BEGINNING?**
HOORAY! LONG LIVE **CAPTAIN BLOOD!**
The *Cinco Llagas,* rechristened the *Arabella,* put out to sea. From that day, the fame of her ran like ripples across the face of the Caribbean. And thus was born the legend of *Captain Blood*.

SPANISH TRANSLATIONS COURTESY LANCE TOOKS & TRANSLATED.NET

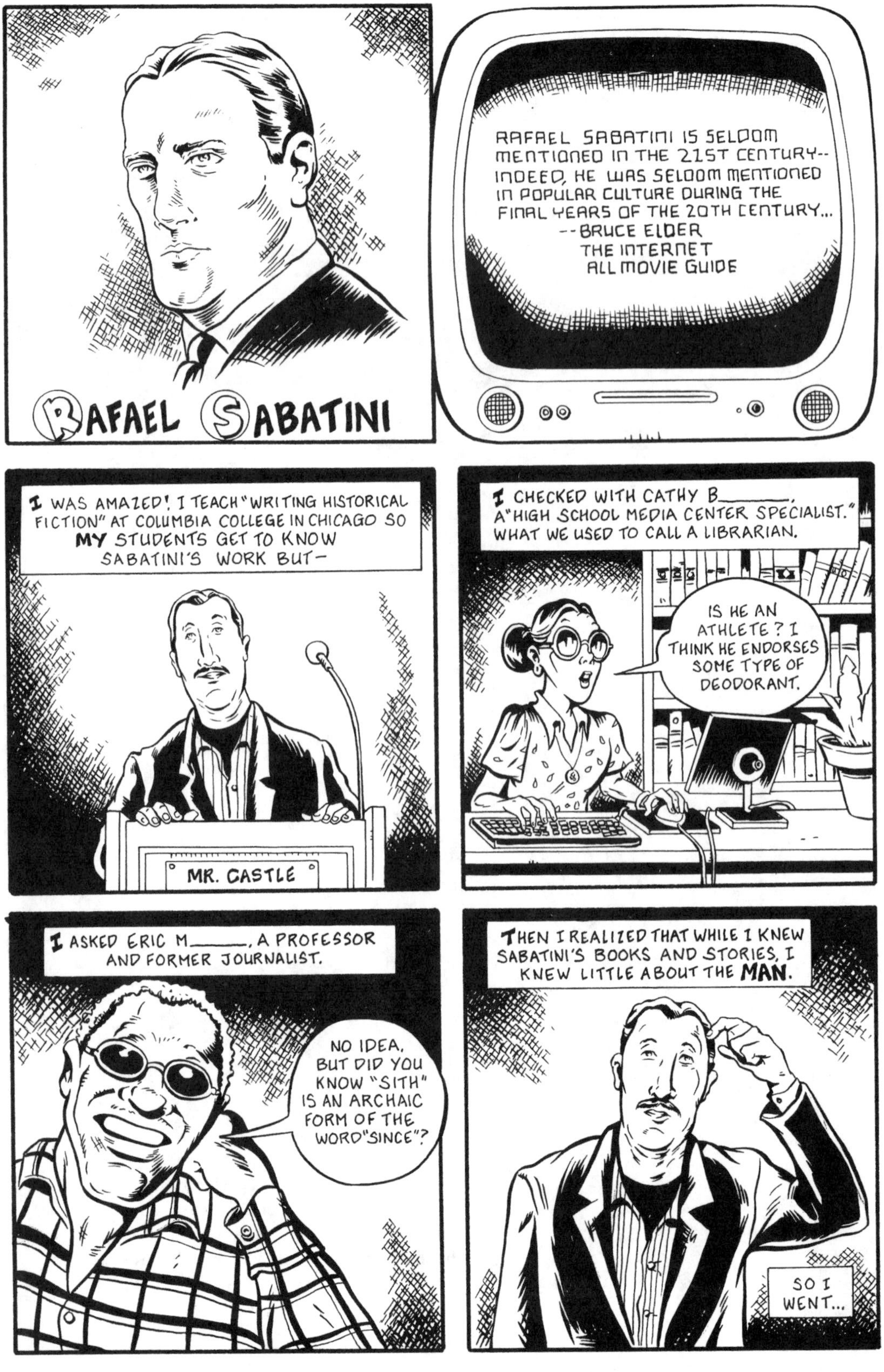
RAFAEL SABATINI
RAFAEL SABATINI IS SELDOM MENTIONED IN THE 21ST CENTURY-- INDEED, HE WAS SELDOM MENTIONED IN POPULAR CULTURE DURING THE FINAL YEARS OF THE 20TH CENTURY... --BRUCE ELDER THE INTERNET ALL MOVIE GUIDE
I WAS AMAZED! I TEACH "WRITING HISTORICAL FICTION" AT COLUMBIA COLLEGE IN CHICAGO SO MY STUDENTS GET TO KNOW SABATINI'S WORK BUT-
MR. CASTLE
I CHECKED WITH CATHY B______, A "HIGH SCHOOL MEDIA CENTER SPECIALIST." WHAT WE USED TO CALL A LIBRARIAN.
IS HE AN ATHLETE? I THINK HE ENDORSES SOME TYPE OF DEODORANT.
I ASKED ERIC M______, A PROFESSOR AND FORMER JOURNALIST.
NO IDEA. BUT DID YOU KNOW "SITH" IS AN ARCHAIC FORM OF THE WORD "SINCE"?
THEN I REALIZED THAT WHILE I KNEW SABATINI'S BOOKS AND STORIES, I KNEW LITTLE ABOUT THE MAN.
SO I WENT...

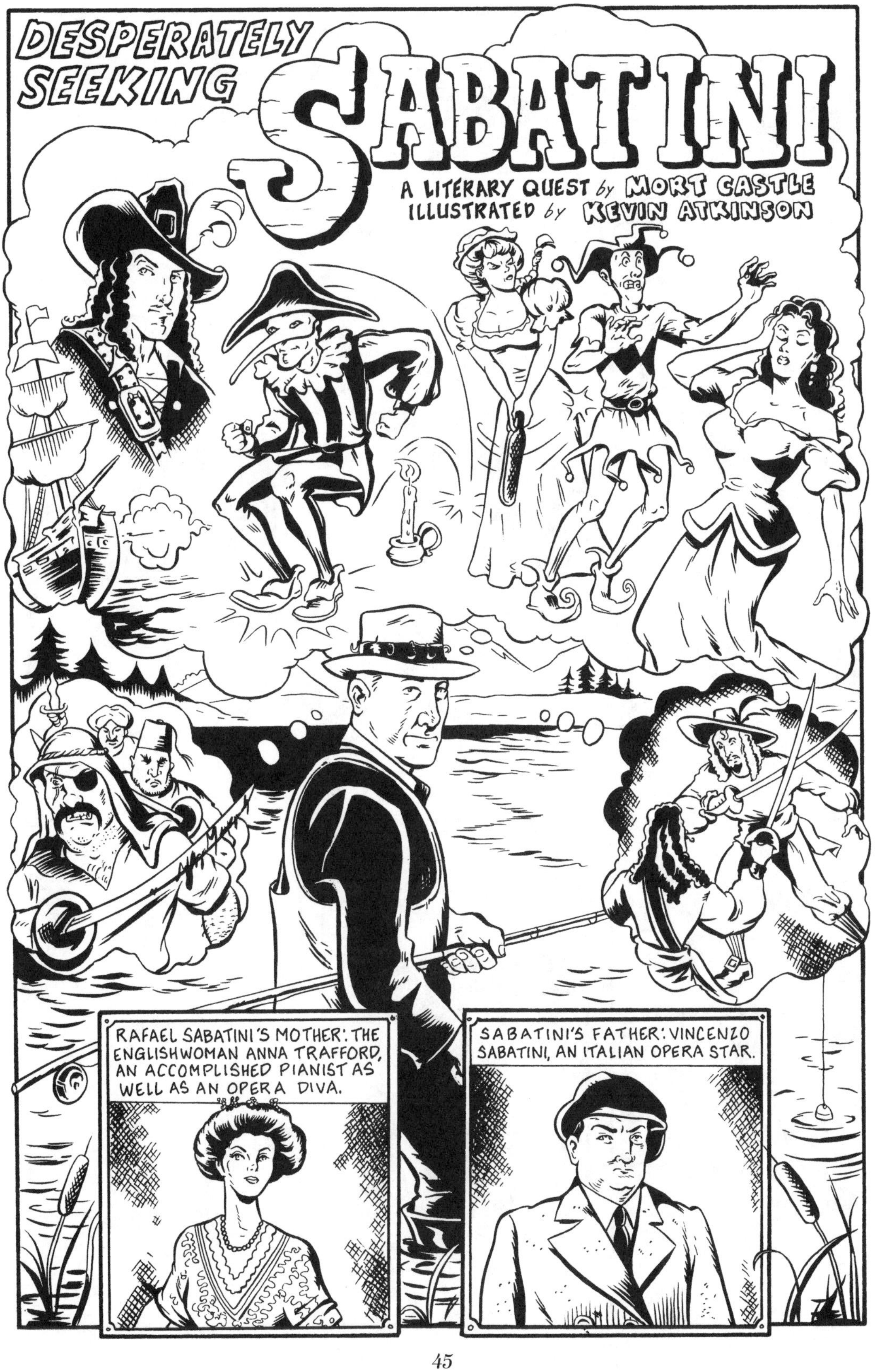
DESPERATELY SEEKING SABATINI
A LITERARY QUEST by MORT CASTLE
ILLUSTRATED by KEVIN ATKINSON
RAFAEL SABATINI'S MOTHER: THE ENGLISHWOMAN ANNA TRAFFORD, AN ACCOMPLISHED PIANIST AS WELL AS AN OPERA DIVA.
SABATINI'S FATHER: VINCENZO SABATINI, AN ITALIAN OPERA STAR.

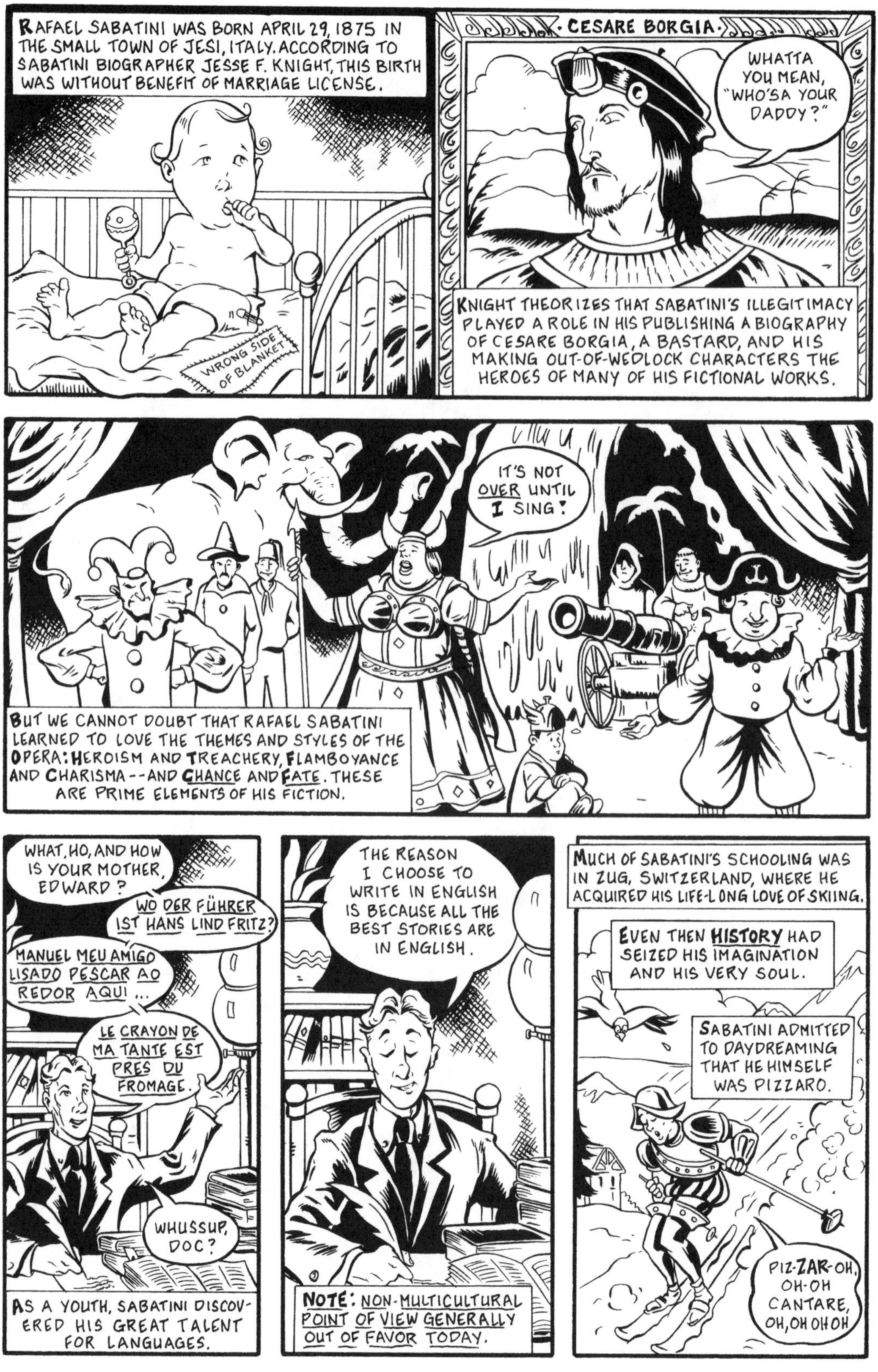
RAFAEL SABATINI WAS BORN APRIL 29, 1875 IN THE SMALL TOWN OF JESI, ITALY. ACCORDING TO SABATINI BIOGRAPHER JESSE F. KNIGHT, THIS BIRTH WAS WITHOUT BENEFIT OF MARRIAGE LICENSE.
WRONG SIDE OF BLANKET
· CESARE BORGIA ·
WHATTA YOU MEAN, "WHO'SA YOUR DADDY?"
KNIGHT THEORIZES THAT SABATINI'S ILLEGITIMACY PLAYED A ROLE IN HIS PUBLISHING A BIOGRAPHY OF CESARE BORGIA, A BASTARD, AND HIS MAKING OUT-OF-WEDLOCK CHARACTERS THE HEROES OF MANY OF HIS FICTIONAL WORKS.
IT'S NOT OVER UNTIL I SING!
BUT WE CANNOT DOUBT THAT RAFAEL SABATINI LEARNED TO LOVE THE THEMES AND STYLES OF THE OPERA: HEROISM AND TREACHERY, FLAMBOYANCE AND CHARISMA -- AND CHANCE AND FATE. THESE ARE PRIME ELEMENTS OF HIS FICTION.
WHAT, HO, AND HOW IS YOUR MOTHER, EDWARD?
WO DER FÜHRER IST HANS LIND FRITZ?
MANUEL MEU AMIGO LISADO PESCAR AO REDOR AQUI...
LE CRAYON DE MA TANTE EST PRES DU FROMAGE.
WHUSSUP, DOC?
AS A YOUTH, SABATINI DISCOVERED HIS GREAT TALENT FOR LANGUAGES.
THE REASON I CHOOSE TO WRITE IN ENGLISH IS BECAUSE ALL THE BEST STORIES ARE IN ENGLISH.
NOTE: NON-MULTICULTURAL POINT OF VIEW GENERALLY OUT OF FAVOR TODAY.
MUCH OF SABATINI'S SCHOOLING WAS IN ZUG, SWITZERLAND, WHERE HE ACQUIRED HIS LIFE-LONG LOVE OF SKIING.
EVEN THEN HISTORY HAD SEIZED HIS IMAGINATION AND HIS VERY SOUL.
SABATINI ADMITTED TO DAYDREAMING THAT HE HIMSELF WAS PIZZARO.
PIZ-ZAR-OH, OH-OH CANTARE, OH, OH OH OH

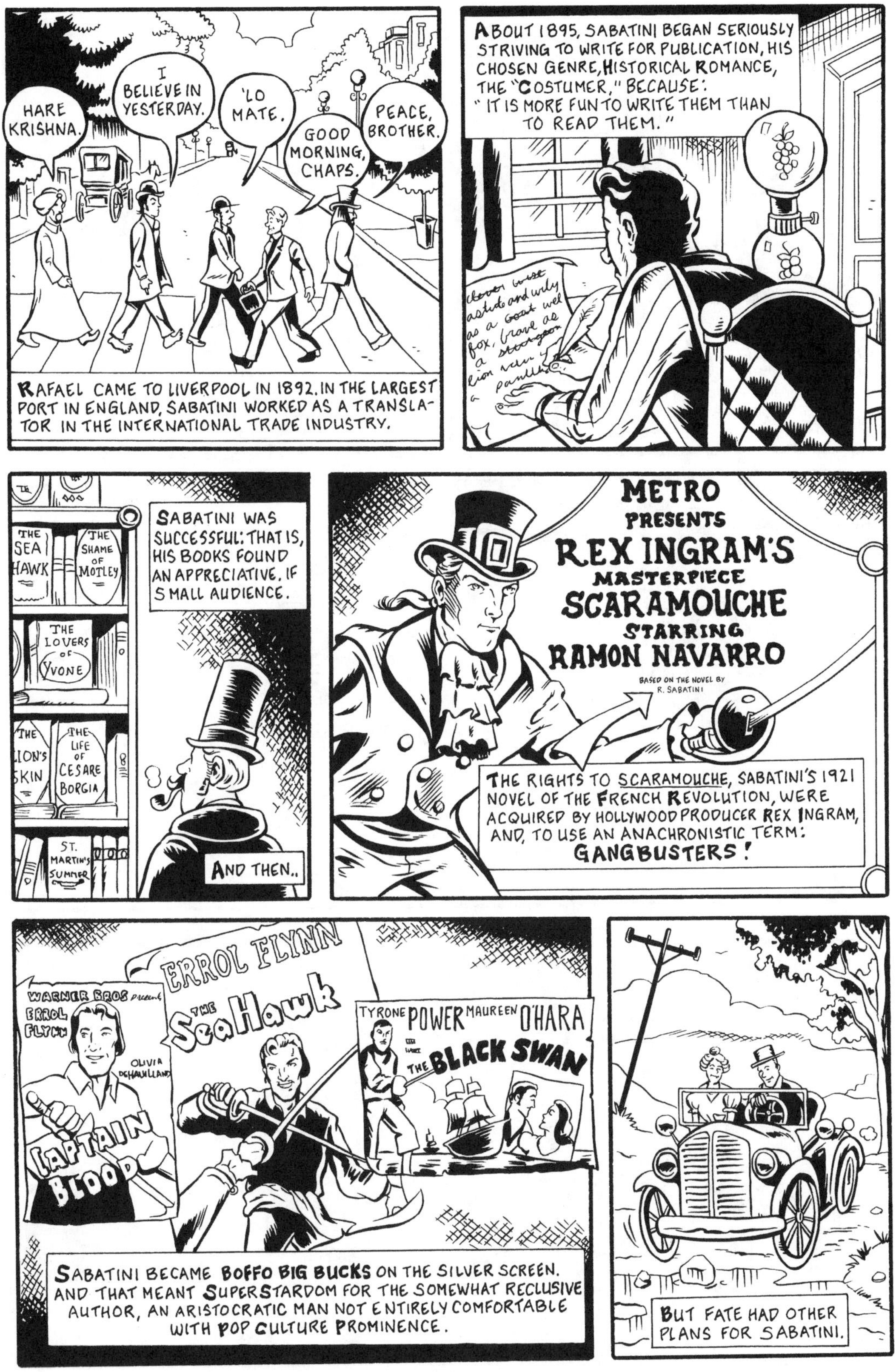
HARE KRISHNA.
I BELIEVE IN YESTERDAY.
'LO MATE.
GOOD MORNING, CHAPS.
PEACE, BROTHER.
RAFAEL CAME TO LIVERPOOL IN 1892. IN THE LARGEST PORT IN ENGLAND, SABATINI WORKED AS A TRANSLATOR IN THE INTERNATIONAL TRADE INDUSTRY.
ABOUT 1895, SABATINI BEGAN SERIOUSLY STRIVING TO WRITE FOR PUBLICATION, HIS CHOSEN GENRE, HISTORICAL ROMANCE, THE "COSTUMER," BECAUSE: "IT IS MORE FUN TO WRITE THEM THAN TO READ THEM."
THE SEA HAWK
THE SHAME OF MOTLEY
THE LOVERS OF YVONE
THE LION'S SKIN
THE LIFE OF CESARE BORGIA
ST. MARTIN'S SUMMER
SABATINI WAS SUCCESSFUL: THAT IS, HIS BOOKS FOUND AN APPRECIATIVE, IF SMALL AUDIENCE.
AND THEN..
METRO PRESENTS REX INGRAM'S MASTERPIECE SCARAMOUCHE STARRING RAMON NAVARRO
BASED ON THE NOVEL BY R. SABATINI
THE RIGHTS TO SCARAMOUCHE, SABATINI'S 1921 NOVEL OF THE FRENCH REVOLUTION, WERE ACQUIRED BY HOLLYWOOD PRODUCER REX INGRAM, AND, TO USE AN ANACHRONISTIC TERM: GANGBUSTERS!
WARNER BROS presents ERROL FLYNN
OLIVIA DEHAVILLAND
CAPTAIN BLOOD
ERROL FLYNN
THE SeaHawk
TYRONE POWER MAUREEN O'HARA
THE BLACK SWAN
SABATINI BECAME BOFFO BIG BUCKS ON THE SILVER SCREEN. AND THAT MEANT SUPERSTARDOM FOR THE SOMEWHAT RECLUSIVE AUTHOR, AN ARISTOCRATIC MAN NOT ENTIRELY COMFORTABLE WITH POP CULTURE PROMINENCE.
BUT FATE HAD OTHER PLANS FOR SABATINI.

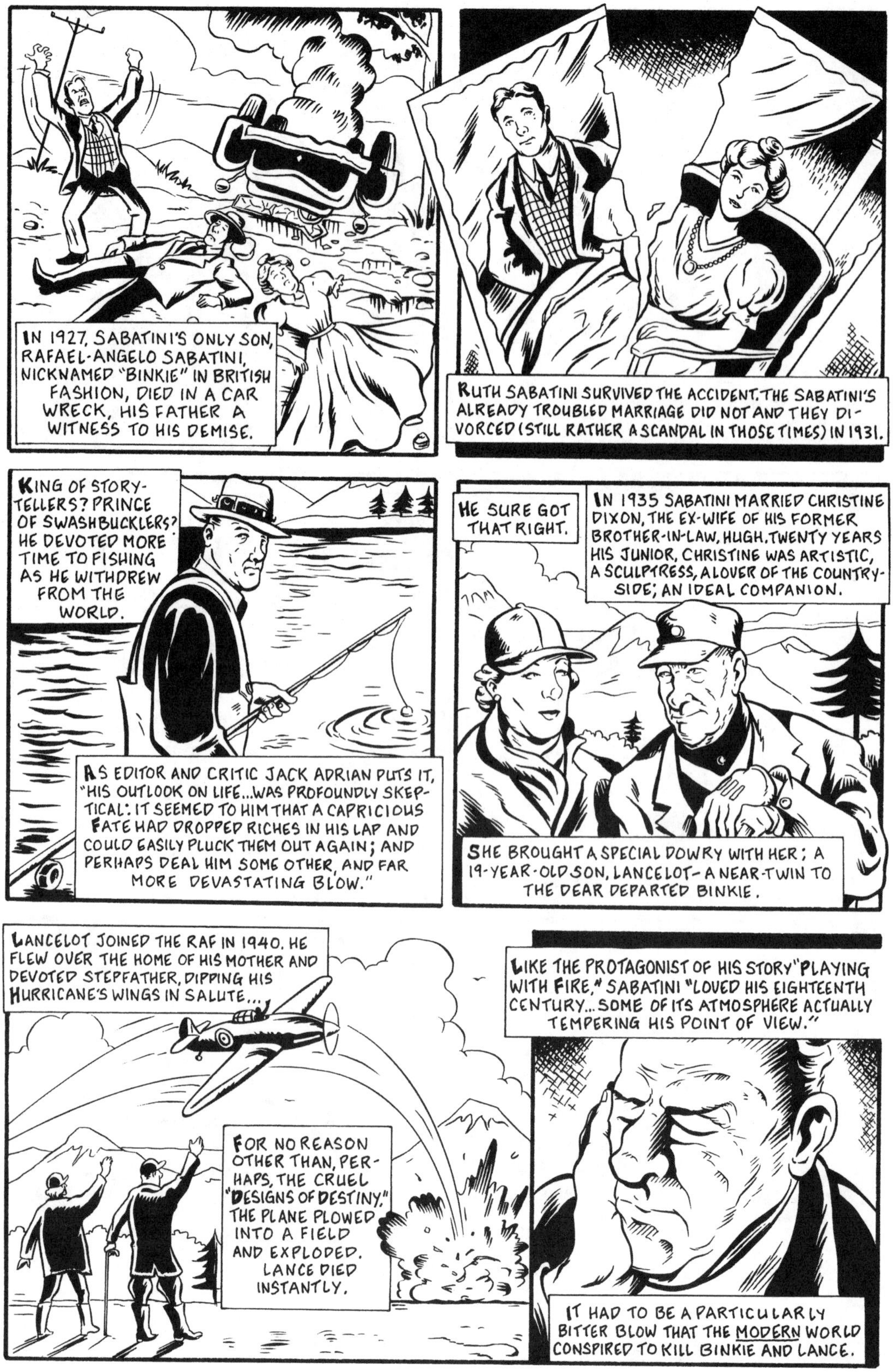
IN 1927, SABATINI'S ONLY SON, RAFAEL-ANGELO SABATINI, NICKNAMED "BINKIE" IN BRITISH FASHION, DIED IN A CAR WRECK, HIS FATHER A WITNESS TO HIS DEMISE.
RUTH SABATINI SURVIVED THE ACCIDENT. THE SABATINI'S ALREADY TROUBLED MARRIAGE DID NOT AND THEY DIVORCED (STILL RATHER A SCANDAL IN THOSE TIMES) IN 1931.
KING OF STORY-TELLERS? PRINCE OF SWASHBUCKLERS? HE DEVOTED MORE TIME TO FISHING AS HE WITHDREW FROM THE WORLD.
AS EDITOR AND CRITIC JACK ADRIAN PUTS IT, "HIS OUTLOOK ON LIFE...WAS PROFOUNDLY SKEPTICAL: IT SEEMED TO HIM THAT A CAPRICIOUS FATE HAD DROPPED RICHES IN HIS LAP AND COULD EASILY PLUCK THEM OUT AGAIN; AND PERHAPS DEAL HIM SOME OTHER, AND FAR MORE DEVASTATING BLOW."
HE SURE GOT THAT RIGHT.
IN 1935 SABATINI MARRIED CHRISTINE DIXON, THE EX-WIFE OF HIS FORMER BROTHER-IN-LAW, HUGH. TWENTY YEARS HIS JUNIOR, CHRISTINE WAS ARTISTIC, A SCULPTRESS, A LOVER OF THE COUNTRYSIDE; AN IDEAL COMPANION.
SHE BROUGHT A SPECIAL DOWRY WITH HER; A 19-YEAR-OLD SON, LANCELOT- A NEAR-TWIN TO THE DEAR DEPARTED BINKIE.
LANCELOT JOINED THE RAF IN 1940. HE FLEW OVER THE HOME OF HIS MOTHER AND DEVOTED STEPFATHER, DIPPING HIS HURRICANE'S WINGS IN SALUTE...
FOR NO REASON OTHER THAN, PERHAPS, THE CRUEL "DESIGNS OF DESTINY," THE PLANE PLOWED INTO A FIELD AND EXPLODED. LANCE DIED INSTANTLY.
LIKE THE PROTAGONIST OF HIS STORY "PLAYING WITH FIRE," SABATINI "LOVED HIS EIGHTEENTH CENTURY... SOME OF ITS ATMOSPHERE ACTUALLY TEMPERING HIS POINT OF VIEW."
IT HAD TO BE A PARTICULARLY BITTER BLOW THAT THE MODERN WORLD CONSPIRED TO KILL BINKIE AND LANCE.

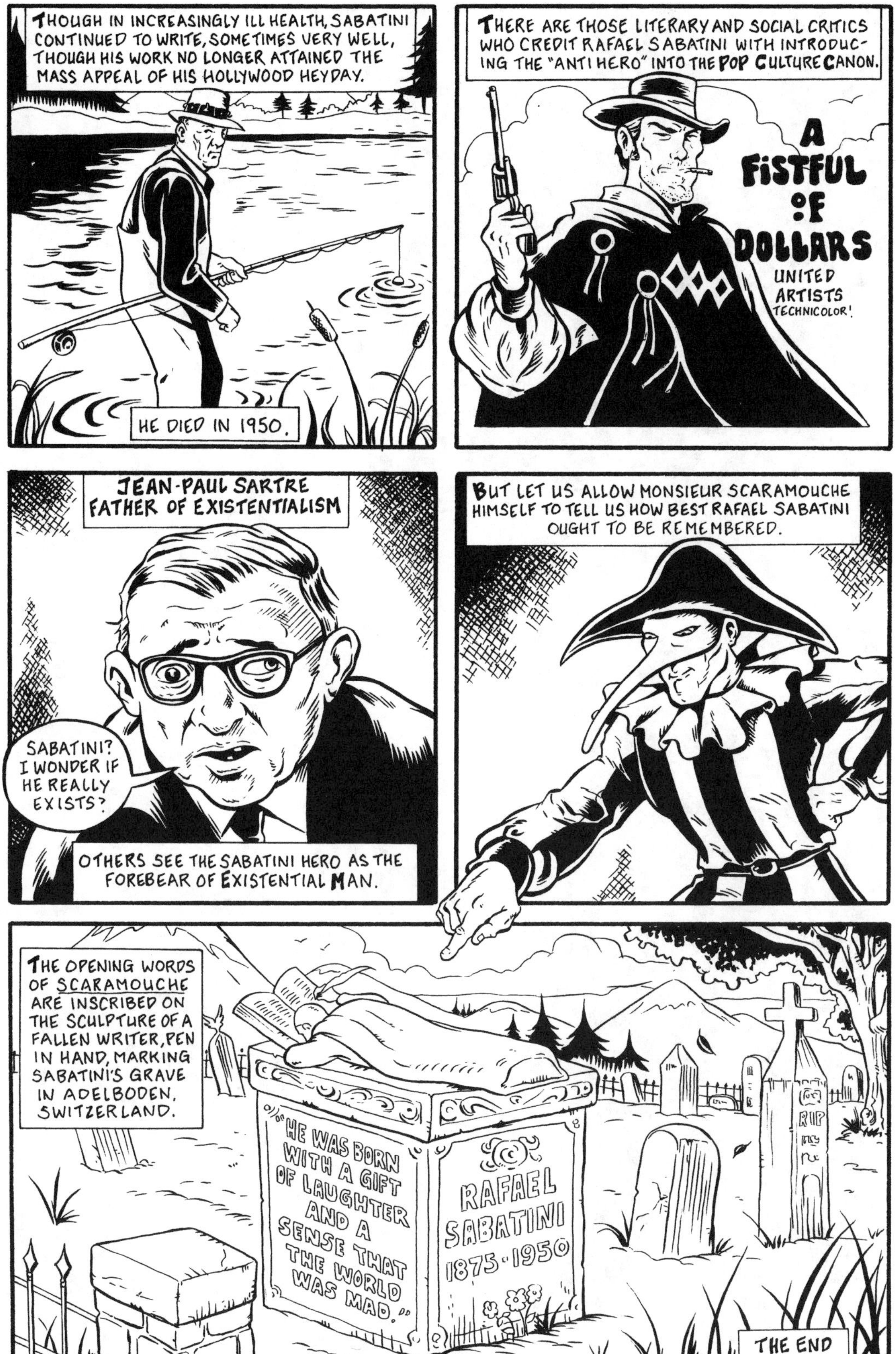
THOUGH IN INCREASINGLY ILL HEALTH, SABATINI CONTINUED TO WRITE, SOMETIMES VERY WELL, THOUGH HIS WORK NO LONGER ATTAINED THE MASS APPEAL OF HIS HOLLYWOOD HEYDAY.
HE DIED IN 1950.
THERE ARE THOSE LITERARY AND SOCIAL CRITICS WHO CREDIT RAFAEL SABATINI WITH INTRODUCING THE "ANTI HERO" INTO THE POP CULTURE CANON.
A FISTFUL OF DOLLARS
UNITED ARTISTS
TECHNICOLOR!
JEAN-PAUL SARTRE FATHER OF EXISTENTIALISM
SABATINI? I WONDER IF HE REALLY EXISTS?
OTHERS SEE THE SABATINI HERO AS THE FOREBEAR OF EXISTENTIAL MAN.
BUT LET US ALLOW MONSIEUR SCARAMOUCHE HIMSELF TO TELL US HOW BEST RAFAEL SABATINI OUGHT TO BE REMEMBERED.
THE OPENING WORDS OF SCARAMOUCHE ARE INSCRIBED ON THE SCULPTURE OF A FALLEN WRITER, PEN IN HAND, MARKING SABATINI'S GRAVE IN ADELBODEN, SWITZERLAND.
"HE WAS BORN WITH A GIFT OF LAUGHTER AND A SENSE THAT THE WORLD WAS MAD."
RAFAEL SABATINI 1875 · 1950
RIP
THE END

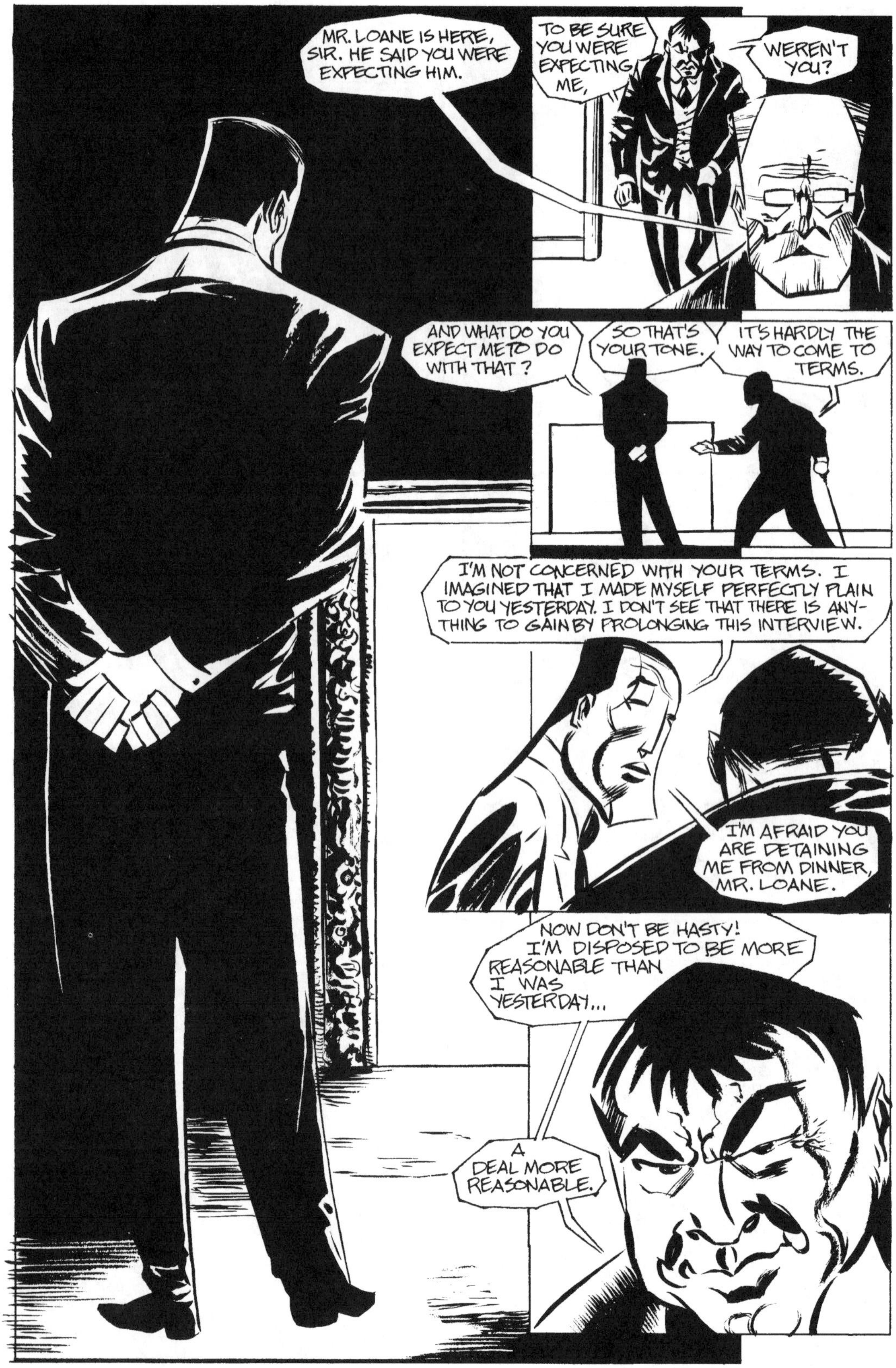
MR. LOANE IS HERE, SIR. HE SAID YOU WERE EXPECTING HIM.
TO BE SURE YOU WERE EXPECTING ME,
WEREN'T YOU?
AND WHAT DO YOU EXPECT ME TO DO WITH THAT ?
SO THAT'S YOUR TONE.
IT'S HARDLY THE WAY TO COME TO TERMS.
I'M NOT CONCERNED WITH YOUR TERMS. I IMAGINED THAT I MADE MYSELF PERFECTLY PLAIN TO YOU YESTERDAY. I DON'T SEE THAT THERE IS ANYTHING TO GAIN BY PROLONGING THIS INTERVIEW.
I'M AFRAID YOU ARE DETAINING ME FROM DINNER, MR. LOANE.
NOW DON'T BE HASTY! I'M DISPOSED TO BE MORE REASONABLE THAN I WAS YESTERDAY...
A DEAL MORE REASONABLE.

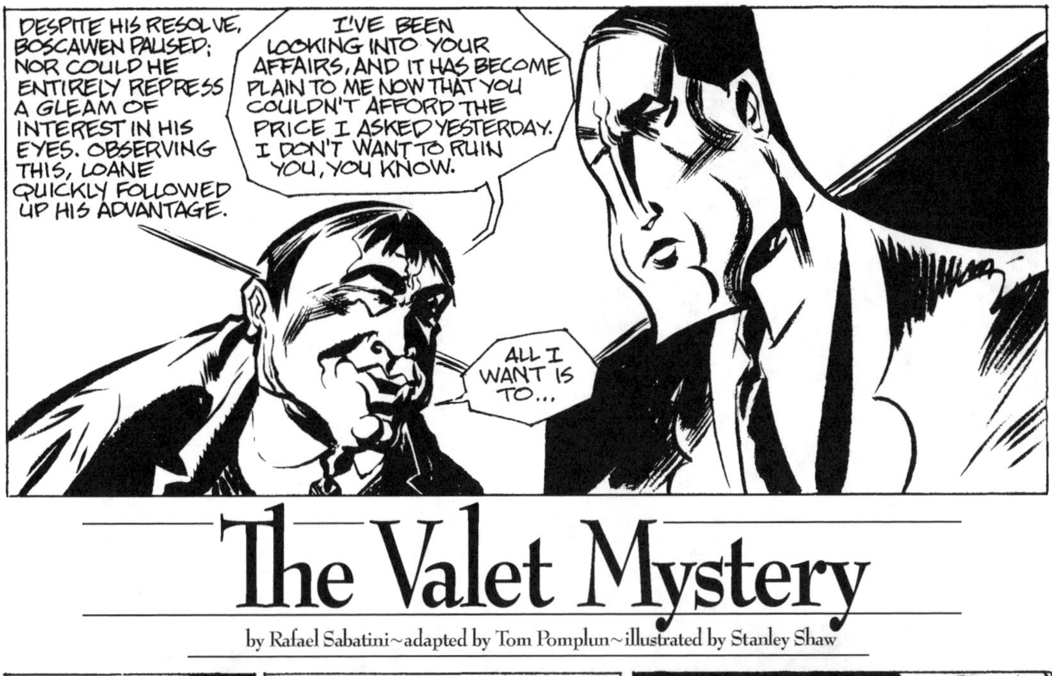
DESPITE HIS RESOLVE, BOSCAWEN PAUSED; NOR COULD HE ENTIRELY REPRESS A GLEAM OF INTEREST IN HIS EYES. OBSERVING THIS, LOANE QUICKLY FOLLOWED UP HIS ADVANTAGE.
I'VE BEEN LOOKING INTO YOUR AFFAIRS, AND IT HAS BECOME PLAIN TO ME NOW THAT YOU COULDN'T AFFORD THE PRICE I ASKED YESTERDAY. I DON'T WANT TO RUIN YOU, YOU KNOW.
ALL I WANT IS TO...

The Valet Mystery

by Rafael Sabatini~adapted by Tom Pomplun~illustrated by Stanley Shaw

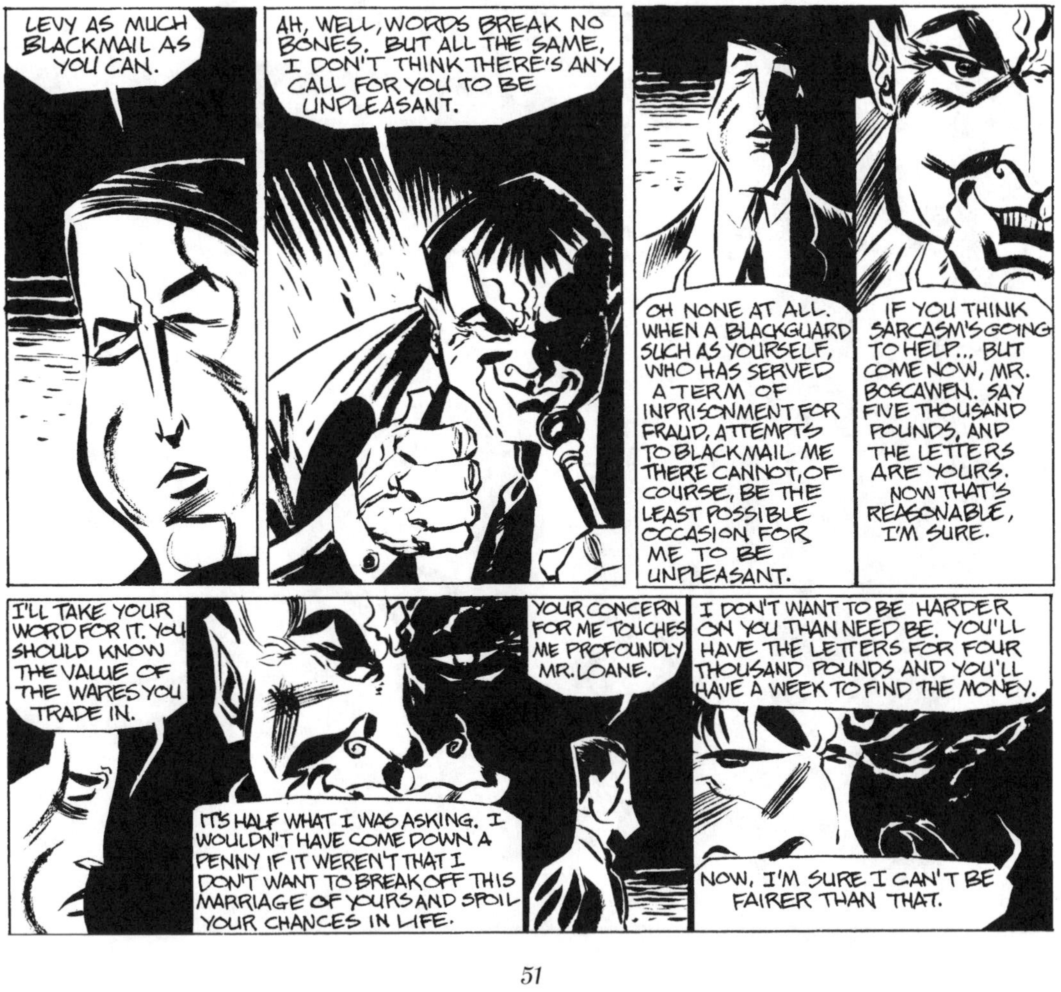
LEVY AS MUCH BLACKMAIL AS YOU CAN.
AH, WELL, WORDS BREAK NO BONES. BUT ALL THE SAME, I DON'T THINK THERE'S ANY CALL FOR YOU TO BE UNPLEASANT.
OH NONE AT ALL. WHEN A BLACKGUARD SUCH AS YOURSELF, WHO HAS SERVED A TERM OF INPRISONMENT FOR FRAUD, ATTEMPTS TO BLACKMAIL ME THERE CANNOT, OF COURSE, BE THE LEAST POSSIBLE OCCASION FOR ME TO BE UNPLEASANT.
IF YOU THINK SARCASM'S GOING TO HELP... BUT COME NOW, MR. BOSCAWEN. SAY FIVE THOUSAND POUNDS, AND THE LETTERS ARE YOURS. NOW THAT'S REASONABLE, I'M SURE.
I'LL TAKE YOUR WORD FOR IT. YOU SHOULD KNOW THE VALUE OF THE WARES YOU TRADE IN.
IT'S HALF WHAT I WAS ASKING. I WOULDN'T HAVE COME DOWN A PENNY IF IT WEREN'T THAT I DON'T WANT TO BREAK OFF THIS MARRIAGE OF YOURS AND SPOIL YOUR CHANCES IN LIFE.
YOUR CONCERN FOR ME TOUCHES ME PROFOUNDLY MR. LOANE.
I DON'T WANT TO BE HARDER ON YOU THAN NEED BE. YOU'LL HAVE THE LETTERS FOR FOUR THOUSAND POUNDS AND YOU'LL HAVE A WEEK TO FIND THE MONEY.
NOW, I'M SURE I CAN'T BE FAIRER THAN THAT.

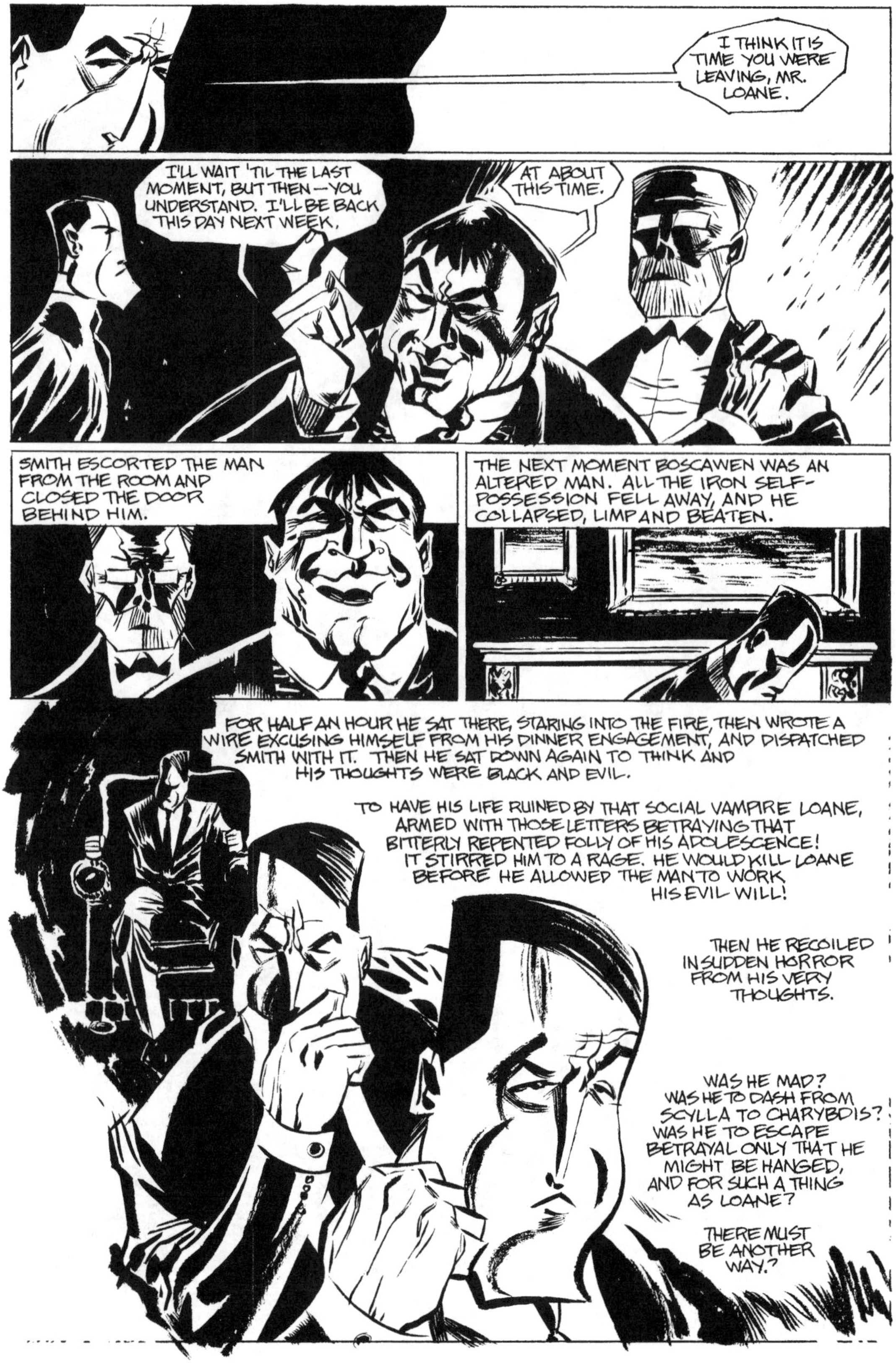
I THINK IT IS TIME YOU WERE LEAVING, MR. LOANE.
I'LL WAIT 'TIL THE LAST MOMENT, BUT THEN — YOU UNDERSTAND. I'LL BE BACK THIS DAY NEXT WEEK,
AT ABOUT THIS TIME.
SMITH ESCORTED THE MAN FROM THE ROOM AND CLOSED THE DOOR BEHIND HIM.
THE NEXT MOMENT BOSCAWEN WAS AN ALTERED MAN. ALL THE IRON SELF-POSSESSION FELL AWAY, AND HE COLLAPSED, LIMP AND BEATEN.
FOR HALF AN HOUR HE SAT THERE, STARING INTO THE FIRE, THEN WROTE A WIRE EXCUSING HIMSELF FROM HIS DINNER ENGAGEMENT, AND DISPATCHED SMITH WITH IT. THEN HE SAT DOWN AGAIN TO THINK AND HIS THOUGHTS WERE BLACK AND EVIL.
TO HAVE HIS LIFE RUINED BY THAT SOCIAL VAMPIRE LOANE, ARMED WITH THOSE LETTERS BETRAYING THAT BITTERLY REPENTED FOLLY OF HIS ADOLESCENCE! IT STIRRED HIM TO A RAGE. HE WOULD KILL LOANE BEFORE HE ALLOWED THE MAN TO WORK HIS EVIL WILL!
THEN HE RECOILED IN SUDDEN HORROR FROM HIS VERY THOUGHTS.
WAS HE MAD? WAS HE TO DASH FROM SCYLLA TO CHARYBDIS? WAS HE TO ESCAPE BETRAYAL ONLY THAT HE MIGHT BE HANGED, AND FOR SUCH A THING AS LOANE?
THERE MUST BE ANOTHER WAY?

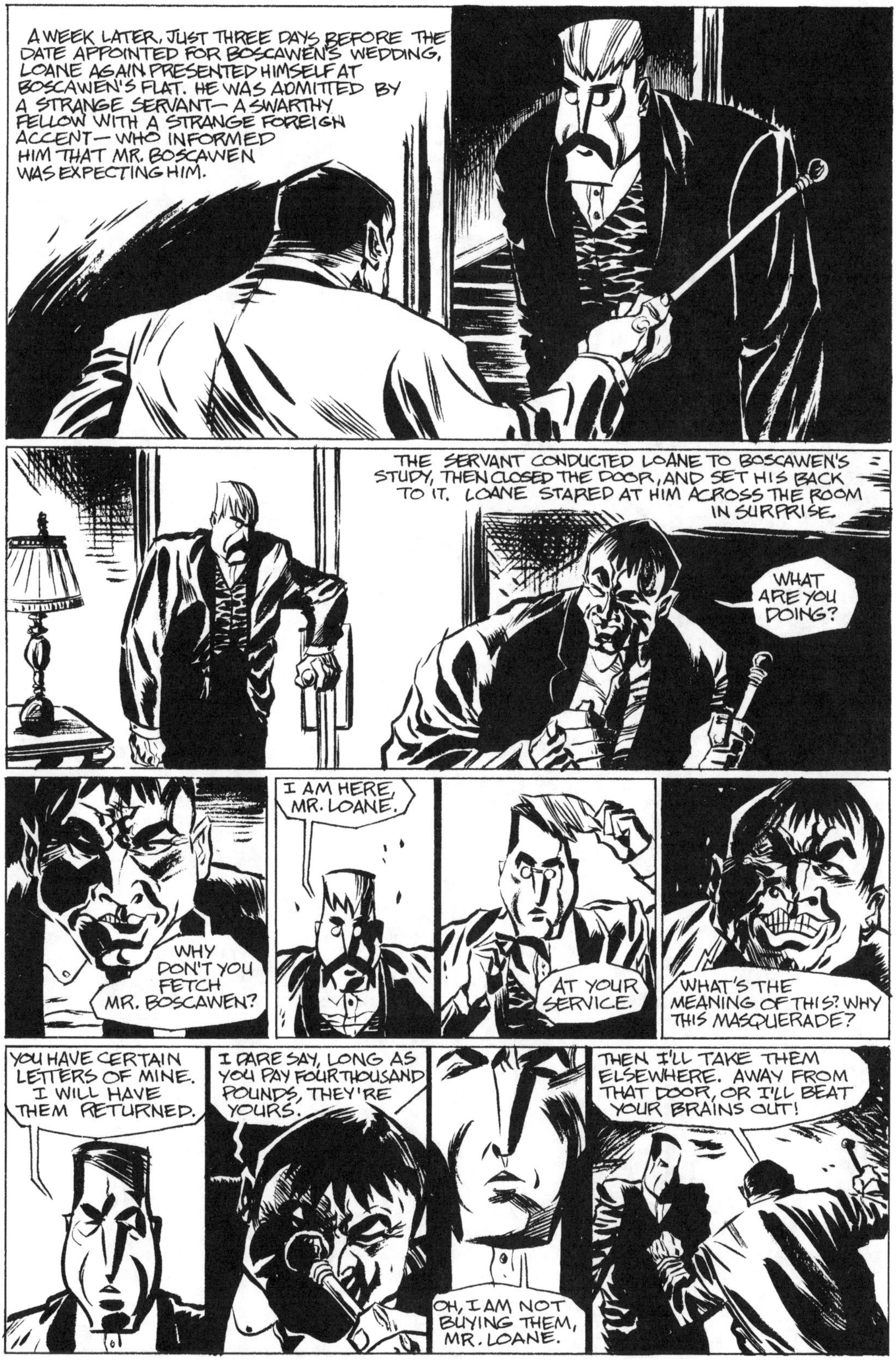
A WEEK LATER, JUST THREE DAYS BEFORE THE DATE APPOINTED FOR BOSCAWEN'S WEDDING, LOANE AGAIN PRESENTED HIMSELF AT BOSCAWEN'S FLAT. HE WAS ADMITTED BY A STRANGE SERVANT— A SWARTHY FELLOW WITH A STRANGE FOREIGN ACCENT— WHO INFORMED HIM THAT MR. BOSCAWEN WAS EXPECTING HIM.
THE SERVANT CONDUCTED LOANE TO BOSCAWEN'S STUDY, THEN CLOSED THE DOOR, AND SET HIS BACK TO IT. LOANE STARED AT HIM ACROSS THE ROOM IN SURPRISE.
WHAT ARE YOU DOING?
WHY DON'T YOU FETCH MR. BOSCAWEN?
I AM HERE, MR. LOANE.
AT YOUR SERVICE.
WHAT'S THE MEANING OF THIS? WHY THIS MASQUERADE?
YOU HAVE CERTAIN LETTERS OF MINE. I WILL HAVE THEM RETURNED.
I DARE SAY, LONG AS YOU PAY FOUR THOUSAND POUNDS, THEY'RE YOURS.
OH, I AM NOT BUYING THEM, MR. LOANE.
THEN I'LL TAKE THEM ELSEWHERE. AWAY FROM THAT DOOR, OR I'LL BEAT YOUR BRAINS OUT!

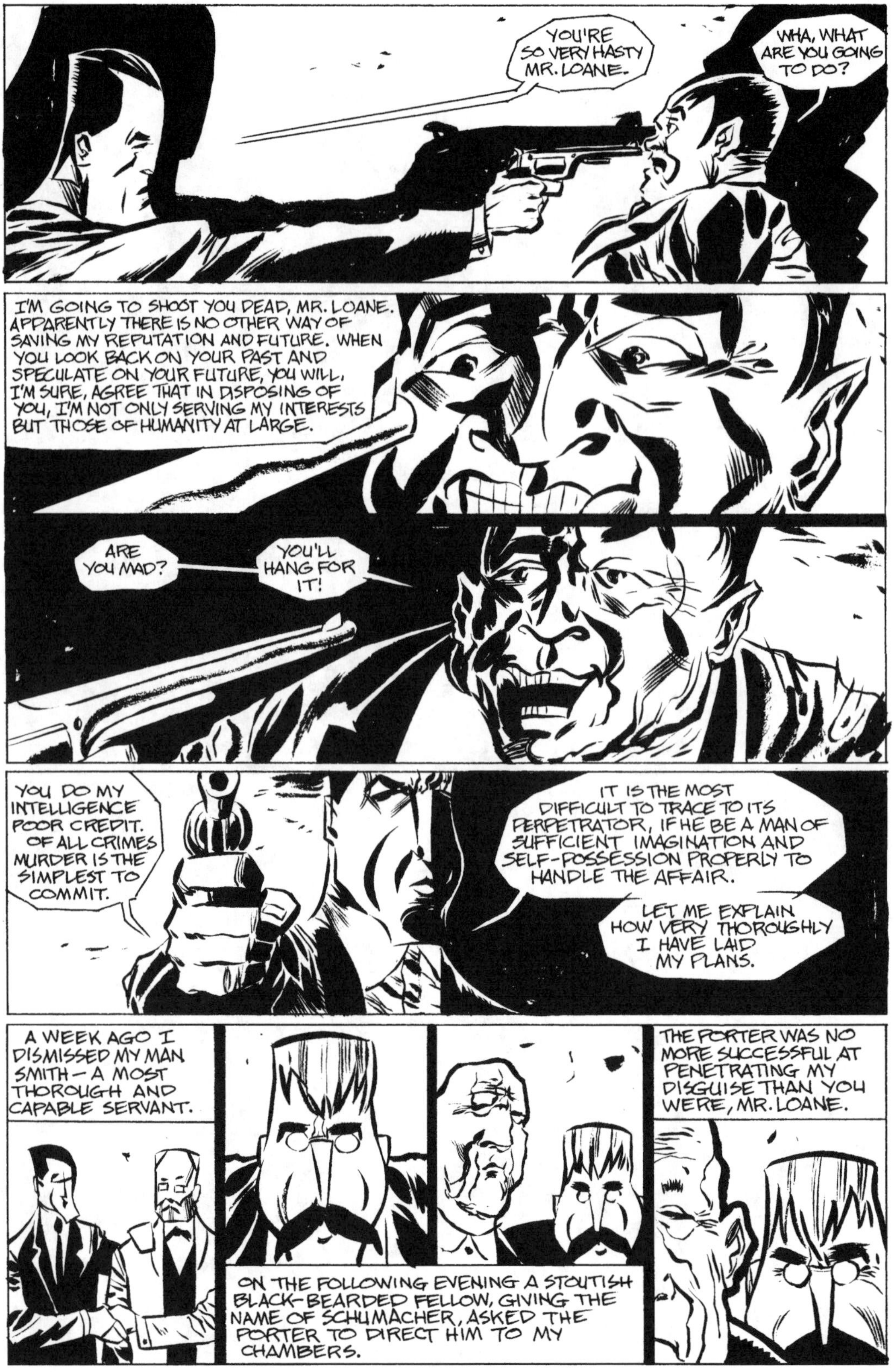
YOU'RE SO VERY HASTY MR. LOANE.
WHA, WHAT ARE YOU GOING TO DO?
I'M GOING TO SHOOT YOU DEAD, MR. LOANE. APPARENTLY THERE IS NO OTHER WAY OF SAVING MY REPUTATION AND FUTURE. WHEN YOU LOOK BACK ON YOUR PAST AND SPECULATE ON YOUR FUTURE, YOU WILL, I'M SURE, AGREE THAT IN DISPOSING OF YOU, I'M NOT ONLY SERVING MY INTERESTS BUT THOSE OF HUMANITY AT LARGE.
ARE YOU MAD?
YOU'LL HANG FOR IT!
YOU DO MY INTELLIGENCE POOR CREDIT. OF ALL CRIMES MURDER IS THE SIMPLEST TO COMMIT.
IT IS THE MOST DIFFICULT TO TRACE TO ITS PERPETRATOR, IF HE BE A MAN OF SUFFICIENT IMAGINATION AND SELF-POSSESSION PROPERLY TO HANDLE THE AFFAIR.
LET ME EXPLAIN HOW VERY THOROUGHLY I HAVE LAID MY PLANS.
A WEEK AGO I DISMISSED MY MAN SMITH — A MOST THOROUGH AND CAPABLE SERVANT.
ON THE FOLLOWING EVENING A STOUTISH BLACK-BEARDED FELLOW, GIVING THE NAME OF SCHUMACHER, ASKED THE PORTER TO DIRECT HIM TO MY CHAMBERS.
THE PORTER WAS NO MORE SUCCESSFUL AT PENETRATING MY DISGUISE THAN YOU WERE, MR. LOANE.

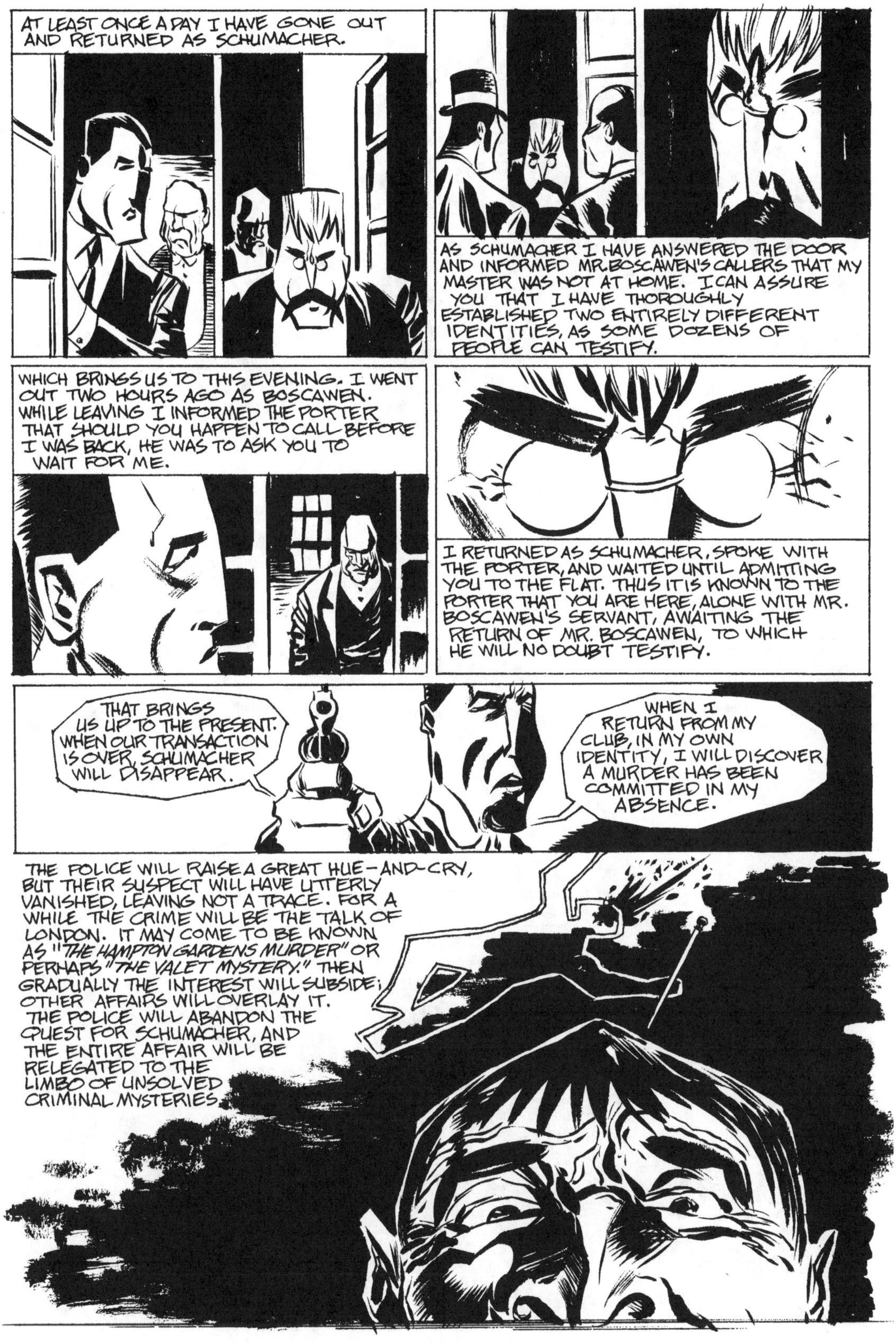
AT LEAST ONCE A DAY I HAVE GONE OUT AND RETURNED AS SCHUMACHER.
AS SCHUMACHER I HAVE ANSWERED THE DOOR AND INFORMED MR. BOSCAWEN'S CALLERS THAT MY MASTER WAS NOT AT HOME. I CAN ASSURE YOU THAT I HAVE THOROUGHLY ESTABLISHED TWO ENTIRELY DIFFERENT IDENTITIES, AS SOME DOZENS OF PEOPLE CAN TESTIFY.
WHICH BRINGS US TO THIS EVENING. I WENT OUT TWO HOURS AGO AS BOSCAWEN. WHILE LEAVING I INFORMED THE PORTER THAT SHOULD YOU HAPPEN TO CALL BEFORE I WAS BACK, HE WAS TO ASK YOU TO WAIT FOR ME.
I RETURNED AS SCHUMACHER, SPOKE WITH THE PORTER, AND WAITED UNTIL ADMITTING YOU TO THE FLAT. THUS IT IS KNOWN TO THE PORTER THAT YOU ARE HERE, ALONE WITH MR. BOSCAWEN'S SERVANT, AWAITING THE RETURN OF MR. BOSCAWEN, TO WHICH HE WILL NO DOUBT TESTIFY.
THAT BRINGS US UP TO THE PRESENT. WHEN OUR TRANSACTION IS OVER, SCHUMACHER WILL DISAPPEAR.
WHEN I RETURN FROM MY CLUB, IN MY OWN IDENTITY, I WILL DISCOVER A MURDER HAS BEEN COMMITTED IN MY ABSENCE.
THE POLICE WILL RAISE A GREAT HUE-AND-CRY, BUT THEIR SUSPECT WILL HAVE UTTERLY VANISHED, LEAVING NOT A TRACE. FOR A WHILE THE CRIME WILL BE THE TALK OF LONDON. IT MAY COME TO BE KNOWN AS "THE HAMPTON GARDENS MURDER" OR PERHAPS "THE VALET MYSTERY." THEN GRADUALLY THE INTEREST WILL SUBSIDE; OTHER AFFAIRS WILL OVERLAY IT. THE POLICE WILL ABANDON THE QUEST FOR SCHUMACHER, AND THE ENTIRE AFFAIR WILL BE RELEGATED TO THE LIMBO OF UNSOLVED CRIMINAL MYSTERIES.

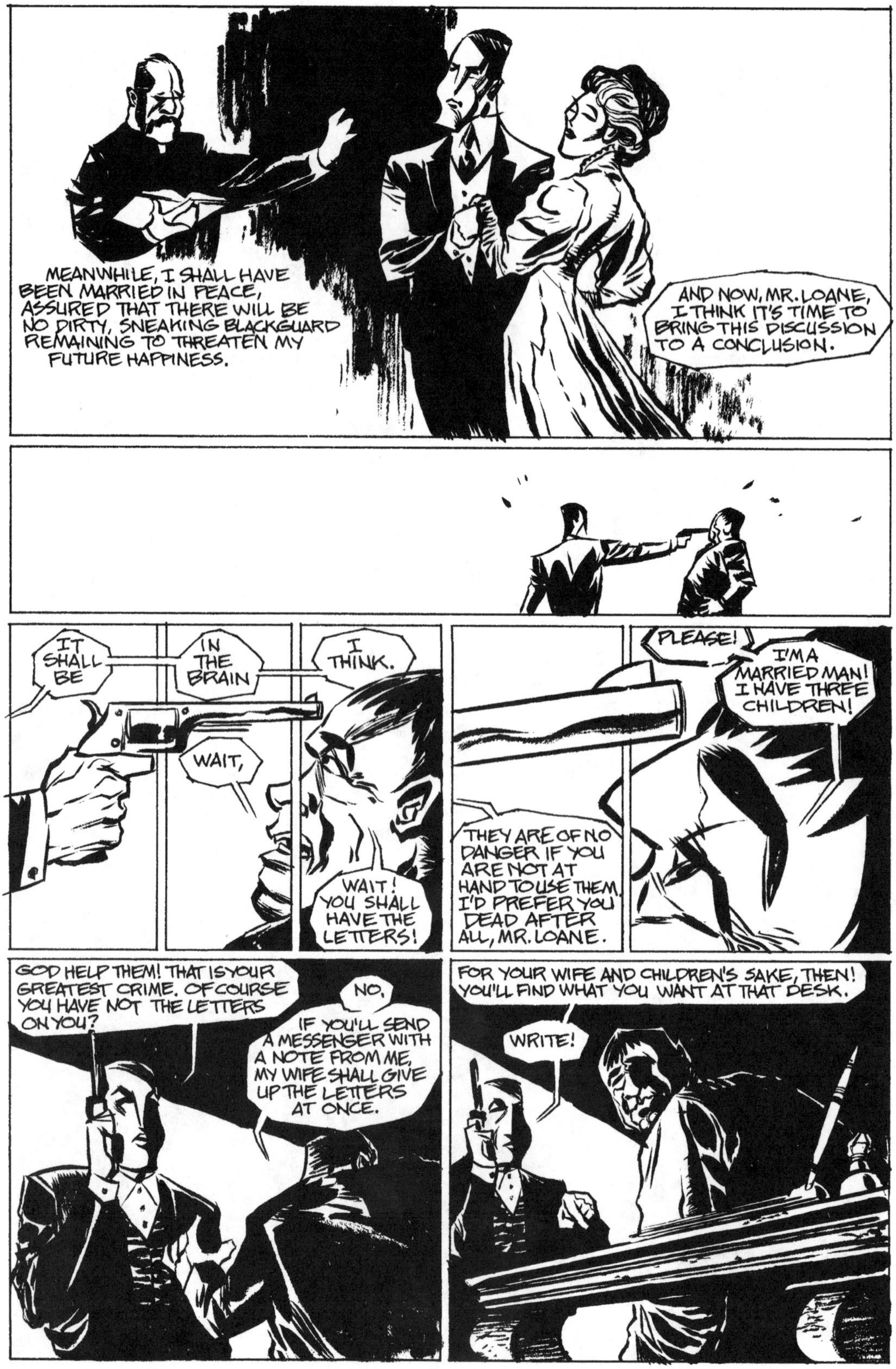
MEANWHILE, I SHALL HAVE BEEN MARRIED IN PEACE, ASSURED THAT THERE WILL BE NO DIRTY, SNEAKING BLACKGUARD REMAINING TO THREATEN MY FUTURE HAPPINESS.
AND NOW, MR. LOANE, I THINK IT'S TIME TO BRING THIS DISCUSSION TO A CONCLUSION.
IT SHALL BE
IN THE BRAIN
I THINK.
WAIT,
WAIT! YOU SHALL HAVE THE LETTERS!
THEY ARE OF NO DANGER IF YOU ARE NOT AT HAND TO USE THEM. I'D PREFER YOU DEAD AFTER ALL, MR. LOANE.
PLEASE!
I'M A MARRIED MAN! I HAVE THREE CHILDREN!
GOD HELP THEM! THAT IS YOUR GREATEST CRIME. OF COURSE YOU HAVE NOT THE LETTERS ON YOU?
NO,
IF YOU'LL SEND A MESSENGER WITH A NOTE FROM ME, MY WIFE SHALL GIVE UP THE LETTERS AT ONCE.
FOR YOUR WIFE AND CHILDREN'S SAKE, THEN! YOU'LL FIND WHAT YOU WANT AT THAT DESK.
WRITE!

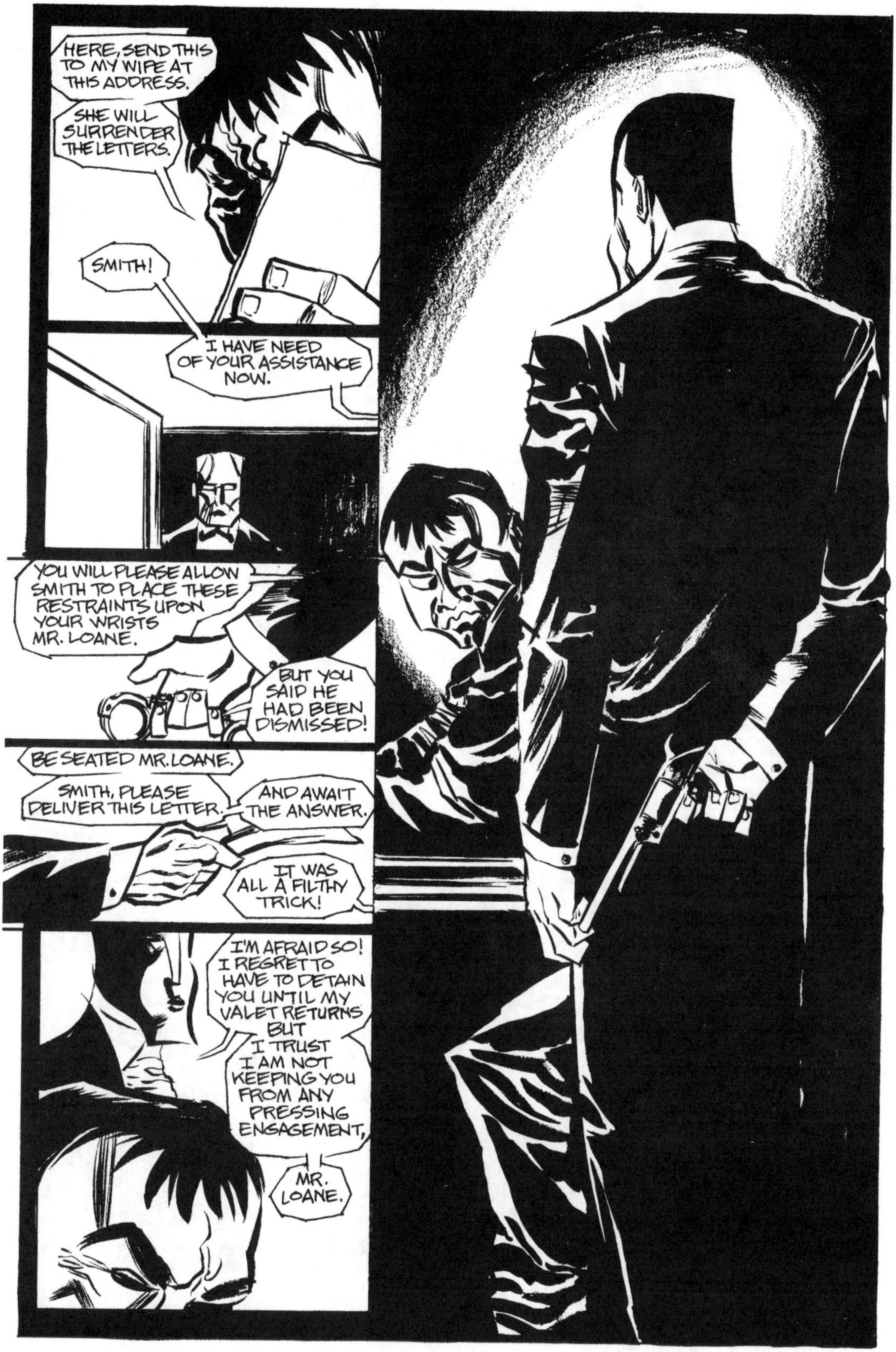
HERE, SEND THIS TO MY WIFE AT THIS ADDRESS.
SHE WILL SURRENDER THE LETTERS.
SMITH!
I HAVE NEED OF YOUR ASSISTANCE NOW.
YOU WILL PLEASE ALLOW SMITH TO PLACE THESE RESTRAINTS UPON YOUR WRISTS MR. LOANE.
BUT YOU SAID HE HAD BEEN DISMISSED!
BE SEATED MR. LOANE.
SMITH, PLEASE DELIVER THIS LETTER.
AND AWAIT THE ANSWER.
IT WAS ALL A FILTHY TRICK!
I'M AFRAID SO! I REGRET TO HAVE TO DETAIN YOU UNTIL MY VALET RETURNS BUT I TRUST I AM NOT KEEPING YOU FROM ANY PRESSING ENGAGEMENT,
MR. LOANE.

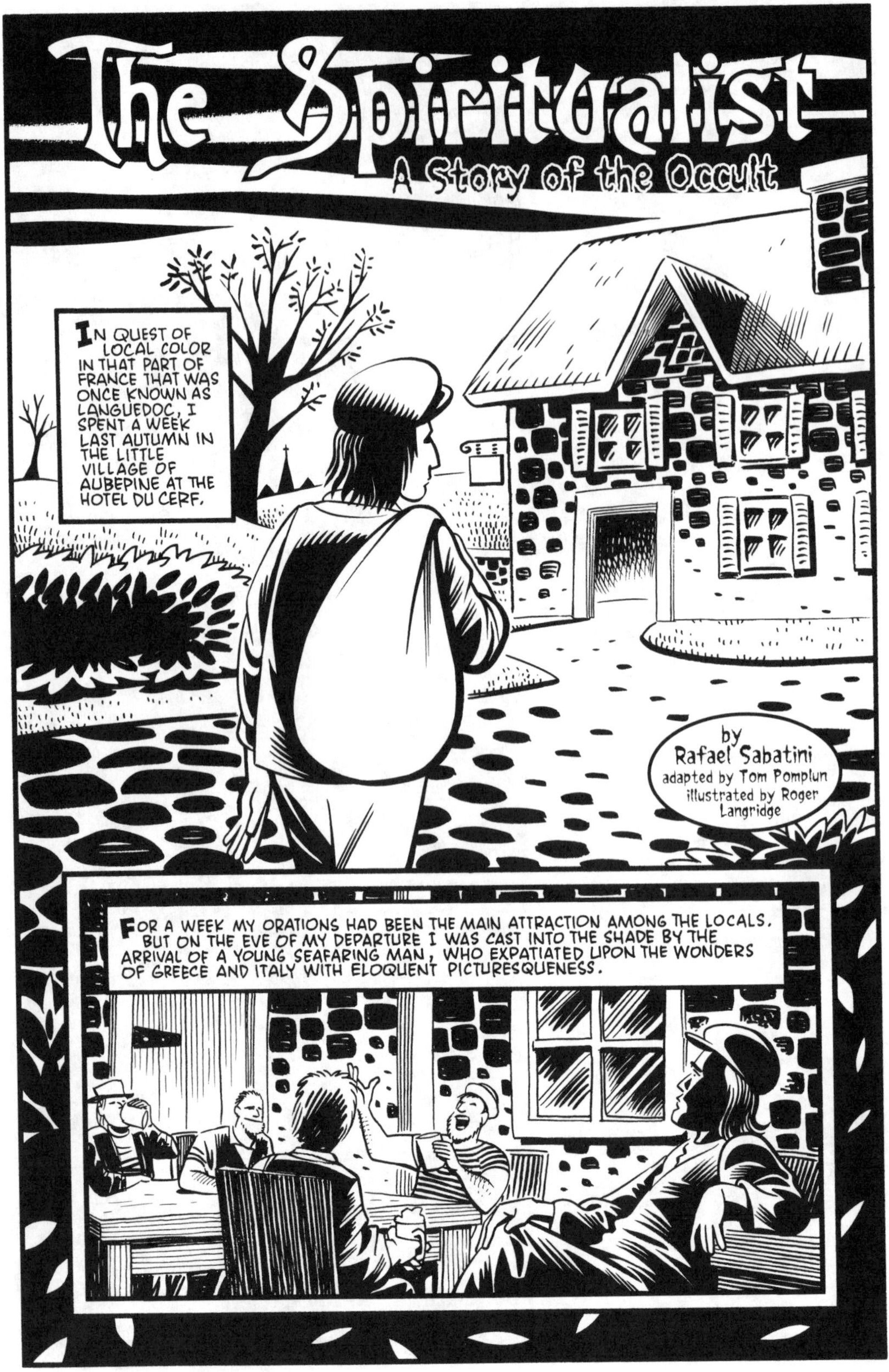
The Spiritualist
A Story of the Occult
In quest of local color in that part of France that was once known as Languedoc, I spent a week last autumn in the little village of Aubepine at the Hotel du Cerf.
by Rafael Sabatini
adapted by Tom Pomplun
illustrated by Roger Langridge
For a week my orations had been the main attraction among the locals. But on the eve of my departure I was cast into the shade by the arrival of a young seafaring man, who expatiated upon the wonders of Greece and Italy with eloquent picturesqueness.

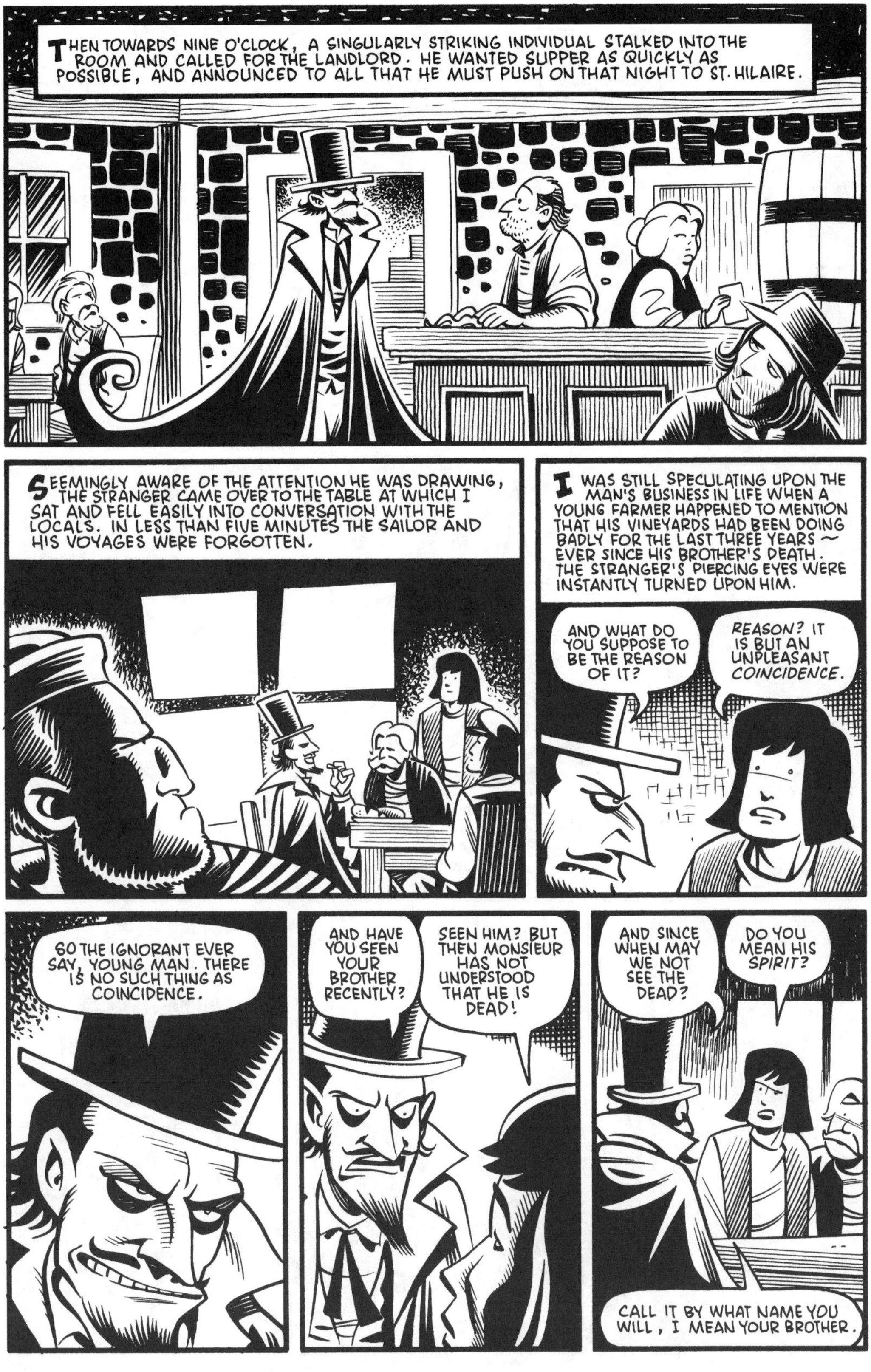
THEN TOWARDS NINE O'CLOCK, A SINGULARLY STRIKING INDIVIDUAL STALKED INTO THE ROOM AND CALLED FOR THE LANDLORD. HE WANTED SUPPER AS QUICKLY AS POSSIBLE, AND ANNOUNCED TO ALL THAT HE MUST PUSH ON THAT NIGHT TO ST. HILAIRE.
SEEMINGLY AWARE OF THE ATTENTION HE WAS DRAWING, THE STRANGER CAME OVER TO THE TABLE AT WHICH I SAT AND FELL EASILY INTO CONVERSATION WITH THE LOCALS. IN LESS THAN FIVE MINUTES THE SAILOR AND HIS VOYAGES WERE FORGOTTEN.
I WAS STILL SPECULATING UPON THE MAN'S BUSINESS IN LIFE WHEN A YOUNG FARMER HAPPENED TO MENTION THAT HIS VINEYARDS HAD BEEN DOING BADLY FOR THE LAST THREE YEARS ~ EVER SINCE HIS BROTHER'S DEATH. THE STRANGER'S PIERCING EYES WERE INSTANTLY TURNED UPON HIM.
AND WHAT DO YOU SUPPOSE TO BE THE REASON OF IT?
REASON? IT IS BUT AN UNPLEASANT COINCIDENCE.
SO THE IGNORANT EVER SAY, YOUNG MAN. THERE IS NO SUCH THING AS COINCIDENCE.
AND HAVE YOU SEEN YOUR BROTHER RECENTLY?
SEEN HIM? BUT THEN MONSIEUR HAS NOT UNDERSTOOD THAT HE IS DEAD!
AND SINCE WHEN MAY WE NOT SEE THE DEAD?
DO YOU MEAN HIS SPIRIT?
CALL IT BY WHAT NAME YOU WILL, I MEAN YOUR BROTHER.

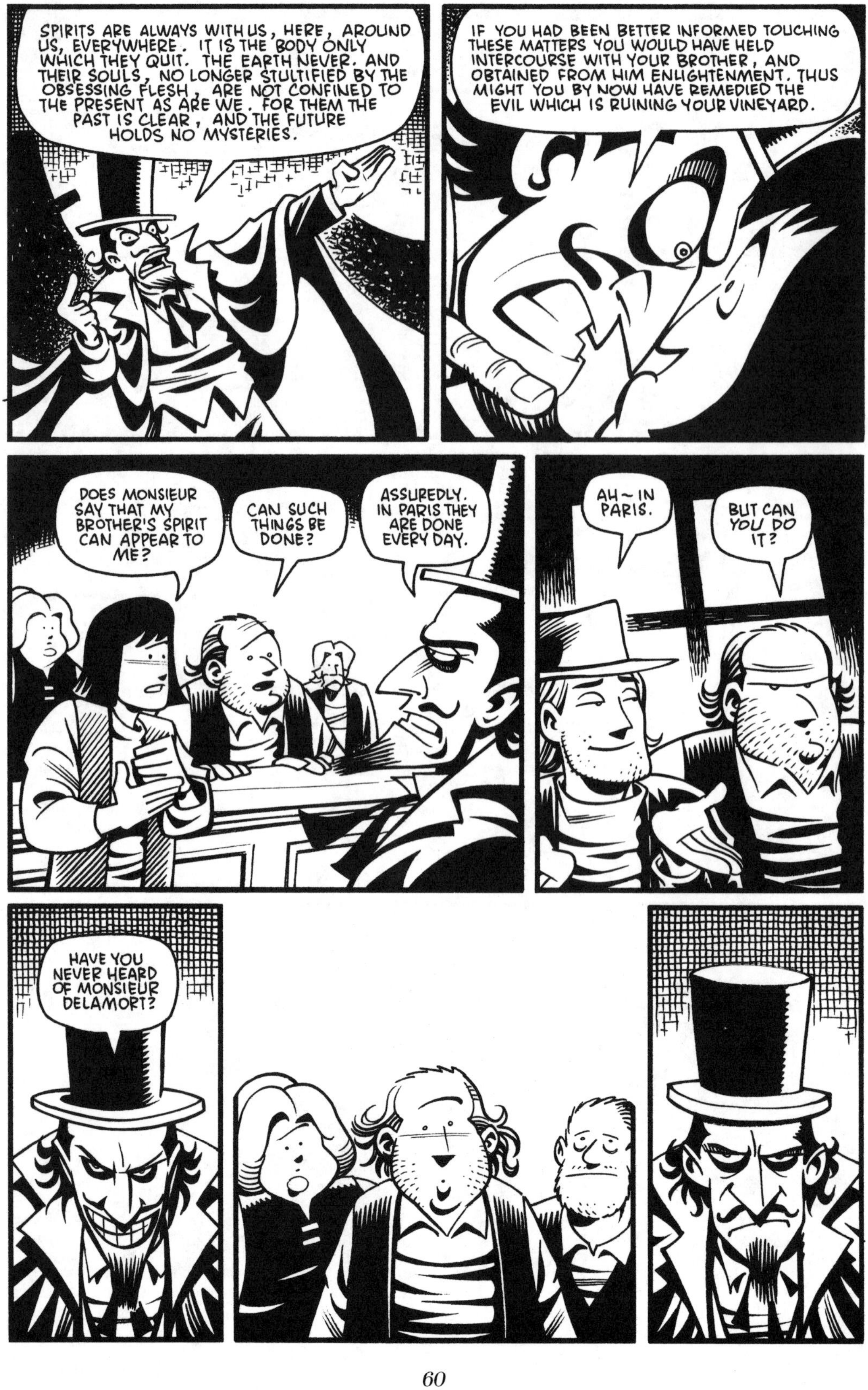
SPIRITS ARE ALWAYS WITH US, HERE, AROUND US, EVERYWHERE. IT IS THE BODY ONLY WHICH THEY QUIT. THE EARTH NEVER. AND THEIR SOULS, NO LONGER STULTIFIED BY THE OBSESSING FLESH, ARE NOT CONFINED TO THE PRESENT AS ARE WE. FOR THEM THE PAST IS CLEAR, AND THE FUTURE HOLDS NO MYSTERIES.
IF YOU HAD BEEN BETTER INFORMED TOUCHING THESE MATTERS YOU WOULD HAVE HELD INTERCOURSE WITH YOUR BROTHER, AND OBTAINED FROM HIM ENLIGHTENMENT. THUS MIGHT YOU BY NOW HAVE REMEDIED THE EVIL WHICH IS RUINING YOUR VINEYARD.
DOES MONSIEUR SAY THAT MY BROTHER'S SPIRIT CAN APPEAR TO ME?
CAN SUCH THINGS BE DONE?
ASSUREDLY. IN PARIS THEY ARE DONE EVERY DAY.
AH ~ IN PARIS.
BUT CAN YOU DO IT?
HAVE YOU NEVER HEARD OF MONSIEUR DELAMORT?

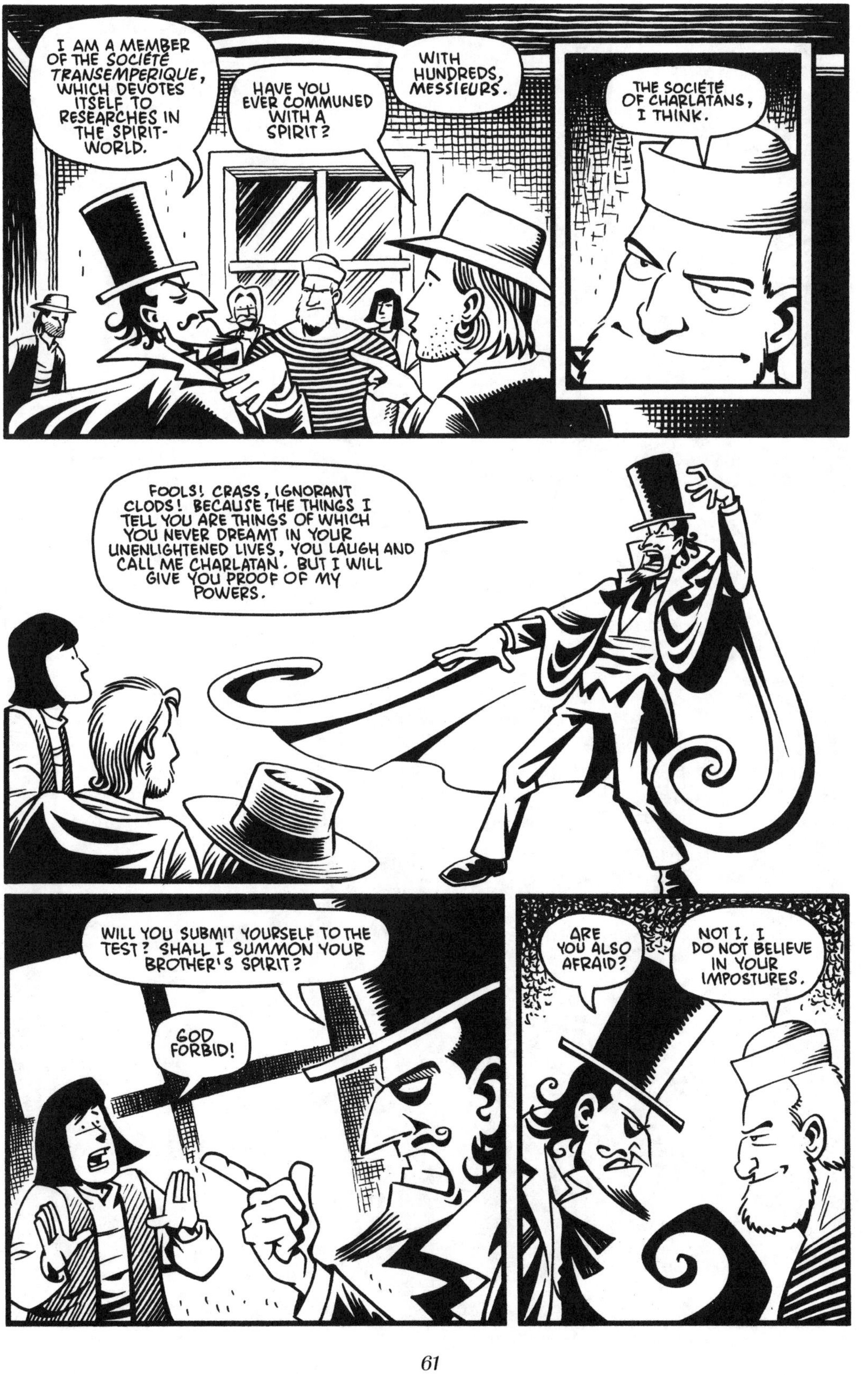
I AM A MEMBER OF THE *SOCIÉTÉ TRANSEMPERIQUE*, WHICH DEVOTES ITSELF TO RESEARCHES IN THE SPIRIT-WORLD.
HAVE YOU EVER COMMUNED WITH A SPIRIT?
WITH HUNDREDS, MESSIEURS.
THE SOCIÉTÉ OF CHARLATANS, I THINK.
FOOLS! CRASS, IGNORANT CLODS! BECAUSE THE THINGS I TELL YOU ARE THINGS OF WHICH YOU NEVER DREAMT IN YOUR UNENLIGHTENED LIVES, YOU LAUGH AND CALL ME CHARLATAN. BUT I WILL GIVE YOU PROOF OF MY POWERS.
WILL YOU SUBMIT YOURSELF TO THE TEST? SHALL I SUMMON YOUR BROTHER'S SPIRIT?
GOD FORBID!
ARE YOU ALSO AFRAID?
NOT I, I DO NOT BELIEVE IN YOUR IMPOSTURES.

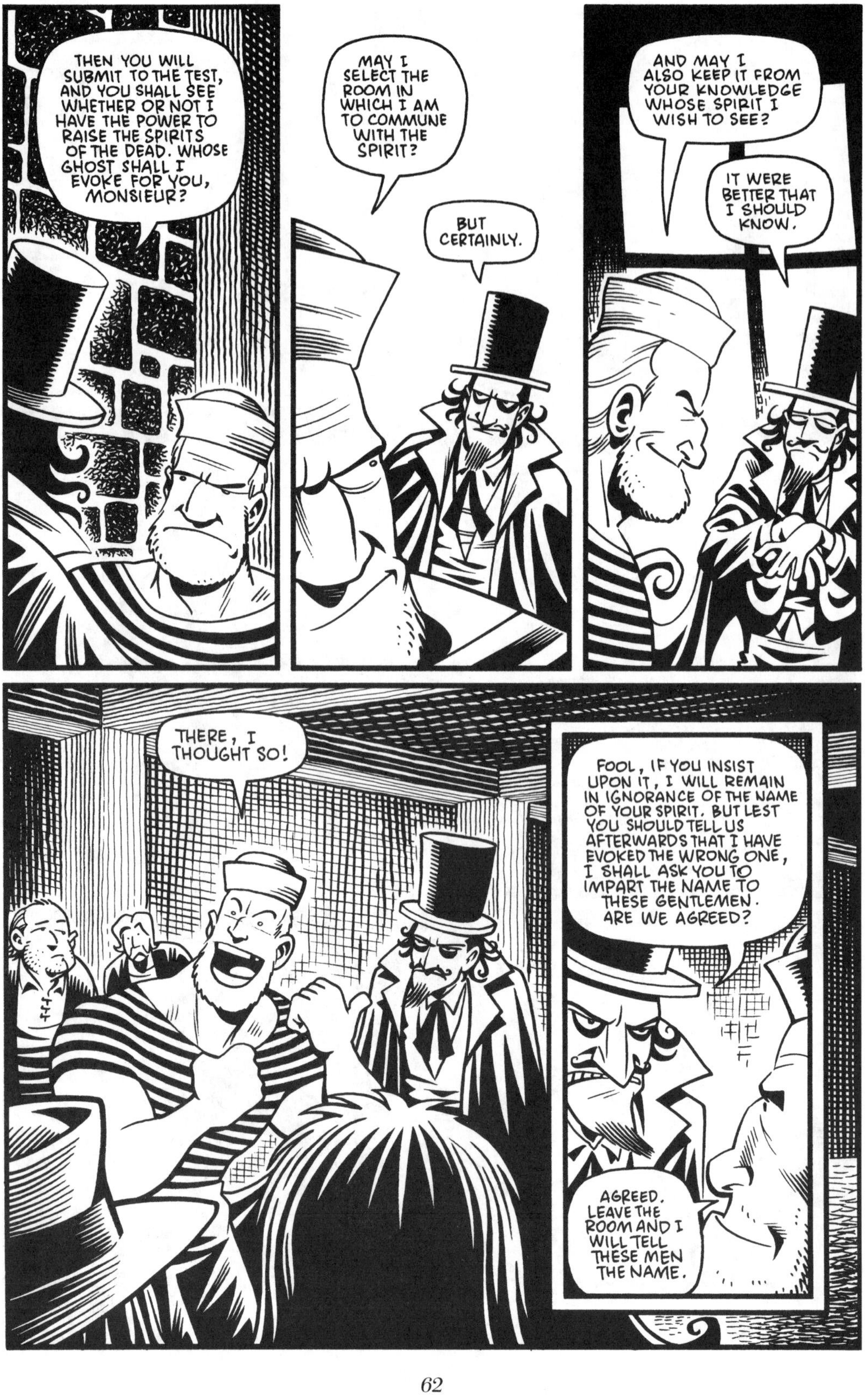
THEN YOU WILL SUBMIT TO THE TEST, AND YOU SHALL SEE WHETHER OR NOT I HAVE THE POWER TO RAISE THE SPIRITS OF THE DEAD. WHOSE GHOST SHALL I EVOKE FOR YOU, MONSIEUR?
MAY I SELECT THE ROOM IN WHICH I AM TO COMMUNE WITH THE SPIRIT?
BUT CERTAINLY.
AND MAY I ALSO KEEP IT FROM YOUR KNOWLEDGE WHOSE SPIRIT I WISH TO SEE?
IT WERE BETTER THAT I SHOULD KNOW.
THERE, I THOUGHT SO!
FOOL, IF YOU INSIST UPON IT, I WILL REMAIN IN IGNORANCE OF THE NAME OF YOUR SPIRIT. BUT LEST YOU SHOULD TELL US AFTERWARDS THAT I HAVE EVOKED THE WRONG ONE, I SHALL ASK YOU TO IMPART THE NAME TO THESE GENTLEMEN. ARE WE AGREED?
AGREED. LEAVE THE ROOM AND I WILL TELL THESE MEN THE NAME.

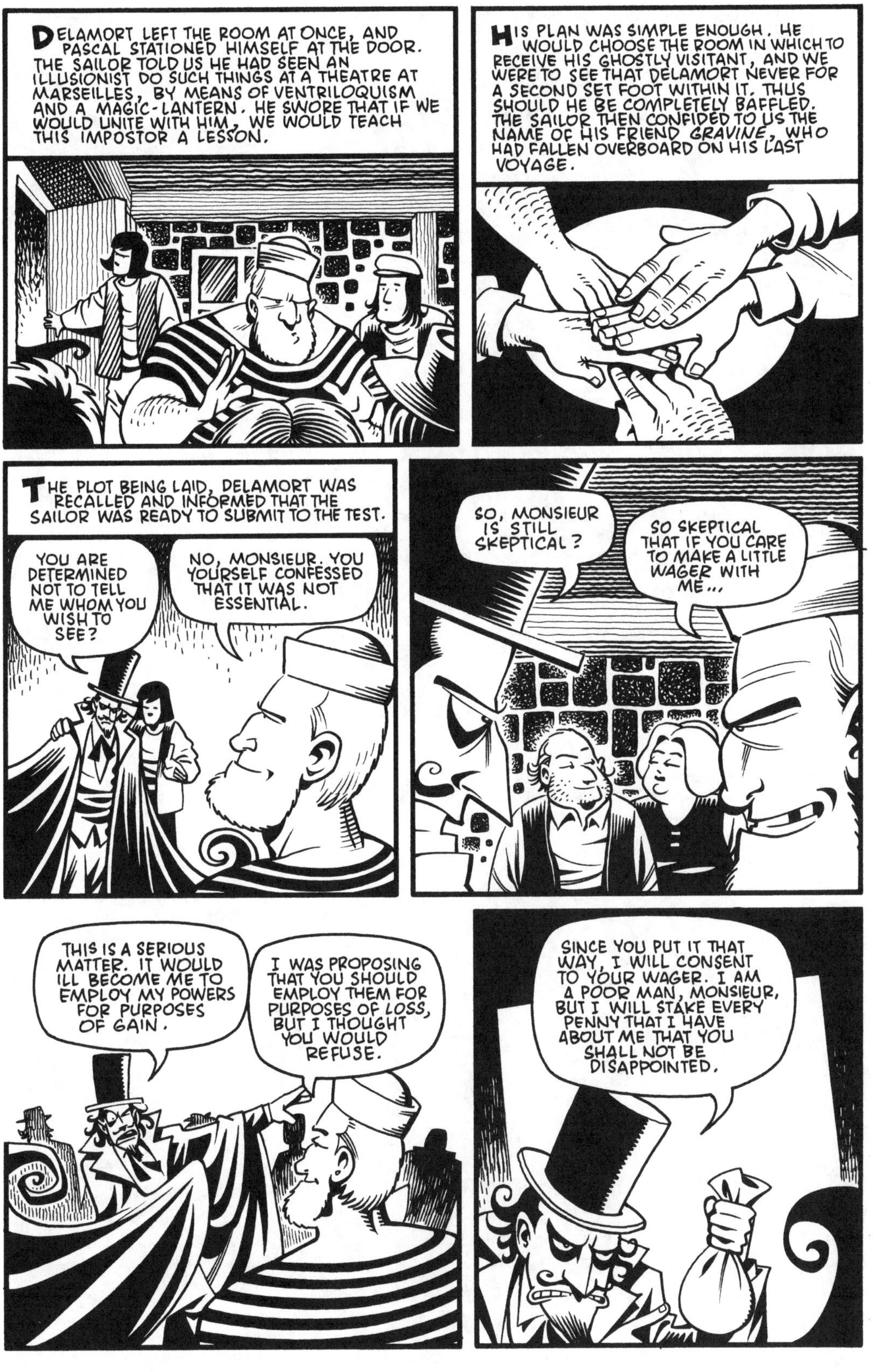
DELAMORT LEFT THE ROOM AT ONCE, AND PASCAL STATIONED HIMSELF AT THE DOOR. THE SAILOR TOLD US HE HAD SEEN AN ILLUSIONIST DO SUCH THINGS AT A THEATRE AT MARSEILLES, BY MEANS OF VENTRILOQUISM AND A MAGIC-LANTERN. HE SWORE THAT IF WE WOULD UNITE WITH HIM, WE WOULD TEACH THIS IMPOSTOR A LESSON.
HIS PLAN WAS SIMPLE ENOUGH. HE WOULD CHOOSE THE ROOM IN WHICH TO RECEIVE HIS GHOSTLY VISITANT, AND WE WERE TO SEE THAT DELAMORT NEVER FOR A SECOND SET FOOT WITHIN IT. THUS SHOULD HE BE COMPLETELY BAFFLED. THE SAILOR THEN CONFIDED TO US THE NAME OF HIS FRIEND *GRAVINE*, WHO HAD FALLEN OVERBOARD ON HIS LAST VOYAGE.
THE PLOT BEING LAID, DELAMORT WAS RECALLED AND INFORMED THAT THE SAILOR WAS READY TO SUBMIT TO THE TEST.
YOU ARE DETERMINED NOT TO TELL ME WHOM YOU WISH TO SEE?
NO, MONSIEUR. YOU YOURSELF CONFESSED THAT IT WAS NOT ESSENTIAL.
SO, MONSIEUR IS STILL SKEPTICAL?
SO SKEPTICAL THAT IF YOU CARE TO MAKE A LITTLE WAGER WITH ME...
THIS IS A SERIOUS MATTER. IT WOULD ILL BECOME ME TO EMPLOY MY POWERS FOR PURPOSES OF GAIN.
I WAS PROPOSING THAT YOU SHOULD EMPLOY THEM FOR PURPOSES OF *LOSS*, BUT I THOUGHT YOU WOULD REFUSE.
SINCE YOU PUT IT THAT WAY, I WILL CONSENT TO YOUR WAGER. I AM A POOR MAN, MONSIEUR, BUT I WILL STAKE EVERY PENNY THAT I HAVE ABOUT ME THAT YOU SHALL NOT BE DISAPPOINTED.

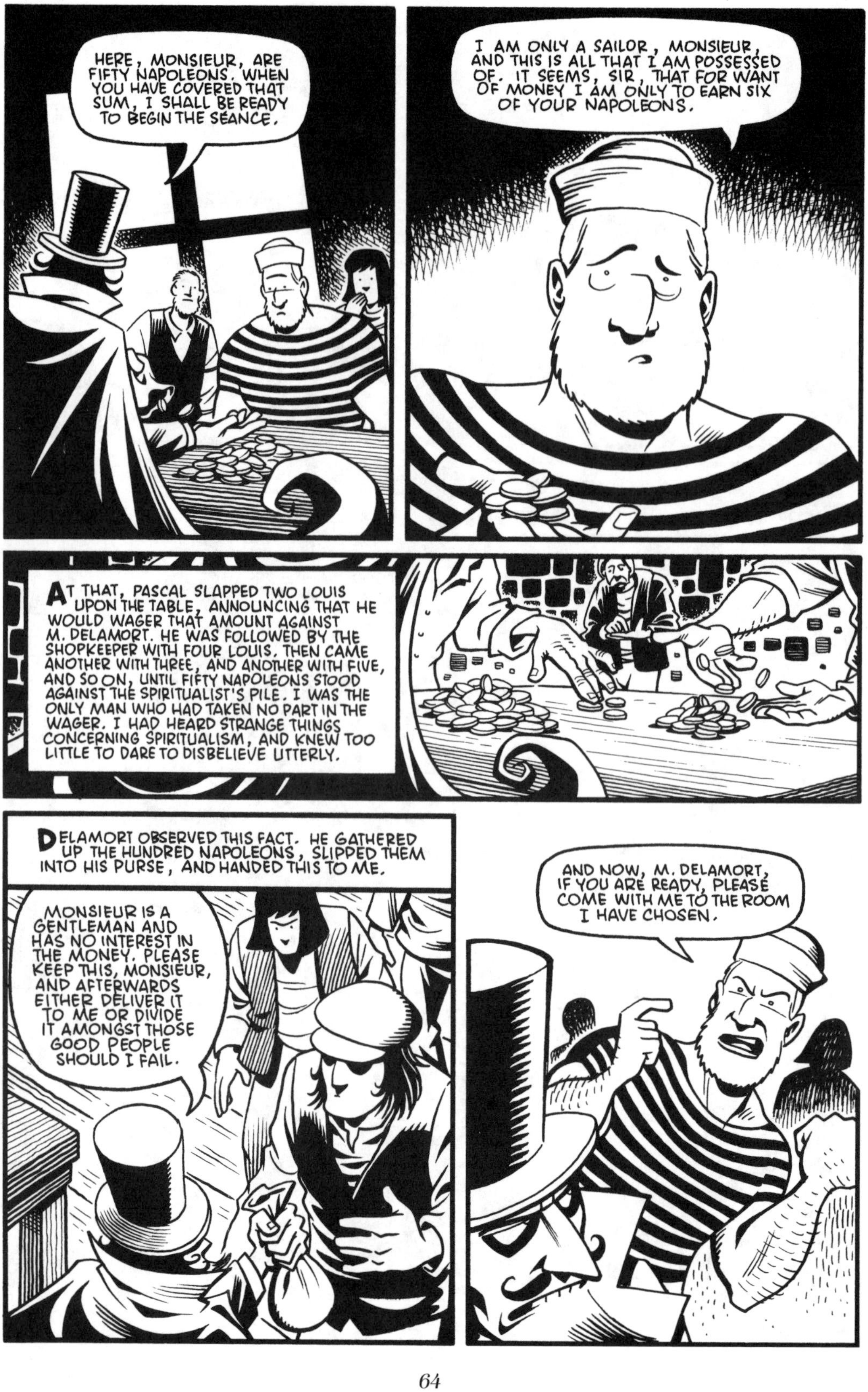
HERE, MONSIEUR, ARE FIFTY NAPOLEONS. WHEN YOU HAVE COVERED THAT SUM, I SHALL BE READY TO BEGIN THE SÉANCE.
I AM ONLY A SAILOR, MONSIEUR, AND THIS IS ALL THAT I AM POSSESSED OF. IT SEEMS, SIR, THAT FOR WANT OF MONEY I AM ONLY TO EARN SIX OF YOUR NAPOLEONS.
AT THAT, PASCAL SLAPPED TWO LOUIS UPON THE TABLE, ANNOUNCING THAT HE WOULD WAGER THAT AMOUNT AGAINST M. DELAMORT. HE WAS FOLLOWED BY THE SHOPKEEPER WITH FOUR LOUIS. THEN CAME ANOTHER WITH THREE, AND ANOTHER WITH FIVE, AND SO ON, UNTIL FIFTY NAPOLEONS STOOD AGAINST THE SPIRITUALIST'S PILE. I WAS THE ONLY MAN WHO HAD TAKEN NO PART IN THE WAGER. I HAD HEARD STRANGE THINGS CONCERNING SPIRITUALISM, AND KNEW TOO LITTLE TO DARE TO DISBELIEVE UTTERLY.
DELAMORT OBSERVED THIS FACT. HE GATHERED UP THE HUNDRED NAPOLEONS, SLIPPED THEM INTO HIS PURSE, AND HANDED THIS TO ME.
MONSIEUR IS A GENTLEMAN AND HAS NO INTEREST IN THE MONEY. PLEASE KEEP THIS, MONSIEUR, AND AFTERWARDS EITHER DELIVER IT TO ME OR DIVIDE IT AMONGST THOSE GOOD PEOPLE SHOULD I FAIL.
AND NOW, M. DELAMORT, IF YOU ARE READY, PLEASE COME WITH ME TO THE ROOM I HAVE CHOSEN.

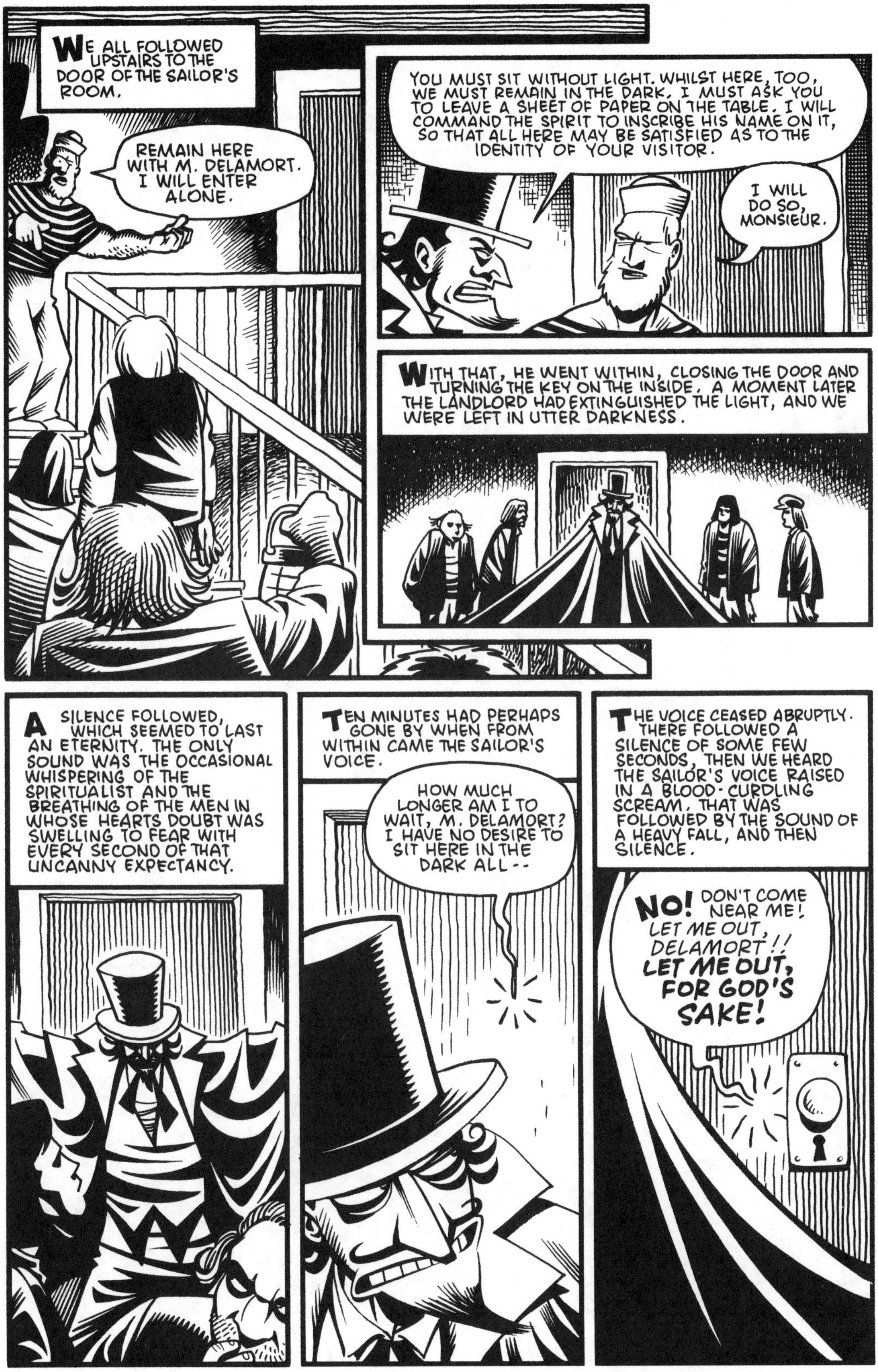
WE ALL FOLLOWED UPSTAIRS TO THE DOOR OF THE SAILOR'S ROOM.
REMAIN HERE WITH M. DELAMORT. I WILL ENTER ALONE.
YOU MUST SIT WITHOUT LIGHT. WHILST HERE, TOO, WE MUST REMAIN IN THE DARK. I MUST ASK YOU TO LEAVE A SHEET OF PAPER ON THE TABLE. I WILL COMMAND THE SPIRIT TO INSCRIBE HIS NAME ON IT, SO THAT ALL HERE MAY BE SATISFIED AS TO THE IDENTITY OF YOUR VISITOR.
I WILL DO SO, MONSIEUR.
WITH THAT, HE WENT WITHIN, CLOSING THE DOOR AND TURNING THE KEY ON THE INSIDE. A MOMENT LATER THE LANDLORD HAD EXTINGUISHED THE LIGHT, AND WE WERE LEFT IN UTTER DARKNESS.
A SILENCE FOLLOWED, WHICH SEEMED TO LAST AN ETERNITY. THE ONLY SOUND WAS THE OCCASIONAL WHISPERING OF THE SPIRITUALIST AND THE BREATHING OF THE MEN IN WHOSE HEARTS DOUBT WAS SWELLING TO FEAR WITH EVERY SECOND OF THAT UNCANNY EXPECTANCY.
TEN MINUTES HAD PERHAPS GONE BY WHEN FROM WITHIN CAME THE SAILOR'S VOICE.
HOW MUCH LONGER AM I TO WAIT, M. DELAMORT? I HAVE NO DESIRE TO SIT HERE IN THE DARK ALL --
THE VOICE CEASED ABRUPTLY. THERE FOLLOWED A SILENCE OF SOME FEW SECONDS, THEN WE HEARD THE SAILOR'S VOICE RAISED IN A BLOOD-CURDLING SCREAM. THAT WAS FOLLOWED BY THE SOUND OF A HEAVY FALL, AND THEN SILENCE.
NO! DON'T COME NEAR ME! LET ME OUT, DELAMORT!! LET ME OUT, FOR GOD'S SAKE!

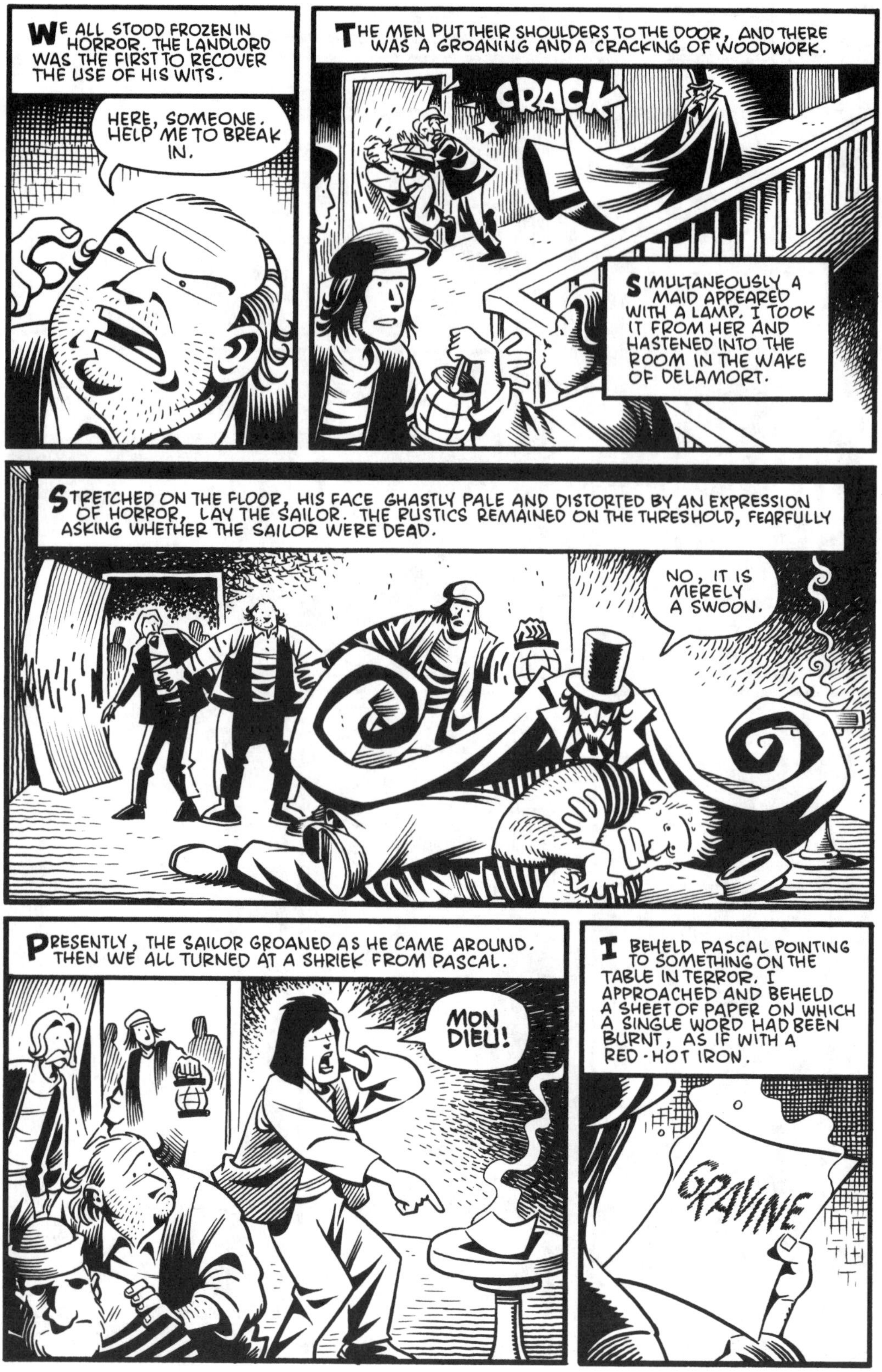
WE ALL STOOD FROZEN IN HORROR. THE LANDLORD WAS THE FIRST TO RECOVER THE USE OF HIS WITS.
HERE, SOMEONE. HELP ME TO BREAK IN.
THE MEN PUT THEIR SHOULDERS TO THE DOOR, AND THERE WAS A GROANING AND A CRACKING OF WOODWORK.
CRACK
SIMULTANEOUSLY A MAID APPEARED WITH A LAMP. I TOOK IT FROM HER AND HASTENED INTO THE ROOM IN THE WAKE OF DELAMORT.
STRETCHED ON THE FLOOR, HIS FACE GHASTLY PALE AND DISTORTED BY AN EXPRESSION OF HORROR, LAY THE SAILOR. THE RUSTICS REMAINED ON THE THRESHOLD, FEARFULLY ASKING WHETHER THE SAILOR WERE DEAD.
NO, IT IS MERELY A SWOON.
PRESENTLY, THE SAILOR GROANED AS HE CAME AROUND. THEN WE ALL TURNED AT A SHRIEK FROM PASCAL.
MON DIEU!
I BEHELD PASCAL POINTING TO SOMETHING ON THE TABLE IN TERROR. I APPROACHED AND BEHELD A SHEET OF PAPER ON WHICH A SINGLE WORD HAD BEEN BURNT, AS IF WITH A RED-HOT IRON.
GRAVINE

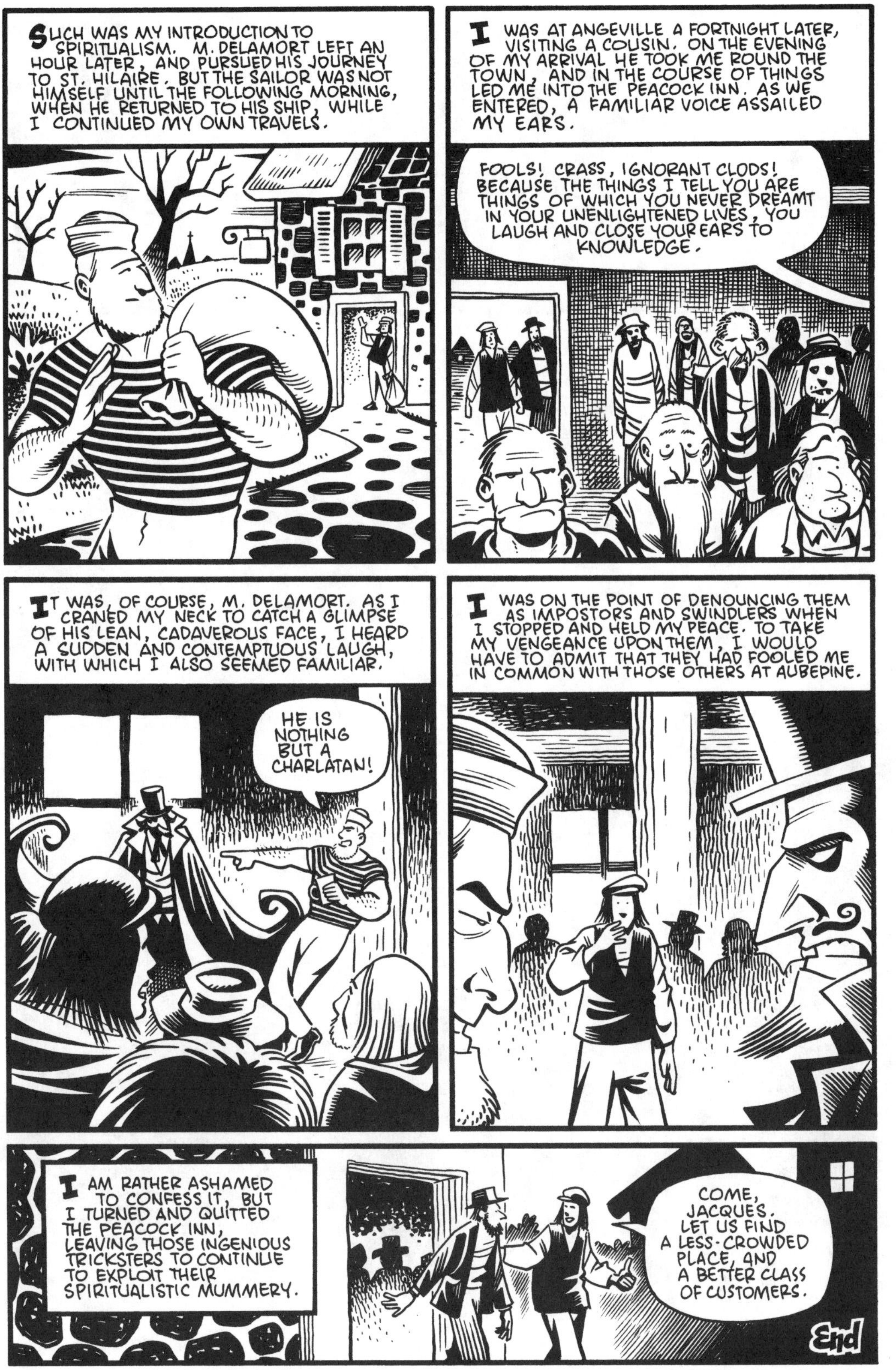
SUCH WAS MY INTRODUCTION TO SPIRITUALISM. M. DELAMORT LEFT AN HOUR LATER, AND PURSUED HIS JOURNEY TO ST. HILAIRE. BUT THE SAILOR WAS NOT HIMSELF UNTIL THE FOLLOWING MORNING, WHEN HE RETURNED TO HIS SHIP, WHILE I CONTINUED MY OWN TRAVELS.
I WAS AT ANGEVILLE A FORTNIGHT LATER, VISITING A COUSIN. ON THE EVENING OF MY ARRIVAL HE TOOK ME ROUND THE TOWN, AND IN THE COURSE OF THINGS LED ME INTO THE PEACOCK INN. AS WE ENTERED, A FAMILIAR VOICE ASSAILED MY EARS.
FOOLS! CRASS, IGNORANT CLODS! BECAUSE THE THINGS I TELL YOU ARE THINGS OF WHICH YOU NEVER DREAMT IN YOUR UNENLIGHTENED LIVES, YOU LAUGH AND CLOSE YOUR EARS TO KNOWLEDGE.
IT WAS, OF COURSE, M. DELAMORT. AS I CRANED MY NECK TO CATCH A GLIMPSE OF HIS LEAN, CADAVEROUS FACE, I HEARD A SUDDEN AND CONTEMPTUOUS LAUGH, WITH WHICH I ALSO SEEMED FAMILIAR.
HE IS NOTHING BUT A CHARLATAN!
I WAS ON THE POINT OF DENOUNCING THEM AS IMPOSTORS AND SWINDLERS WHEN I STOPPED AND HELD MY PEACE. TO TAKE MY VENGEANCE UPON THEM, I WOULD HAVE TO ADMIT THAT THEY HAD FOOLED ME IN COMMON WITH THOSE OTHERS AT AUBEPINE.
I AM RATHER ASHAMED TO CONFESS IT, BUT I TURNED AND QUITTED THE PEACOCK INN, LEAVING THOSE INGENIOUS TRICKSTERS TO CONTINUE TO EXPLOIT THEIR SPIRITUALISTIC MUMMERY.
COME, JACQUES. LET US FIND A LESS-CROWDED PLACE, AND A BETTER CLASS OF CUSTOMERS.
End

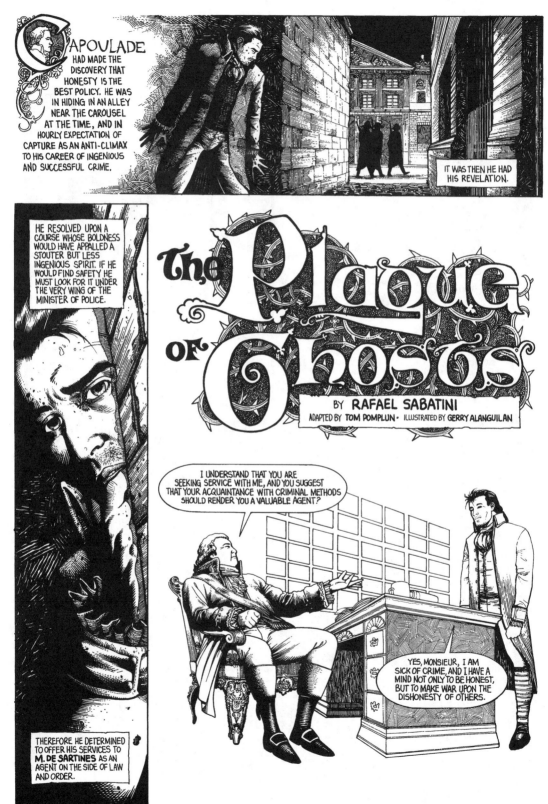

CAPOULADE HAD MADE THE DISCOVERY THAT HONESTY IS THE BEST POLICY. HE WAS IN HIDING IN AN ALLEY NEAR THE CAROUSEL AT THE TIME, AND IN HOURLY EXPECTATION OF CAPTURE AS AN ANTI-CLIMAX TO HIS CAREER OF INGENIOUS AND SUCCESSFUL CRIME.

IT WAS THEN HE HAD HIS REVELATION.

HE RESOLVED UPON A COURSE WHOSE BOLDNESS WOULD HAVE APPALLED A STOUTER BUT LESS INGENIOUS SPIRIT. IF HE WOULD FIND SAFETY HE MUST LOOK FOR IT UNDER THE VERY WING OF THE MINISTER OF POLICE.

The Plague of Ghosts

BY RAFAEL SABATINI

ADAPTED BY TOM POMPLUN • ILLUSTRATED BY GERRY ALANGUILAN

I UNDERSTAND THAT YOU ARE SEEKING SERVICE WITH ME, AND YOU SUGGEST THAT YOUR ACQUAINTANCE WITH CRIMINAL METHODS SHOULD RENDER YOU A VALUABLE AGENT?

YES, MONSIEUR, I AM SICK OF CRIME, AND I HAVE A MIND NOT ONLY TO BE HONEST, BUT TO MAKE WAR UPON THE DISHONESTY OF OTHERS.

THEREFORE HE DETERMINED TO OFFER HIS SERVICES TO M. DE SARTINES AS AN AGENT ON THE SIDE OF LAW AND ORDER.

68

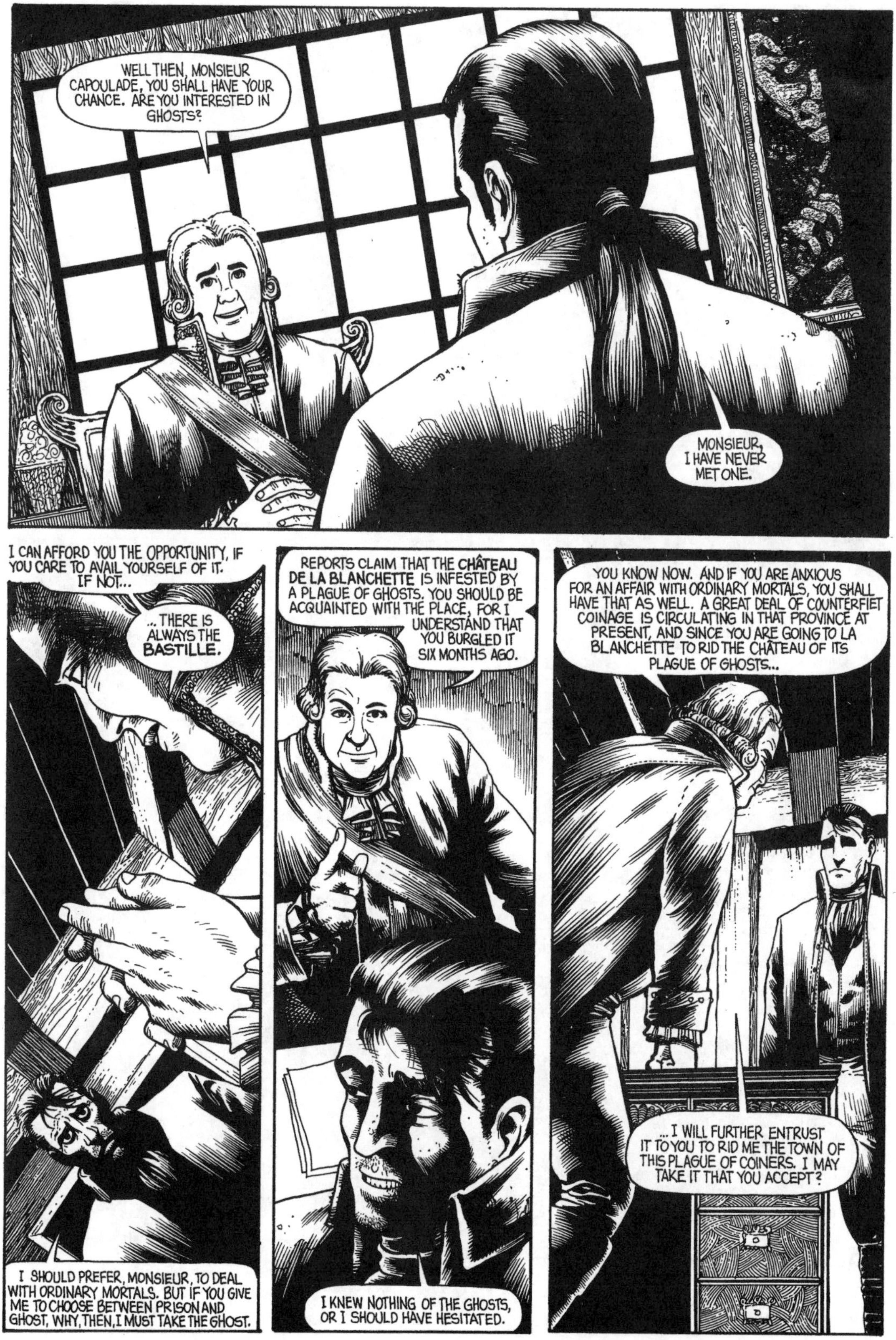
WELL THEN, MONSIEUR CAPOULADE, YOU SHALL HAVE YOUR CHANCE. ARE YOU INTERESTED IN GHOSTS?
MONSIEUR, I HAVE NEVER MET ONE.
I CAN AFFORD YOU THE OPPORTUNITY, IF YOU CARE TO AVAIL YOURSELF OF IT. IF NOT...
...THERE IS ALWAYS THE BASTILLE.
I SHOULD PREFER, MONSIEUR, TO DEAL WITH ORDINARY MORTALS. BUT IF YOU GIVE ME TO CHOOSE BETWEEN PRISON AND GHOST, WHY, THEN, I MUST TAKE THE GHOST.
REPORTS CLAIM THAT THE CHÂTEAU DE LA BLANCHETTE IS INFESTED BY A PLAGUE OF GHOSTS. YOU SHOULD BE ACQUAINTED WITH THE PLACE, FOR I UNDERSTAND THAT YOU BURGLED IT SIX MONTHS AGO.
I KNEW NOTHING OF THE GHOSTS, OR I SHOULD HAVE HESITATED.
YOU KNOW NOW. AND IF YOU ARE ANXIOUS FOR AN AFFAIR WITH ORDINARY MORTALS, YOU SHALL HAVE THAT AS WELL. A GREAT DEAL OF COUNTERFIET COINAGE IS CIRCULATING IN THAT PROVINCE AT PRESENT, AND SINCE YOU ARE GOING TO LA BLANCHETTE TO RID THE CHÂTEAU OF ITS PLAGUE OF GHOSTS...
...I WILL FURTHER ENTRUST IT TO YOU TO RID ME THE TOWN OF THIS PLAGUE OF COINERS. I MAY TAKE IT THAT YOU ACCEPT?

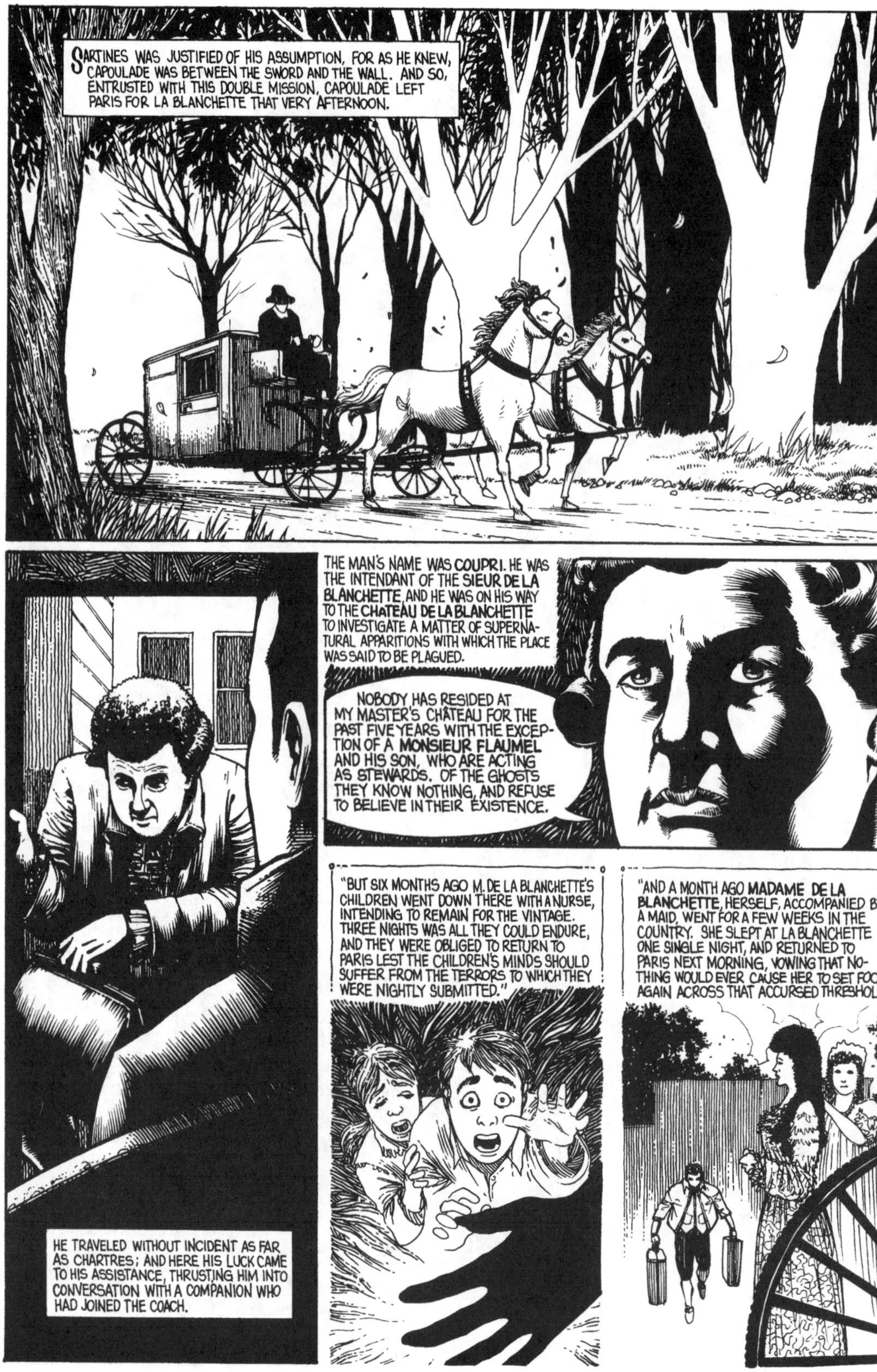
SARTINES WAS JUSTIFIED OF HIS ASSUMPTION, FOR AS HE KNEW, CAPOULADE WAS BETWEEN THE SWORD AND THE WALL. AND SO, ENTRUSTED WITH THIS DOUBLE MISSION, CAPOULADE LEFT PARIS FOR LA BLANCHETTE THAT VERY AFTERNOON.
HE TRAVELED WITHOUT INCIDENT AS FAR AS CHARTRES; AND HERE HIS LUCK CAME TO HIS ASSISTANCE, THRUSTING HIM INTO CONVERSATION WITH A COMPANION WHO HAD JOINED THE COACH.
THE MAN'S NAME WAS COUPRI. HE WAS THE INTENDANT OF THE SIEUR DE LA BLANCHETTE, AND HE WAS ON HIS WAY TO THE CHATEAU DE LA BLANCHETTE TO INVESTIGATE A MATTER OF SUPERNATURAL APPARITIONS WITH WHICH THE PLACE WAS SAID TO BE PLAGUED.
NOBODY HAS RESIDED AT MY MASTER'S CHÂTEAU FOR THE PAST FIVE YEARS WITH THE EXCEPTION OF A MONSIEUR FLAUMEL AND HIS SON, WHO ARE ACTING AS STEWARDS. OF THE GHOSTS THEY KNOW NOTHING, AND REFUSE TO BELIEVE IN THEIR EXISTENCE.
"BUT SIX MONTHS AGO M. DE LA BLANCHETTE'S CHILDREN WENT DOWN THERE WITH A NURSE, INTENDING TO REMAIN FOR THE VINTAGE. THREE NIGHTS WAS ALL THEY COULD ENDURE, AND THEY WERE OBLIGED TO RETURN TO PARIS LEST THE CHILDREN'S MINDS SHOULD SUFFER FROM THE TERRORS TO WHICH THEY WERE NIGHTLY SUBMITTED."
"AND A MONTH AGO MADAME DE LA BLANCHETTE, HERSELF, ACCOMPANIED BY A MAID, WENT FOR A FEW WEEKS IN THE COUNTRY. SHE SLEPT AT LA BLANCHETTE ONE SINGLE NIGHT, AND RETURNED TO PARIS NEXT MORNING, VOWING THAT NOTHING WOULD EVER CAUSE HER TO SET FOOT AGAIN ACROSS THAT ACCURSED THRESHOLD."

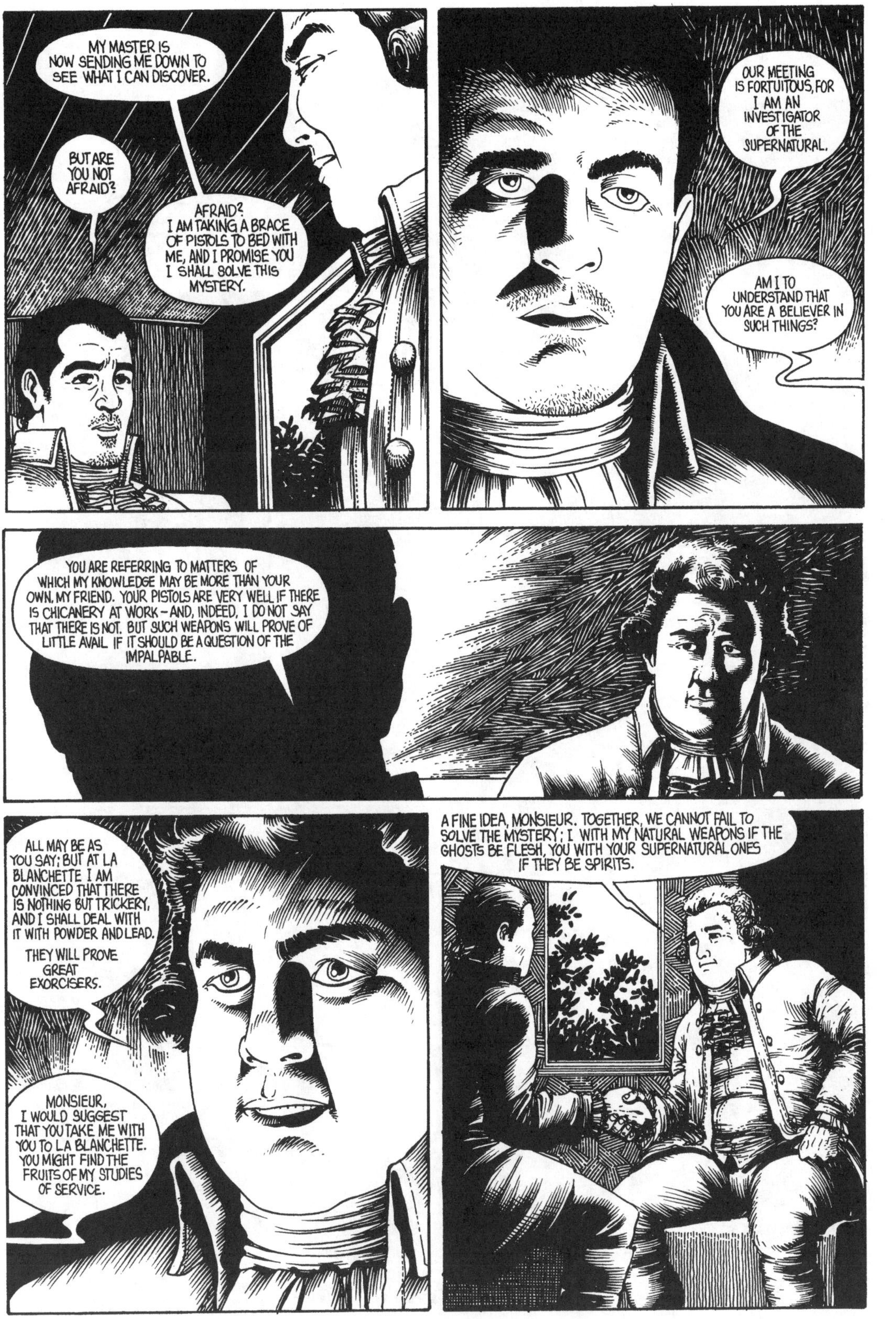
MY MASTER IS NOW SENDING ME DOWN TO SEE WHAT I CAN DISCOVER.
BUT ARE YOU NOT AFRAID?
AFRAID? I AM TAKING A BRACE OF PISTOLS TO BED WITH ME, AND I PROMISE YOU I SHALL SOLVE THIS MYSTERY.
OUR MEETING IS FORTUITOUS, FOR I AM AN INVESTIGATOR OF THE SUPERNATURAL.
AM I TO UNDERSTAND THAT YOU ARE A BELIEVER IN SUCH THINGS?
YOU ARE REFERRING TO MATTERS OF WHICH MY KNOWLEDGE MAY BE MORE THAN YOUR OWN, MY FRIEND. YOUR PISTOLS ARE VERY WELL IF THERE IS CHICANERY AT WORK – AND, INDEED, I DO NOT SAY THAT THERE IS NOT. BUT SUCH WEAPONS WILL PROVE OF LITTLE AVAIL IF IT SHOULD BE A QUESTION OF THE IMPALPABLE.
ALL MAY BE AS YOU SAY; BUT AT LA BLANCHETTE I AM CONVINCED THAT THERE IS NOTHING BUT TRICKERY, AND I SHALL DEAL WITH IT WITH POWDER AND LEAD.
THEY WILL PROVE GREAT EXORCISERS.
MONSIEUR, I WOULD SUGGEST THAT YOU TAKE ME WITH YOU TO LA BLANCHETTE. YOU MIGHT FIND THE FRUITS OF MY STUDIES OF SERVICE.
A FINE IDEA, MONSIEUR. TOGETHER, WE CANNOT FAIL TO SOLVE THE MYSTERY; I WITH MY NATURAL WEAPONS IF THE GHOSTS BE FLESH, YOU WITH YOUR SUPERNATURAL ONES IF THEY BE SPIRITS.

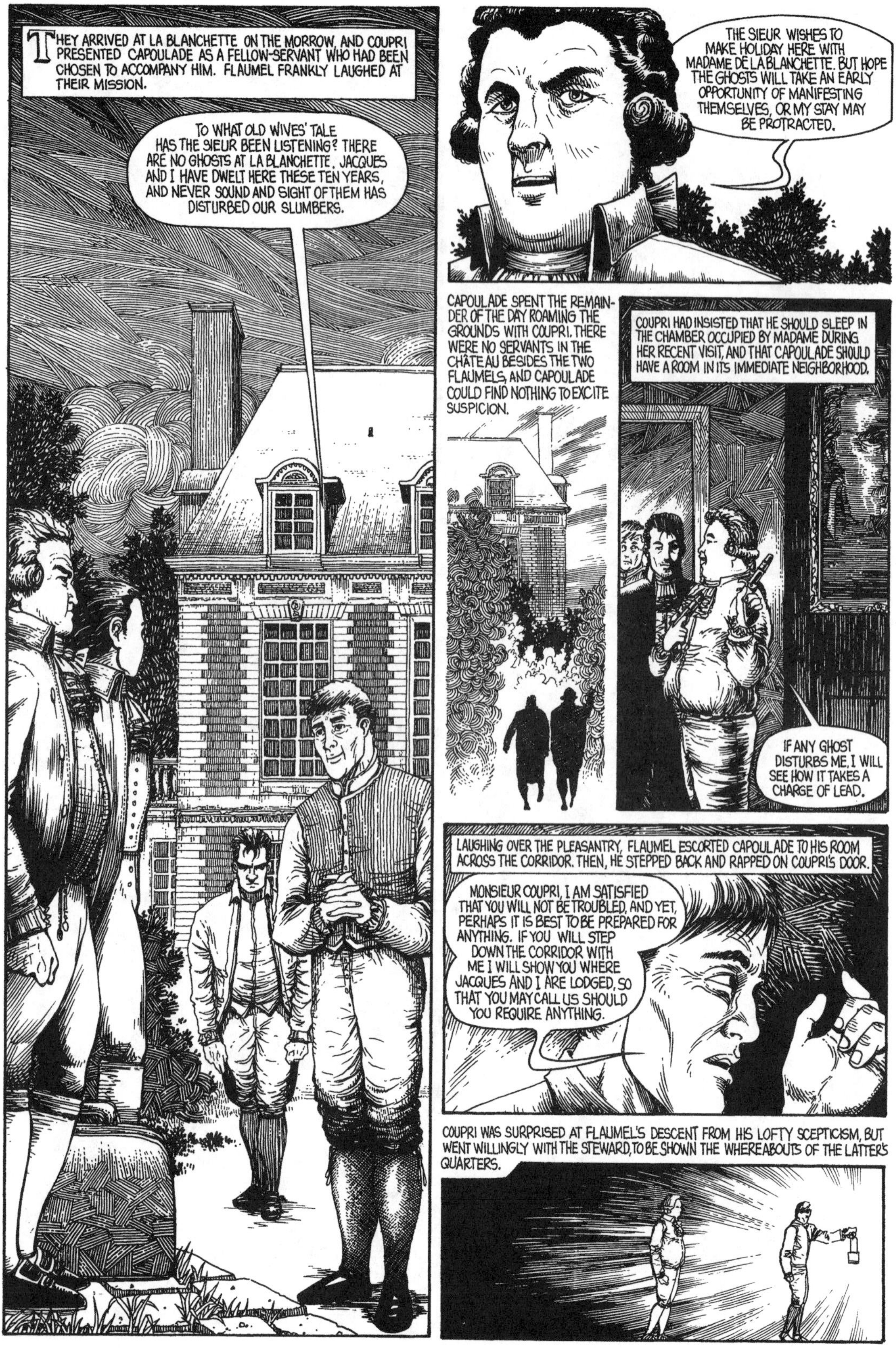
THEY ARRIVED AT LA BLANCHETTE ON THE MORROW, AND COUPRI PRESENTED CAPOULADE AS A FELLOW-SERVANT WHO HAD BEEN CHOSEN TO ACCOMPANY HIM. FLAUMEL FRANKLY LAUGHED AT THEIR MISSION.
TO WHAT OLD WIVES' TALE HAS THE SIEUR BEEN LISTENING? THERE ARE NO GHOSTS AT LA BLANCHETTE. JACQUES AND I HAVE DWELT HERE THESE TEN YEARS, AND NEVER SOUND AND SIGHT OF THEM HAS DISTURBED OUR SLUMBERS.
THE SIEUR WISHES TO MAKE HOLIDAY HERE WITH MADAME DE LA BLANCHETTE. BUT HOPE THE GHOSTS WILL TAKE AN EARLY OPPORTUNITY OF MANIFESTING THEMSELVES, OR MY STAY MAY BE PROTRACTED.
CAPOULADE SPENT THE REMAINDER OF THE DAY ROAMING THE GROUNDS WITH COUPRI. THERE WERE NO SERVANTS IN THE CHÂTEAU BESIDES THE TWO FLAUMELS, AND CAPOULADE COULD FIND NOTHING TO EXCITE SUSPICION.
COUPRI HAD INSISTED THAT HE SHOULD SLEEP IN THE CHAMBER OCCUPIED BY MADAME DURING HER RECENT VISIT, AND THAT CAPOULADE SHOULD HAVE A ROOM IN ITS IMMEDIATE NEIGHBORHOOD.
IF ANY GHOST DISTURBS ME, I WILL SEE HOW IT TAKES A CHARGE OF LEAD.
LAUGHING OVER THE PLEASANTRY, FLAUMEL ESCORTED CAPOULADE TO HIS ROOM ACROSS THE CORRIDOR. THEN, HE STEPPED BACK AND RAPPED ON COUPRI'S DOOR.
MONSIEUR COUPRI, I AM SATISFIED THAT YOU WILL NOT BE TROUBLED, AND YET, PERHAPS IT IS BEST TO BE PREPARED FOR ANYTHING. IF YOU WILL STEP DOWN THE CORRIDOR WITH ME I WILL SHOW YOU WHERE JACQUES AND I ARE LODGED, SO THAT YOU MAY CALL US SHOULD YOU REQUIRE ANYTHING.
COUPRI WAS SURPRISED AT FLAUMEL'S DESCENT FROM HIS LOFTY SCEPTICISM, BUT WENT WILLINGLY WITH THE STEWARD, TO BE SHOWN THE WHEREABOUTS OF THE LATTER'S QUARTERS.

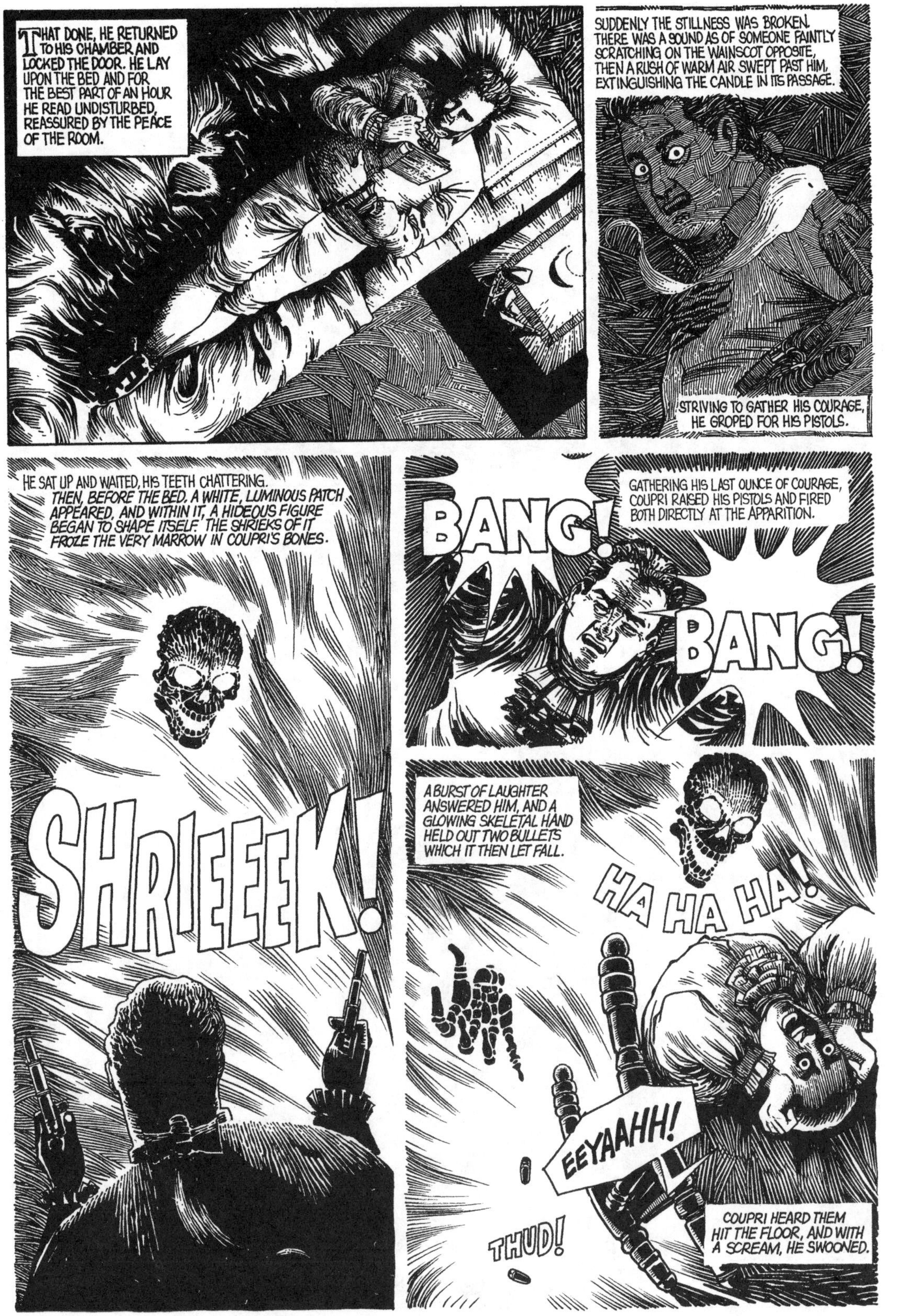
THAT DONE, HE RETURNED TO HIS CHAMBER AND LOCKED THE DOOR. HE LAY UPON THE BED AND FOR THE BEST PART OF AN HOUR HE READ UNDISTURBED, REASSURED BY THE PEACE OF THE ROOM.
SUDDENLY THE STILLNESS WAS BROKEN. THERE WAS A SOUND AS OF SOMEONE FAINTLY SCRATCHING ON THE WAINSCOT OPPOSITE, THEN A RUSH OF WARM AIR SWEPT PAST HIM, EXTINGUISHING THE CANDLE IN ITS PASSAGE.
STRIVING TO GATHER HIS COURAGE, HE GROPED FOR HIS PISTOLS.
HE SAT UP AND WAITED, HIS TEETH CHATTERING. THEN, BEFORE THE BED, A WHITE, LUMINOUS PATCH APPEARED, AND WITHIN IT, A HIDEOUS FIGURE BEGAN TO SHAPE ITSELF. THE SHRIEKS OF IT FROZE THE VERY MARROW IN COUPRI'S BONES.
SHRIEEEK!
GATHERING HIS LAST OUNCE OF COURAGE, COUPRI RAISED HIS PISTOLS AND FIRED BOTH DIRECTLY AT THE APPARITION.
BANG!
BANG!
A BURST OF LAUGHTER ANSWERED HIM, AND A GLOWING SKELETAL HAND HELD OUT TWO BULLETS WHICH IT THEN LET FALL.
HA HA HA HA!
EEYAAHH!
THUD!
COUPRI HEARD THEM HIT THE FLOOR, AND WITH A SCREAM, HE SWOONED.

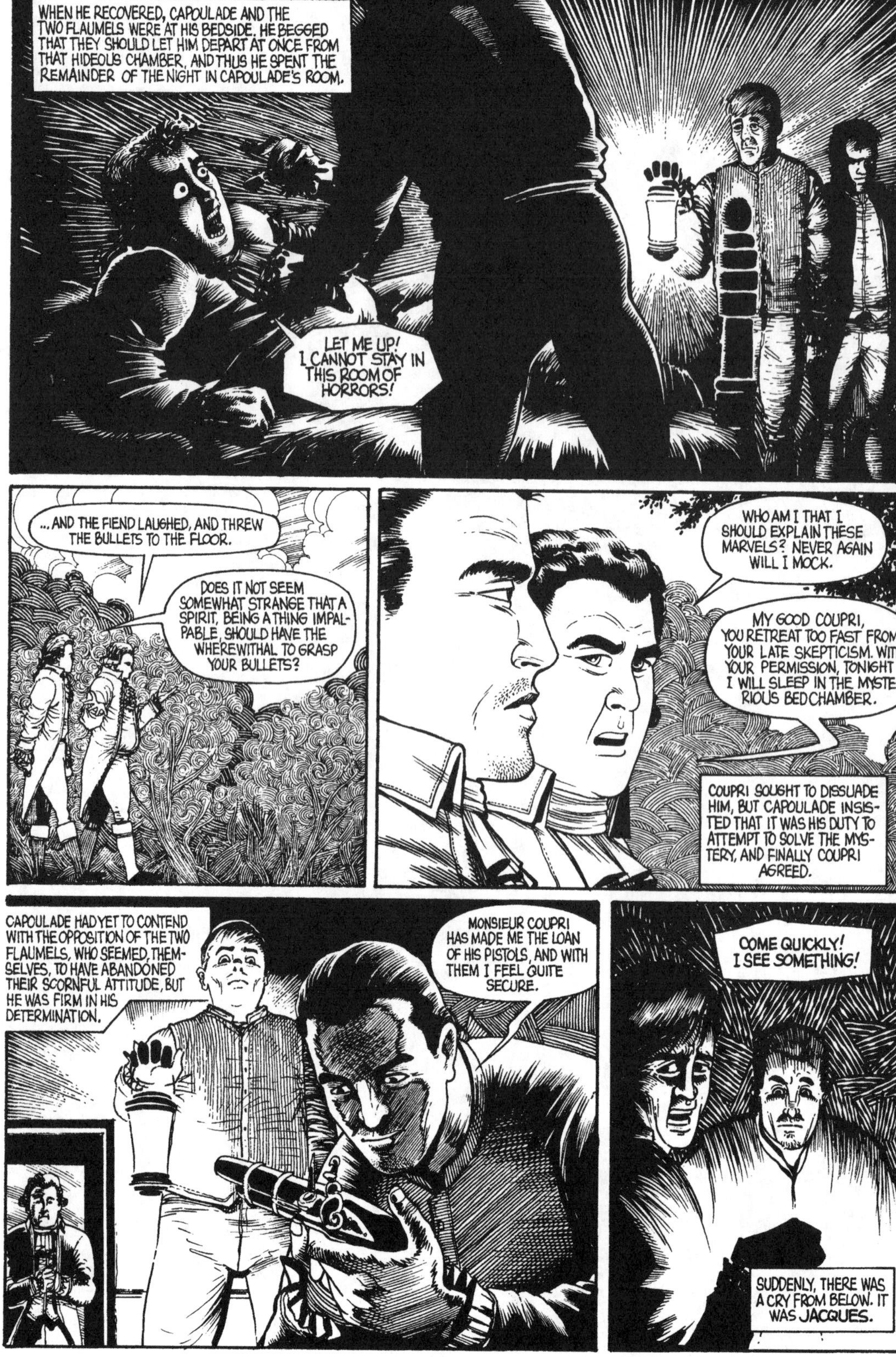
WHEN HE RECOVERED, CAPOULADE AND THE TWO FLAUMELS WERE AT HIS BEDSIDE. HE BEGGED THAT THEY SHOULD LET HIM DEPART AT ONCE FROM THAT HIDEOUS CHAMBER, AND THUS HE SPENT THE REMAINDER OF THE NIGHT IN CAPOULADE'S ROOM.
LET ME UP! I CANNOT STAY IN THIS ROOM OF HORRORS!
...AND THE FIEND LAUGHED, AND THREW THE BULLETS TO THE FLOOR.
DOES IT NOT SEEM SOMEWHAT STRANGE THAT A SPIRIT, BEING A THING IMPALPABLE, SHOULD HAVE THE WHEREWITHAL TO GRASP YOUR BULLETS?
WHO AM I THAT I SHOULD EXPLAIN THESE MARVELS? NEVER AGAIN WILL I MOCK.
MY GOOD COUPRI, YOU RETREAT TOO FAST FROM YOUR LATE SKEPTICISM. WITH YOUR PERMISSION, TONIGHT I WILL SLEEP IN THE MYSTERIOUS BEDCHAMBER.
COUPRI SOUGHT TO DISSUADE HIM, BUT CAPOULADE INSISTED THAT IT WAS HIS DUTY TO ATTEMPT TO SOLVE THE MYSTERY, AND FINALLY COUPRI AGREED.
CAPOULADE HAD YET TO CONTEND WITH THE OPPOSITION OF THE TWO FLAUMELS, WHO SEEMED, THEMSELVES, TO HAVE ABANDONED THEIR SCORNFUL ATTITUDE, BUT HE WAS FIRM IN HIS DETERMINATION.
MONSIEUR COUPRI HAS MADE ME THE LOAN OF HIS PISTOLS, AND WITH THEM I FEEL QUITE SECURE.
COME QUICKLY! I SEE SOMETHING!
SUDDENLY, THERE WAS A CRY FROM BELOW. IT WAS JACQUES.

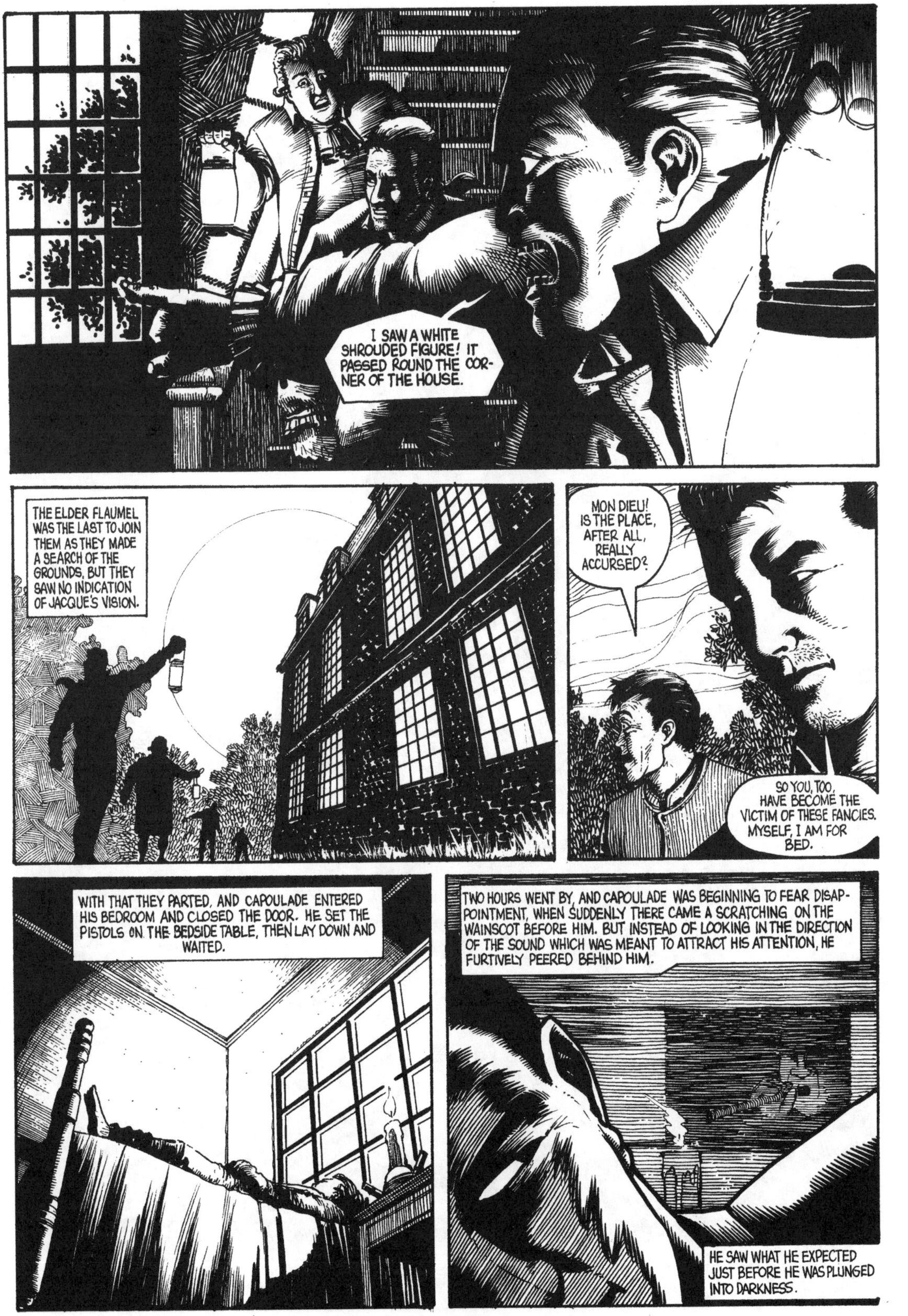
I SAW A WHITE SHROUDED FIGURE! IT PASSED ROUND THE CORNER OF THE HOUSE.
THE ELDER FLAUMEL WAS THE LAST TO JOIN THEM AS THEY MADE A SEARCH OF THE GROUNDS, BUT THEY SAW NO INDICATION OF JACQUE'S VISION.
MON DIEU! IS THE PLACE, AFTER ALL, REALLY ACCURSED?
SO YOU, TOO, HAVE BECOME THE VICTIM OF THESE FANCIES. MYSELF, I AM FOR BED.
WITH THAT THEY PARTED, AND CAPOULADE ENTERED HIS BEDROOM AND CLOSED THE DOOR. HE SET THE PISTOLS ON THE BEDSIDE TABLE, THEN LAY DOWN AND WAITED.
TWO HOURS WENT BY, AND CAPOULADE WAS BEGINNING TO FEAR DISAPPOINTMENT, WHEN SUDDENLY THERE CAME A SCRATCHING ON THE WAINSCOT BEFORE HIM. BUT INSTEAD OF LOOKING IN THE DIRECTION OF THE SOUND WHICH WAS MEANT TO ATTRACT HIS ATTENTION, HE FURTIVELY PEERED BEHIND HIM.
HE SAW WHAT HE EXPECTED JUST BEFORE HE WAS PLUNGED INTO DARKNESS.

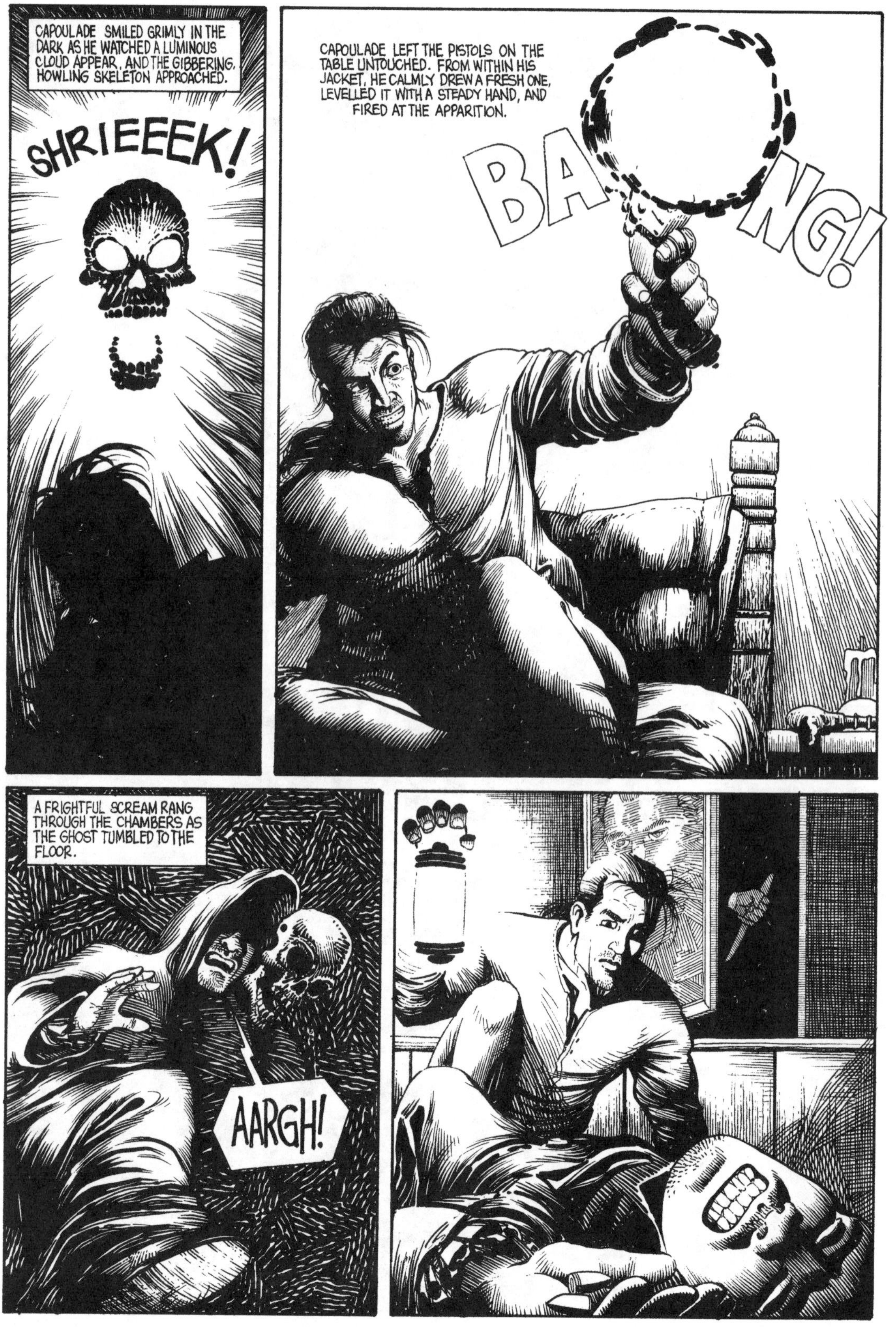
CAPOULADE SMILED GRIMLY IN THE DARK AS HE WATCHED A LUMINOUS CLOUD APPEAR, AND THE GIBBERING, HOWLING SKELETON APPROACHED.
SHRIEEEK!
CAPOULADE LEFT THE PISTOLS ON THE TABLE UNTOUCHED. FROM WITHIN HIS JACKET, HE CALMLY DREW A FRESH ONE, LEVELLED IT WITH A STEADY HAND, AND FIRED AT THE APPARITION.
BANG!
A FRIGHTFUL SCREAM RANG THROUGH THE CHAMBERS AS THE GHOST TUMBLED TO THE FLOOR.
AARGH!

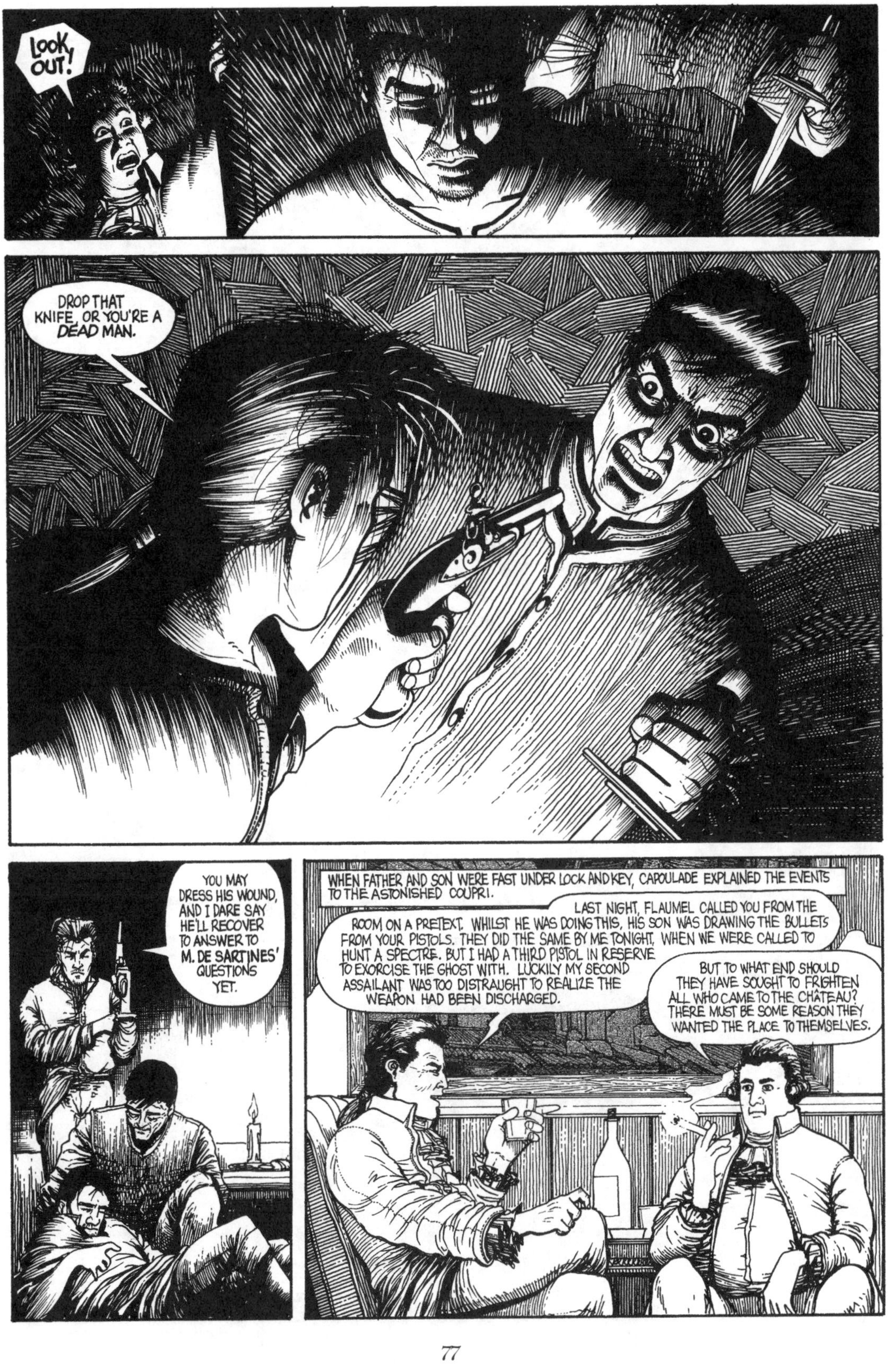
LOOK OUT!
DROP THAT KNIFE, OR YOU'RE A DEAD MAN.
YOU MAY DRESS HIS WOUND, AND I DARE SAY HE'LL RECOVER TO ANSWER TO M. DE SARTINES' QUESTIONS YET.
WHEN FATHER AND SON WERE FAST UNDER LOCK AND KEY, CAPOULADE EXPLAINED THE EVENTS TO THE ASTONISHED COUPRI.
LAST NIGHT, FLAUMEL CALLED YOU FROM THE ROOM ON A PRETEXT. WHILST HE WAS DOING THIS, HIS SON WAS DRAWING THE BULLETS FROM YOUR PISTOLS. THEY DID THE SAME BY ME TONIGHT, WHEN WE WERE CALLED TO HUNT A SPECTRE. BUT I HAD A THIRD PISTOL IN RESERVE TO EXORCISE THE GHOST WITH. LUCKILY MY SECOND ASSAILANT WAS TOO DISTRAUGHT TO REALIZE THE WEAPON HAD BEEN DISCHARGED.
BUT TO WHAT END SHOULD THEY HAVE SOUGHT TO FRIGHTEN ALL WHO CAME TO THE CHÂTEAU? THERE MUST BE SOME REASON THEY WANTED THE PLACE TO THEMSELVES.

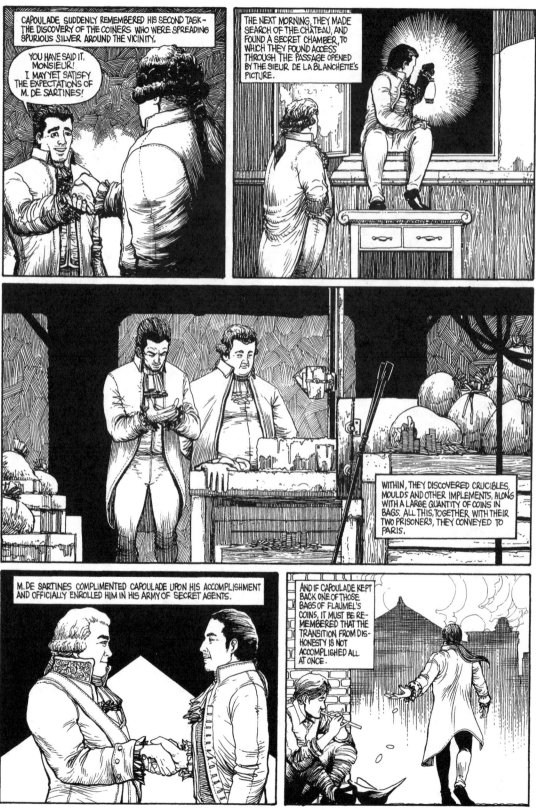

CAPOULADE SUDDENLY REMEMBERED HIS SECOND TASK – THE DISCOVERY OF THE COINERS WHO WERE SPREADING SPURIOUS SILVER AROUND THE VICINITY.

YOU HAVE SAID IT, MONSIEUR! I MAY YET SATISFY THE EXPECTATIONS OF M. DE SARTINES!

THE NEXT MORNING, THEY MADE SEARCH OF THE CHÂTEAU, AND FOUND A SECRET CHAMBER, TO WHICH THEY FOUND ACCESS THROUGH THE PASSAGE OPENED BY THE SIEUR DE LA BLANCHETTE'S PICTURE.

WITHIN, THEY DISCOVERED CRUCIBLES, MOULDS AND OTHER IMPLEMENTS, ALONG WITH A LARGE QUANTITY OF COINS IN BAGS. ALL THIS, TOGETHER WITH THEIR TWO PRISONERS, THEY CONVEYED TO PARIS.

M. DE SARTINES COMPLIMENTED CAPOULADE UPON HIS ACCOMPLISHMENT AND OFFICIALLY ENROLLED HIM IN HIS ARMY OF SECRET AGENTS.

AND IF CAPOULADE KEPT BACK ONE OF THOSE BAGS OF FLAUMEL'S COINS, IT MUST BE REMEMBERED THAT THE TRANSITION FROM DISHONESTY IS NOT ACCOMPLISHED ALL AT ONCE.

ILLUSTRATIONS ©2006 GERRY ALANGUILAN

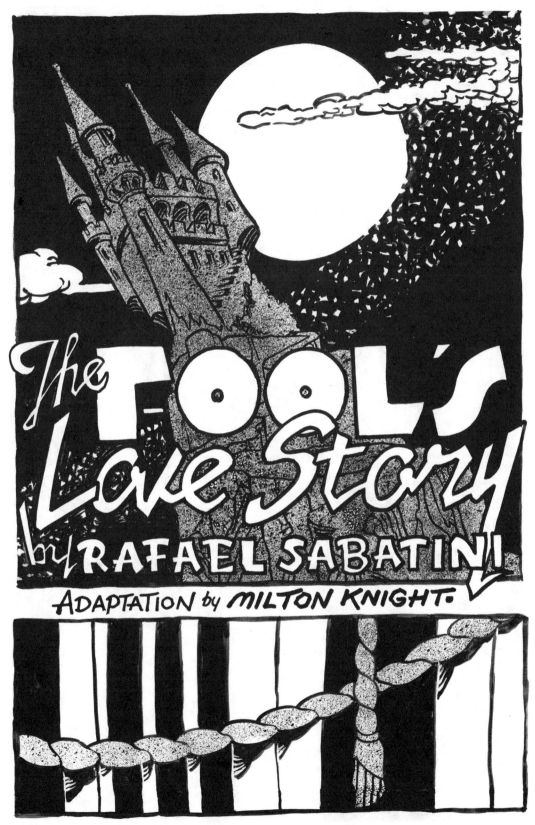

The Fool's Love Story by Rafael Sabatini

Adaptation by Milton Knight.

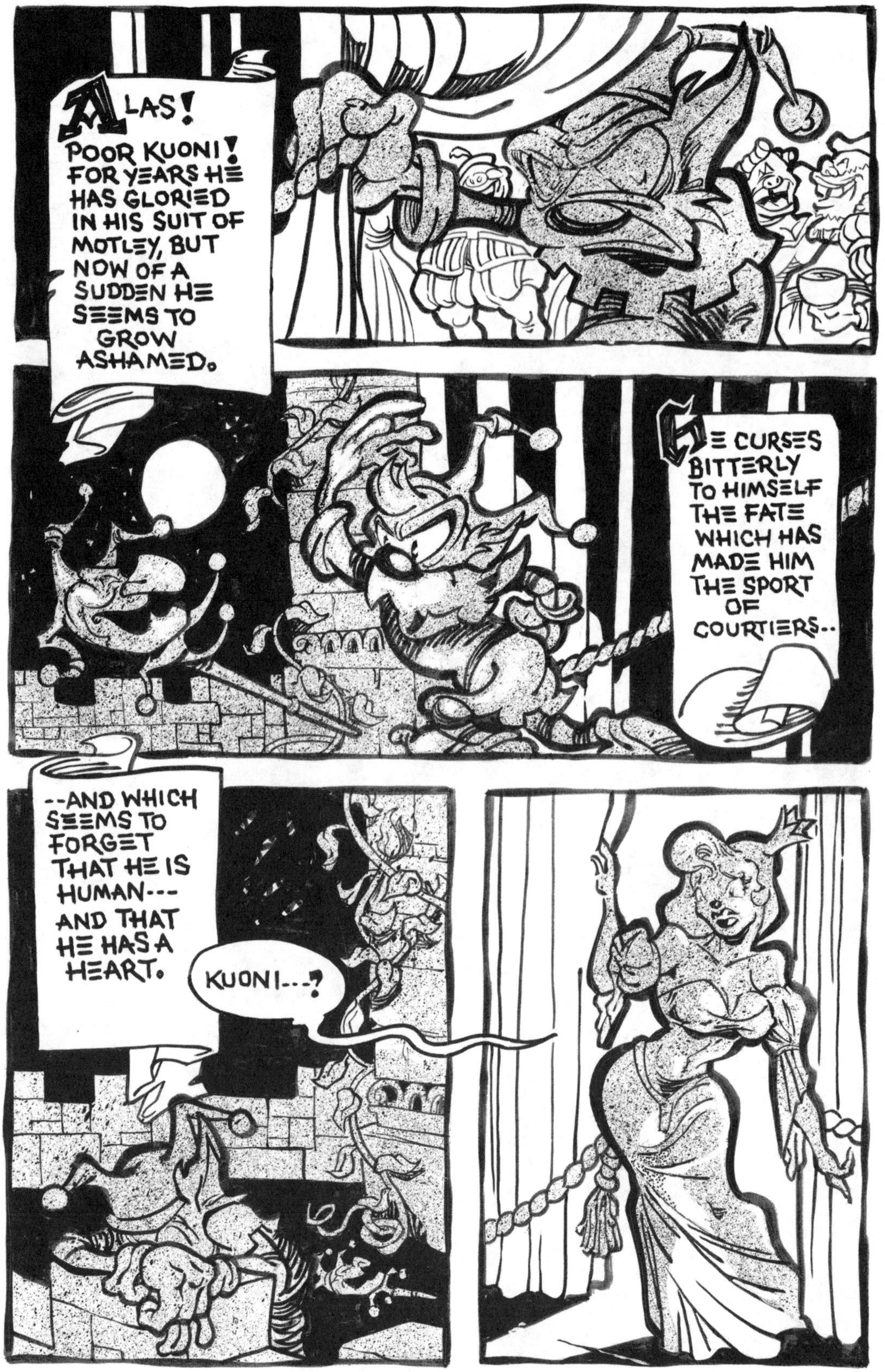
ALAS! POOR KUONI! FOR YEARS HE HAS GLORIED IN HIS SUIT OF MOTLEY, BUT NOW OF A SUDDEN HE SEEMS TO GROW ASHAMED.
HE CURSES BITTERLY TO HIMSELF THE FATE WHICH HAS MADE HIM THE SPORT OF COURTIERS--
--AND WHICH SEEMS TO FORGET THAT HE IS HUMAN--- AND THAT HE HAS A HEART.
KUONI--?

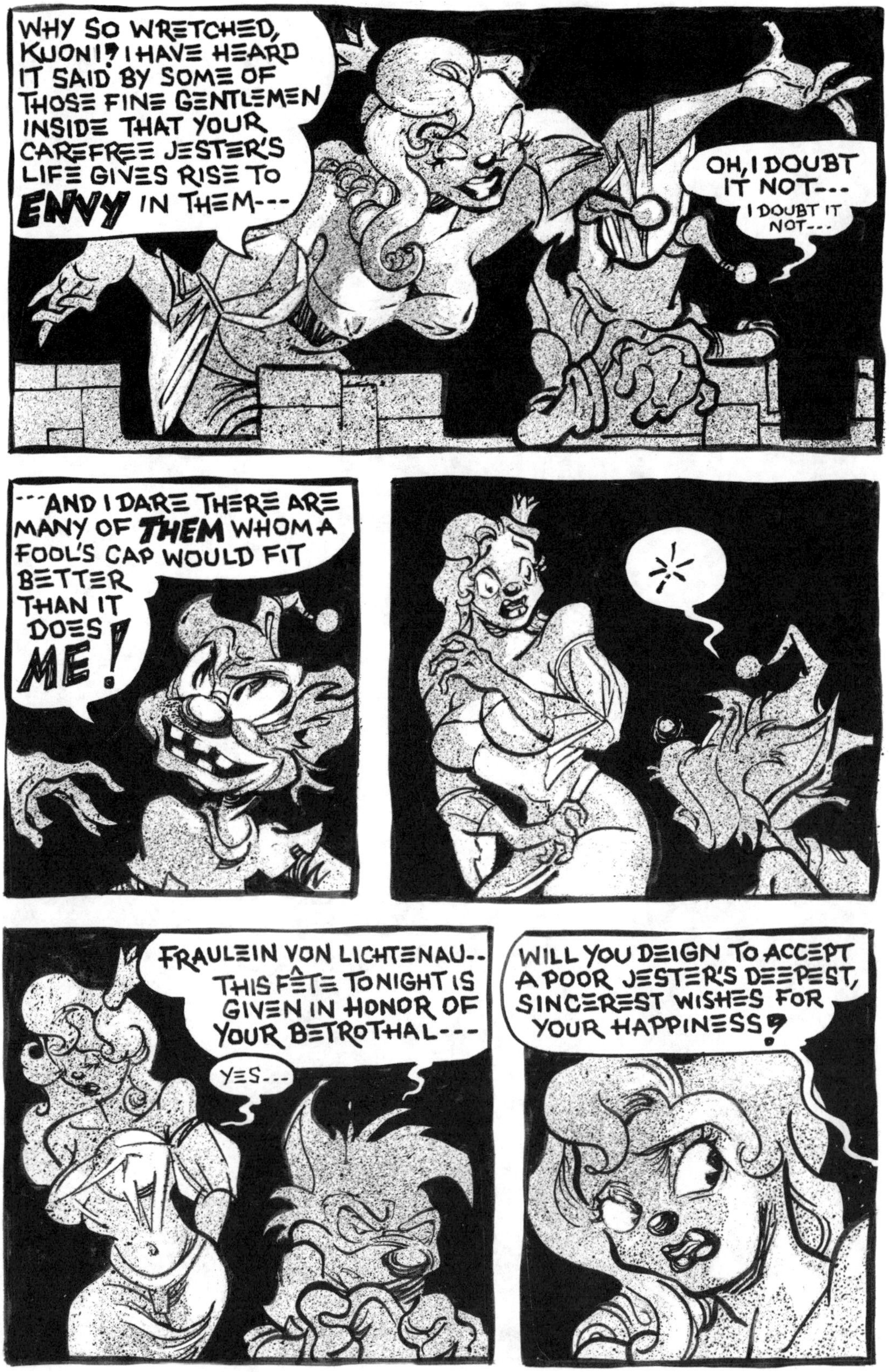
WHY SO WRETCHED, KUONI? I HAVE HEARD IT SAID BY SOME OF THOSE FINE GENTLEMEN INSIDE THAT YOUR CAREFREE JESTER'S LIFE GIVES RISE TO ENVY IN THEM---
OH, I DOUBT IT NOT---
I DOUBT IT NOT---
---AND I DARE THERE ARE MANY OF THEM WHOM A FOOL'S CAP WOULD FIT BETTER THAN IT DOES ME!
!
FRAULEIN VON LICHTENAU-- THIS FÊTE TONIGHT IS GIVEN IN HONOR OF YOUR BETROTHAL---
YES---
WILL YOU DEIGN TO ACCEPT A POOR JESTER'S DEEPEST, SINCEREST WISHES FOR YOUR HAPPINESS?

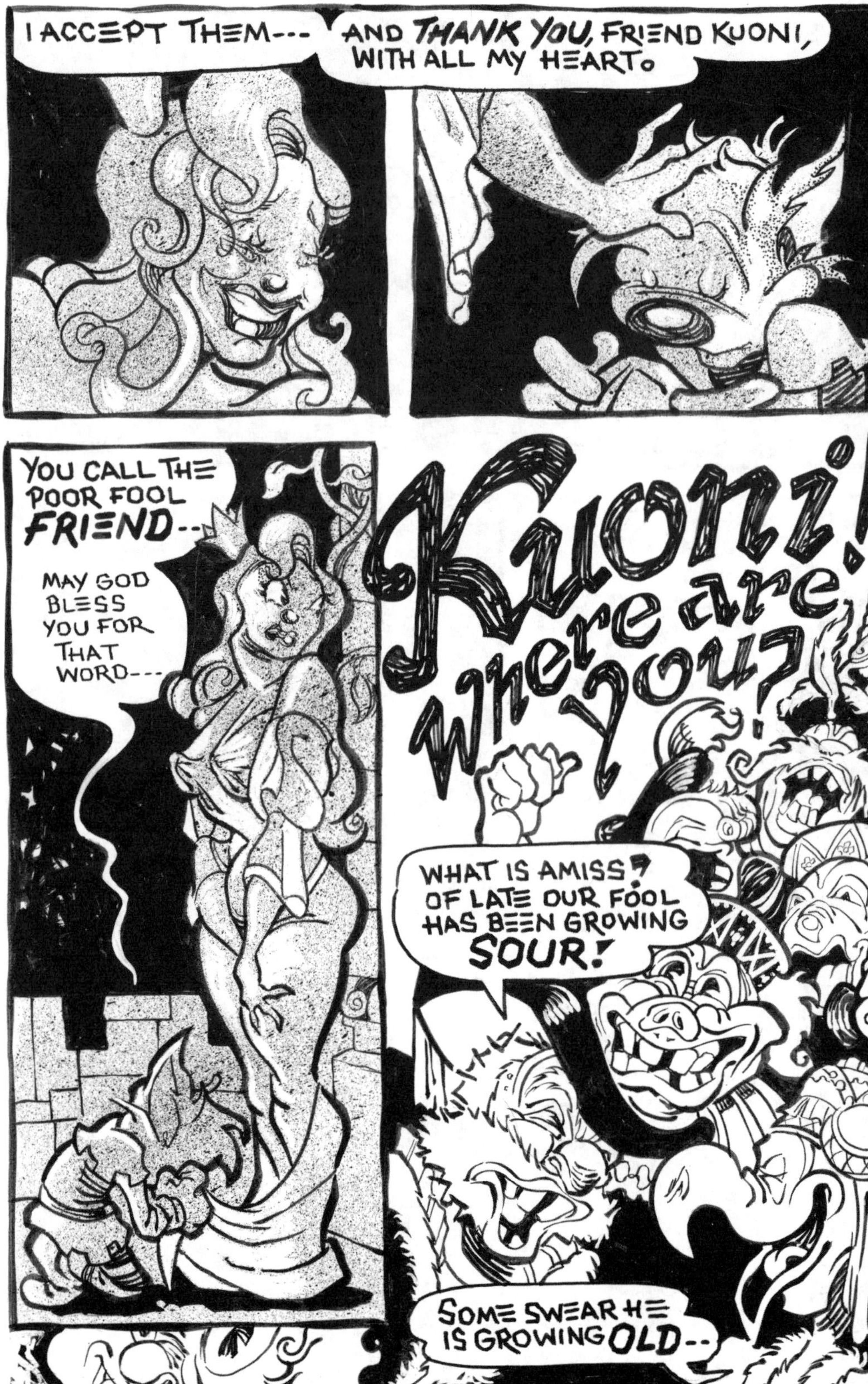
I ACCEPT THEM---
AND THANK YOU, FRIEND KUONI, WITH ALL MY HEART.
YOU CALL THE POOR FOOL FRIEND--
MAY GOD BLESS YOU FOR THAT WORD---
Kuoni! where are you?
WHAT IS AMISS? OF LATE OUR FOOL HAS BEEN GROWING SOUR!
SOME SWEAR HE IS GROWING OLD--

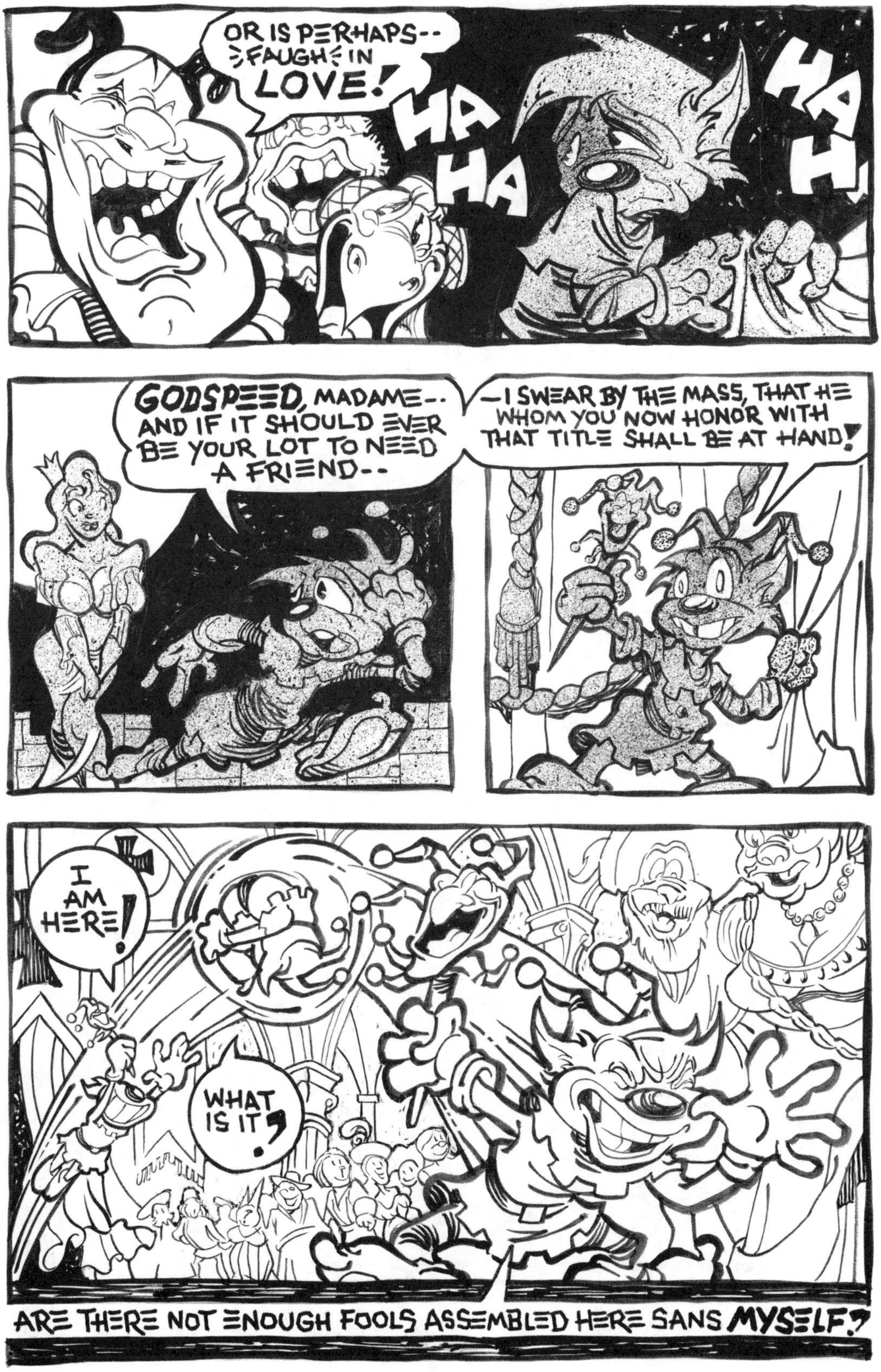
OR IS PERHAPS-- FAUGH IN LOVE!
HA HA
HA HA
GODSPEED, MADAME-- AND IF IT SHOULD EVER BE YOUR LOT TO NEED A FRIEND--
—I SWEAR BY THE MASS, THAT HE WHOM YOU NOW HONOR WITH THAT TITLE SHALL BE AT HAND!
I AM HERE!
WHAT IS IT?
ARE THERE NOT ENOUGH FOOLS ASSEMBLED HERE SANS MYSELF?

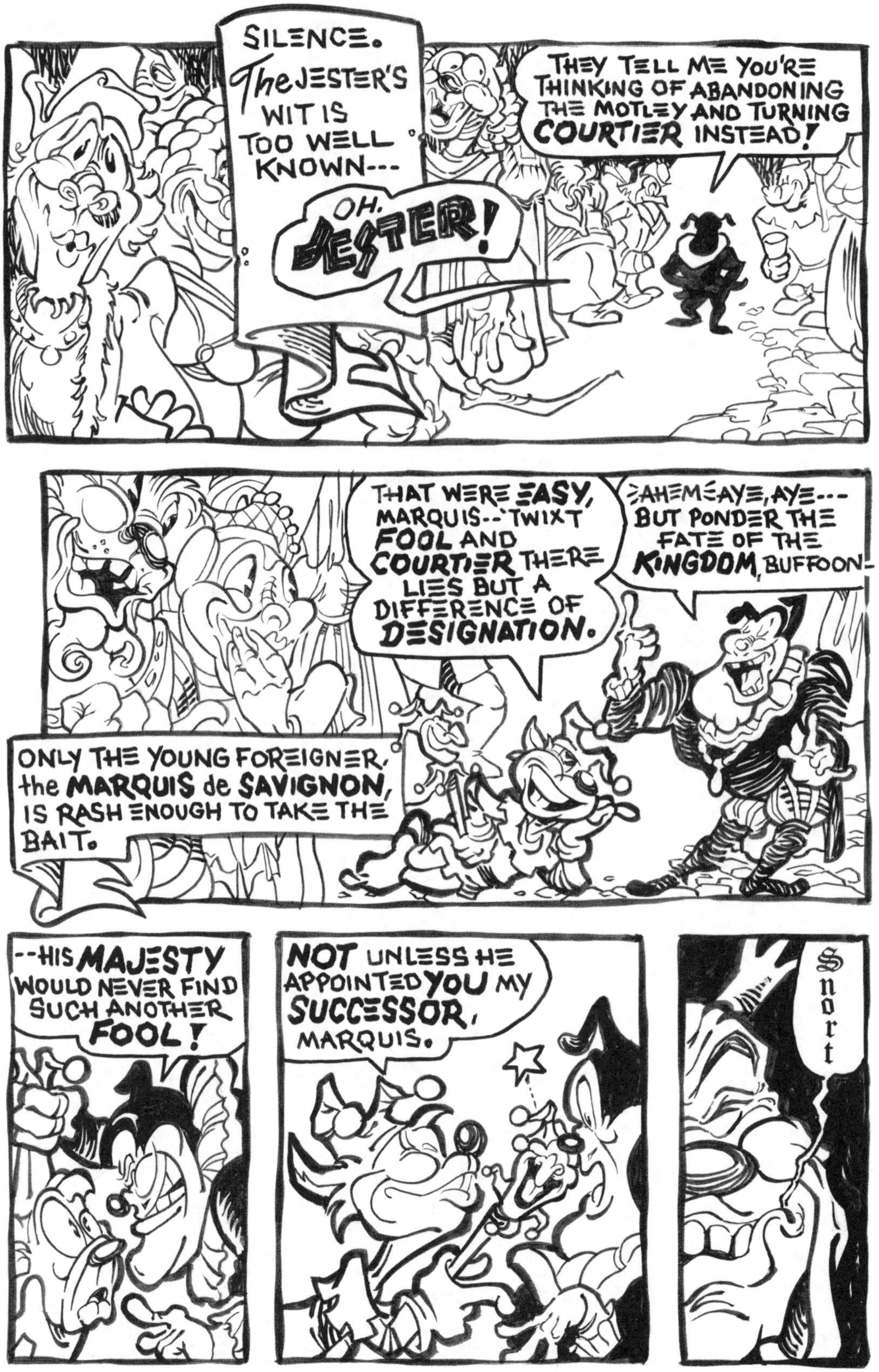
SILENCE. The JESTER'S WIT IS TOO WELL KNOWN---
OH, JESTER!
THEY TELL ME YOU'RE THINKING OF ABANDONING THE MOTLEY AND TURNING COURTIER INSTEAD!
THAT WERE EASY, MARQUIS--'TWIXT FOOL AND COURTIER THERE LIES BUT A DIFFERENCE OF DESIGNATION.
AHEM AYE, AYE--- BUT PONDER THE FATE OF THE KINGDOM, BUFFOON-
ONLY THE YOUNG FOREIGNER, the MARQUIS de SAVIGNON, IS RASH ENOUGH TO TAKE THE BAIT.
--HIS MAJESTY WOULD NEVER FIND SUCH ANOTHER FOOL!
NOT UNLESS HE APPOINTED YOU MY SUCCESSOR, MARQUIS.
Snort

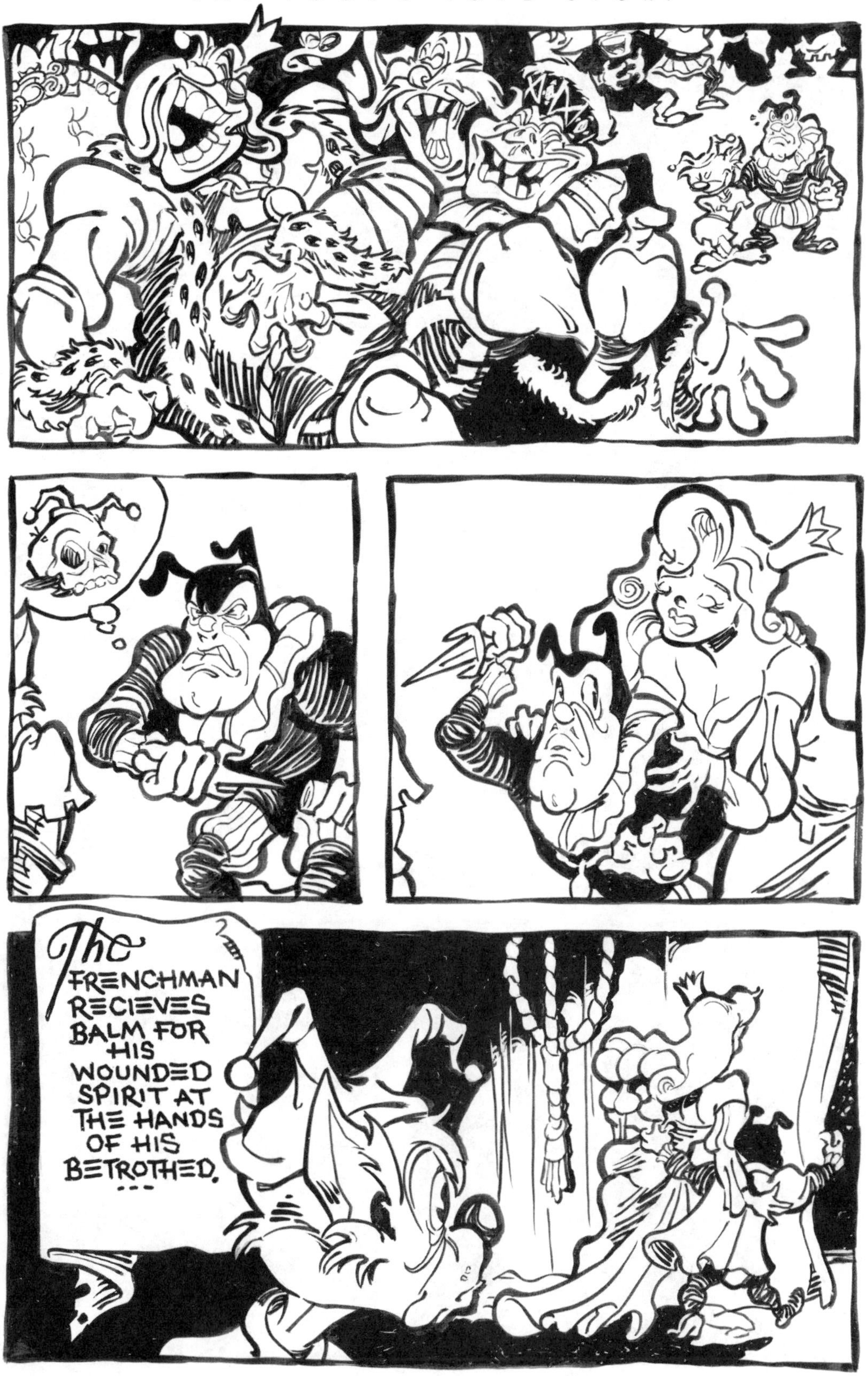
The FRENCHMAN RECIEVES BALM FOR HIS WOUNDED SPIRIT AT THE HANDS OF HIS BETROTHED. ---

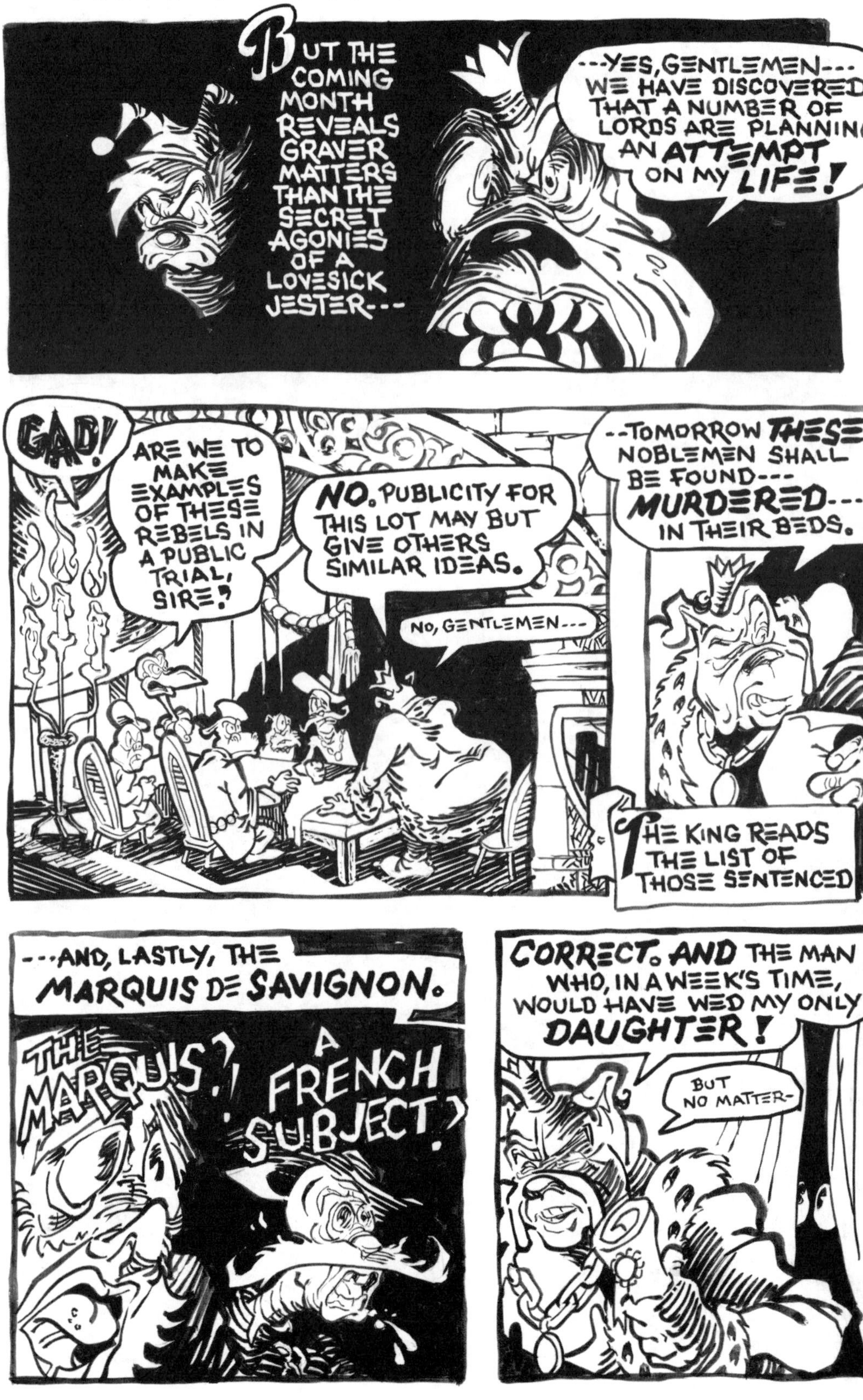
BUT THE COMING MONTH REVEALS GRAVER MATTERS THAN THE SECRET AGONIES OF A LOVESICK JESTER---
---YES, GENTLEMEN--- WE HAVE DISCOVERED THAT A NUMBER OF LORDS ARE PLANNING AN ATTEMPT ON MY LIFE!
GAD!
ARE WE TO MAKE EXAMPLES OF THESE REBELS IN A PUBLIC TRIAL, SIRE?
NO. PUBLICITY FOR THIS LOT MAY BUT GIVE OTHERS SIMILAR IDEAS.
NO, GENTLEMEN---
--TOMORROW THESE NOBLEMEN SHALL BE FOUND--- MURDERED--- IN THEIR BEDS.
THE KING READS THE LIST OF THOSE SENTENCED
---AND, LASTLY, THE MARQUIS DE SAVIGNON.
THE MARQUIS?!
A FRENCH SUBJECT?
CORRECT. AND THE MAN WHO, IN A WEEK'S TIME, WOULD HAVE WED MY ONLY DAUGHTER!
BUT NO MATTER-

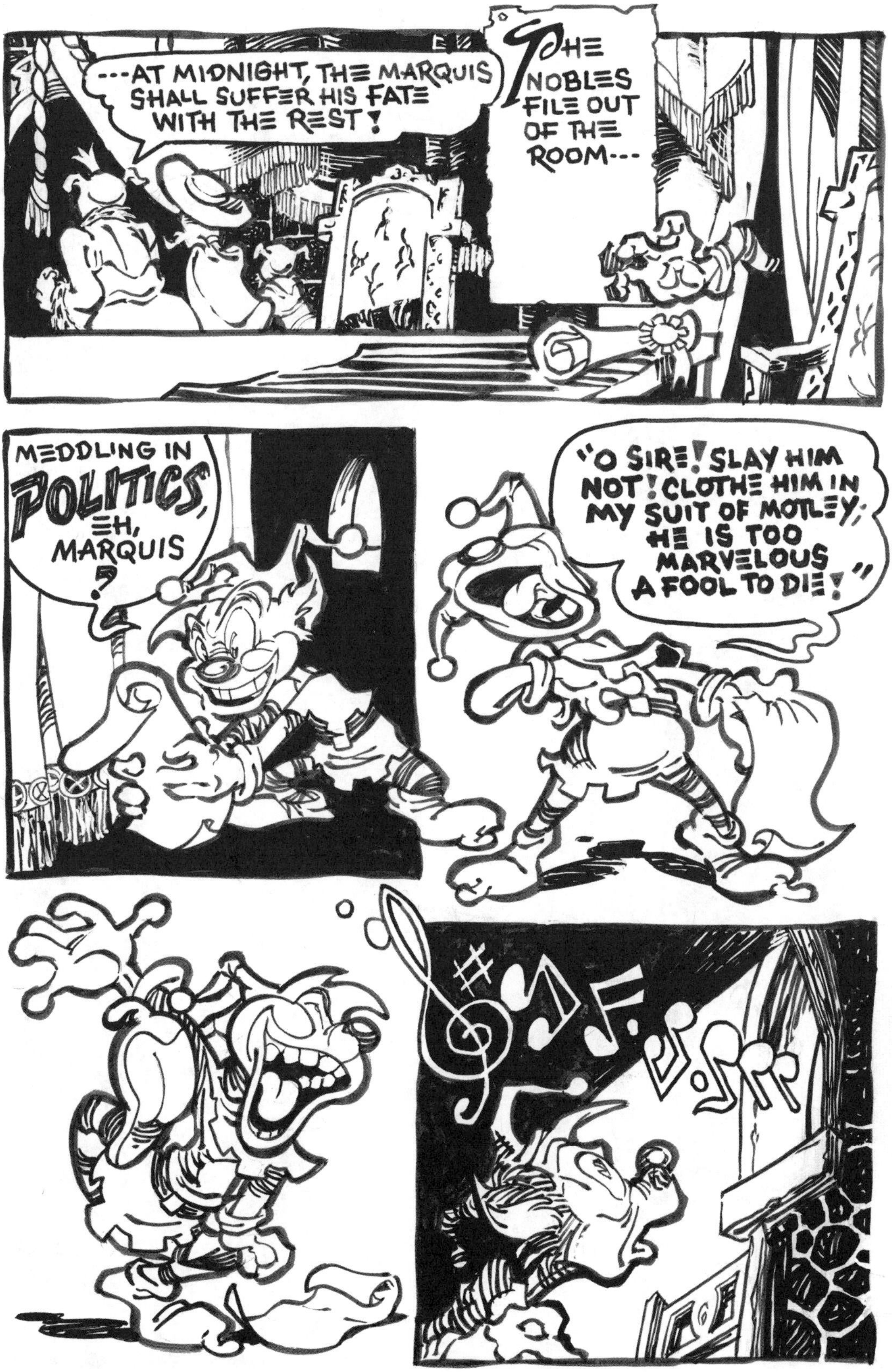
---AT MIDNIGHT, THE MARQUIS SHALL SUFFER HIS FATE WITH THE REST!
THE NOBLES FILE OUT OF THE ROOM---
MEDDLING IN POLITICS, EH, MARQUIS?
"O SIRE! SLAY HIM NOT! CLOTHE HIM IN MY SUIT OF MOTLEY; HE IS TOO MARVELOUS A FOOL TO DIE!"

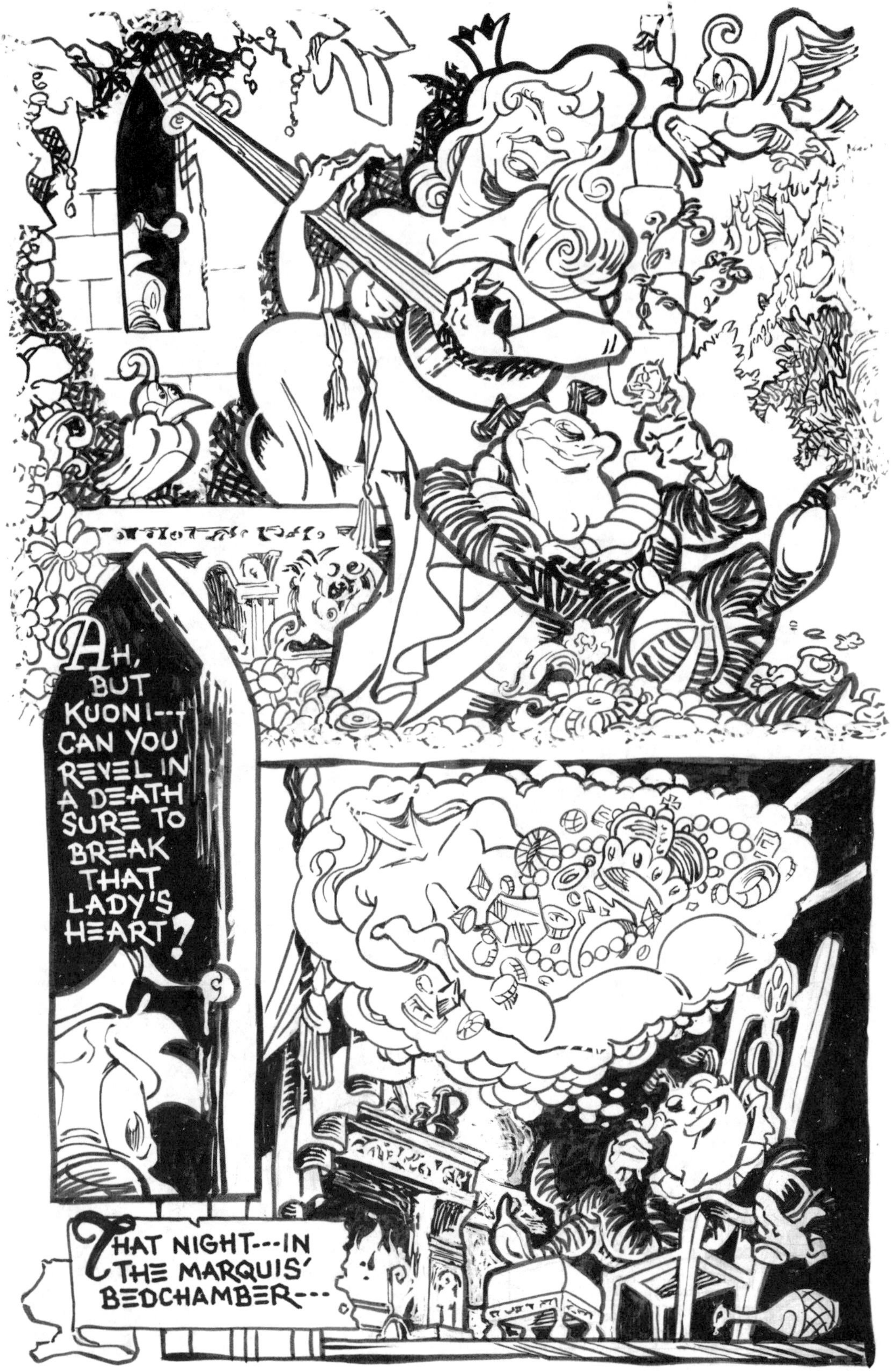
AH, BUT KUONI--- CAN YOU REVEL IN A DEATH SURE TO BREAK THAT LADY'S HEART?
THAT NIGHT---IN THE MARQUIS' BEDCHAMBER---

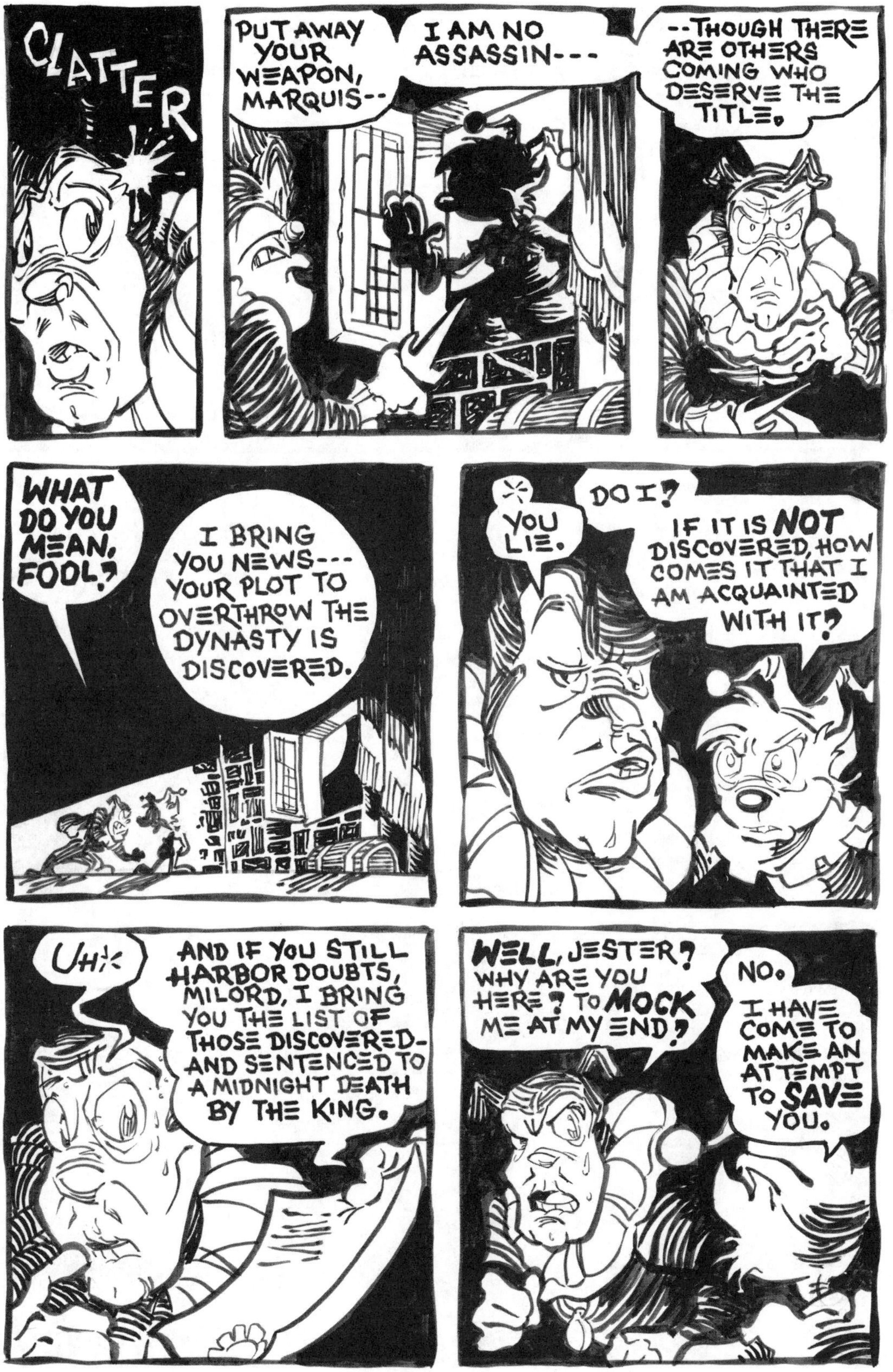
CLATTER
PUT AWAY YOUR WEAPON, MARQUIS--
I AM NO ASSASSIN---
--THOUGH THERE ARE OTHERS COMING WHO DESERVE THE TITLE.
WHAT DO YOU MEAN, FOOL?
I BRING YOU NEWS--- YOUR PLOT TO OVERTHROW THE DYNASTY IS DISCOVERED.
YOU LIE.
DO I?
IF IT IS NOT DISCOVERED, HOW COMES IT THAT I AM ACQUAINTED WITH IT?
UH!
AND IF YOU STILL HARBOR DOUBTS, MILORD, I BRING YOU THE LIST OF THOSE DISCOVERED- AND SENTENCED TO A MIDNIGHT DEATH BY THE KING.
WELL, JESTER? WHY ARE YOU HERE? TO MOCK ME AT MY END?
NO.
I HAVE COME TO MAKE AN ATTEMPT TO SAVE YOU.

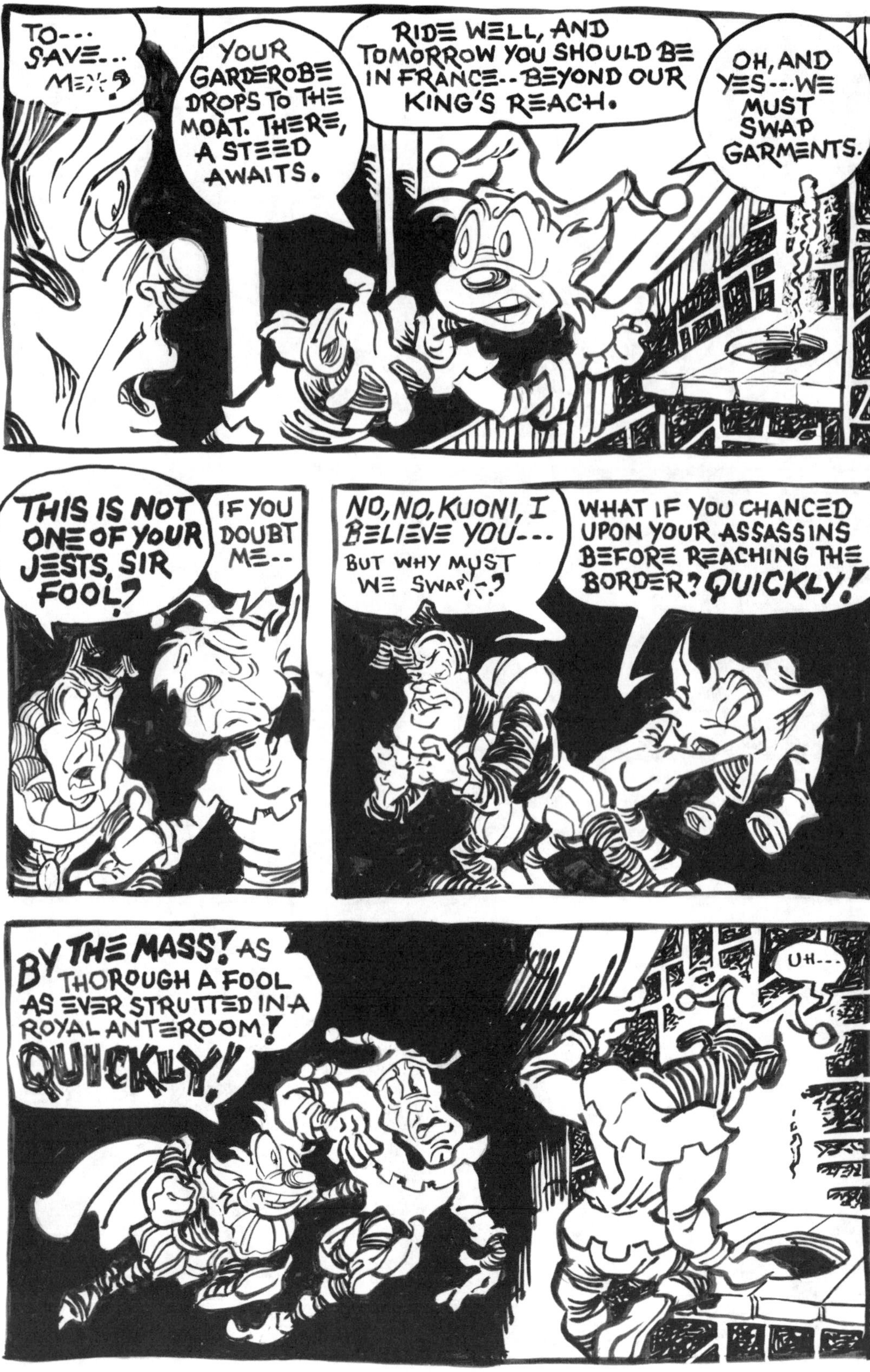
TO--- SAVE... ME?
YOUR GARDEROBE DROPS TO THE MOAT. THERE, A STEED AWAITS.
RIDE WELL, AND TOMORROW YOU SHOULD BE IN FRANCE-- BEYOND OUR KING'S REACH.
OH, AND YES---WE MUST SWAP GARMENTS.
THIS IS NOT ONE OF YOUR JESTS, SIR FOOL?
IF YOU DOUBT ME--
NO, NO, KUONI, I BELIEVE YOU---
BUT WHY MUST WE SWAP?
WHAT IF YOU CHANCED UPON YOUR ASSASSINS BEFORE REACHING THE BORDER? QUICKLY!
BY THE MASS! AS THOROUGH A FOOL AS EVER STRUTTED IN A ROYAL ANTEROOM! QUICKLY!
UH---

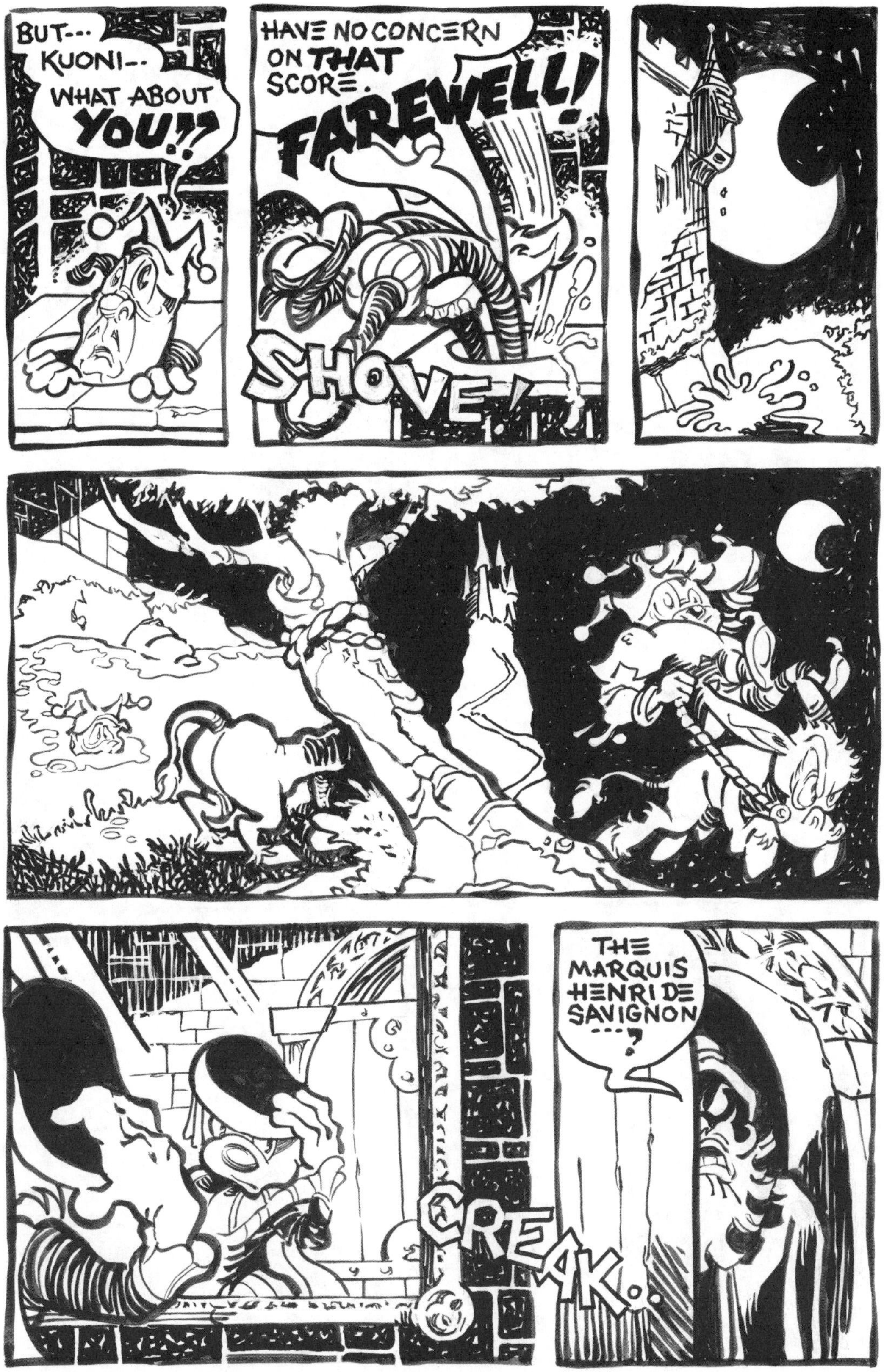
BUT--- KUONI-- WHAT ABOUT YOU.??
HAVE NO CONCERN ON THAT SCORE.
FAREWELL!
SHOVE!
THE MARQUIS HENRI DE SAVIGNON ---?
CREAK..

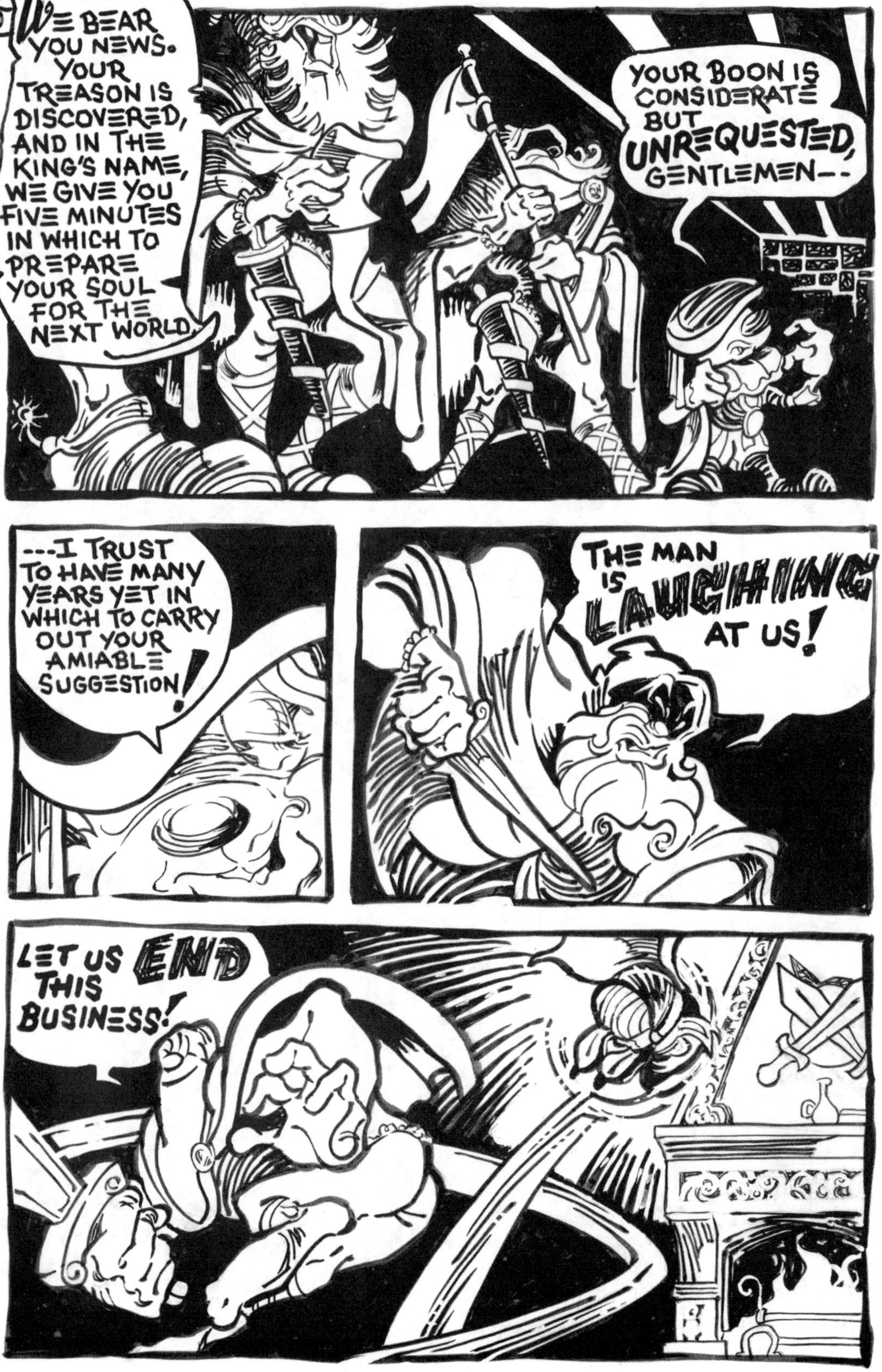
WE BEAR YOU NEWS. YOUR TREASON IS DISCOVERED, AND IN THE KING'S NAME, WE GIVE YOU FIVE MINUTES IN WHICH TO PREPARE YOUR SOUL FOR THE NEXT WORLD.
YOUR BOON IS CONSIDERATE BUT UNREQUESTED, GENTLEMEN--
---I TRUST TO HAVE MANY YEARS YET IN WHICH TO CARRY OUT YOUR AMIABLE SUGGESTION!
THE MAN IS LAUGHING AT US!
LET US END THIS BUSINESS!

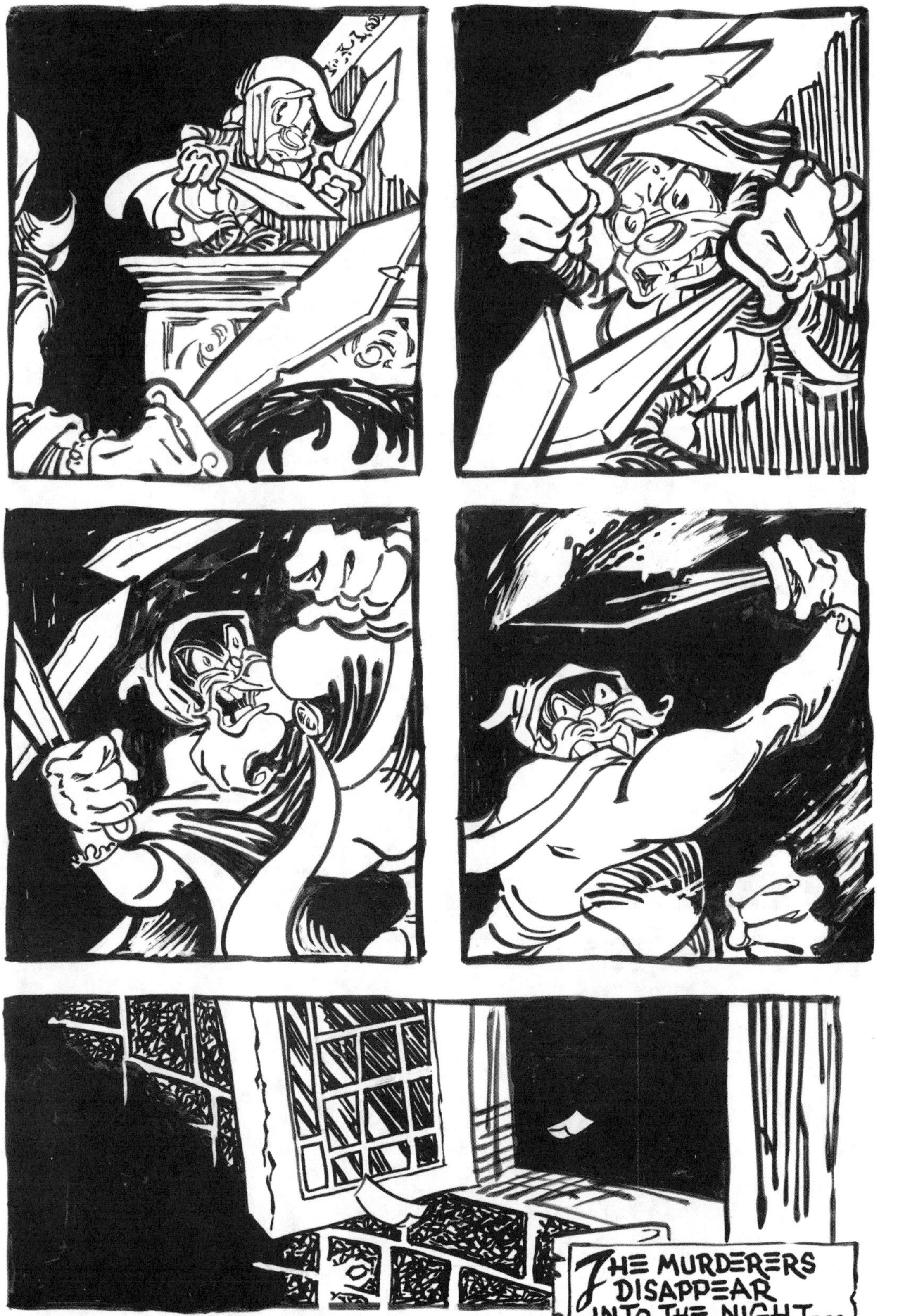
THE MURDERERS DISAPPEAR INTO THE NIGHT---

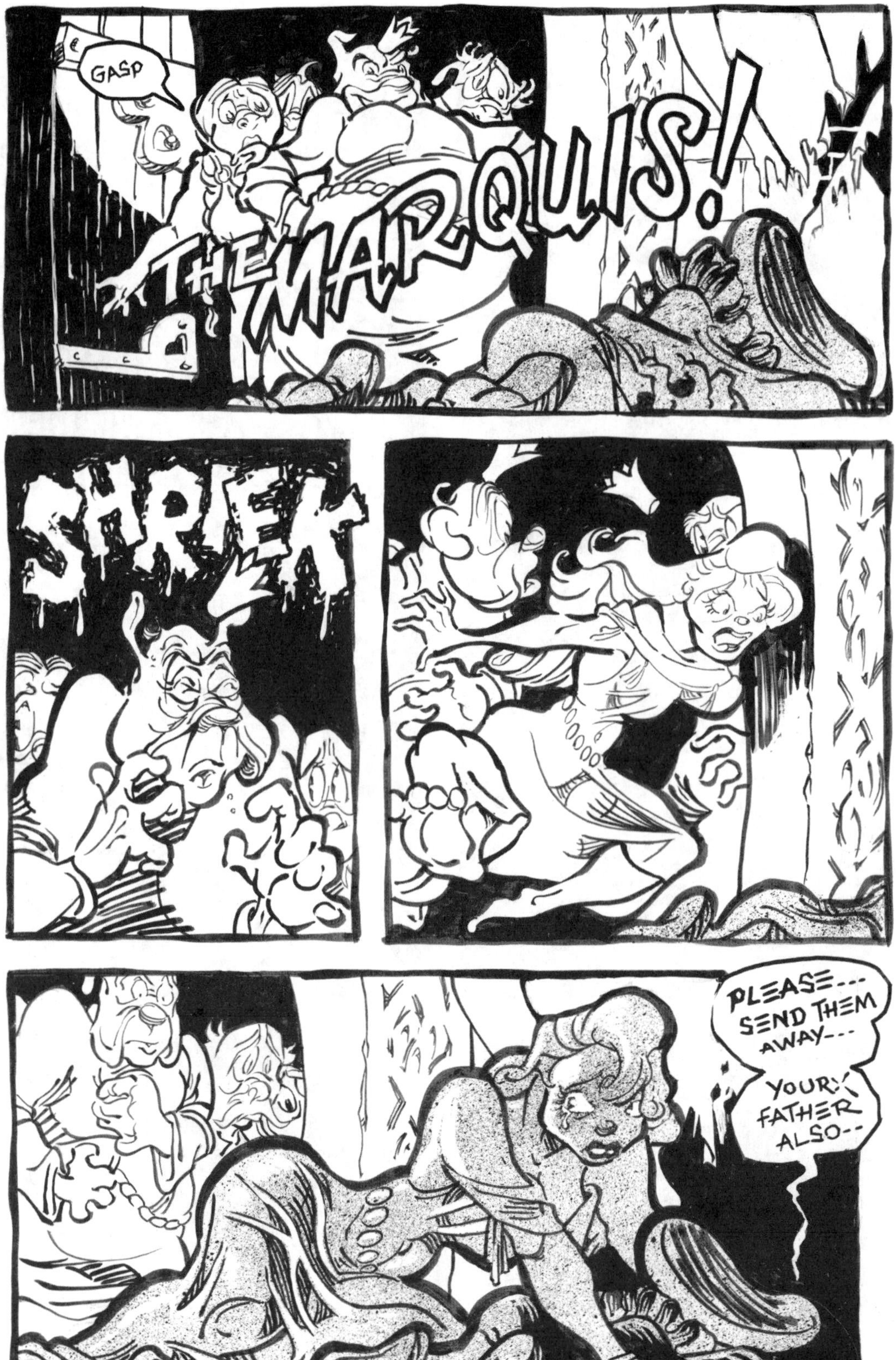
GASP
THE MARQUIS!
SHREEK
PLEASE... SEND THEM AWAY...
YOUR FATHER ALSO--

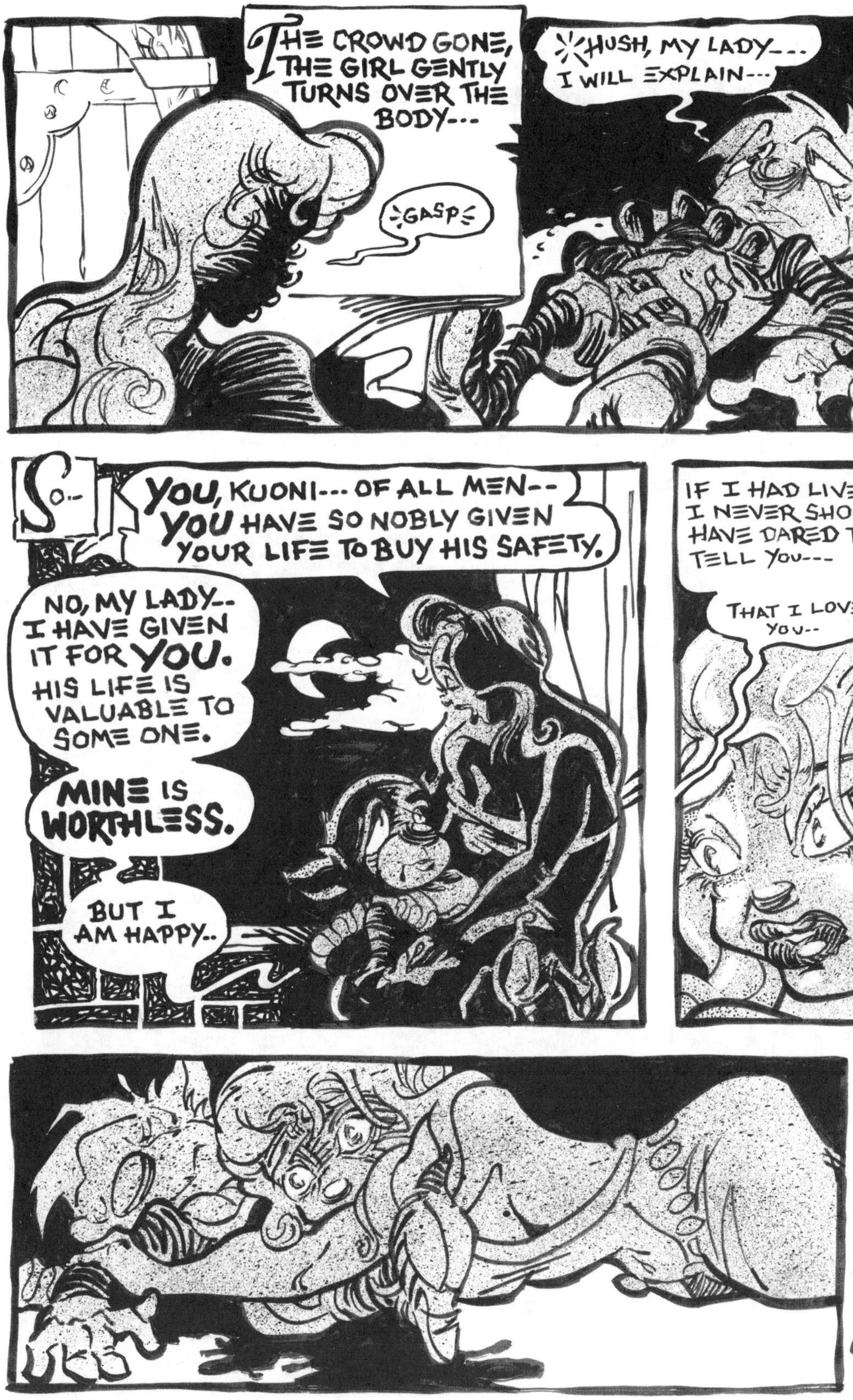
THE CROWD GONE, THE GIRL GENTLY TURNS OVER THE BODY---
GASP
HUSH, MY LADY---
I WILL EXPLAIN---
SO--
YOU, KUONI--- OF ALL MEN-- YOU HAVE SO NOBLY GIVEN YOUR LIFE TO BUY HIS SAFETY.
NO, MY LADY-- I HAVE GIVEN IT FOR YOU. HIS LIFE IS VALUABLE TO SOME ONE.
MINE IS WORTHLESS.
BUT I AM HAPPY..
IF I HAD LIVED, I NEVER SHOULD HAVE DARED TO TELL YOU---
THAT I LOVE YOU--
K.

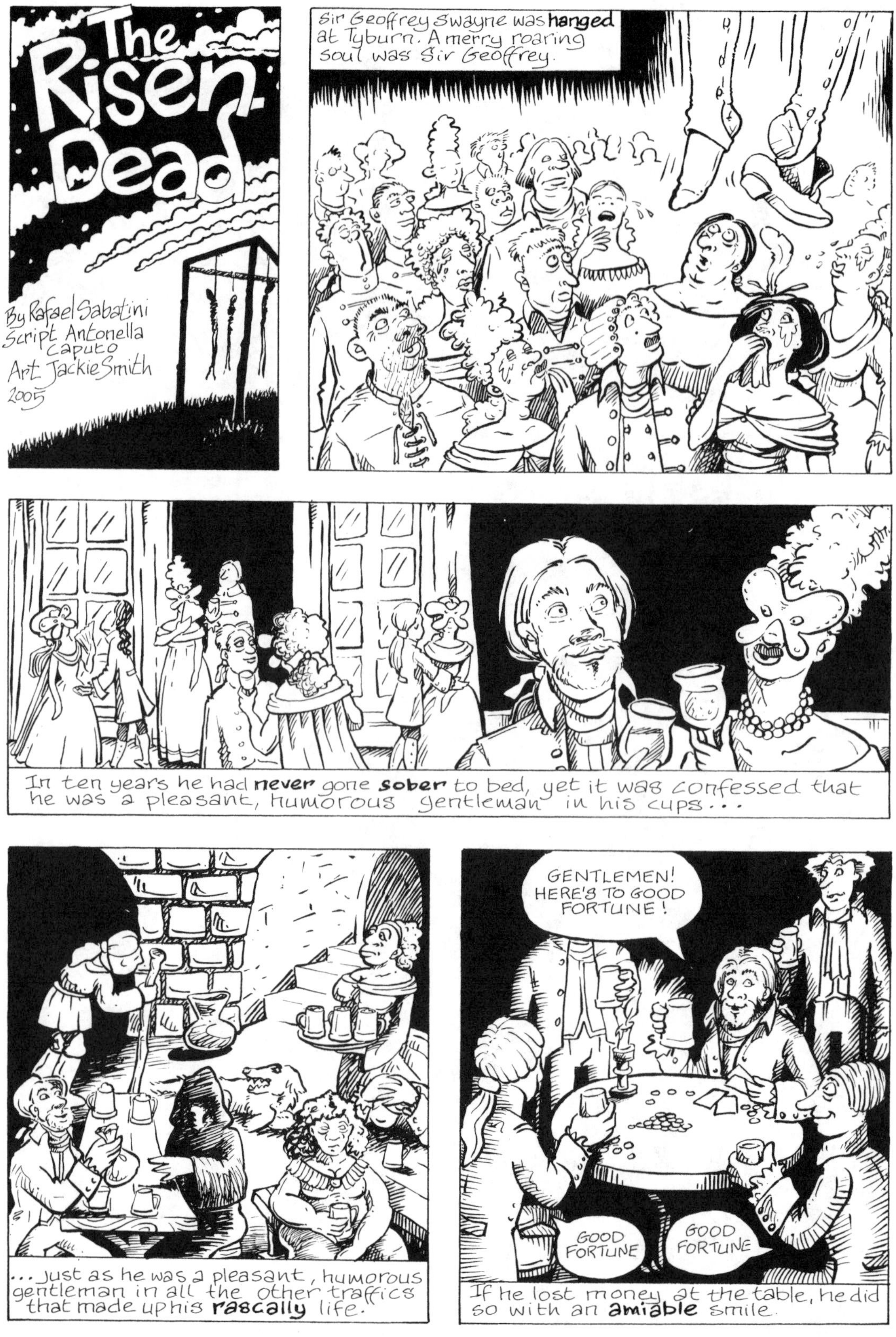
The Risen Dead
By Rafael Sabatini
Script Antonella Caputo
Art Jackie Smith
2005
Sir Geoffrey Swayne was hanged at Tyburn. A merry roaring soul was Sir Geoffrey.
In ten years he had never gone sober to bed, yet it was confessed that he was a pleasant, humorous gentleman in his cups...
...just as he was a pleasant, humorous gentleman in all the other traffics that made up his rascally life.
GENTLEMEN! HERE'S TO GOOD FORTUNE!
GOOD FORTUNE
GOOD FORTUNE
If he lost money at the table, he did so with an amiable smile.

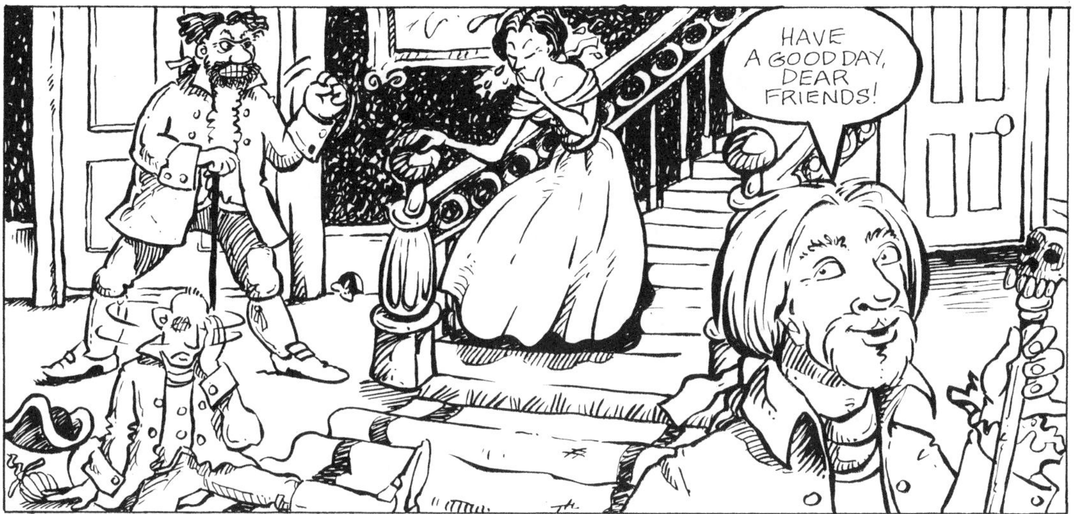
HAVE A GOOD DAY, DEAR FRIENDS!

If he would **beat** his wife, **kick** his servants down the stairs or **grind** the faces of his tenants, yet all these things he did at least with an **engaging** joviality of demeanour.

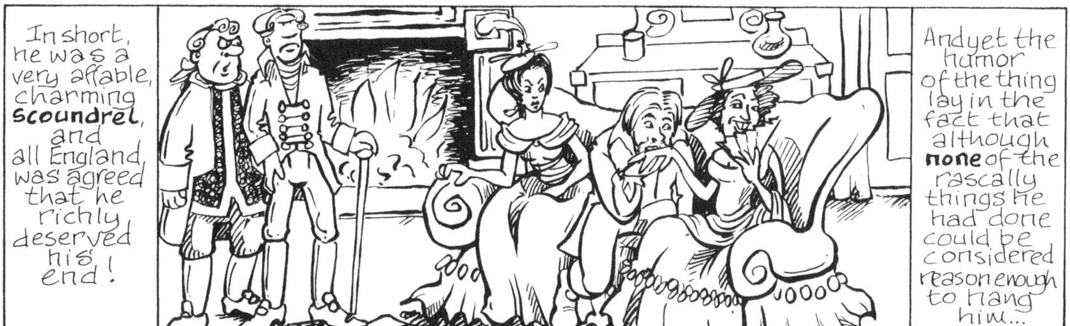
In short, he was a very affable, charming **scoundrel**, and all England was agreed that he richly deserved his end!
And yet the humor of the thing lay in the fact that although **none** of the rascally things he had done could be considered reason enough to hang him...

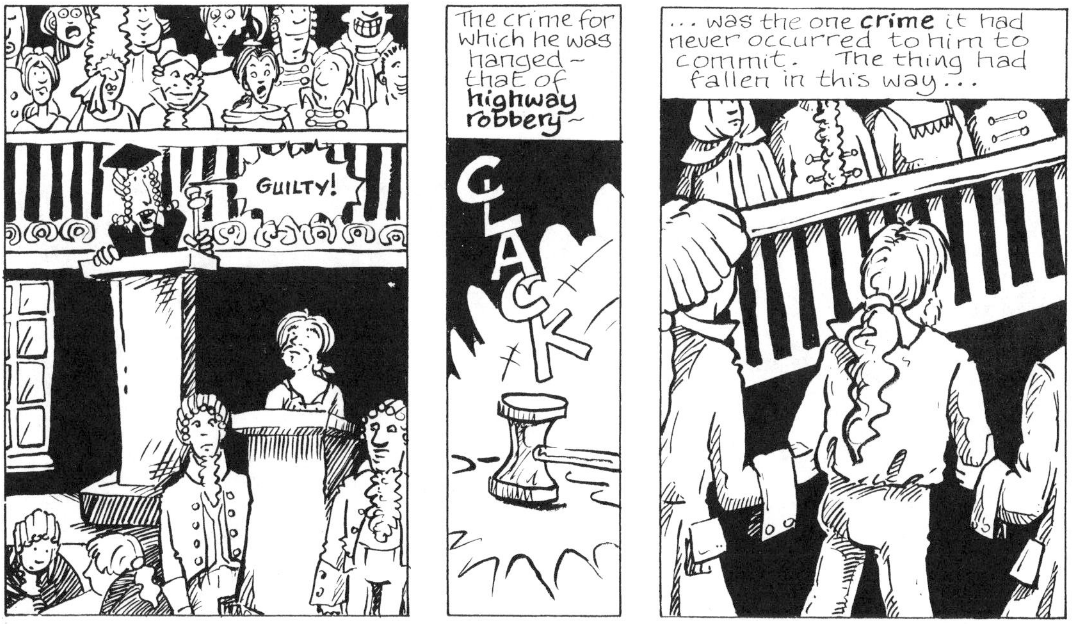
GUILTY!
The crime for which he was hanged ~ that of **highway robbery** ~
CLACK
... was the one **crime** it had never occurred to him to commit. The thing had fallen in this way...

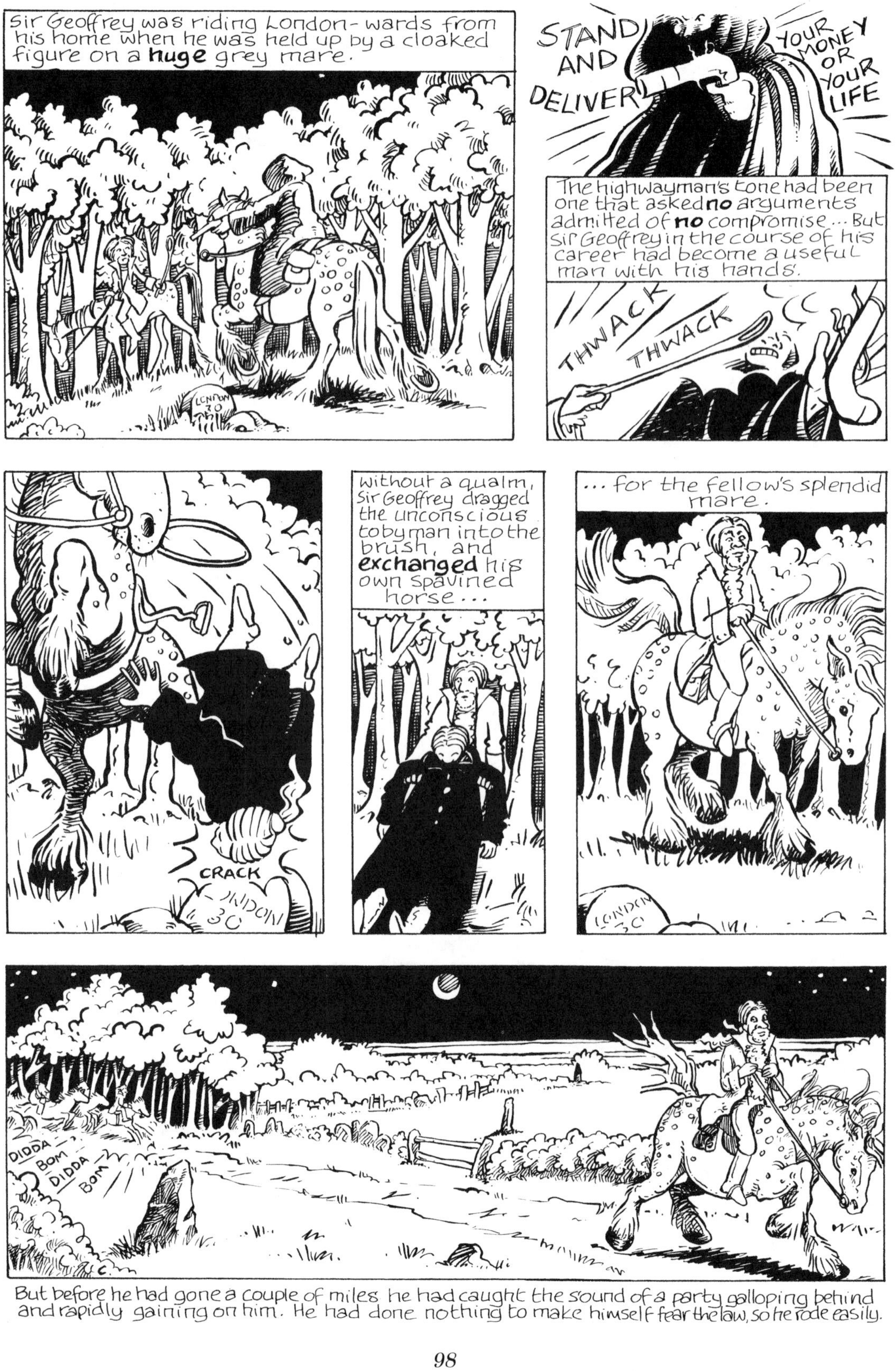
Sir Geoffrey was riding London-wards from his home when he was held up by a cloaked figure on a **huge** grey mare.
LONDON 30
STAND AND DELIVER
YOUR MONEY OR YOUR LIFE
The highwayman's tone had been one that asked **no** arguments admitted of **no** compromise ... But Sir Geoffrey in the course of his career had become a useful man with his hands.
THWACK
THWACK
CRACK
LONDON 30
without a qualm, Sir Geoffrey dragged the unconscious tobyman into the brush, and **exchanged** his own spavined horse ...
... for the fellow's splendid mare.
LONDON 30
DIDDA BOM DIDDA BOM
But before he had gone a couple of miles he had caught the sound of a party galloping behind and rapidly gaining on him. He had done nothing to make himself fear the law, so he rode easily.

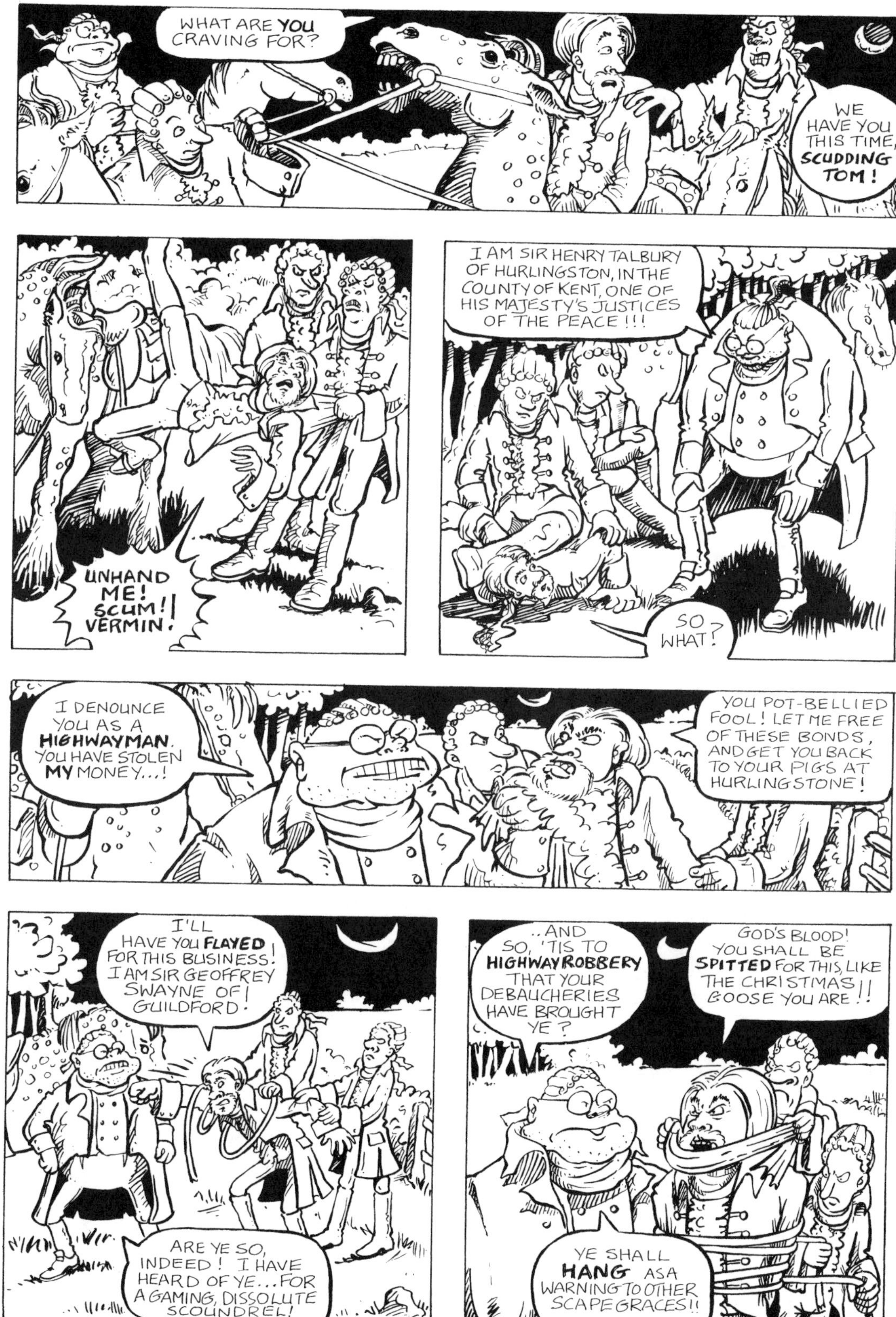
WHAT ARE YOU CRAVING FOR?
WE HAVE YOU THIS TIME, SCUDDING TOM!
UNHAND ME! SCUM! VERMIN!
I AM SIR HENRY TALBURY OF HURLINGSTON, IN THE COUNTY OF KENT, ONE OF HIS MAJESTY'S JUSTICES OF THE PEACE!!!
SO WHAT?
I DENOUNCE YOU AS A HIGHWAYMAN. YOU HAVE STOLEN MY MONEY...!
YOU POT-BELLIED FOOL! LET ME FREE OF THESE BONDS, AND GET YOU BACK TO YOUR PIGS AT HURLINGSTONE!
I'LL HAVE YOU FLAYED FOR THIS BUSINESS! I AM SIR GEOFFREY SWAYNE OF GUILDFORD!
ARE YE SO, INDEED! I HAVE HEARD OF YE... FOR A GAMING, DISSOLUTE SCOUNDREL!
..AND SO, 'TIS TO HIGHWAY ROBBERY THAT YOUR DEBAUCHERIES HAVE BROUGHT YE?
GOD'S BLOOD! YOU SHALL BE SPITTED FOR THIS, LIKE THE CHRISTMAS GOOSE YOU ARE!!
YE SHALL HANG AS A WARNING TO OTHER SCAPEGRACES!!

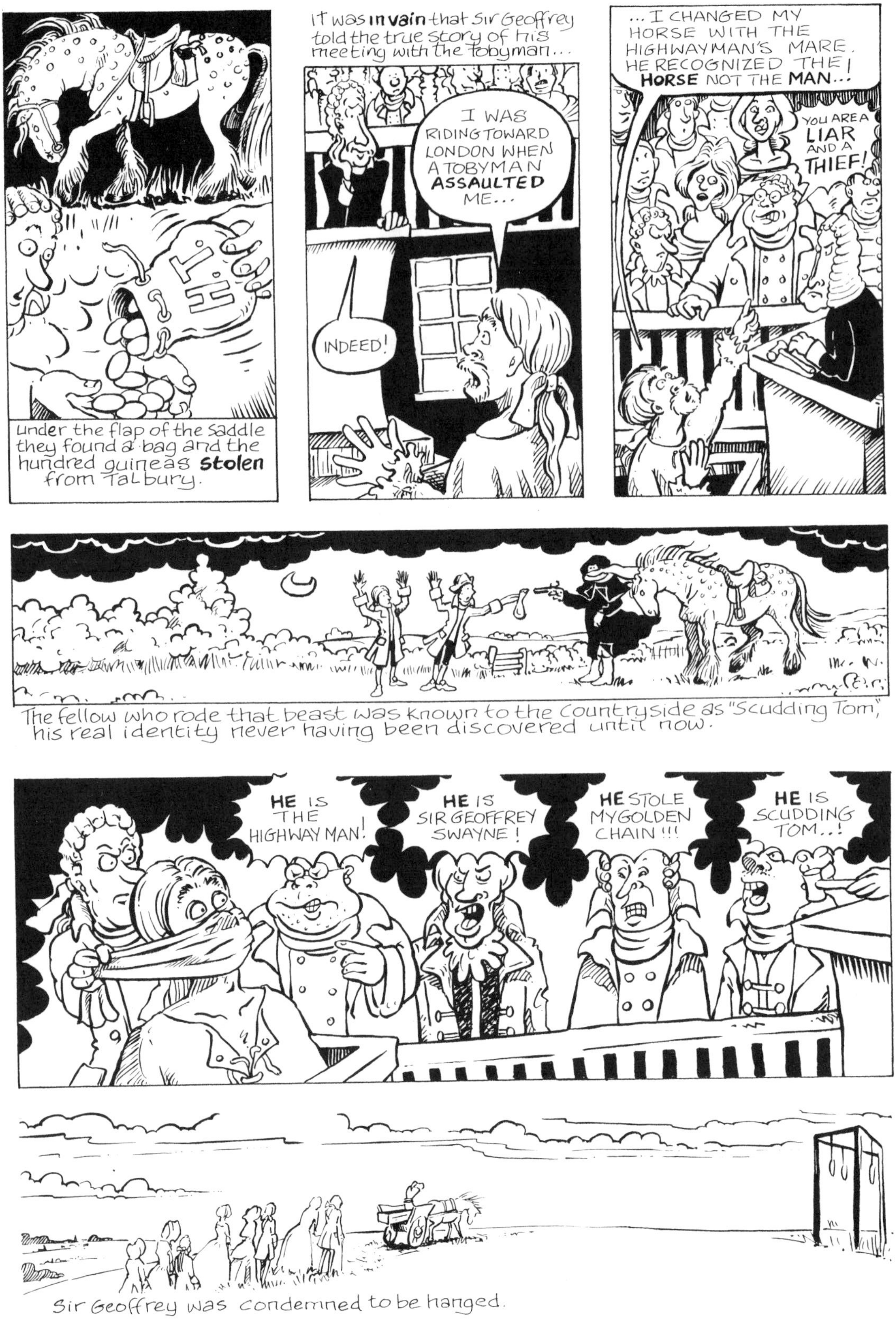
Under the flap of the saddle they found a bag and the hundred guineas **stolen** from Talbury.
It was **in vain** that Sir Geoffrey told the true story of his meeting with the tobyman...
I WAS RIDING TOWARD LONDON WHEN A TOBYMAN **ASSAULTED** ME...
INDEED!
...I CHANGED MY HORSE WITH THE HIGHWAYMAN'S MARE. HE RECOGNIZED THE **HORSE** NOT THE **MAN**...
YOU ARE A **LIAR** AND A **THIEF!**
The fellow who rode that beast was known to the Countryside as "Scudding Tom," his real identity never having been discovered until now.
HE IS THE HIGHWAYMAN!
HE IS SIR GEOFFREY SWAYNE!
HE STOLE MY GOLDEN CHAIN!!!
HE IS SCUDDING TOM..!
Sir Geoffrey was condemned to be hanged.

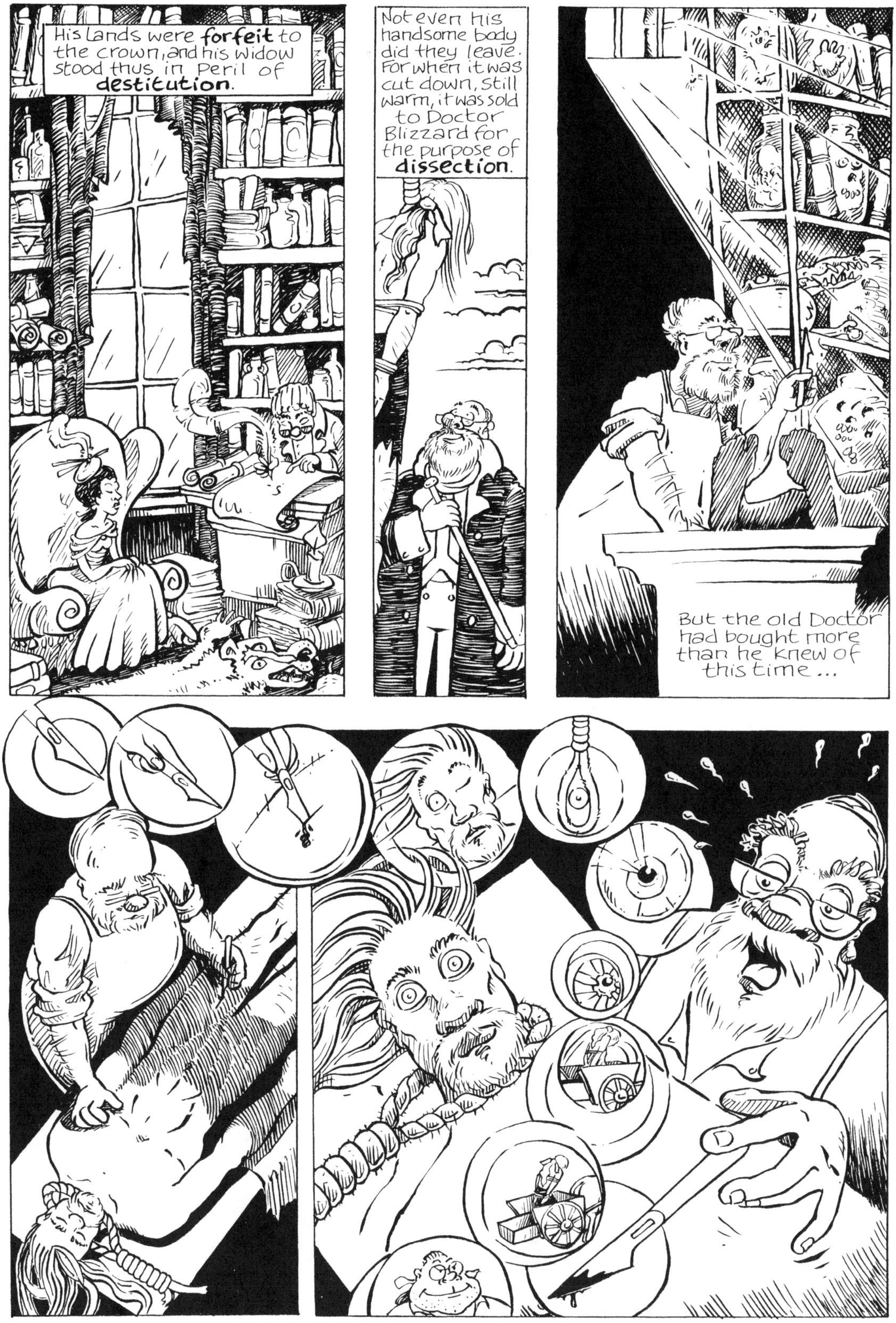
His lands were **forfeit** to the crown, and his widow stood thus in Peril of **destitution**.
Not even his handsome body did they leave. For when it was cut down, still warm, it was sold to Doctor Blizzard for the purpose of **dissection**.
But the old Doctor had bought more than he knew of this time ...

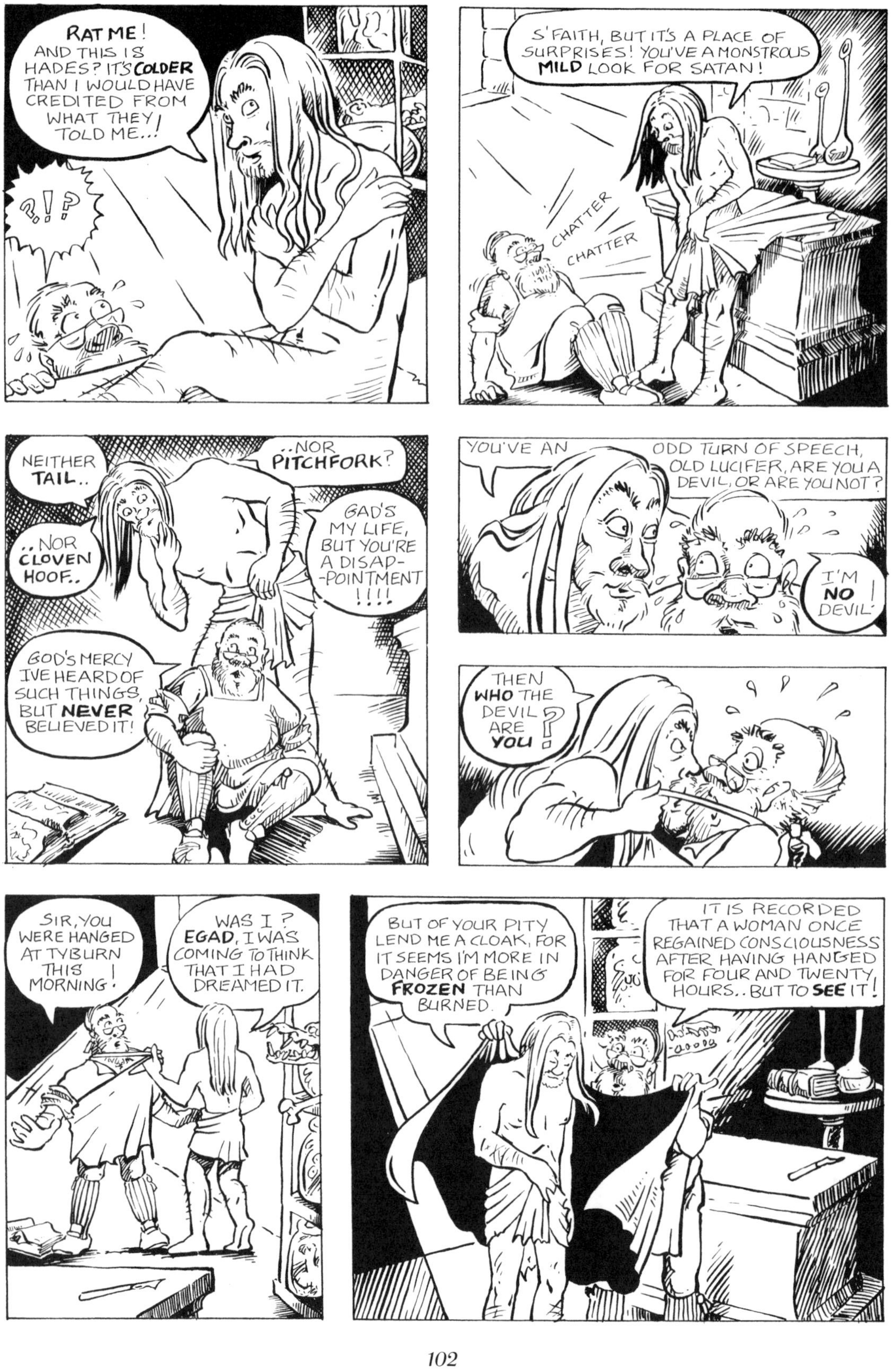
RAT ME! AND THIS IS HADES? IT'S COLDER THAN I WOULD HAVE CREDITED FROM WHAT THEY TOLD ME...!
?!?
S'FAITH, BUT IT'S A PLACE OF SURPRISES! YOU'VE A MONSTROUS MILD LOOK FOR SATAN!
CHATTER
CHATTER
NEITHER TAIL..
..NOR PITCHFORK?
..NOR CLOVEN HOOF..
GAD'S MY LIFE, BUT YOU'RE A DISAP-POINTMENT!!!!
GOD'S MERCY I'VE HEARD OF SUCH THINGS, BUT NEVER BELIEVED IT!
YOU'VE AN ODD TURN OF SPEECH, OLD LUCIFER, ARE YOU A DEVIL, OR ARE YOU NOT?
I'M NO DEVIL!
THEN WHO THE DEVIL ARE YOU?
SIR, YOU WERE HANGED AT TYBURN THIS MORNING!
WAS I? EGAD, I WAS COMING TO THINK THAT I HAD DREAMED IT.
BUT OF YOUR PITY LEND ME A CLOAK, FOR IT SEEMS I'M MORE IN DANGER OF BEING FROZEN THAN BURNED.
IT IS RECORDED THAT A WOMAN ONCE REGAINED CONSCIOUSNESS AFTER HAVING HANGED FOR FOUR AND TWENTY HOURS.. BUT TO SEE IT!

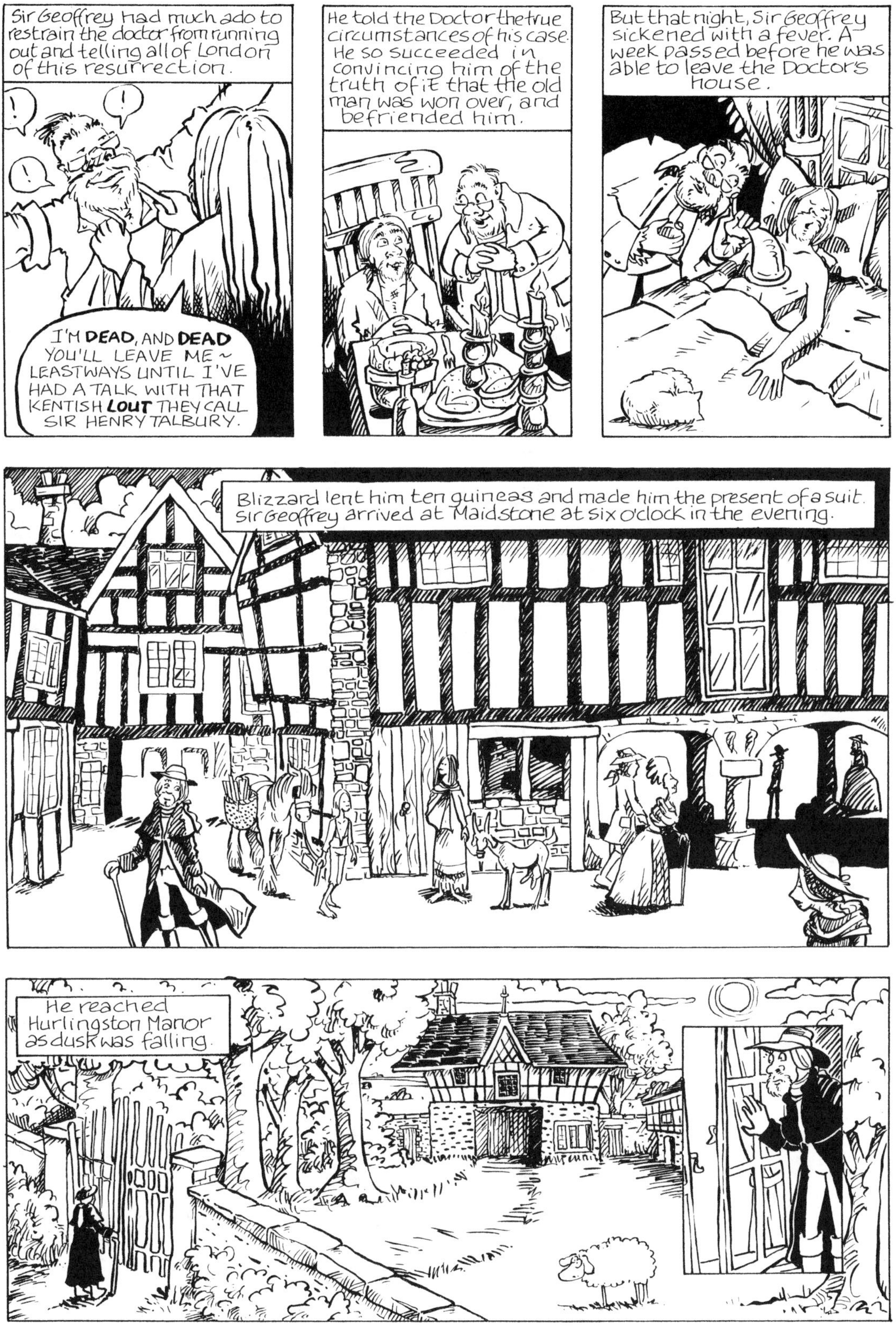
Sir Geoffrey had much ado to restrain the doctor from running out and telling all of London of this resurrection.
!
!
!
I'M DEAD, AND DEAD YOU'LL LEAVE ME ~ LEASTWAYS UNTIL I'VE HAD A TALK WITH THAT KENTISH LOUT THEY CALL SIR HENRY TALBURY.
He told the Doctor the true circumstances of his case. He so succeeded in convincing him of the truth of it that the old man was won over, and befriended him.
But that night, Sir Geoffrey sickened with a fever. A week passed before he was able to leave the Doctor's house.
Blizzard lent him ten guineas and made him the present of a suit. Sir Geoffrey arrived at Maidstone at six o'clock in the evening.
He reached Hurlingston Manor as dusk was falling.

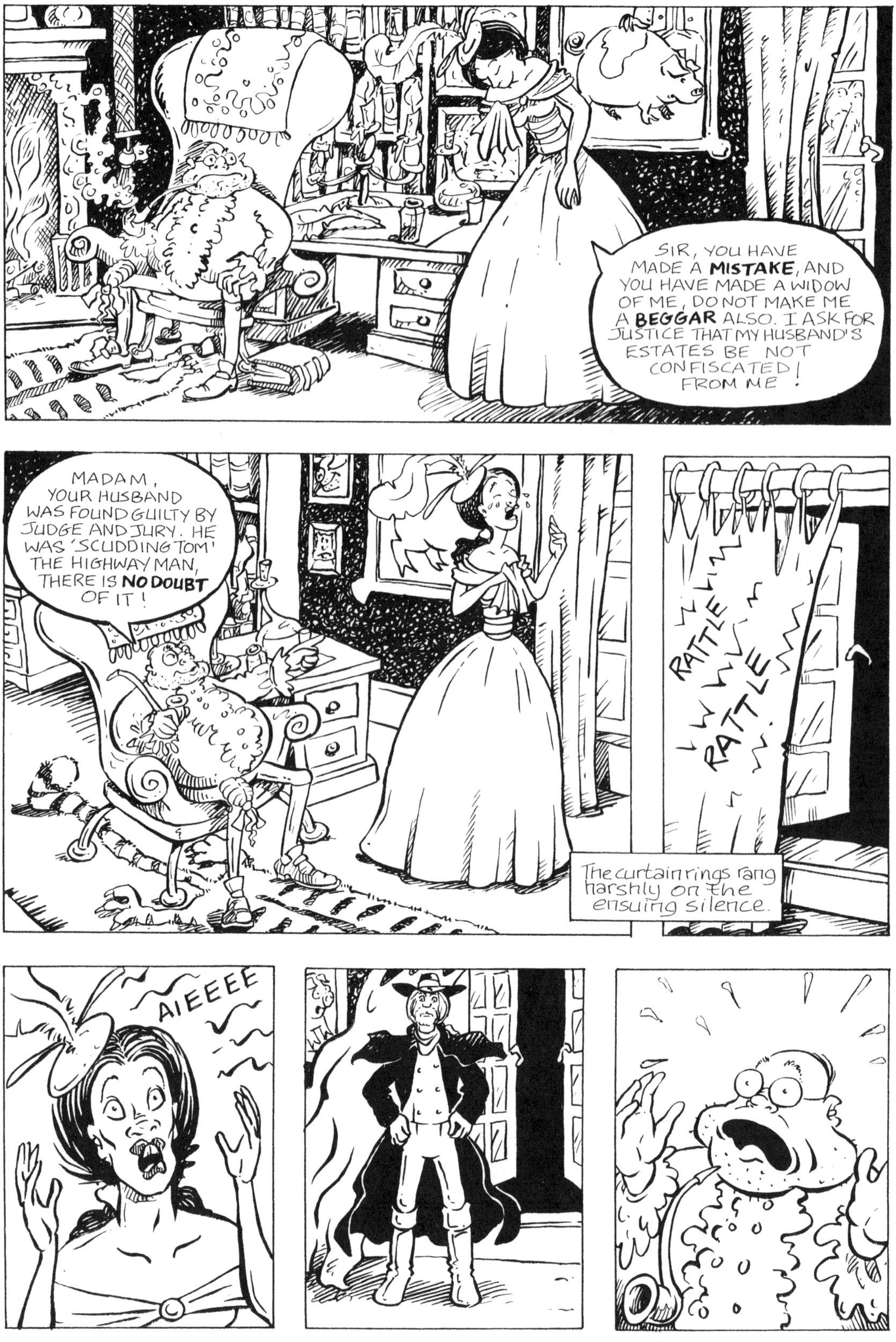
SIR, YOU HAVE MADE A MISTAKE, AND YOU HAVE MADE A WIDOW OF ME, DO NOT MAKE ME A BEGGAR ALSO. I ASK FOR JUSTICE THAT MY HUSBAND'S ESTATES BE NOT CONFISCATED FROM ME!
MADAM, YOUR HUSBAND WAS FOUND GUILTY BY JUDGE AND JURY. HE WAS 'SCUDDING TOM' THE HIGHWAY MAN, THERE IS NO DOUBT OF IT!
RATTLE RATTLE RATTLE
The curtain rings rang harshly on the ensuing silence.
AIEEEE

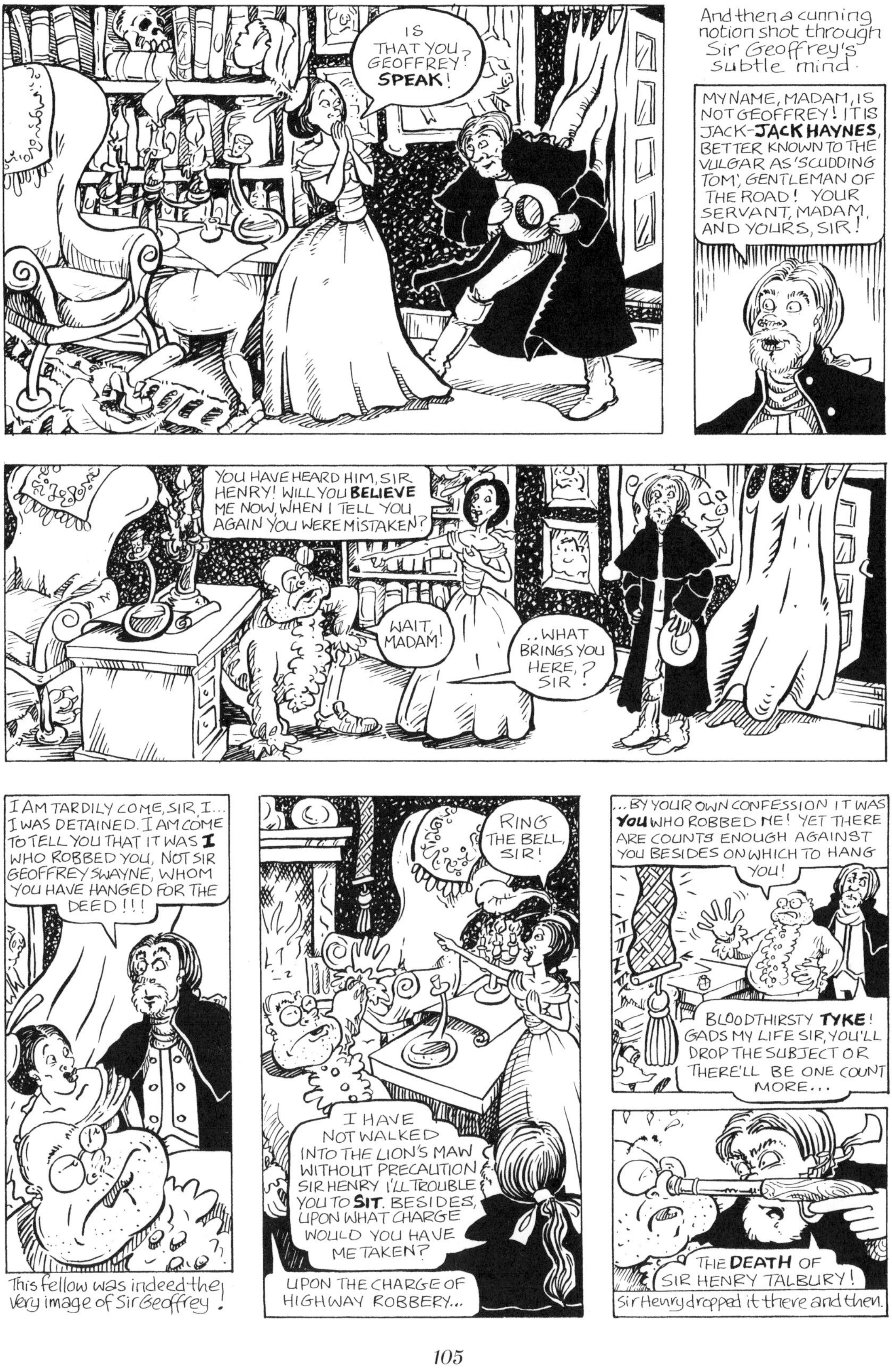
IS THAT YOU GEOFFREY? SPEAK!
And then a cunning notion shot through Sir Geoffrey's subtle mind.
MY NAME, MADAM, IS NOT GEOFFREY! IT IS JACK-JACK HAYNES, BETTER KNOWN TO THE VULGAR AS 'SCUDDING TOM', GENTLEMAN OF THE ROAD! YOUR SERVANT, MADAM, AND YOURS, SIR!
YOU HAVE HEARD HIM, SIR HENRY! WILL YOU BELIEVE ME NOW, WHEN I TELL YOU AGAIN YOU WERE MISTAKEN?
WAIT, MADAM!
..WHAT BRINGS YOU HERE, SIR?
I AM TARDILY COME, SIR, I... I WAS DETAINED. I AM COME TO TELL YOU THAT IT WAS I WHO ROBBED YOU, NOT SIR GEOFFREY SWAYNE, WHOM YOU HAVE HANGED FOR THE DEED!!!
This fellow was indeed the very image of Sir Geoffrey!
RING THE BELL, SIR!
I HAVE NOT WALKED INTO THE LION'S MAW WITHOUT PRECAUTION SIR HENRY I'LL TROUBLE YOU TO SIT. BESIDES, UPON WHAT CHARGE WOULD YOU HAVE ME TAKEN?
UPON THE CHARGE OF HIGHWAY ROBBERY...
...BY YOUR OWN CONFESSION IT WAS YOU WHO ROBBED ME! YET THERE ARE COUNTS ENOUGH AGAINST YOU BESIDES ON WHICH TO HANG YOU!
BLOODTHIRSTY TYKE! GADS MY LIFE SIR, YOU'LL DROP THE SUBJECT OR THERE'LL BE ONE COUNT MORE...
THE DEATH OF SIR HENRY TALBURY!
Sir Henry dropped it there and then.

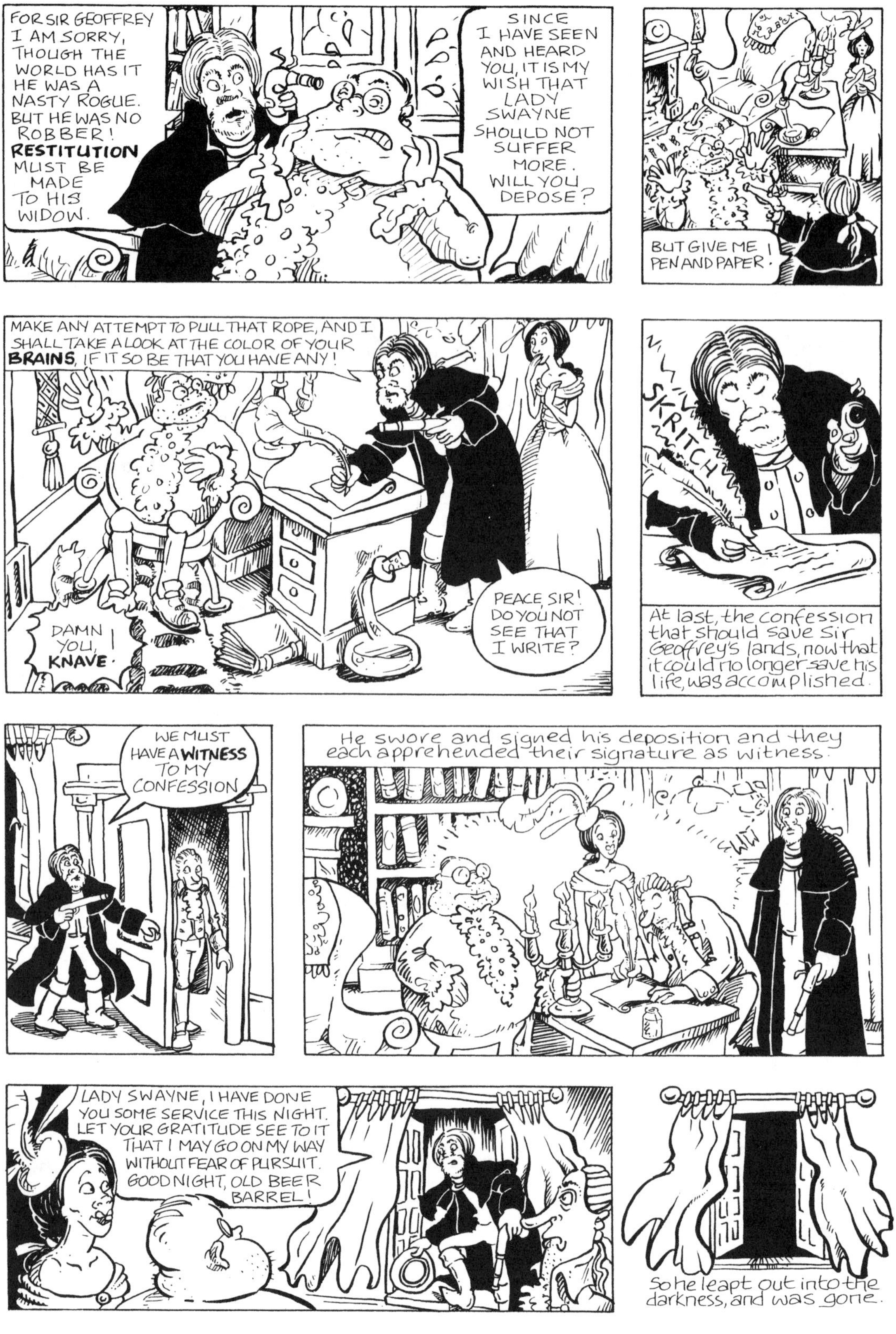
FOR SIR GEOFFREY I AM SORRY, THOUGH THE WORLD HAS IT HE WAS A NASTY ROGUE. BUT HE WAS NO ROBBER! **RESTITUTION** MUST BE MADE TO HIS WIDOW.
SINCE I HAVE SEEN AND HEARD YOU, IT IS MY WISH THAT LADY SWAYNE SHOULD NOT SUFFER MORE. WILL YOU DEPOSE?
BUT GIVE ME PEN AND PAPER!
MAKE ANY ATTEMPT TO PULL THAT ROPE, AND I SHALL TAKE A LOOK AT THE COLOR OF YOUR **BRAINS**, IF IT SO BE THAT YOU HAVE ANY!
DAMN YOU, **KNAVE**!
PEACE, SIR! DO YOU NOT SEE THAT I WRITE?
SKRITCH
At last, the confession that should save Sir Geoffrey's lands, now that it could no longer save his life, was accomplished.
WE MUST HAVE A **WITNESS** TO MY CONFESSION
He swore and signed his deposition and they each apprehended their signature as witness.
LADY SWAYNE, I HAVE DONE YOU SOME SERVICE THIS NIGHT. LET YOUR GRATITUDE SEE TO IT THAT I MAY GO ON MY WAY WITHOUT FEAR OF PURSUIT. GOOD NIGHT, OLD BEER BARREL!
So he leapt out into the darkness, and was gone.

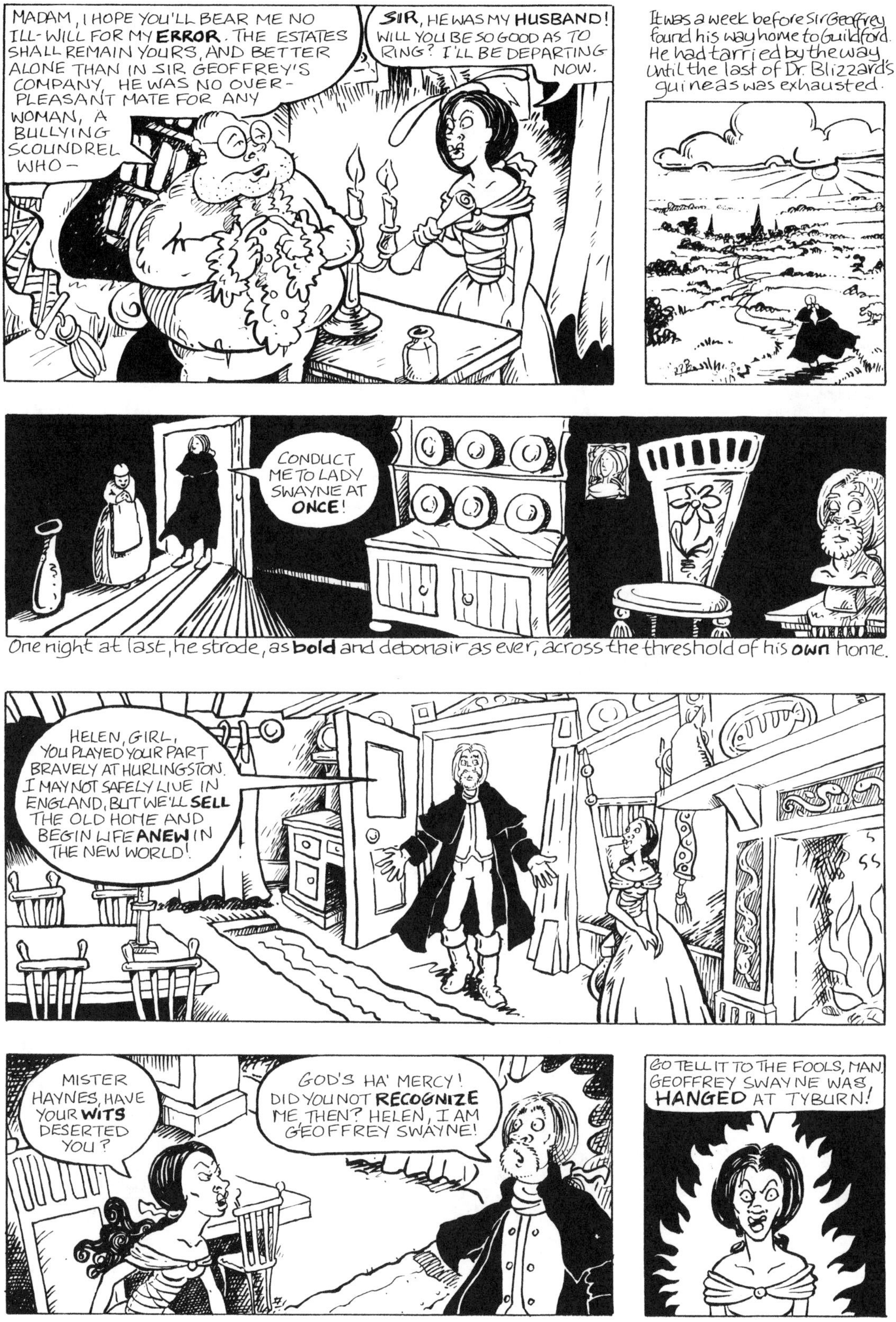
MADAM, I HOPE YOU'LL BEAR ME NO ILL-WILL FOR MY ERROR. THE ESTATES SHALL REMAIN YOURS, AND BETTER ALONE THAN IN SIR GEOFFREY'S COMPANY. HE WAS NO OVER-PLEASANT MATE FOR ANY WOMAN, A BULLYING SCOUNDREL WHO—
SIR, HE WAS MY HUSBAND! WILL YOU BE SO GOOD AS TO RING? I'LL BE DEPARTING NOW.
It was a week before Sir Geoffrey found his way home to Guildford. He had tarried by the way until the last of Dr. Blizzard's guineas was exhausted.
CONDUCT ME TO LADY SWAYNE AT ONCE!
One night at last, he strode, as bold and debonair as ever, across the threshold of his own home.
HELEN, GIRL, YOU PLAYED YOUR PART BRAVELY AT HURLINGSTON. I MAY NOT SAFELY LIVE IN ENGLAND, BUT WE'LL SELL THE OLD HOME AND BEGIN LIFE ANEW IN THE NEW WORLD!
MISTER HAYNES, HAVE YOUR WITS DESERTED YOU?
GOD'S HA' MERCY! DID YOU NOT RECOGNIZE ME, THEN? HELEN, I AM GEOFFREY SWAYNE!
GO TELL IT TO THE FOOLS, MAN. GEOFFREY SWAYNE WAS HANGED AT TYBURN!

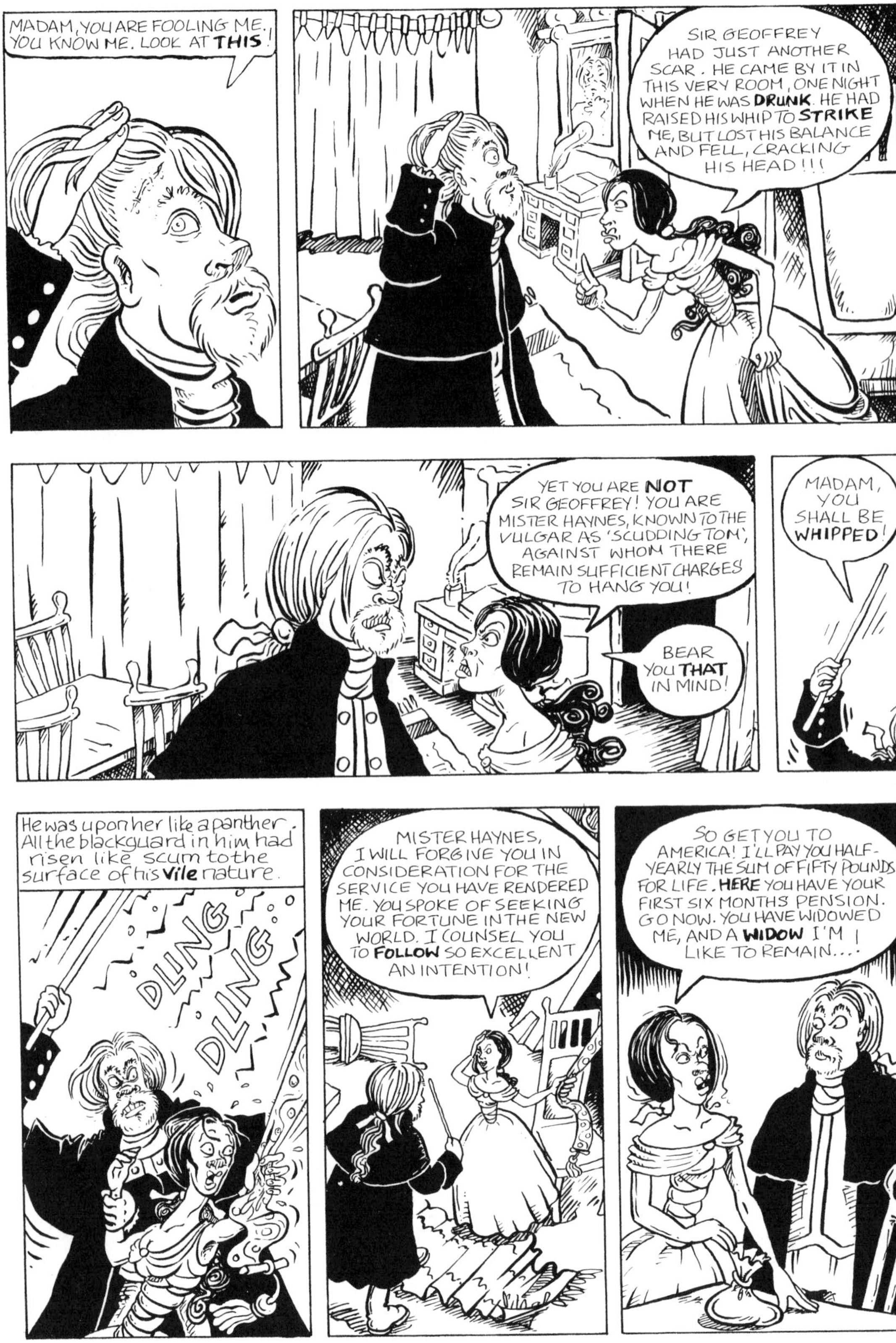
MADAM, YOU ARE FOOLING ME. YOU KNOW ME. LOOK AT **THIS**!
SIR GEOFFREY HAD JUST ANOTHER SCAR. HE CAME BY IT IN THIS VERY ROOM, ONE NIGHT WHEN HE WAS **DRUNK**. HE HAD RAISED HIS WHIP TO **STRIKE** ME, BUT LOST HIS BALANCE AND FELL, CRACKING HIS HEAD!!!
YET YOU ARE **NOT** SIR GEOFFREY! YOU ARE MISTER HAYNES, KNOWN TO THE VULGAR AS 'SCUDDING TOM', AGAINST WHOM THERE REMAIN SUFFICIENT CHARGES TO HANG YOU!
BEAR YOU **THAT** IN MIND!
MADAM, YOU SHALL BE **WHIPPED**!
He was upon her like a panther. All the blackguard in him had risen like scum to the surface of his **Vile** nature.
DLING DLING
MISTER HAYNES, I WILL FORGIVE YOU IN CONSIDERATION FOR THE SERVICE YOU HAVE RENDERED ME. YOU SPOKE OF SEEKING YOUR FORTUNE IN THE NEW WORLD. I COUNSEL YOU TO **FOLLOW** SO EXCELLENT AN INTENTION!
SO GET YOU TO AMERICA! I'LL PAY YOU HALF-YEARLY THE SUM OF FIFTY POUNDS FOR LIFE. **HERE** YOU HAVE YOUR FIRST SIX MONTHS PENSION. GO NOW. YOU HAVE WIDOWED ME, AND A **WIDOW** I'M LIKE TO REMAIN....

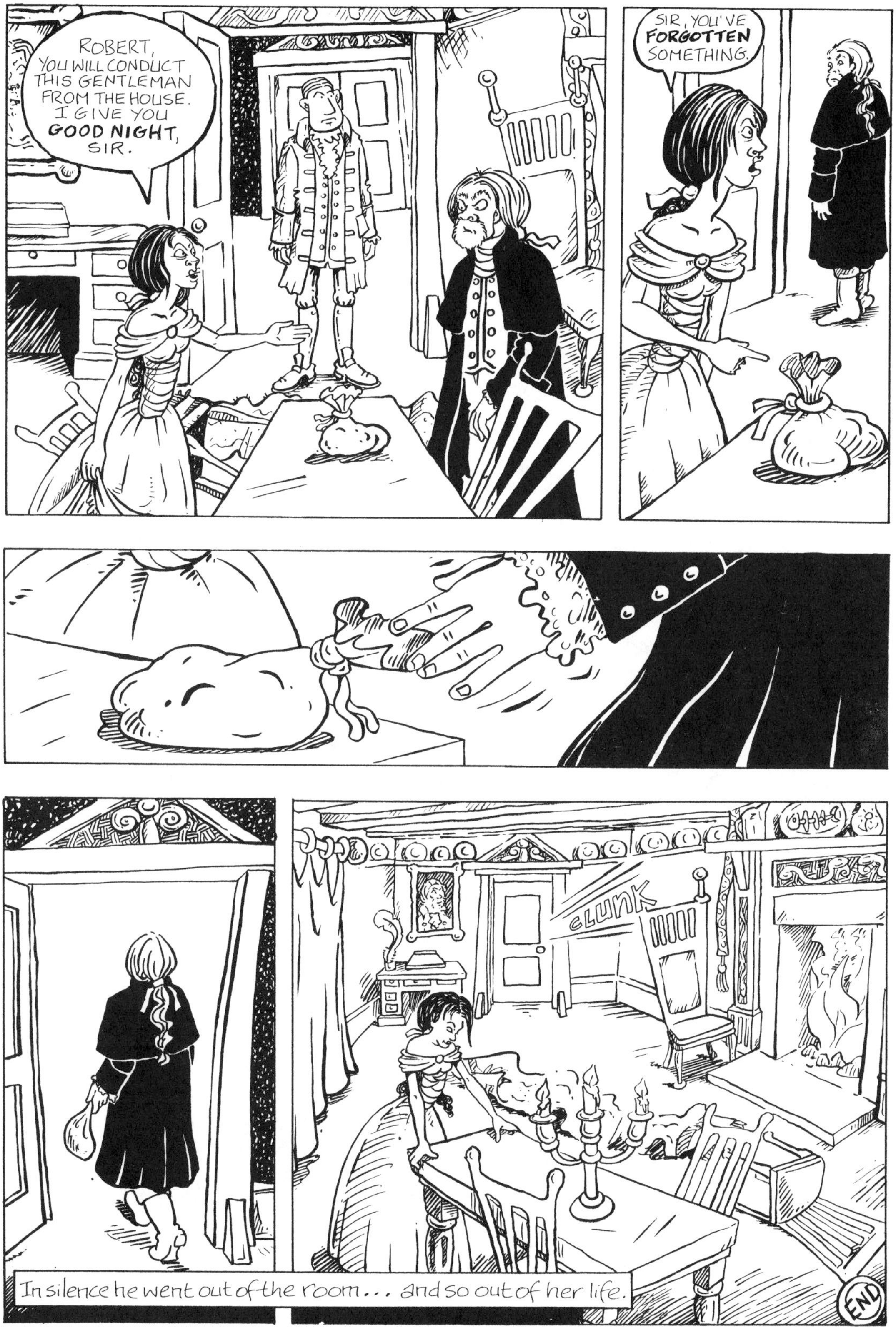
ROBERT, YOU WILL CONDUCT THIS GENTLEMAN FROM THE HOUSE. I GIVE YOU **GOOD NIGHT**, SIR.
SIR, YOU'VE **FORGOTTEN** SOMETHING.
CLUNK
In silence he went out of the room... and so out of her life.
END

ON A LANGUOROUS AFTERNOON IN JULY, ANTHONY ORPINGTON WAS ENTERTAINING TO TEA HIS NEPHEW, THE CELEBRATED STANLEY BICKERSHAW.

RAFAEL SABATINI'S

THE DREAM

ADAPTED BY
TOM POMPLUN

PICTATED BY
RICH TOMMASO

STANLEY BICKERSHAW WAS CELEBRATED FOR HIS RESEARCHES IN THE REALM OF HYPNOTIC PHENOMENA, AND MUCH OF THE WORK HE HAD DONE WAS UNPRECEDENTED. NEVERTHELESS, HE REMAINED POOR, FOR WHILE HE HAD WON BUSHELS OF LAURELS, BICKERSHAW HAD MADE THE DISAPPOINTING DISCOVERY THAT THE PLANT IS A PURELY ORNAMENTAL ONE, INCAPABLE OF BEARING FRUIT. CONSEQUENTLY HIS APPEALS FOR ASSISTANCE TO HIS WEALTHY UNCLE RECURRED WITH THE REGULARITY OF THE SEASONS.

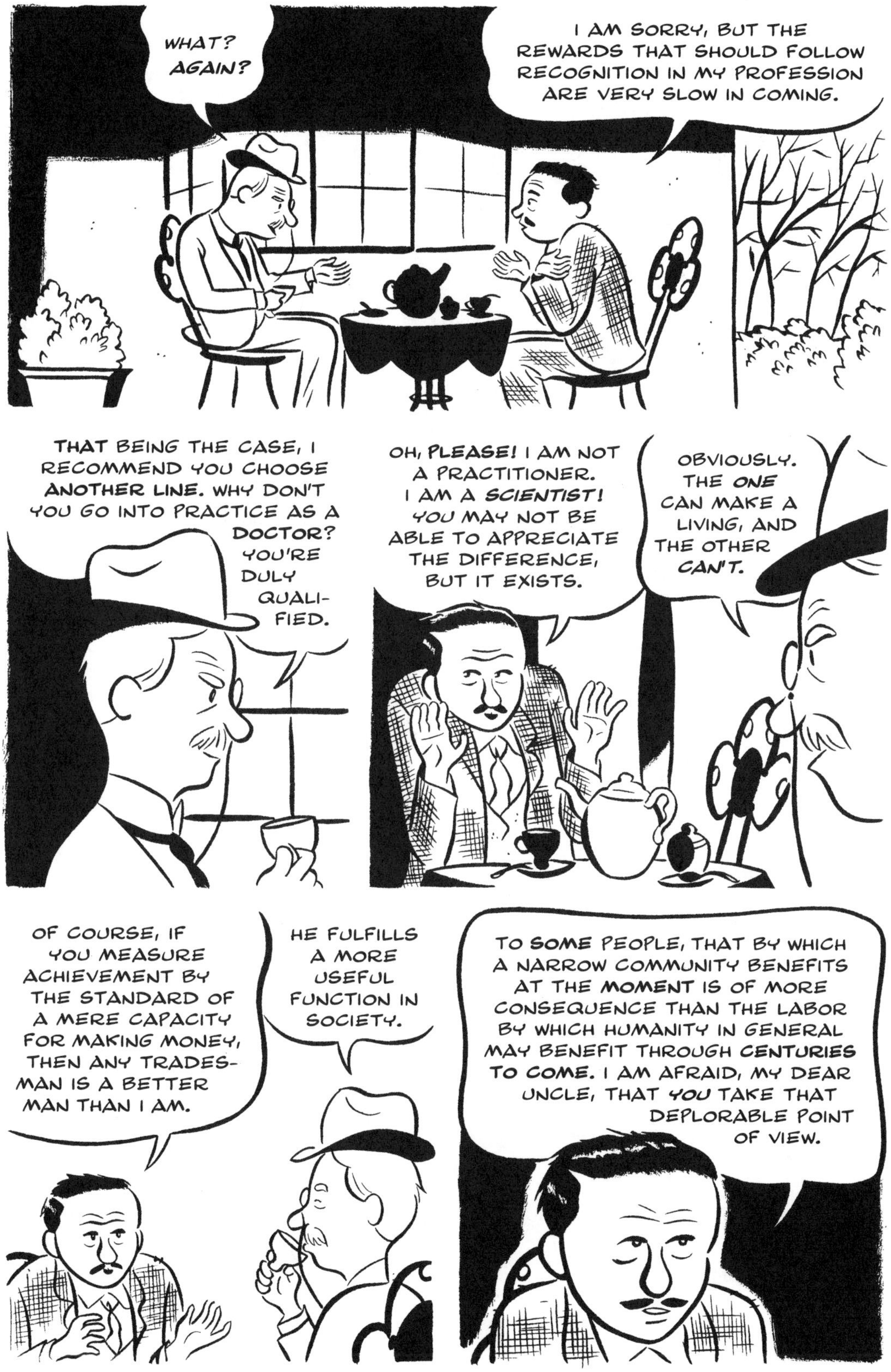
WHAT? AGAIN?
I AM SORRY, BUT THE REWARDS THAT SHOULD FOLLOW RECOGNITION IN MY PROFESSION ARE VERY SLOW IN COMING.
THAT BEING THE CASE, I RECOMMEND YOU CHOOSE ANOTHER LINE. WHY DON'T YOU GO INTO PRACTICE AS A DOCTOR? YOU'RE DULY QUALI-FIED.
OH, PLEASE! I AM NOT A PRACTITIONER. I AM A SCIENTIST! YOU MAY NOT BE ABLE TO APPRECIATE THE DIFFERENCE, BUT IT EXISTS.
OBVIOUSLY. THE ONE CAN MAKE A LIVING, AND THE OTHER CAN'T.
OF COURSE, IF YOU MEASURE ACHIEVEMENT BY THE STANDARD OF A MERE CAPACITY FOR MAKING MONEY, THEN ANY TRADES-MAN IS A BETTER MAN THAN I AM.
HE FULFILLS A MORE USEFUL FUNCTION IN SOCIETY.
TO SOME PEOPLE, THAT BY WHICH A NARROW COMMUNITY BENEFITS AT THE MOMENT IS OF MORE CONSEQUENCE THAN THE LABOR BY WHICH HUMANITY IN GENERAL MAY BENEFIT THROUGH CENTURIES TO COME. I AM AFRAID, MY DEAR UNCLE, THAT YOU TAKE THAT DEPLORABLE POINT OF VIEW.

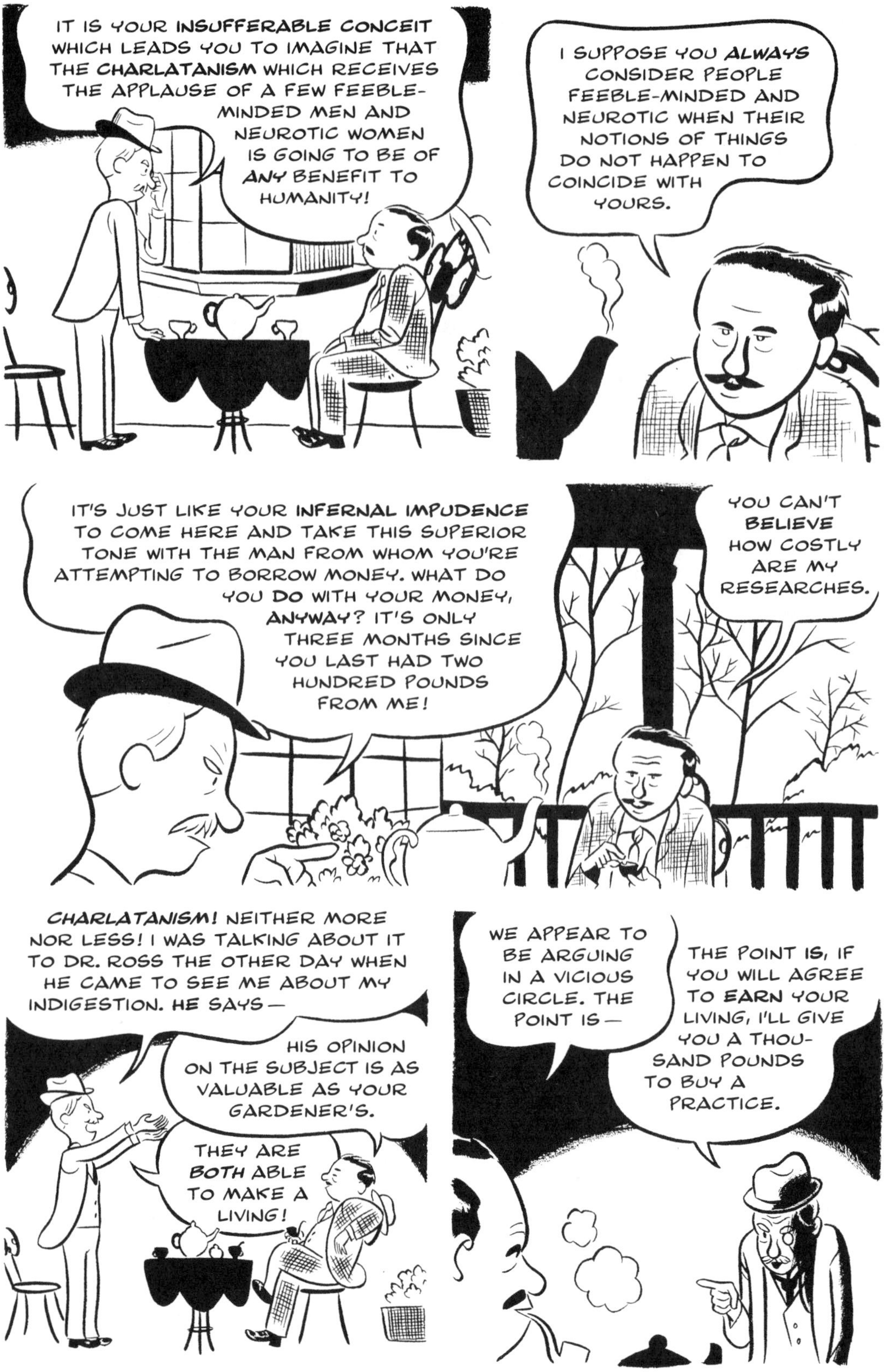
IT IS YOUR INSUFFERABLE CONCEIT WHICH LEADS YOU TO IMAGINE THAT THE CHARLATANISM WHICH RECEIVES THE APPLAUSE OF A FEW FEEBLE-MINDED MEN AND NEUROTIC WOMEN IS GOING TO BE OF ANY BENEFIT TO HUMANITY!
I SUPPOSE YOU ALWAYS CONSIDER PEOPLE FEEBLE-MINDED AND NEUROTIC WHEN THEIR NOTIONS OF THINGS DO NOT HAPPEN TO COINCIDE WITH YOURS.
IT'S JUST LIKE YOUR INFERNAL IMPUDENCE TO COME HERE AND TAKE THIS SUPERIOR TONE WITH THE MAN FROM WHOM YOU'RE ATTEMPTING TO BORROW MONEY. WHAT DO YOU DO WITH YOUR MONEY, ANYWAY? IT'S ONLY THREE MONTHS SINCE YOU LAST HAD TWO HUNDRED POUNDS FROM ME!
YOU CAN'T BELIEVE HOW COSTLY ARE MY RESEARCHES.
CHARLATANISM! NEITHER MORE NOR LESS! I WAS TALKING ABOUT IT TO DR. ROSS THE OTHER DAY WHEN HE CAME TO SEE ME ABOUT MY INDIGESTION. HE SAYS—
HIS OPINION ON THE SUBJECT IS AS VALUABLE AS YOUR GARDENER'S.
THEY ARE BOTH ABLE TO MAKE A LIVING!
WE APPEAR TO BE ARGUING IN A VICIOUS CIRCLE. THE POINT IS—
THE POINT IS, IF YOU WILL AGREE TO EARN YOUR LIVING, I'LL GIVE YOU A THOUSAND POUNDS TO BUY A PRACTICE.

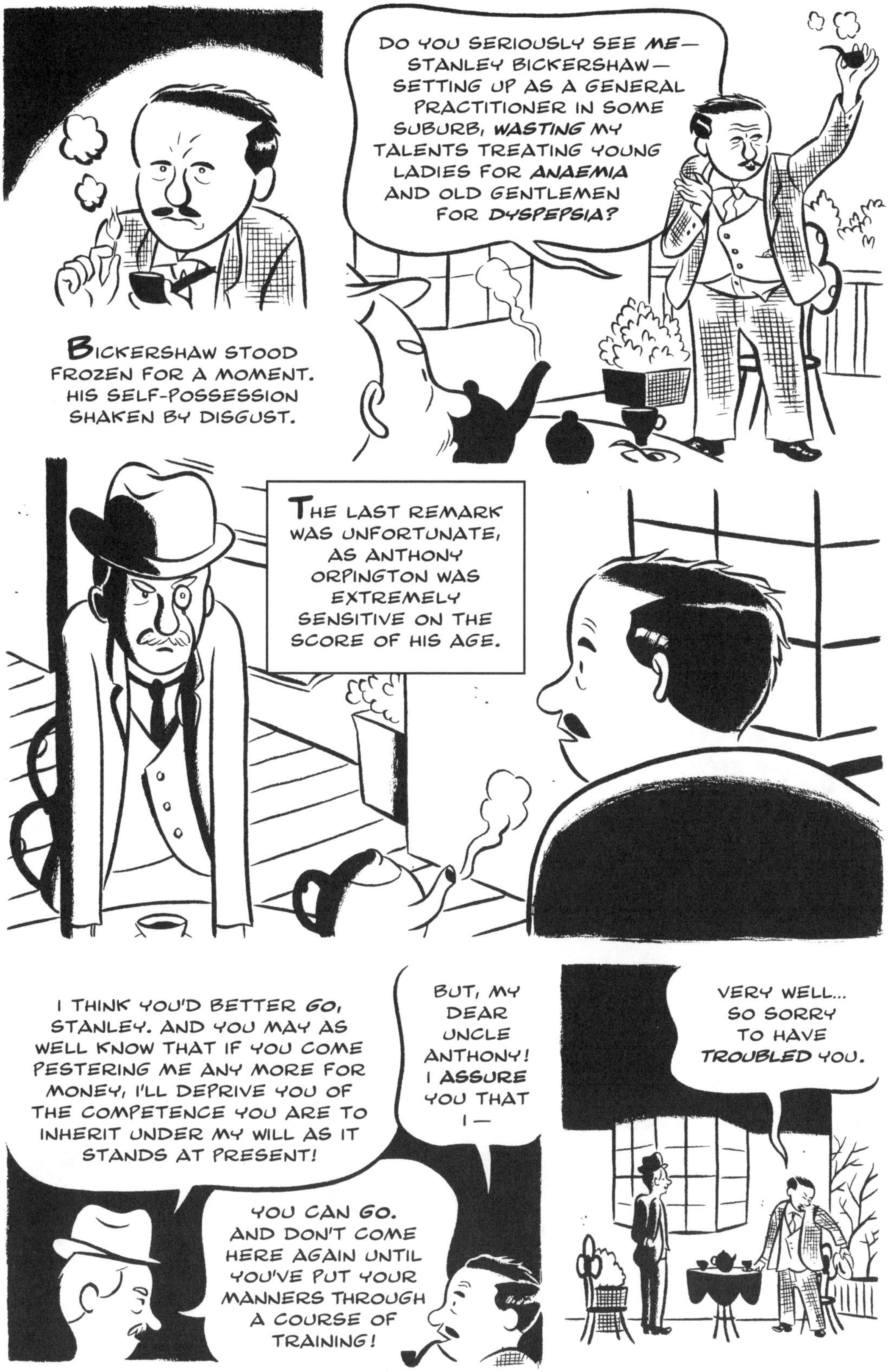
BICKERSHAW STOOD FROZEN FOR A MOMENT. HIS SELF-POSSESSION SHAKEN BY DISGUST.
DO YOU SERIOUSLY SEE ME— STANLEY BICKERSHAW— SETTING UP AS A GENERAL PRACTITIONER IN SOME SUBURB, WASTING MY TALENTS TREATING YOUNG LADIES FOR ANAEMIA AND OLD GENTLEMEN FOR DYSPEPSIA?
THE LAST REMARK WAS UNFORTUNATE, AS ANTHONY ORPINGTON WAS EXTREMELY SENSITIVE ON THE SCORE OF HIS AGE.
I THINK YOU'D BETTER GO, STANLEY. AND YOU MAY AS WELL KNOW THAT IF YOU COME PESTERING ME ANY MORE FOR MONEY, I'LL DEPRIVE YOU OF THE COMPETENCE YOU ARE TO INHERIT UNDER MY WILL AS IT STANDS AT PRESENT!
BUT, MY DEAR UNCLE ANTHONY! I ASSURE YOU THAT I—
YOU CAN GO. AND DON'T COME HERE AGAIN UNTIL YOU'VE PUT YOUR MANNERS THROUGH A COURSE OF TRAINING!
VERY WELL... SO SORRY TO HAVE TROUBLED YOU.

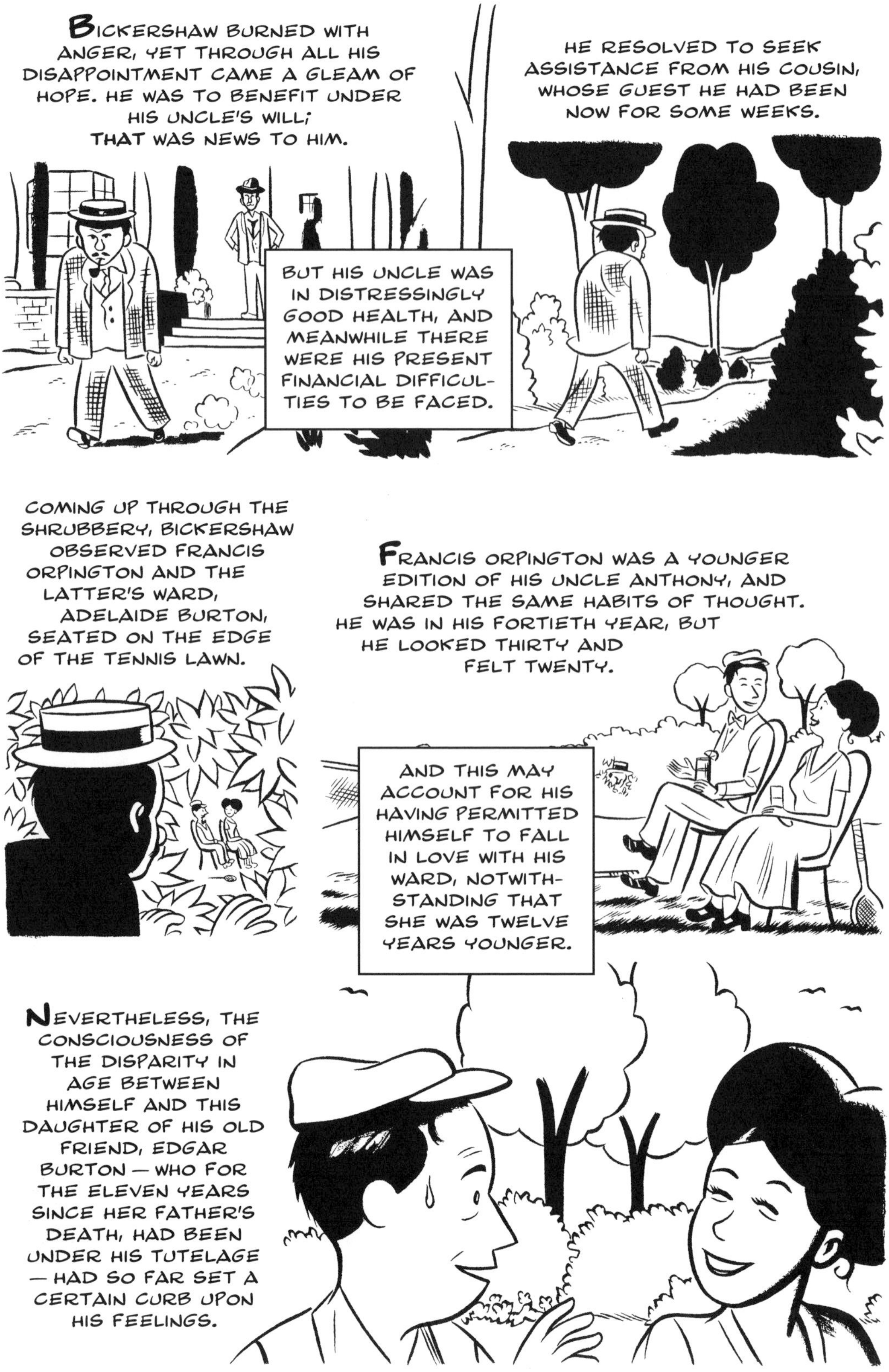
BICKERSHAW BURNED WITH ANGER, YET THROUGH ALL HIS DISAPPOINTMENT CAME A GLEAM OF HOPE. HE WAS TO BENEFIT UNDER HIS UNCLE'S WILL; THAT WAS NEWS TO HIM.
BUT HIS UNCLE WAS IN DISTRESSINGLY GOOD HEALTH, AND MEANWHILE THERE WERE HIS PRESENT FINANCIAL DIFFICULTIES TO BE FACED.
HE RESOLVED TO SEEK ASSISTANCE FROM HIS COUSIN, WHOSE GUEST HE HAD BEEN NOW FOR SOME WEEKS.
COMING UP THROUGH THE SHRUBBERY, BICKERSHAW OBSERVED FRANCIS ORPINGTON AND THE LATTER'S WARD, ADELAIDE BURTON, SEATED ON THE EDGE OF THE TENNIS LAWN.
FRANCIS ORPINGTON WAS A YOUNGER EDITION OF HIS UNCLE ANTHONY, AND SHARED THE SAME HABITS OF THOUGHT. HE WAS IN HIS FORTIETH YEAR, BUT HE LOOKED THIRTY AND FELT TWENTY.
AND THIS MAY ACCOUNT FOR HIS HAVING PERMITTED HIMSELF TO FALL IN LOVE WITH HIS WARD, NOTWITHSTANDING THAT SHE WAS TWELVE YEARS YOUNGER.
NEVERTHELESS, THE CONSCIOUSNESS OF THE DISPARITY IN AGE BETWEEN HIMSELF AND THIS DAUGHTER OF HIS OLD FRIEND, EDGAR BURTON — WHO FOR THE ELEVEN YEARS SINCE HER FATHER'S DEATH, HAD BEEN UNDER HIS TUTELAGE — HAD SO FAR SET A CERTAIN CURB UPON HIS FEELINGS.

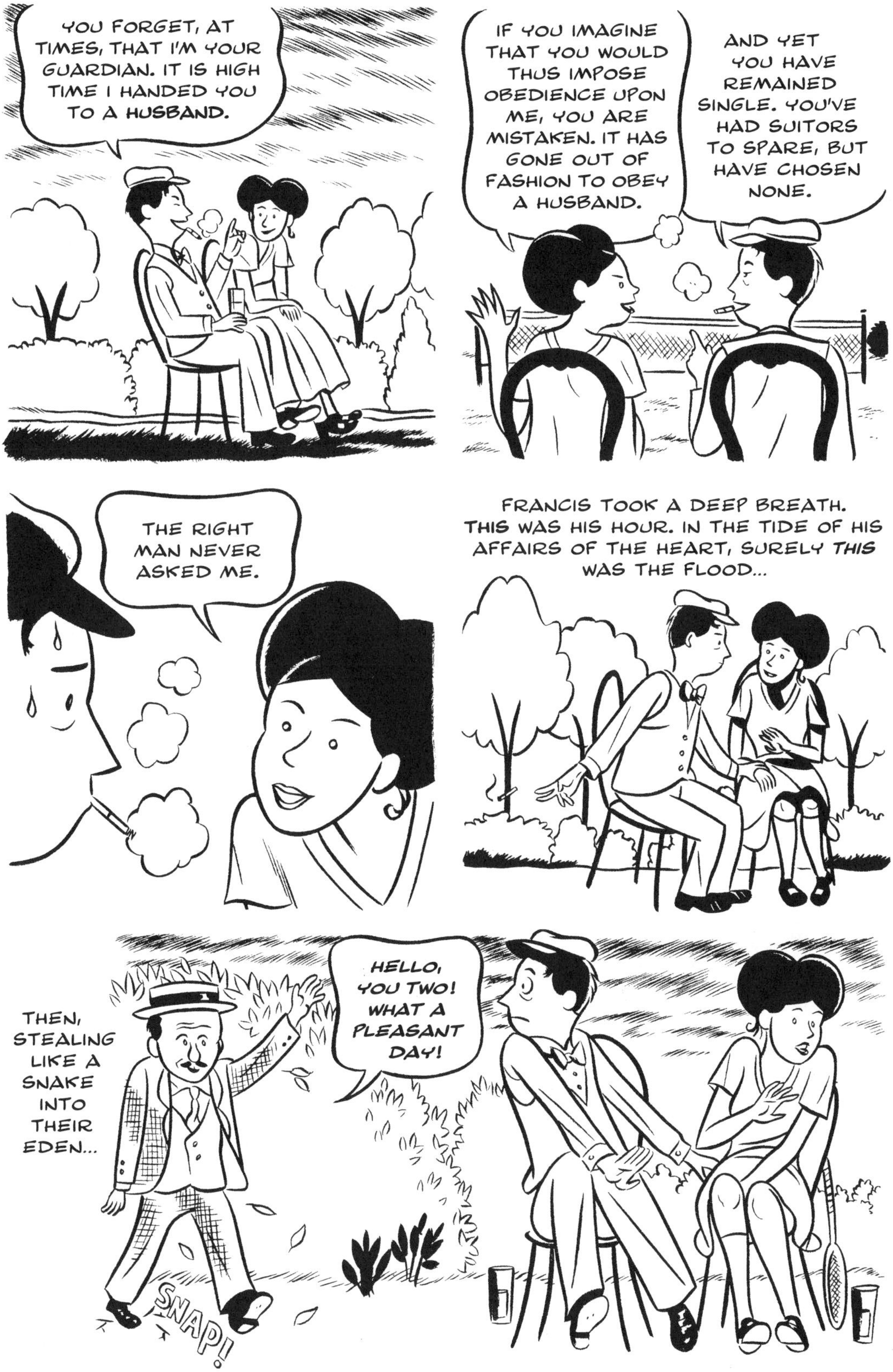
YOU FORGET, AT TIMES, THAT I'M YOUR GUARDIAN. IT IS HIGH TIME I HANDED YOU TO A HUSBAND.
IF YOU IMAGINE THAT YOU WOULD THUS IMPOSE OBEDIENCE UPON ME, YOU ARE MISTAKEN. IT HAS GONE OUT OF FASHION TO OBEY A HUSBAND.
AND YET YOU HAVE REMAINED SINGLE. YOU'VE HAD SUITORS TO SPARE, BUT HAVE CHOSEN NONE.
THE RIGHT MAN NEVER ASKED ME.
FRANCIS TOOK A DEEP BREATH. THIS WAS HIS HOUR. IN THE TIDE OF HIS AFFAIRS OF THE HEART, SURELY THIS WAS THE FLOOD...
THEN, STEALING LIKE A SNAKE INTO THEIR EDEN...
HELLO, YOU TWO! WHAT A PLEASANT DAY!
SNAP!

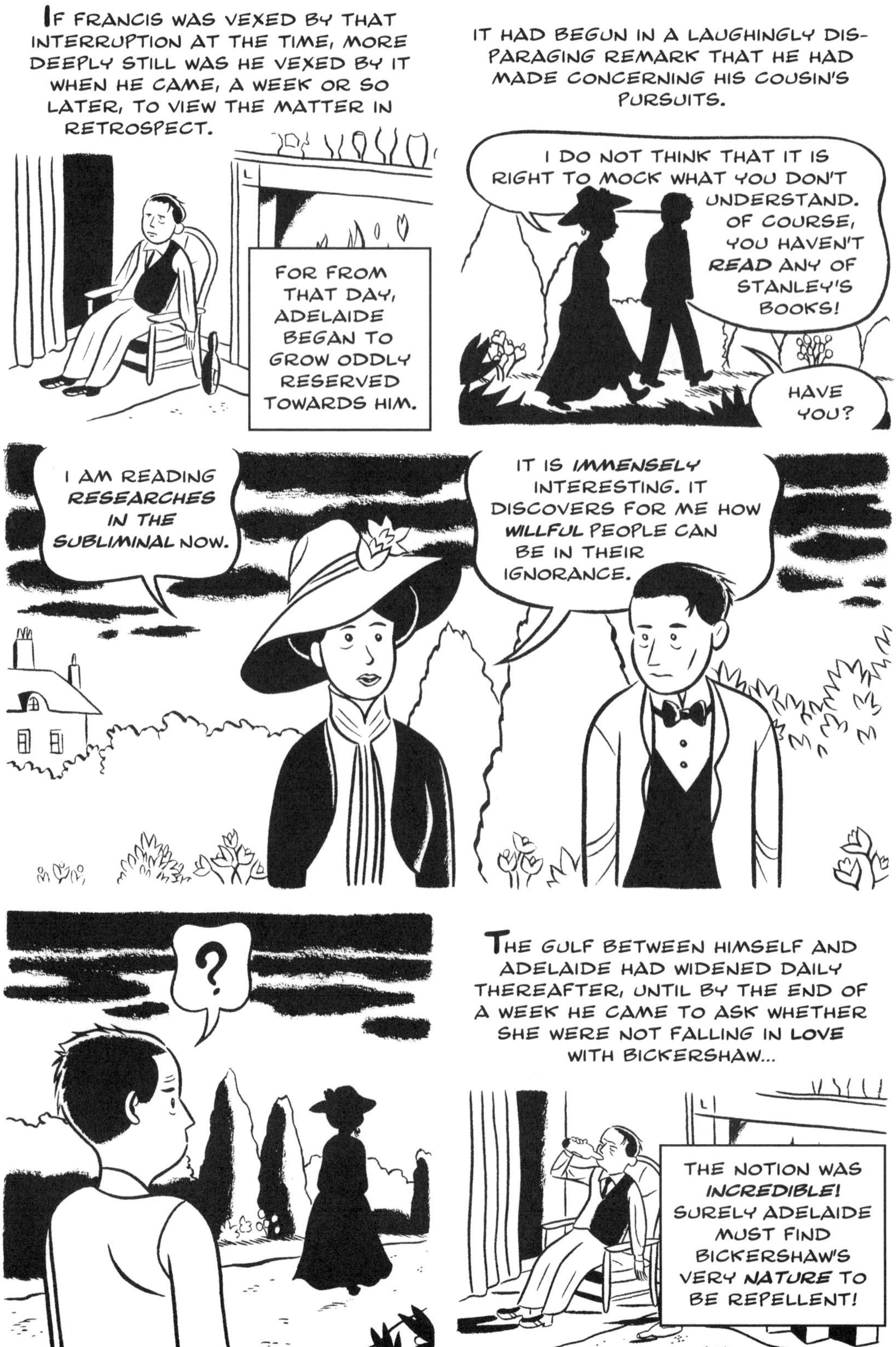
IF FRANCIS WAS VEXED BY THAT INTERRUPTION AT THE TIME, MORE DEEPLY STILL WAS HE VEXED BY IT WHEN HE CAME, A WEEK OR SO LATER, TO VIEW THE MATTER IN RETROSPECT.
FOR FROM THAT DAY, ADELAIDE BEGAN TO GROW ODDLY RESERVED TOWARDS HIM.
IT HAD BEGUN IN A LAUGHINGLY DISPARAGING REMARK THAT HE HAD MADE CONCERNING HIS COUSIN'S PURSUITS.
I DO NOT THINK THAT IT IS RIGHT TO MOCK WHAT YOU DON'T UNDERSTAND. OF COURSE, YOU HAVEN'T READ ANY OF STANLEY'S BOOKS!
HAVE YOU?
I AM READING RESEARCHES IN THE SUBLIMINAL NOW.
IT IS IMMENSELY INTERESTING. IT DISCOVERS FOR ME HOW WILLFUL PEOPLE CAN BE IN THEIR IGNORANCE.
?
THE GULF BETWEEN HIMSELF AND ADELAIDE HAD WIDENED DAILY THEREAFTER, UNTIL BY THE END OF A WEEK HE CAME TO ASK WHETHER SHE WERE NOT FALLING IN LOVE WITH BICKERSHAW...
THE NOTION WAS INCREDIBLE! SURELY ADELAIDE MUST FIND BICKERSHAW'S VERY NATURE TO BE REPELLENT!

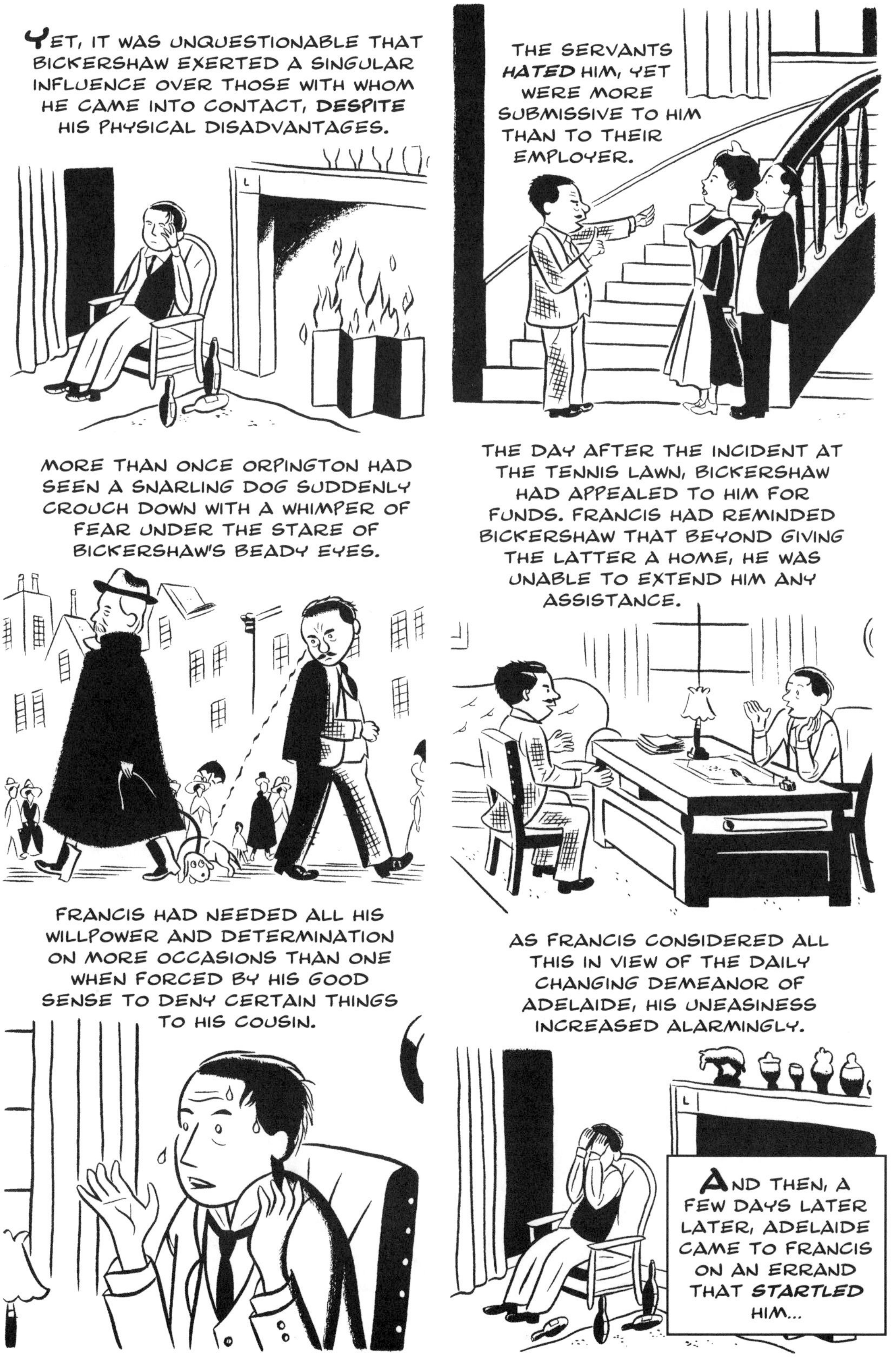
YET, IT WAS UNQUESTIONABLE THAT BICKERSHAW EXERTED A SINGULAR INFLUENCE OVER THOSE WITH WHOM HE CAME INTO CONTACT, DESPITE HIS PHYSICAL DISADVANTAGES.
THE SERVANTS HATED HIM, YET WERE MORE SUBMISSIVE TO HIM THAN TO THEIR EMPLOYER.
MORE THAN ONCE ORPINGTON HAD SEEN A SNARLING DOG SUDDENLY CROUCH DOWN WITH A WHIMPER OF FEAR UNDER THE STARE OF BICKERSHAW'S BEADY EYES.
THE DAY AFTER THE INCIDENT AT THE TENNIS LAWN, BICKERSHAW HAD APPEALED TO HIM FOR FUNDS. FRANCIS HAD REMINDED BICKERSHAW THAT BEYOND GIVING THE LATTER A HOME, HE WAS UNABLE TO EXTEND HIM ANY ASSISTANCE.
FRANCIS HAD NEEDED ALL HIS WILLPOWER AND DETERMINATION ON MORE OCCASIONS THAN ONE WHEN FORCED BY HIS GOOD SENSE TO DENY CERTAIN THINGS TO HIS COUSIN.
AS FRANCIS CONSIDERED ALL THIS IN VIEW OF THE DAILY CHANGING DEMEANOR OF ADELAIDE, HIS UNEASINESS INCREASED ALARMINGLY.
AND THEN, A FEW DAYS LATER LATER, ADELAIDE CAME TO FRANCIS ON AN ERRAND THAT STARTLED HIM...

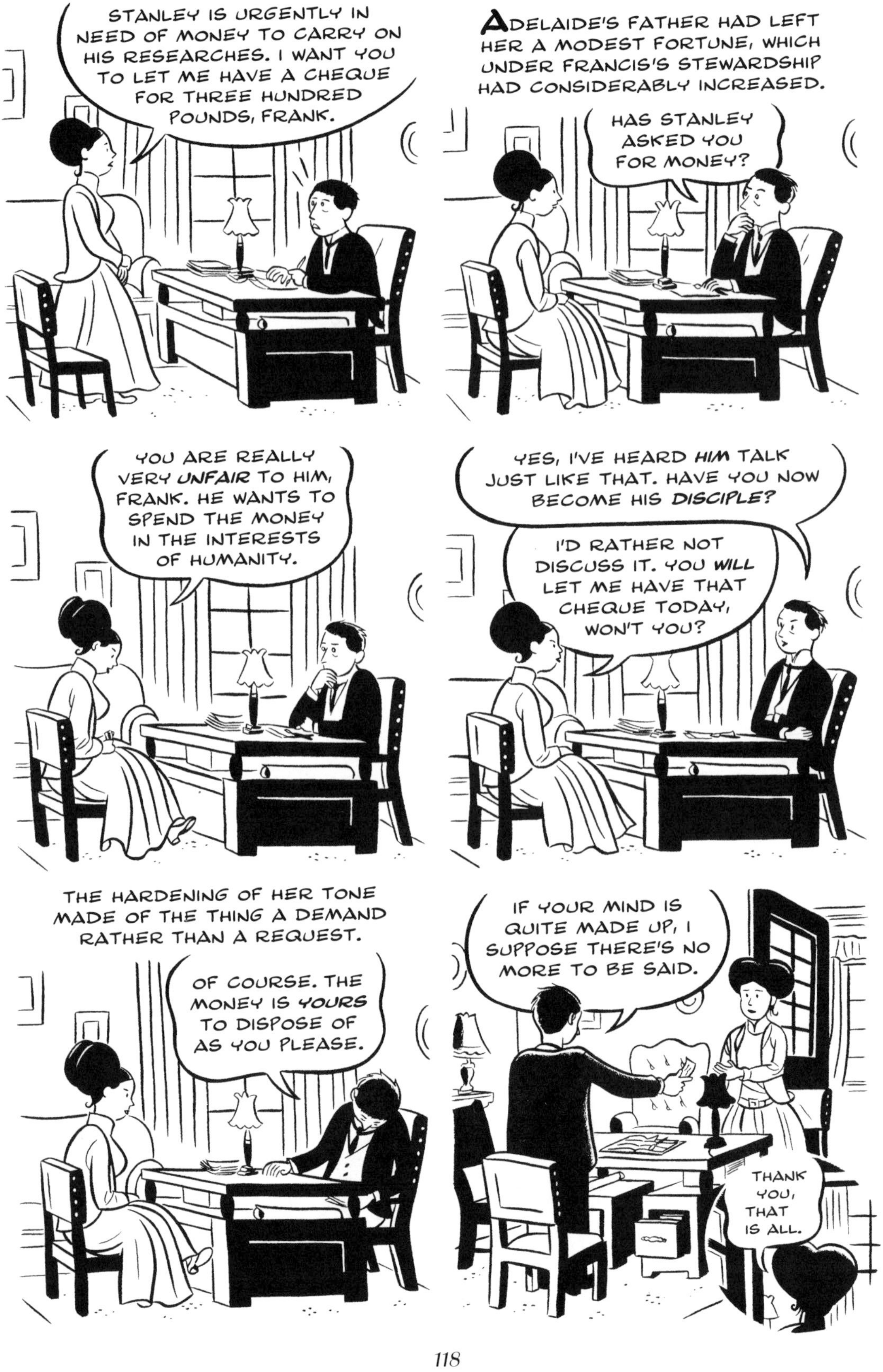
STANLEY IS URGENTLY IN NEED OF MONEY TO CARRY ON HIS RESEARCHES. I WANT YOU TO LET ME HAVE A CHEQUE FOR THREE HUNDRED POUNDS, FRANK.
ADELAIDE'S FATHER HAD LEFT HER A MODEST FORTUNE, WHICH UNDER FRANCIS'S STEWARDSHIP HAD CONSIDERABLY INCREASED.
HAS STANLEY ASKED YOU FOR MONEY?
YOU ARE REALLY VERY *UNFAIR* TO HIM, FRANK. HE WANTS TO SPEND THE MONEY IN THE INTERESTS OF HUMANITY.
YES, I'VE HEARD *HIM* TALK JUST LIKE THAT. HAVE YOU NOW BECOME HIS *DISCIPLE?*
I'D RATHER NOT DISCUSS IT. YOU *WILL* LET ME HAVE THAT CHEQUE TODAY, WON'T YOU?
THE HARDENING OF HER TONE MADE OF THE THING A DEMAND RATHER THAN A REQUEST.
OF COURSE. THE MONEY IS *YOURS* TO DISPOSE OF AS YOU PLEASE.
IF YOUR MIND IS QUITE MADE UP, I SUPPOSE THERE'S NO MORE TO BE SAID.
THANK YOU, THAT IS ALL.

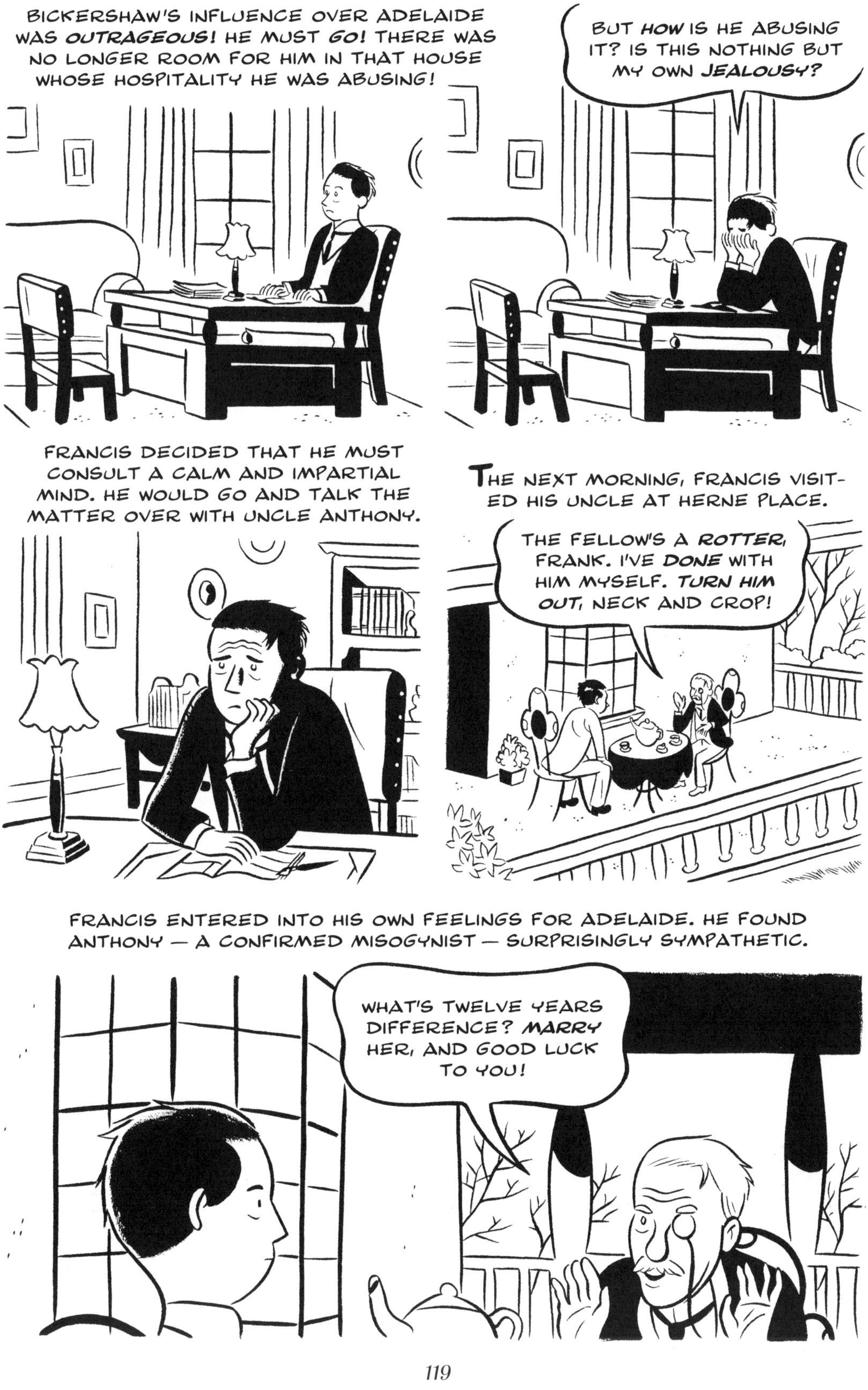
BICKERSHAW'S INFLUENCE OVER ADELAIDE WAS OUTRAGEOUS! HE MUST GO! THERE WAS NO LONGER ROOM FOR HIM IN THAT HOUSE WHOSE HOSPITALITY HE WAS ABUSING!
BUT HOW IS HE ABUSING IT? IS THIS NOTHING BUT MY OWN JEALOUSY?
FRANCIS DECIDED THAT HE MUST CONSULT A CALM AND IMPARTIAL MIND. HE WOULD GO AND TALK THE MATTER OVER WITH UNCLE ANTHONY.
THE NEXT MORNING, FRANCIS VISITED HIS UNCLE AT HERNE PLACE.
THE FELLOW'S A ROTTER, FRANK. I'VE DONE WITH HIM MYSELF. TURN HIM OUT, NECK AND CROP!
FRANCIS ENTERED INTO HIS OWN FEELINGS FOR ADELAIDE. HE FOUND ANTHONY — A CONFIRMED MISOGYNIST — SURPRISINGLY SYMPATHETIC.
WHAT'S TWELVE YEARS DIFFERENCE? MARRY HER, AND GOOD LUCK TO YOU!

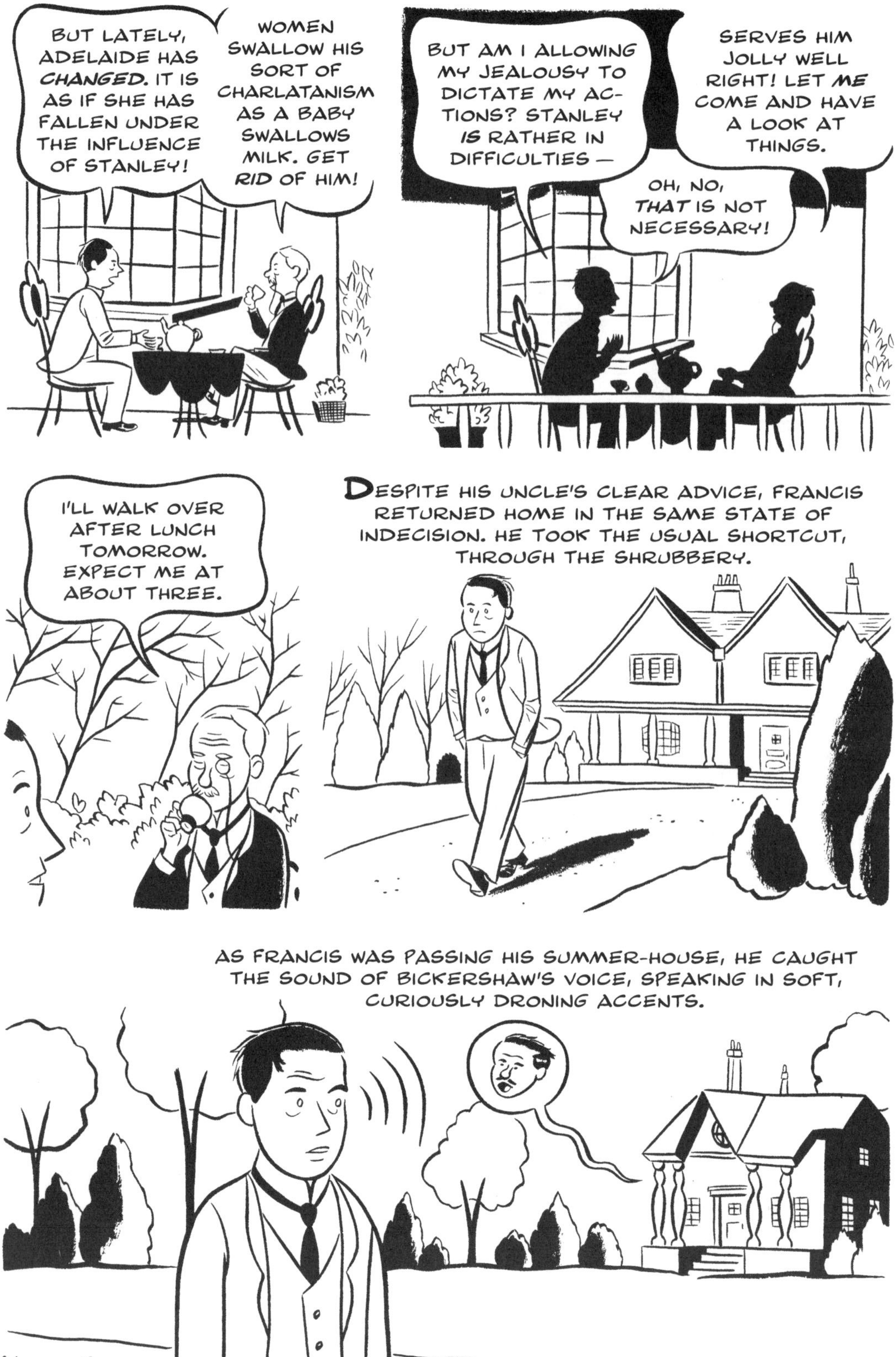
BUT LATELY, ADELAIDE HAS *CHANGED.* IT IS AS IF SHE HAS FALLEN UNDER THE INFLUENCE OF STANLEY!
WOMEN SWALLOW HIS SORT OF CHARLATANISM AS A BABY SWALLOWS MILK. GET *RID* OF HIM!
BUT AM I ALLOWING MY JEALOUSY TO DICTATE MY ACTIONS? STANLEY *IS* RATHER IN DIFFICULTIES —
SERVES HIM JOLLY WELL RIGHT! LET *ME* COME AND HAVE A LOOK AT THINGS.
OH, NO, *THAT* IS NOT NECESSARY!
I'LL WALK OVER AFTER LUNCH TOMORROW. EXPECT ME AT ABOUT THREE.
DESPITE HIS UNCLE'S CLEAR ADVICE, FRANCIS RETURNED HOME IN THE SAME STATE OF INDECISION. HE TOOK THE USUAL SHORTCUT, THROUGH THE SHRUBBERY.
AS FRANCIS WAS PASSING HIS SUMMER-HOUSE, HE CAUGHT THE SOUND OF BICKERSHAW'S VOICE, SPEAKING IN SOFT, CURIOUSLY DRONING ACCENTS.

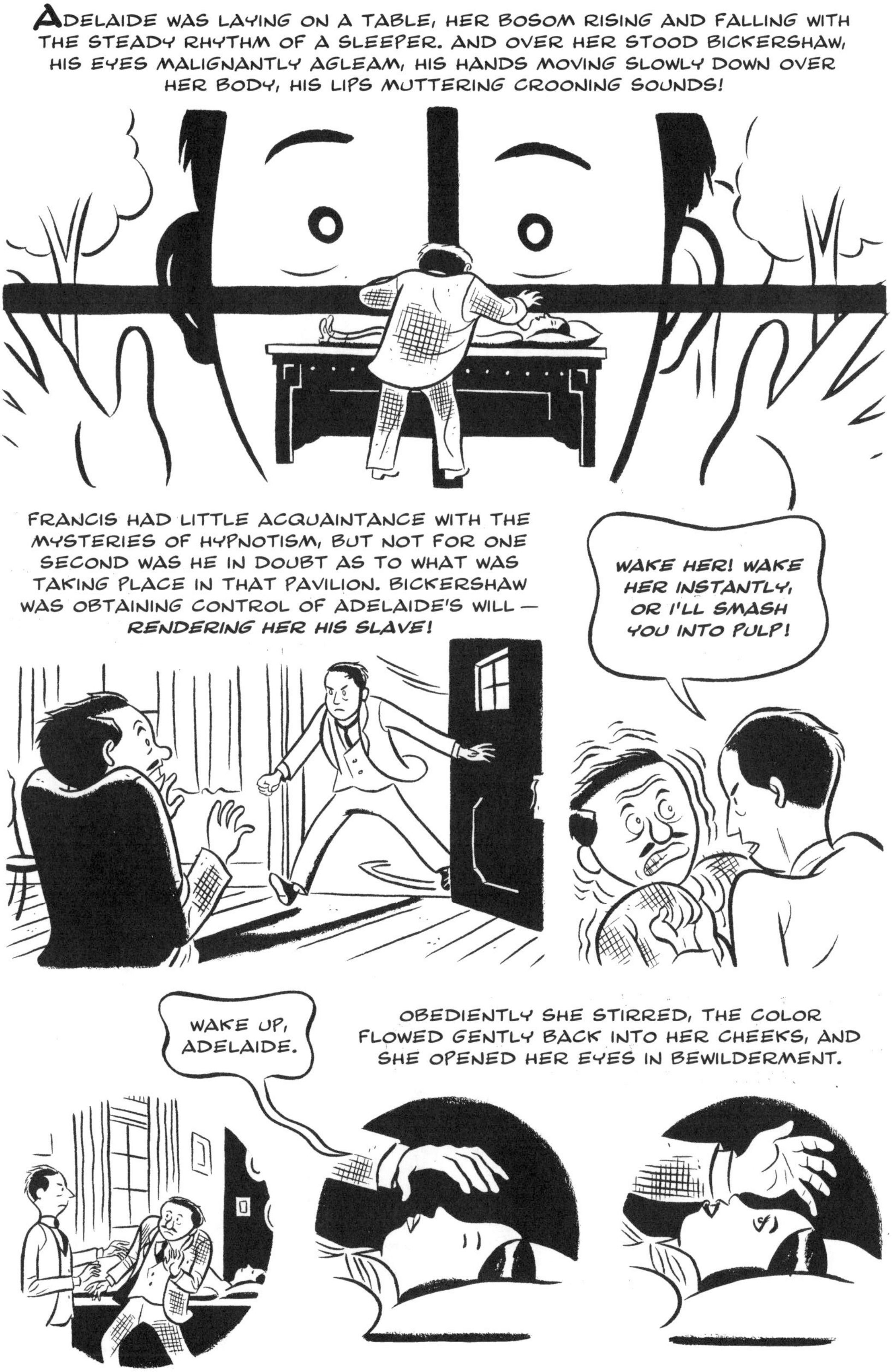
ADELAIDE WAS LAYING ON A TABLE, HER BOSOM RISING AND FALLING WITH THE STEADY RHYTHM OF A SLEEPER. AND OVER HER STOOD BICKERSHAW, HIS EYES MALIGNANTLY AGLEAM, HIS HANDS MOVING SLOWLY DOWN OVER HER BODY, HIS LIPS MUTTERING CROONING SOUNDS!
FRANCIS HAD LITTLE ACQUAINTANCE WITH THE MYSTERIES OF HYPNOTISM, BUT NOT FOR ONE SECOND WAS HE IN DOUBT AS TO WHAT WAS TAKING PLACE IN THAT PAVILION. BICKERSHAW WAS OBTAINING CONTROL OF ADELAIDE'S WILL — RENDERING HER HIS SLAVE!
WAKE HER! WAKE HER INSTANTLY, OR I'LL SMASH YOU INTO PULP!
WAKE UP, ADELAIDE.
OBEDIENTLY SHE STIRRED, THE COLOR FLOWED GENTLY BACK INTO HER CHEEKS, AND SHE OPENED HER EYES IN BEWILDERMENT.

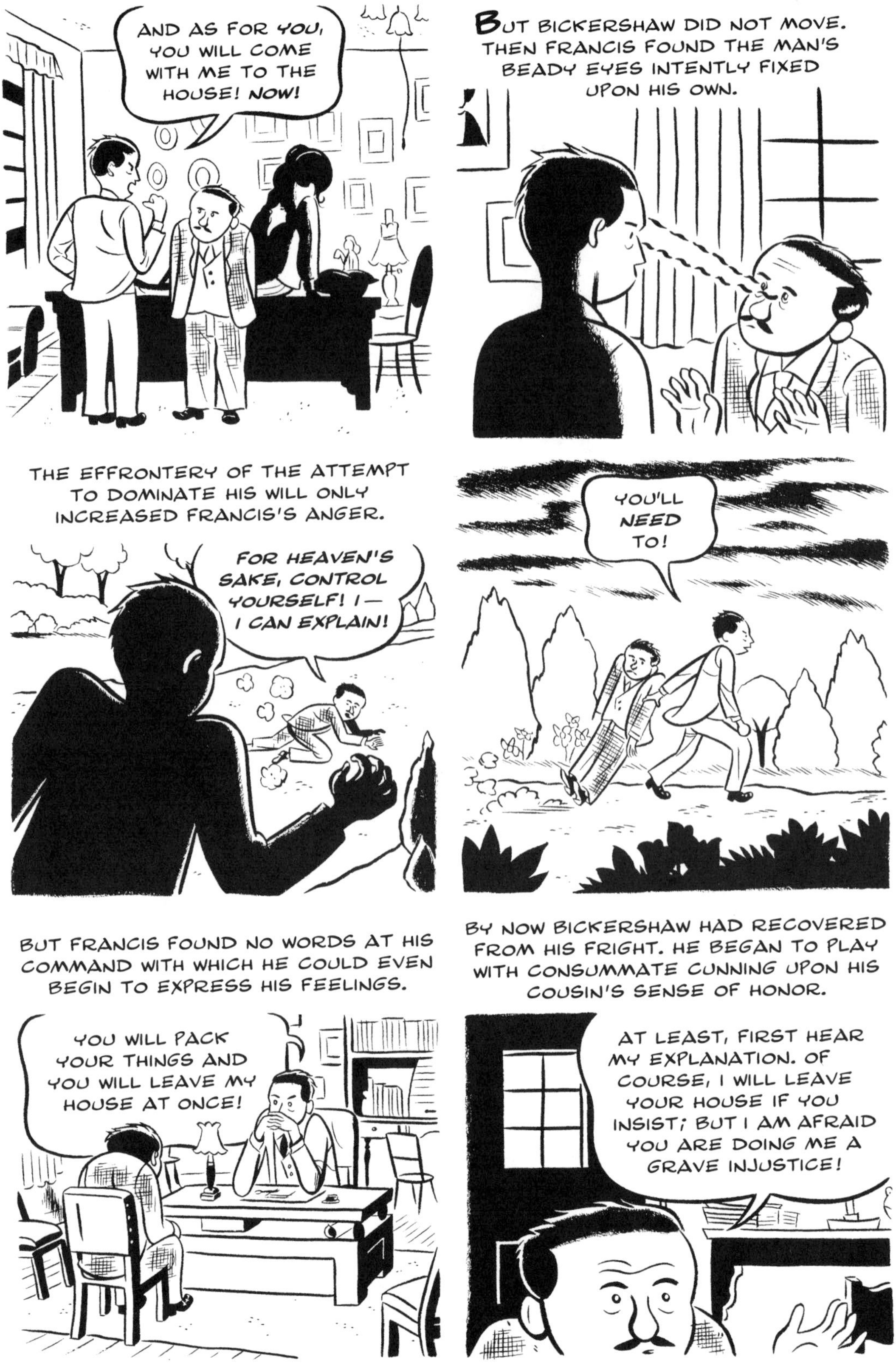
AND AS FOR YOU, YOU WILL COME WITH ME TO THE HOUSE! NOW!
BUT BICKERSHAW DID NOT MOVE. THEN FRANCIS FOUND THE MAN'S BEADY EYES INTENTLY FIXED UPON HIS OWN.
THE EFFRONTERY OF THE ATTEMPT TO DOMINATE HIS WILL ONLY INCREASED FRANCIS'S ANGER.
FOR HEAVEN'S SAKE, CONTROL YOURSELF! I— I CAN EXPLAIN!
YOU'LL NEED TO!
BUT FRANCIS FOUND NO WORDS AT HIS COMMAND WITH WHICH HE COULD EVEN BEGIN TO EXPRESS HIS FEELINGS.
YOU WILL PACK YOUR THINGS AND YOU WILL LEAVE MY HOUSE AT ONCE!
BY NOW BICKERSHAW HAD RECOVERED FROM HIS FRIGHT. HE BEGAN TO PLAY WITH CONSUMMATE CUNNING UPON HIS COUSIN'S SENSE OF HONOR.
AT LEAST, FIRST HEAR MY EXPLANATION. OF COURSE, I WILL LEAVE YOUR HOUSE IF YOU INSIST; BUT I AM AFRAID YOU ARE DOING ME A GRAVE INJUSTICE!

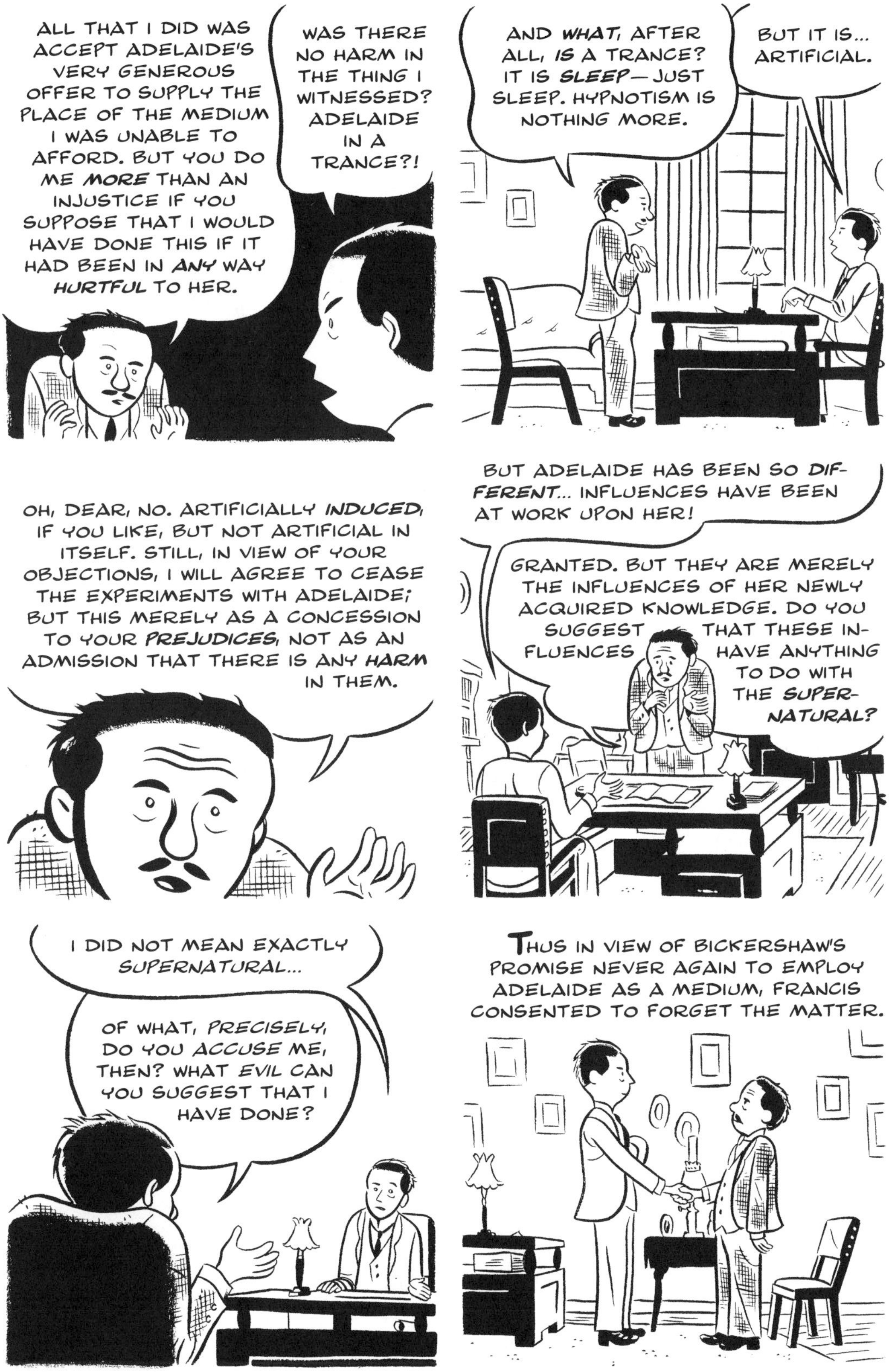
ALL THAT I DID WAS ACCEPT ADELAIDE'S VERY GENEROUS OFFER TO SUPPLY THE PLACE OF THE MEDIUM I WAS UNABLE TO AFFORD. BUT YOU DO ME MORE THAN AN INJUSTICE IF YOU SUPPOSE THAT I WOULD HAVE DONE THIS IF IT HAD BEEN IN ANY WAY HURTFUL TO HER.
WAS THERE NO HARM IN THE THING I WITNESSED? ADELAIDE IN A TRANCE?!
AND WHAT, AFTER ALL, IS A TRANCE? IT IS SLEEP— JUST SLEEP. HYPNOTISM IS NOTHING MORE.
BUT IT IS... ARTIFICIAL.
OH, DEAR, NO. ARTIFICIALLY INDUCED, IF YOU LIKE, BUT NOT ARTIFICIAL IN ITSELF. STILL, IN VIEW OF YOUR OBJECTIONS, I WILL AGREE TO CEASE THE EXPERIMENTS WITH ADELAIDE; BUT THIS MERELY AS A CONCESSION TO YOUR PREJUDICES, NOT AS AN ADMISSION THAT THERE IS ANY HARM IN THEM.
BUT ADELAIDE HAS BEEN SO DIFFERENT... INFLUENCES HAVE BEEN AT WORK UPON HER!
GRANTED. BUT THEY ARE MERELY THE INFLUENCES OF HER NEWLY ACQUIRED KNOWLEDGE. DO YOU SUGGEST THAT THESE INFLUENCES HAVE ANYTHING TO DO WITH THE SUPERNATURAL?
I DID NOT MEAN EXACTLY SUPERNATURAL...
OF WHAT, PRECISELY, DO YOU ACCUSE ME, THEN? WHAT EVIL CAN YOU SUGGEST THAT I HAVE DONE?
THUS IN VIEW OF BICKERSHAW'S PROMISE NEVER AGAIN TO EMPLOY ADELAIDE AS A MEDIUM, FRANCIS CONSENTED TO FORGET THE MATTER.

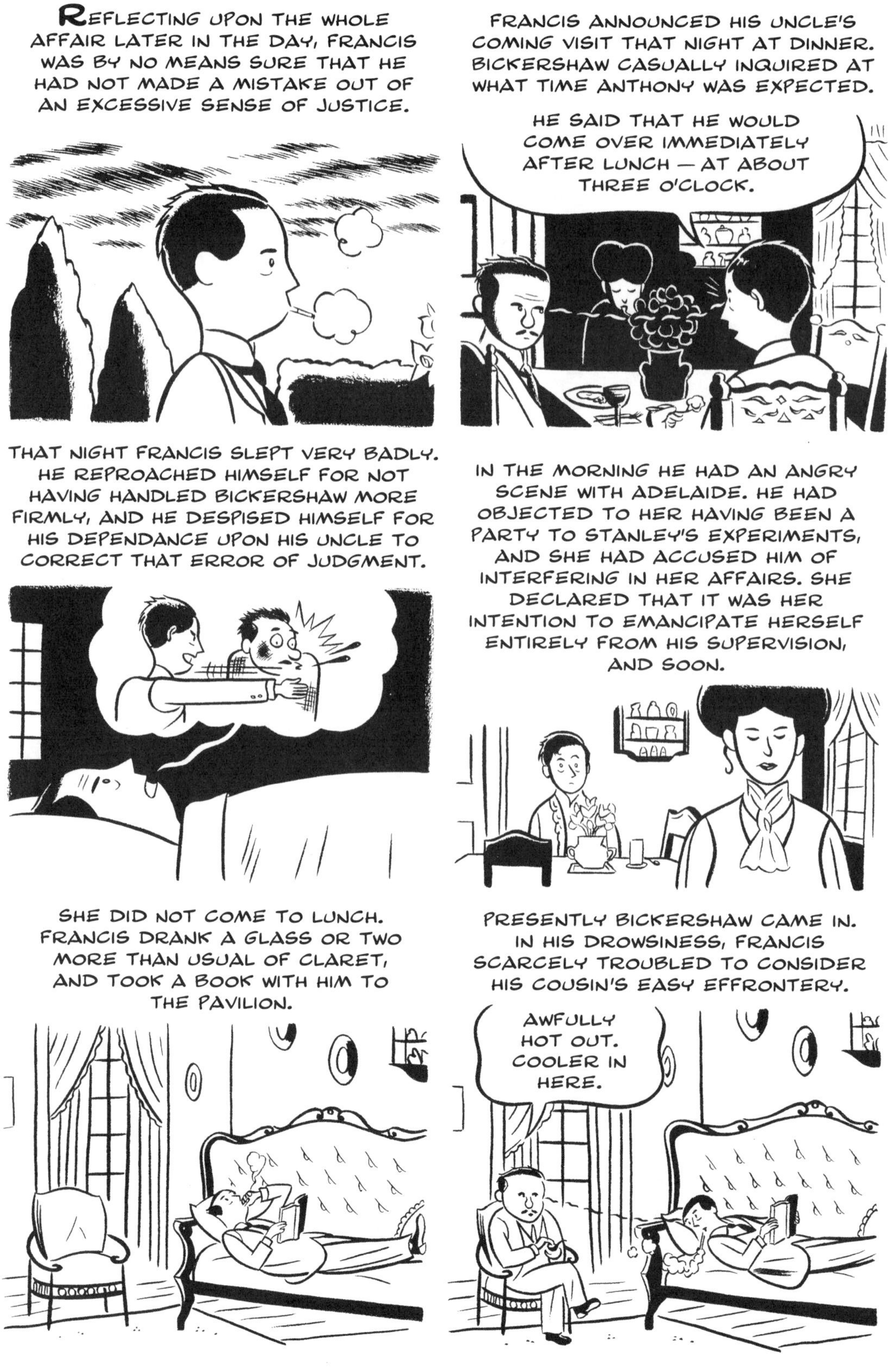
REFLECTING UPON THE WHOLE AFFAIR LATER IN THE DAY, FRANCIS WAS BY NO MEANS SURE THAT HE HAD NOT MADE A MISTAKE OUT OF AN EXCESSIVE SENSE OF JUSTICE.
FRANCIS ANNOUNCED HIS UNCLE'S COMING VISIT THAT NIGHT AT DINNER. BICKERSHAW CASUALLY INQUIRED AT WHAT TIME ANTHONY WAS EXPECTED.
HE SAID THAT HE WOULD COME OVER IMMEDIATELY AFTER LUNCH — AT ABOUT THREE O'CLOCK.
THAT NIGHT FRANCIS SLEPT VERY BADLY. HE REPROACHED HIMSELF FOR NOT HAVING HANDLED BICKERSHAW MORE FIRMLY, AND HE DESPISED HIMSELF FOR HIS DEPENDANCE UPON HIS UNCLE TO CORRECT THAT ERROR OF JUDGMENT.
IN THE MORNING HE HAD AN ANGRY SCENE WITH ADELAIDE. HE HAD OBJECTED TO HER HAVING BEEN A PARTY TO STANLEY'S EXPERIMENTS, AND SHE HAD ACCUSED HIM OF INTERFERING IN HER AFFAIRS. SHE DECLARED THAT IT WAS HER INTENTION TO EMANCIPATE HERSELF ENTIRELY FROM HIS SUPERVISION, AND SOON.
SHE DID NOT COME TO LUNCH. FRANCIS DRANK A GLASS OR TWO MORE THAN USUAL OF CLARET, AND TOOK A BOOK WITH HIM TO THE PAVILION.
PRESENTLY BICKERSHAW CAME IN. IN HIS DROWSINESS, FRANCIS SCARCELY TROUBLED TO CONSIDER HIS COUSIN'S EASY EFFRONTERY.
AWFULLY HOT OUT. COOLER IN HERE.

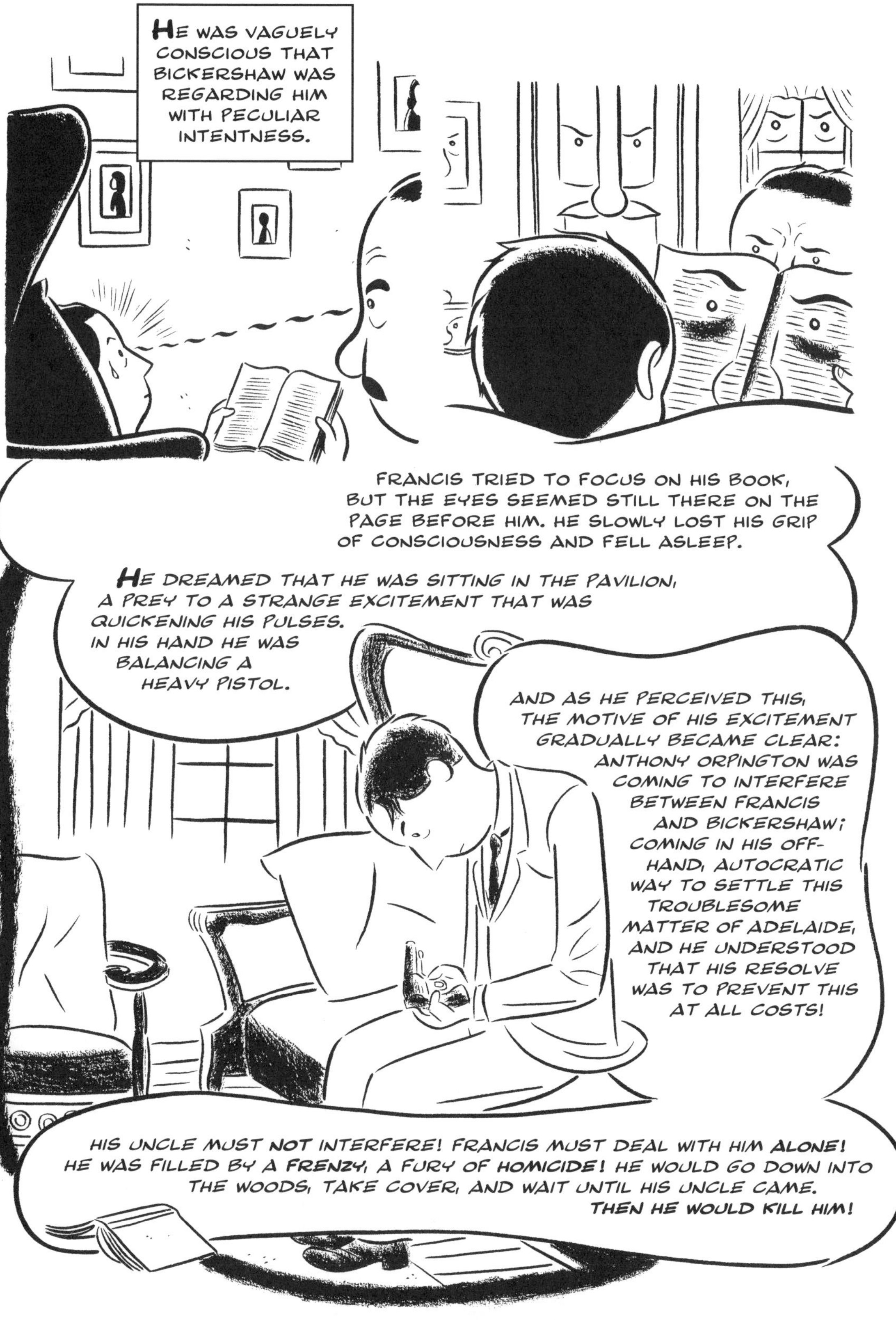
HE WAS VAGUELY CONSCIOUS THAT BICKERSHAW WAS REGARDING HIM WITH PECULIAR INTENTNESS.
FRANCIS TRIED TO FOCUS ON HIS BOOK, BUT THE EYES SEEMED STILL THERE ON THE PAGE BEFORE HIM. HE SLOWLY LOST HIS GRIP OF CONSCIOUSNESS AND FELL ASLEEP.
HE DREAMED THAT HE WAS SITTING IN THE PAVILION, A PREY TO A STRANGE EXCITEMENT THAT WAS QUICKENING HIS PULSES. IN HIS HAND HE WAS BALANCING A HEAVY PISTOL.
AND AS HE PERCEIVED THIS, THE MOTIVE OF HIS EXCITEMENT GRADUALLY BECAME CLEAR: ANTHONY ORPINGTON WAS COMING TO INTERFERE BETWEEN FRANCIS AND BICKERSHAW; COMING IN HIS OFF-HAND, AUTOCRATIC WAY TO SETTLE THIS TROUBLESOME MATTER OF ADELAIDE, AND HE UNDERSTOOD THAT HIS RESOLVE WAS TO PREVENT THIS AT ALL COSTS!
HIS UNCLE MUST NOT INTERFERE! FRANCIS MUST DEAL WITH HIM ALONE! HE WAS FILLED BY A FRENZY, A FURY OF HOMICIDE! HE WOULD GO DOWN INTO THE WOODS, TAKE COVER, AND WAIT UNTIL HIS UNCLE CAME. THEN HE WOULD KILL HIM!

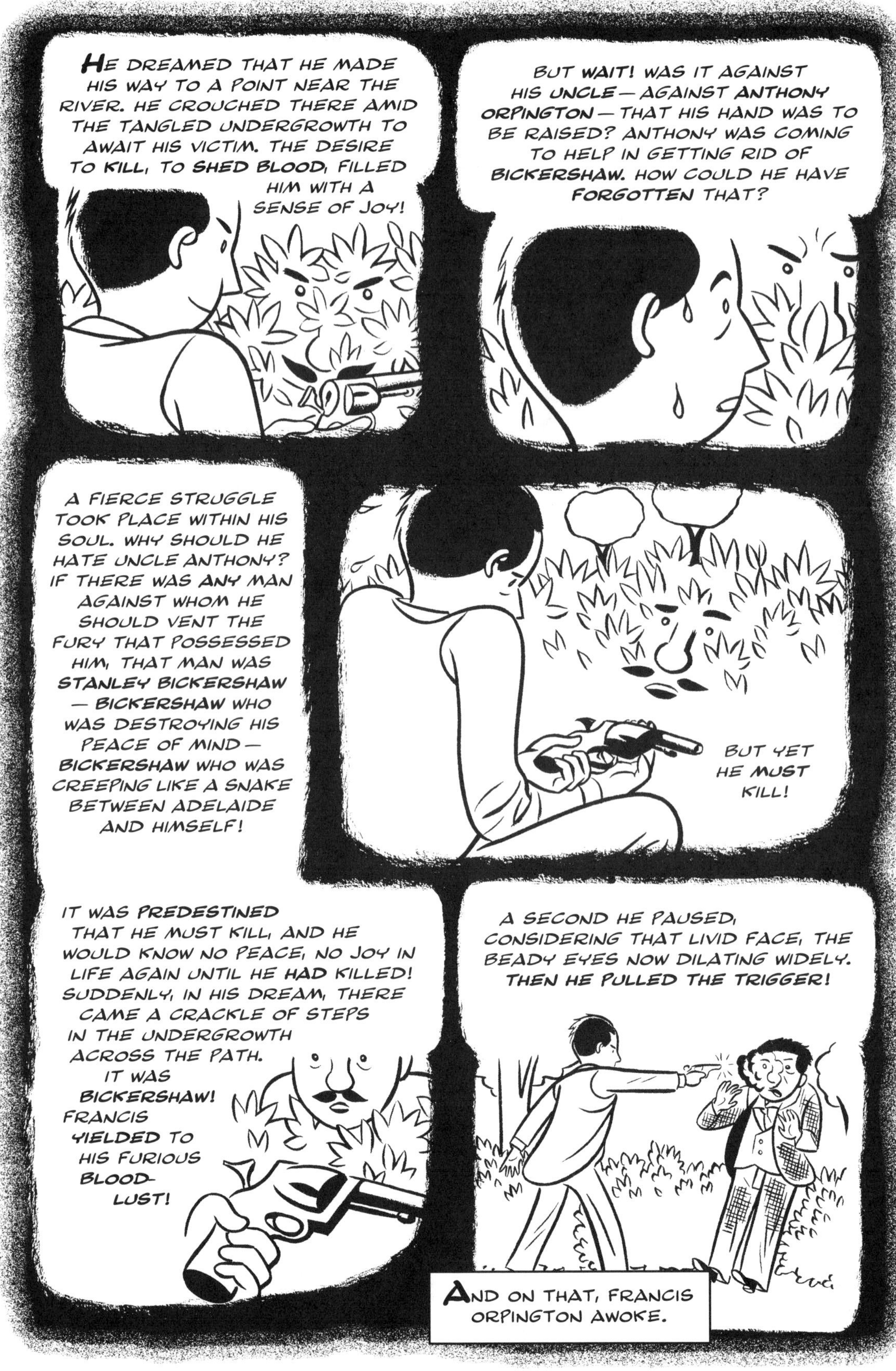
HE DREAMED THAT HE MADE HIS WAY TO A POINT NEAR THE RIVER. HE CROUCHED THERE AMID THE TANGLED UNDERGROWTH TO AWAIT HIS VICTIM. THE DESIRE TO KILL, TO SHED BLOOD, FILLED HIM WITH A SENSE OF JOY!
BUT WAIT! WAS IT AGAINST HIS UNCLE — AGAINST ANTHONY ORPINGTON — THAT HIS HAND WAS TO BE RAISED? ANTHONY WAS COMING TO HELP IN GETTING RID OF BICKERSHAW. HOW COULD HE HAVE FORGOTTEN THAT?
A FIERCE STRUGGLE TOOK PLACE WITHIN HIS SOUL. WHY SHOULD HE HATE UNCLE ANTHONY? IF THERE WAS ANY MAN AGAINST WHOM HE SHOULD VENT THE FURY THAT POSSESSED HIM, THAT MAN WAS STANLEY BICKERSHAW — BICKERSHAW WHO WAS DESTROYING HIS PEACE OF MIND — BICKERSHAW WHO WAS CREEPING LIKE A SNAKE BETWEEN ADELAIDE AND HIMSELF!
BUT YET HE MUST KILL!
IT WAS PREDESTINED THAT HE MUST KILL, AND HE WOULD KNOW NO PEACE, NO JOY IN LIFE AGAIN UNTIL HE HAD KILLED! SUDDENLY, IN HIS DREAM, THERE CAME A CRACKLE OF STEPS IN THE UNDERGROWTH ACROSS THE PATH.
IT WAS BICKERSHAW! FRANCIS YIELDED TO HIS FURIOUS BLOOD-LUST!
A SECOND HE PAUSED, CONSIDERING THAT LIVID FACE, THE BEADY EYES NOW DILATING WIDELY. THEN HE PULLED THE TRIGGER!
AND ON THAT, FRANCIS ORPINGTON AWOKE.

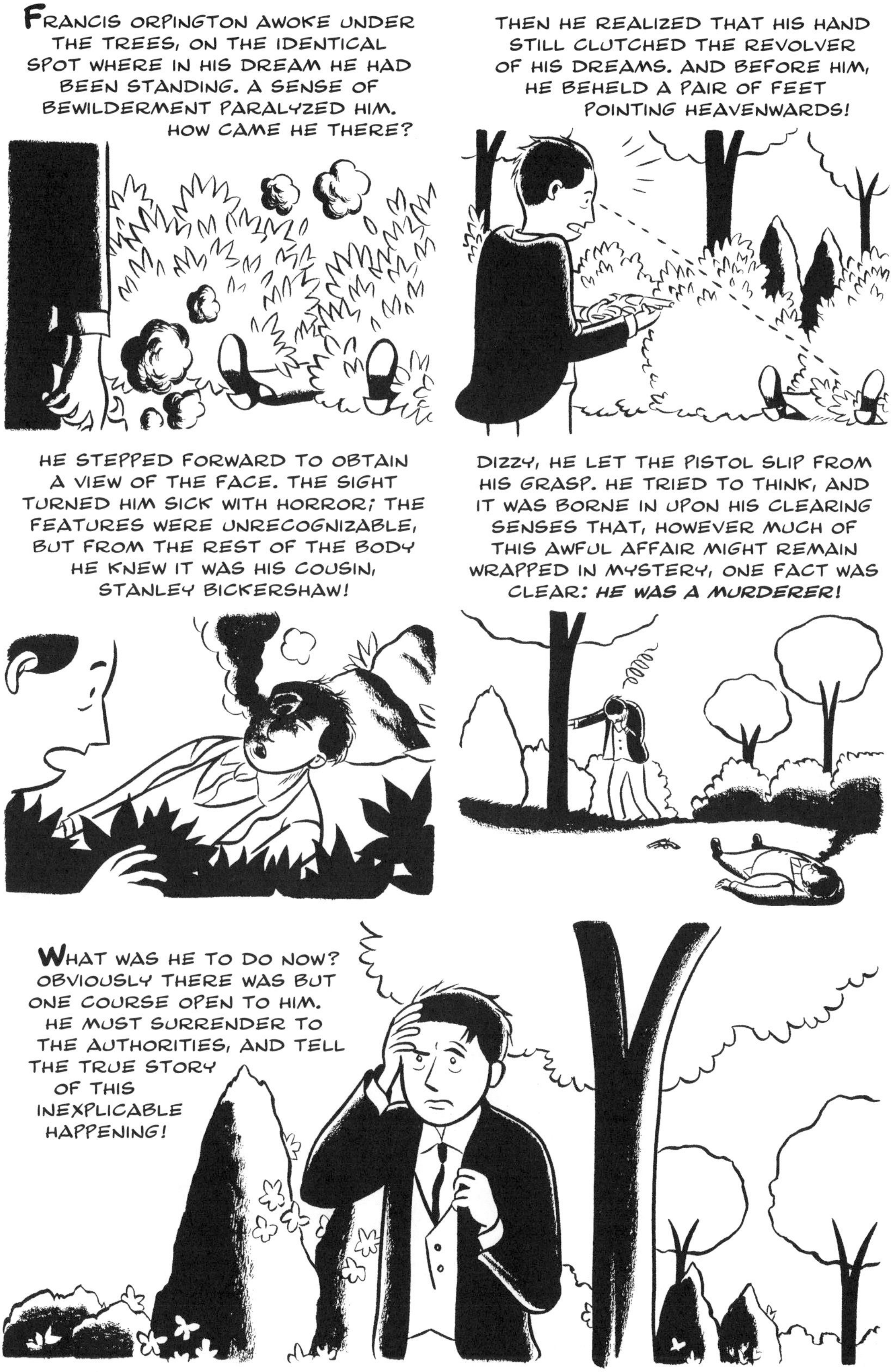
FRANCIS ORPINGTON AWOKE UNDER THE TREES, ON THE IDENTICAL SPOT WHERE IN HIS DREAM HE HAD BEEN STANDING. A SENSE OF BEWILDERMENT PARALYZED HIM. HOW CAME HE THERE?
THEN HE REALIZED THAT HIS HAND STILL CLUTCHED THE REVOLVER OF HIS DREAMS. AND BEFORE HIM, HE BEHELD A PAIR OF FEET POINTING HEAVENWARDS!
HE STEPPED FORWARD TO OBTAIN A VIEW OF THE FACE. THE SIGHT TURNED HIM SICK WITH HORROR; THE FEATURES WERE UNRECOGNIZABLE, BUT FROM THE REST OF THE BODY HE KNEW IT WAS HIS COUSIN, STANLEY BICKERSHAW!
DIZZY, HE LET THE PISTOL SLIP FROM HIS GRASP. HE TRIED TO THINK, AND IT WAS BORNE IN UPON HIS CLEARING SENSES THAT, HOWEVER MUCH OF THIS AWFUL AFFAIR MIGHT REMAIN WRAPPED IN MYSTERY, ONE FACT WAS CLEAR: *HE WAS A MURDERER!*
WHAT WAS HE TO DO NOW? OBVIOUSLY THERE WAS BUT ONE COURSE OPEN TO HIM. HE MUST SURRENDER TO THE AUTHORITIES, AND TELL THE TRUE STORY OF THIS INEXPLICABLE HAPPENING!

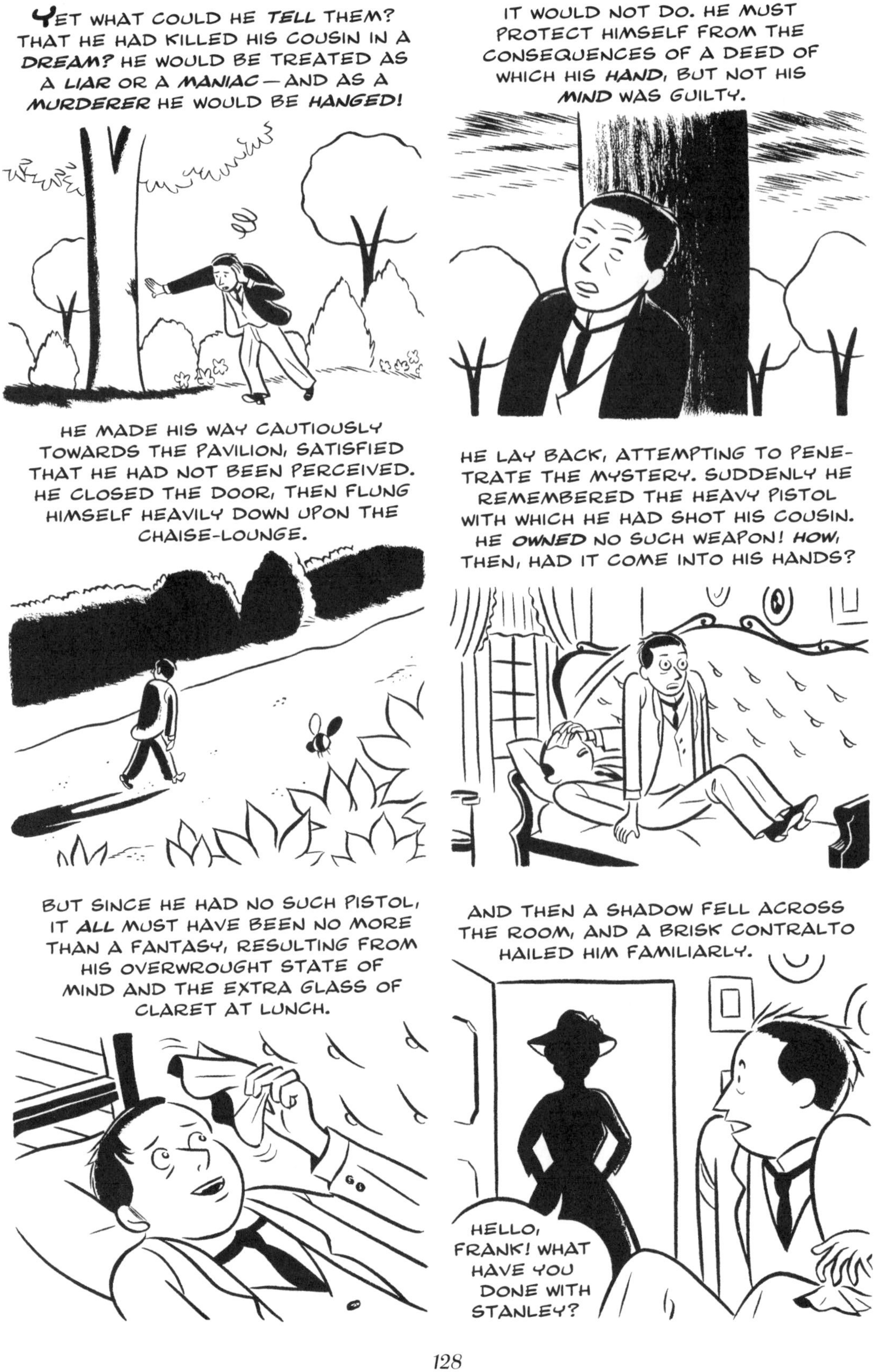
YET WHAT COULD HE TELL THEM? THAT HE HAD KILLED HIS COUSIN IN A DREAM? HE WOULD BE TREATED AS A LIAR OR A MANIAC—AND AS A MURDERER HE WOULD BE HANGED!
IT WOULD NOT DO. HE MUST PROTECT HIMSELF FROM THE CONSEQUENCES OF A DEED OF WHICH HIS HAND, BUT NOT HIS MIND WAS GUILTY.
HE MADE HIS WAY CAUTIOUSLY TOWARDS THE PAVILION, SATISFIED THAT HE HAD NOT BEEN PERCEIVED. HE CLOSED THE DOOR, THEN FLUNG HIMSELF HEAVILY DOWN UPON THE CHAISE-LOUNGE.
HE LAY BACK, ATTEMPTING TO PENETRATE THE MYSTERY. SUDDENLY HE REMEMBERED THE HEAVY PISTOL WITH WHICH HE HAD SHOT HIS COUSIN. HE OWNED NO SUCH WEAPON! HOW, THEN, HAD IT COME INTO HIS HANDS?
BUT SINCE HE HAD NO SUCH PISTOL, IT ALL MUST HAVE BEEN NO MORE THAN A FANTASY, RESULTING FROM HIS OVERWROUGHT STATE OF MIND AND THE EXTRA GLASS OF CLARET AT LUNCH.
AND THEN A SHADOW FELL ACROSS THE ROOM, AND A BRISK CONTRALTO HAILED HIM FAMILIARLY.
HELLO, FRANK! WHAT HAVE YOU DONE WITH STANLEY?

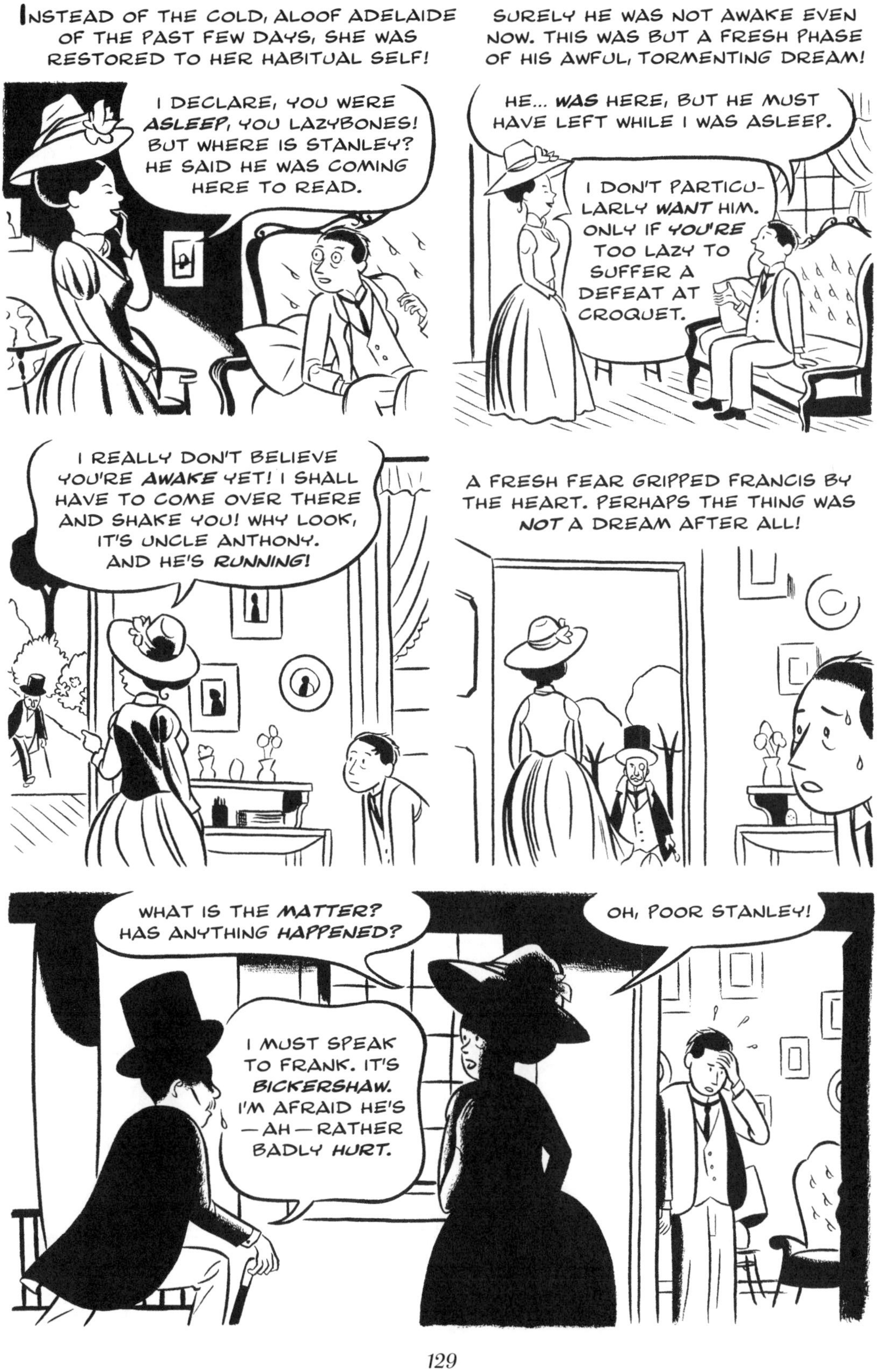
INSTEAD OF THE COLD, ALOOF ADELAIDE OF THE PAST FEW DAYS, SHE WAS RESTORED TO HER HABITUAL SELF!
I DECLARE, YOU WERE ASLEEP, YOU LAZYBONES! BUT WHERE IS STANLEY? HE SAID HE WAS COMING HERE TO READ.
SURELY HE WAS NOT AWAKE EVEN NOW. THIS WAS BUT A FRESH PHASE OF HIS AWFUL, TORMENTING DREAM!
HE... WAS HERE, BUT HE MUST HAVE LEFT WHILE I WAS ASLEEP.
I DON'T PARTICULARLY WANT HIM. ONLY IF YOU'RE TOO LAZY TO SUFFER A DEFEAT AT CROQUET.
I REALLY DON'T BELIEVE YOU'RE AWAKE YET! I SHALL HAVE TO COME OVER THERE AND SHAKE YOU! WHY LOOK, IT'S UNCLE ANTHONY. AND HE'S RUNNING!
A FRESH FEAR GRIPPED FRANCIS BY THE HEART. PERHAPS THE THING WAS NOT A DREAM AFTER ALL!
WHAT IS THE MATTER? HAS ANYTHING HAPPENED?
I MUST SPEAK TO FRANK. IT'S BICKERSHAW. I'M AFRAID HE'S —AH— RATHER BADLY HURT.
OH, POOR STANLEY!

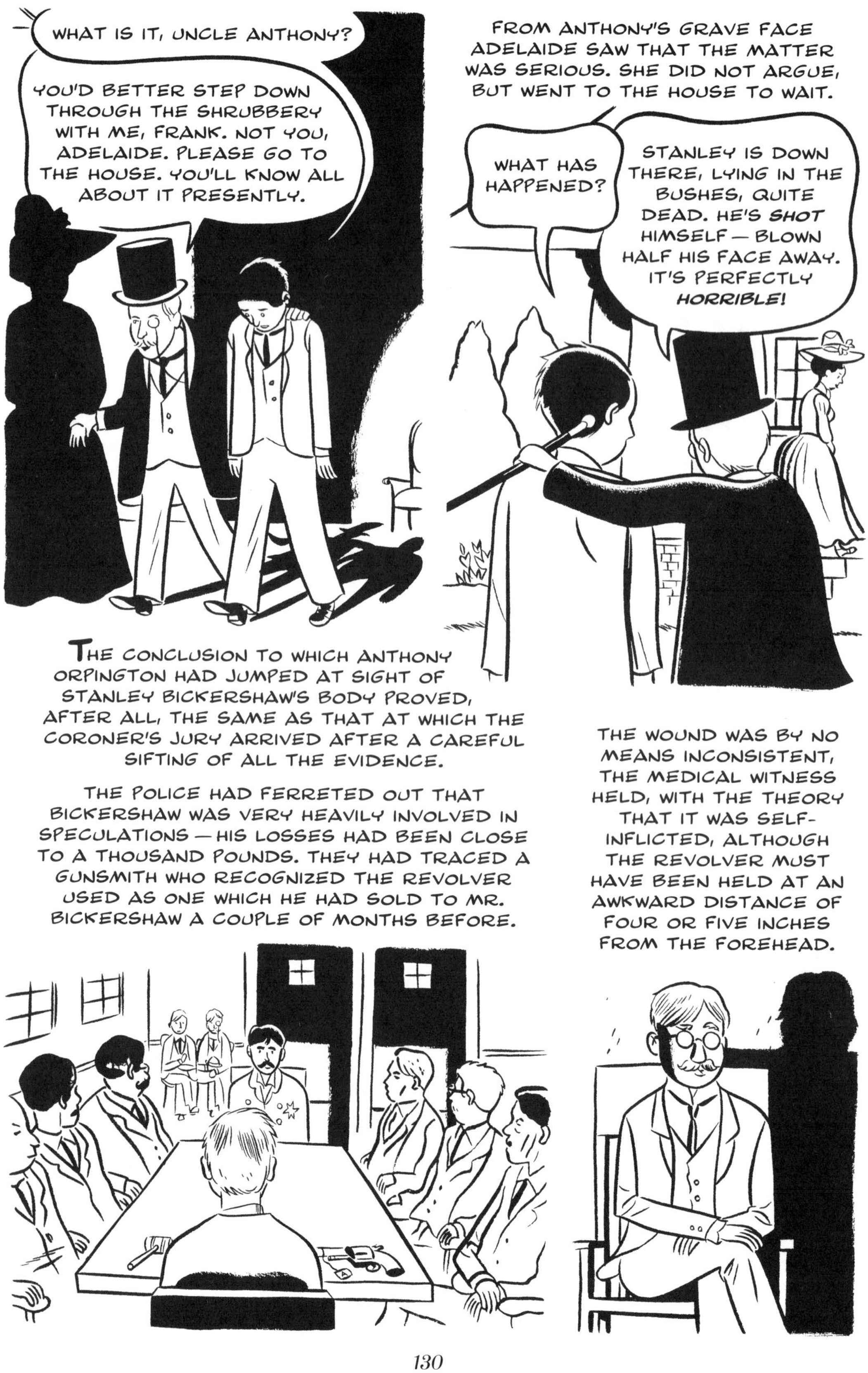
WHAT IS IT, UNCLE ANTHONY?
YOU'D BETTER STEP DOWN THROUGH THE SHRUBBERY WITH ME, FRANK. NOT YOU, ADELAIDE. PLEASE GO TO THE HOUSE. YOU'LL KNOW ALL ABOUT IT PRESENTLY.
FROM ANTHONY'S GRAVE FACE ADELAIDE SAW THAT THE MATTER WAS SERIOUS. SHE DID NOT ARGUE, BUT WENT TO THE HOUSE TO WAIT.
WHAT HAS HAPPENED?
STANLEY IS DOWN THERE, LYING IN THE BUSHES, QUITE DEAD. HE'S *SHOT* HIMSELF — BLOWN HALF HIS FACE AWAY. IT'S PERFECTLY *HORRIBLE!*
THE CONCLUSION TO WHICH ANTHONY ORPINGTON HAD JUMPED AT SIGHT OF STANLEY BICKERSHAW'S BODY PROVED, AFTER ALL, THE SAME AS THAT AT WHICH THE CORONER'S JURY ARRIVED AFTER A CAREFUL SIFTING OF ALL THE EVIDENCE.
THE POLICE HAD FERRETED OUT THAT BICKERSHAW WAS VERY HEAVILY INVOLVED IN SPECULATIONS — HIS LOSSES HAD BEEN CLOSE TO A THOUSAND POUNDS. THEY HAD TRACED A GUNSMITH WHO RECOGNIZED THE REVOLVER USED AS ONE WHICH HE HAD SOLD TO MR. BICKERSHAW A COUPLE OF MONTHS BEFORE.
THE WOUND WAS BY NO MEANS INCONSISTENT, THE MEDICAL WITNESS HELD, WITH THE THEORY THAT IT WAS SELF-INFLICTED, ALTHOUGH THE REVOLVER MUST HAVE BEEN HELD AT AN AWKWARD DISTANCE OF FOUR OR FIVE INCHES FROM THE FOREHEAD.

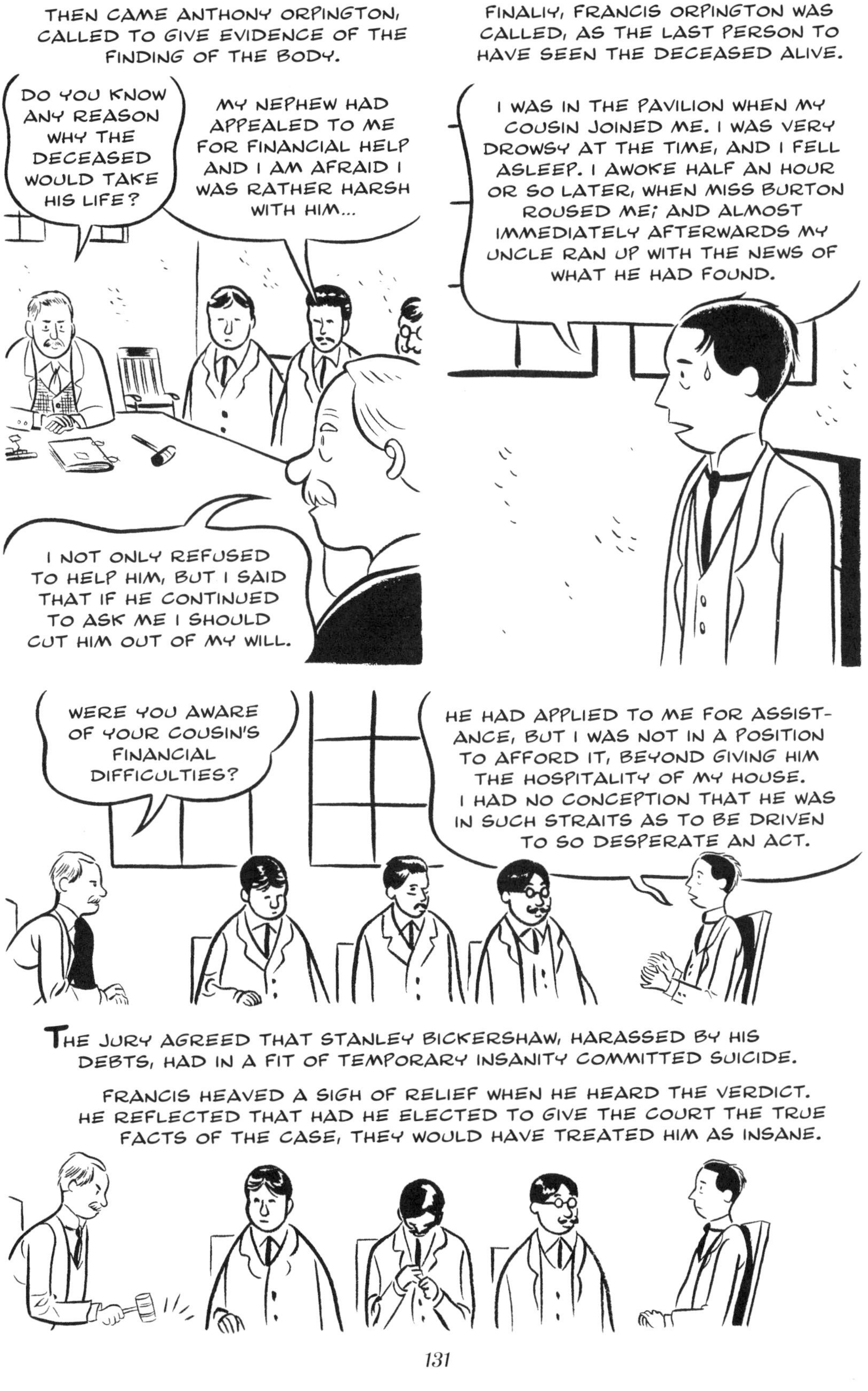
THEN CAME ANTHONY ORPINGTON, CALLED TO GIVE EVIDENCE OF THE FINDING OF THE BODY.
DO YOU KNOW ANY REASON WHY THE DECEASED WOULD TAKE HIS LIFE?
MY NEPHEW HAD APPEALED TO ME FOR FINANCIAL HELP AND I AM AFRAID I WAS RATHER HARSH WITH HIM...
I NOT ONLY REFUSED TO HELP HIM, BUT I SAID THAT IF HE CONTINUED TO ASK ME I SHOULD CUT HIM OUT OF MY WILL.
FINALLY, FRANCIS ORPINGTON WAS CALLED, AS THE LAST PERSON TO HAVE SEEN THE DECEASED ALIVE.
I WAS IN THE PAVILION WHEN MY COUSIN JOINED ME. I WAS VERY DROWSY AT THE TIME, AND I FELL ASLEEP. I AWOKE HALF AN HOUR OR SO LATER, WHEN MISS BURTON ROUSED ME; AND ALMOST IMMEDIATELY AFTERWARDS MY UNCLE RAN UP WITH THE NEWS OF WHAT HE HAD FOUND.
WERE YOU AWARE OF YOUR COUSIN'S FINANCIAL DIFFICULTIES?
HE HAD APPLIED TO ME FOR ASSISTANCE, BUT I WAS NOT IN A POSITION TO AFFORD IT, BEYOND GIVING HIM THE HOSPITALITY OF MY HOUSE. I HAD NO CONCEPTION THAT HE WAS IN SUCH STRAITS AS TO BE DRIVEN TO SO DESPERATE AN ACT.
THE JURY AGREED THAT STANLEY BICKERSHAW, HARASSED BY HIS DEBTS, HAD IN A FIT OF TEMPORARY INSANITY COMMITTED SUICIDE.
FRANCIS HEAVED A SIGH OF RELIEF WHEN HE HEARD THE VERDICT. HE REFLECTED THAT HAD HE ELECTED TO GIVE THE COURT THE TRUE FACTS OF THE CASE, THEY WOULD HAVE TREATED HIM AS INSANE.

INDEED, THERE WERE MOMENTS IN THE DAYS THAT FOLLOWED WHEN HE DID NOT KNOW WHETHER HE SHOULD NOT SO REGARD ***HIMSELF.*** HE EVEN ASKED HIMSELF WHETHER HE HAD NOT BEEN THE SPORT OF SOME FREAK OF ***SECOND SIGHT***, AND HAD ONLY ***IMAGINED*** HIMSELF A PARTICIPATOR.

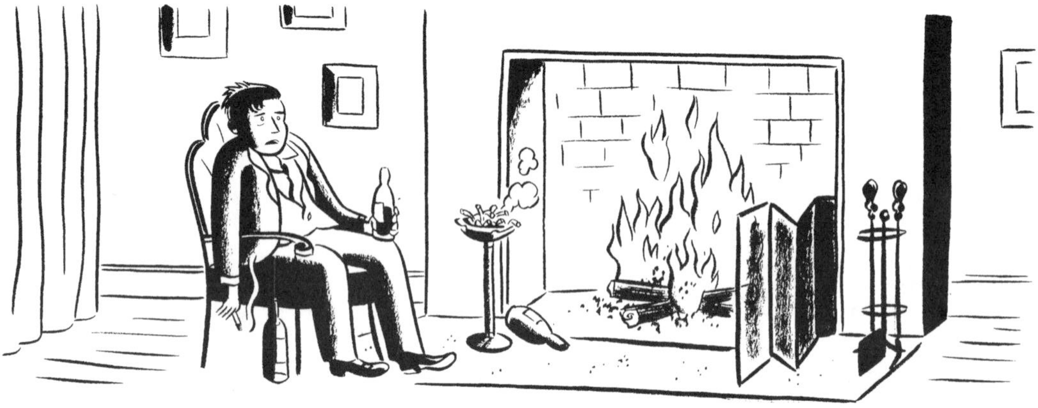

THE THING PREYED UPON HIS MIND, AND DISTURBED HIS NIGHTS WITH HORRID VISIONS OF THE MUTILATED FACE OF BICKERSHAW.

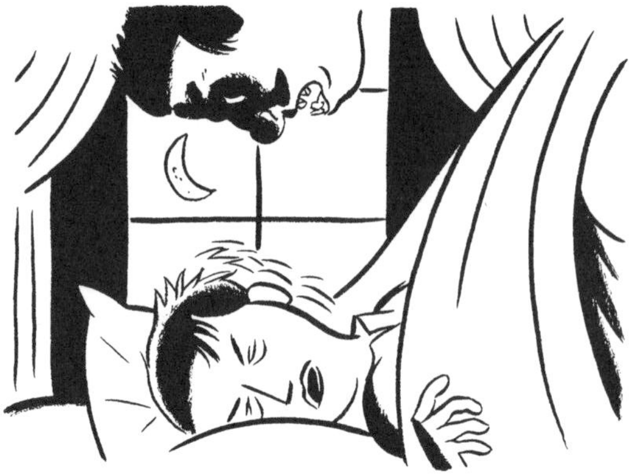

HE GREW NERVOUS AND IRRITABLE, AND HE WOULD SIT FOR HOURS BROODING. ***HAD*** HE OR ***HAD HE NOT*** KILLED BICKERSHAW? HE NO LONGER KNEW.

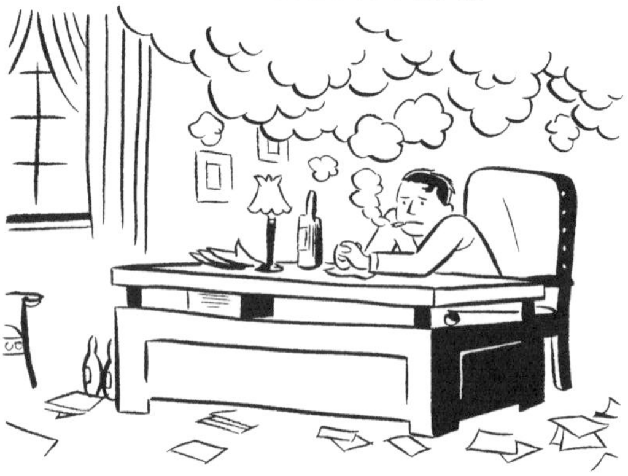

ADELAIDE'S CONCERN FOR HIM GREW WITH HIS DISTEMPER. AND THEN ONE EVENING, A FORTNIGHT AFTER THE INQUEST, SHE FORCED MATTERS TO A CLIMAX.

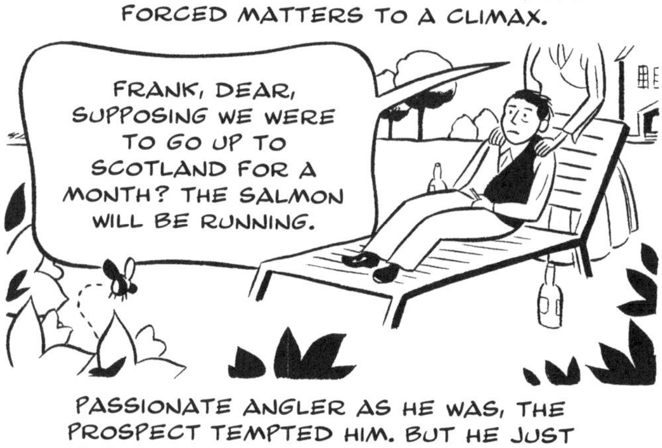
FRANK, DEAR, SUPPOSING WE WERE TO GO UP TO SCOTLAND FOR A MONTH? THE SALMON WILL BE RUNNING.

PASSIONATE ANGLER AS HE WAS, THE PROSPECT TEMPTED HIM. BUT HE JUST SIGHED HEAVILY, WITHOUT ANSWERING.

ADELAIDE LOVED FRANCIS ORPINGTON DEEPLY, AND SHE HAD PRAYED THAT HE MIGHT FIND THE COURAGE TO ASK HER TO BECOME HIS WIFE.

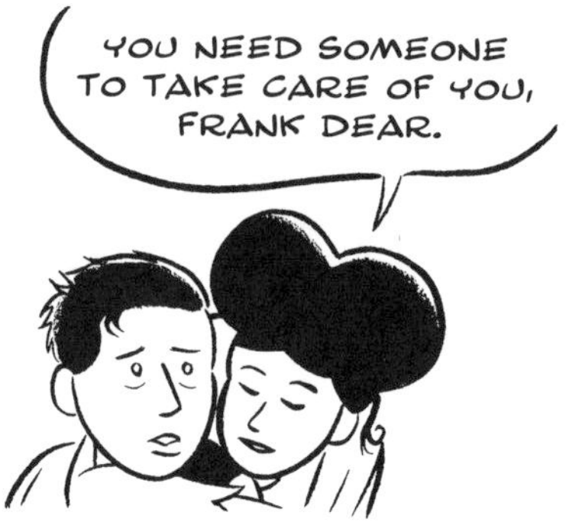
YOU NEED SOMEONE TO TAKE CARE OF YOU, FRANK DEAR.

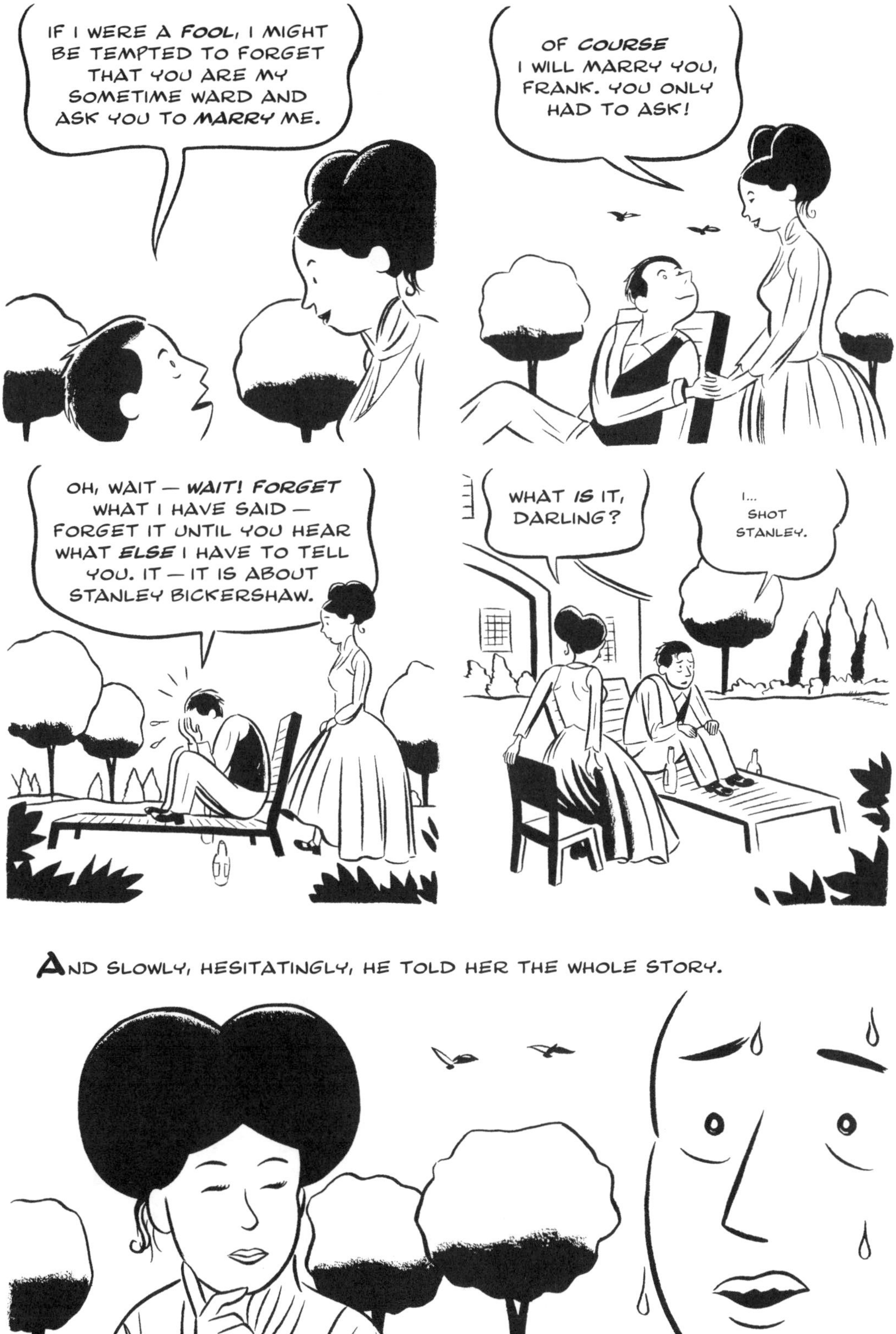
IF I WERE A FOOL, I MIGHT BE TEMPTED TO FORGET THAT YOU ARE MY SOMETIME WARD AND ASK YOU TO MARRY ME.
OF COURSE I WILL MARRY YOU, FRANK. YOU ONLY HAD TO ASK!
OH, WAIT — WAIT! FORGET WHAT I HAVE SAID — FORGET IT UNTIL YOU HEAR WHAT ELSE I HAVE TO TELL YOU. IT — IT IS ABOUT STANLEY BICKERSHAW.
WHAT IS IT, DARLING?
I... SHOT STANLEY.
AND SLOWLY, HESITATINGLY, HE TOLD HER THE WHOLE STORY.

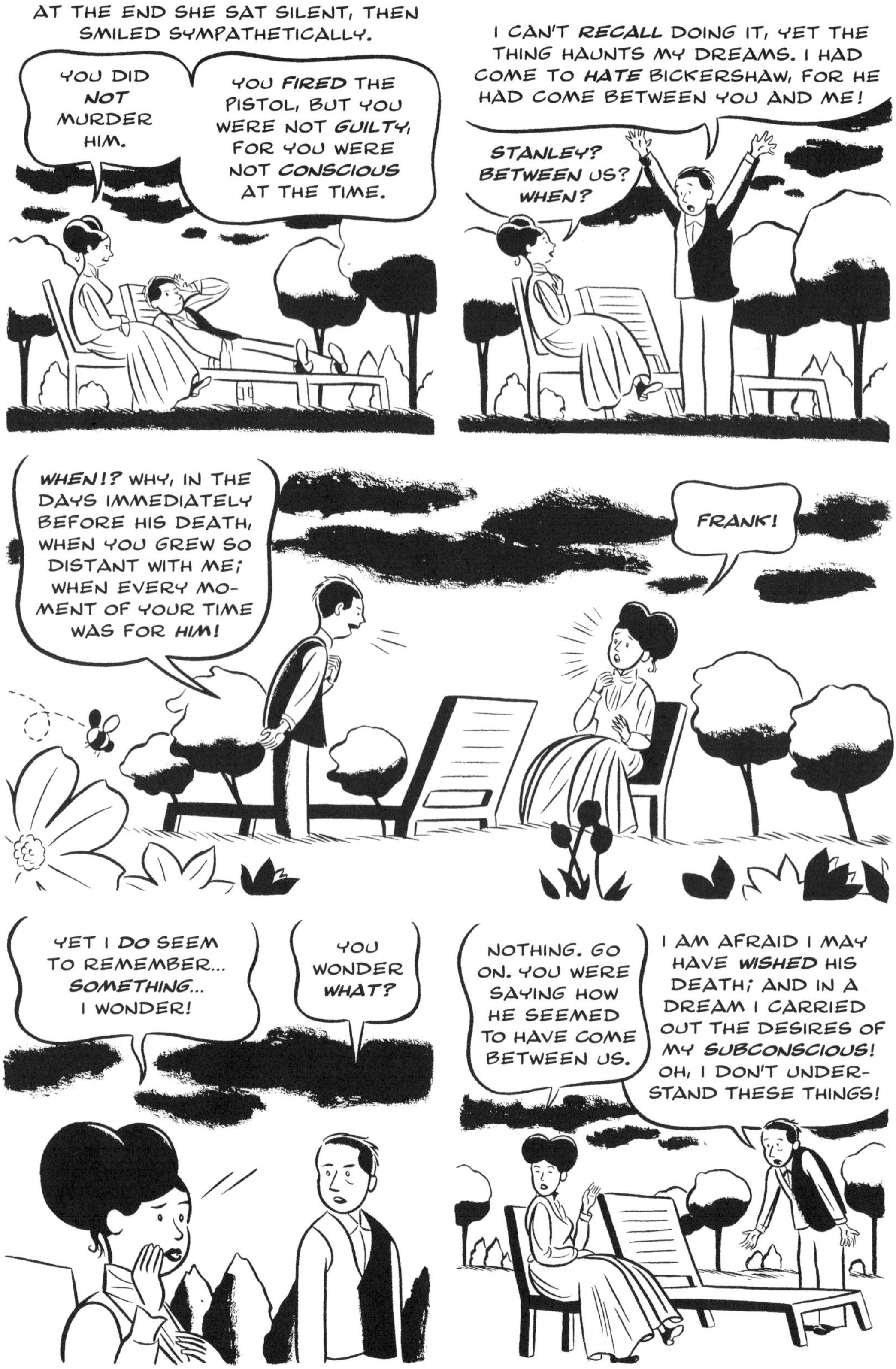
AT THE END SHE SAT SILENT, THEN SMILED SYMPATHETICALLY.
YOU DID NOT MURDER HIM.
YOU FIRED THE PISTOL, BUT YOU WERE NOT GUILTY, FOR YOU WERE NOT CONSCIOUS AT THE TIME.
I CAN'T RECALL DOING IT, YET THE THING HAUNTS MY DREAMS. I HAD COME TO HATE BICKERSHAW, FOR HE HAD COME BETWEEN YOU AND ME!
STANLEY? BETWEEN US? WHEN?
WHEN!? WHY, IN THE DAYS IMMEDIATELY BEFORE HIS DEATH, WHEN YOU GREW SO DISTANT WITH ME; WHEN EVERY MOMENT OF YOUR TIME WAS FOR HIM!
FRANK!
YET I DO SEEM TO REMEMBER... SOMETHING... I WONDER!
YOU WONDER WHAT?
NOTHING. GO ON. YOU WERE SAYING HOW HE SEEMED TO HAVE COME BETWEEN US.
I AM AFRAID I MAY HAVE WISHED HIS DEATH; AND IN A DREAM I CARRIED OUT THE DESIRES OF MY SUBCONSCIOUS! OH, I DON'T UNDERSTAND THESE THINGS!

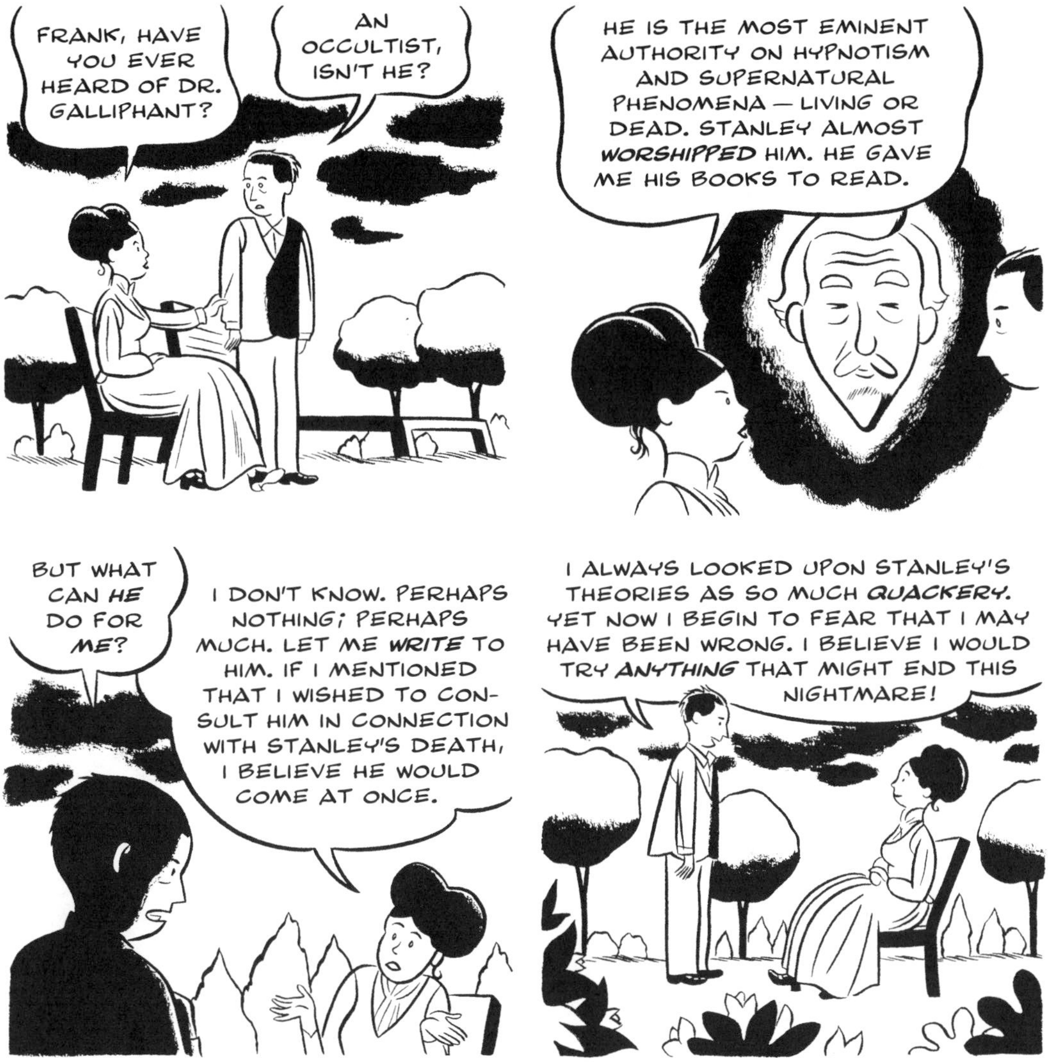
FRANK, HAVE YOU EVER HEARD OF DR. GALLIPHANT?
AN OCCULTIST, ISN'T HE?
HE IS THE MOST EMINENT AUTHORITY ON HYPNOTISM AND SUPERNATURAL PHENOMENA — LIVING OR DEAD. STANLEY ALMOST *WORSHIPPED* HIM. HE GAVE ME HIS BOOKS TO READ.
BUT WHAT CAN *HE* DO FOR *ME*?
I DON'T KNOW. PERHAPS NOTHING; PERHAPS MUCH. LET ME *WRITE* TO HIM. IF I MENTIONED THAT I WISHED TO CONSULT HIM IN CONNECTION WITH STANLEY'S DEATH, I BELIEVE HE WOULD COME AT ONCE.
I ALWAYS LOOKED UPON STANLEY'S THEORIES AS SO MUCH *QUACKERY*. YET NOW I BEGIN TO FEAR THAT I MAY HAVE BEEN WRONG. I BELIEVE I WOULD TRY *ANYTHING* THAT MIGHT END THIS NIGHTMARE!

FRANCIS GAVE WAY; AND HAVING DONE SO, HE BECAME INFECTED BY SOMETHING OF HER OWN FAITH IN THIS FAMOUS MAN. THEY WENT INDOORS, WHERE ADELAIDE WROTE HER LETTER.

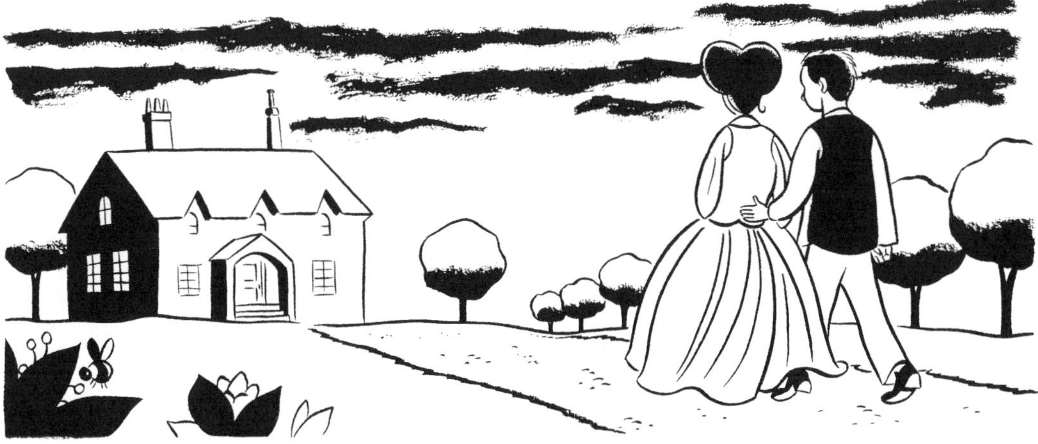

JUST AFTER LUNCH NEXT DAY, THE BUTLER PRESENTED A CARD ON WHICH FRANCIS READ THE NAME OF DR. EMERSON GALLIPHANT.

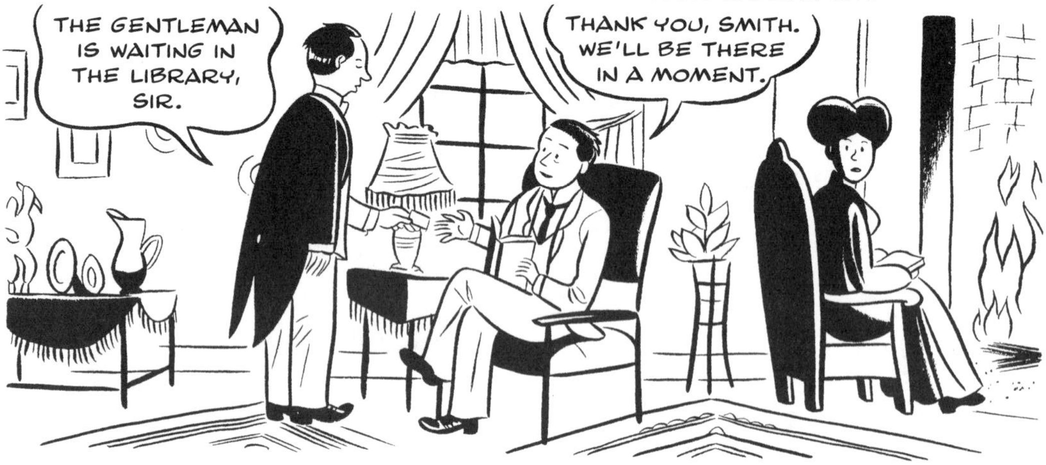
THE GENTLEMAN IS WAITING IN THE LIBRARY, SIR.
THANK YOU, SMITH. WE'LL BE THERE IN A MOMENT.

ORPINGTON WAS MORE THAN FAVORABLY IMPRESSED BY THE MAN WHO SMILED AS HE ASKED TO BE INFORMED IN WHAT HE COULD BE OF SERVICE.

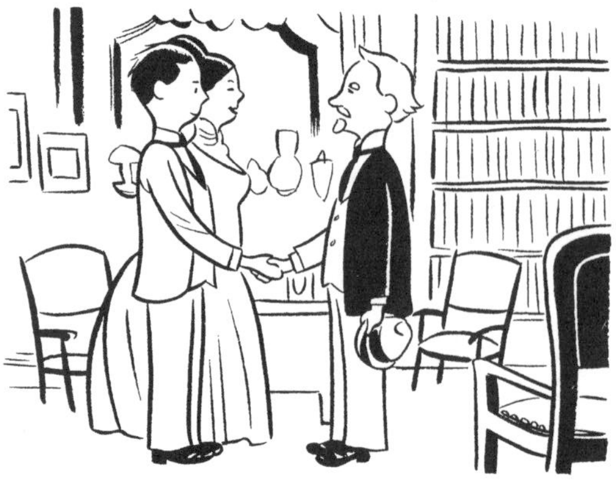

FRANCIS TOLD HIS STORY TO DR. GALLIPHANT, PRECISELY AS HE HAD TOLD IT THE PREVIOUS NIGHT TO ADELAIDE.

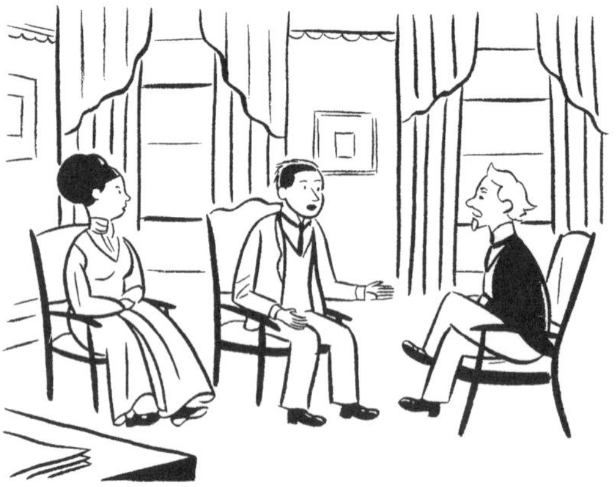

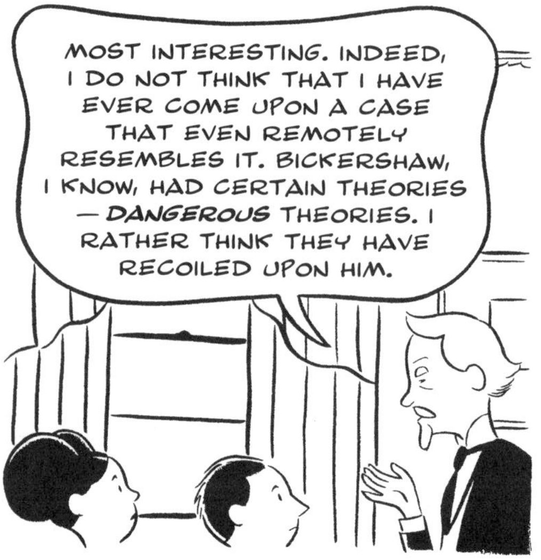
MOST INTERESTING. INDEED, I DO NOT THINK THAT I HAVE EVER COME UPON A CASE THAT EVEN REMOTELY RESEMBLES IT. BICKERSHAW, I KNOW, HAD CERTAIN THEORIES — *DANGEROUS* THEORIES. I RATHER THINK THEY HAVE RECOILED UPON HIM.

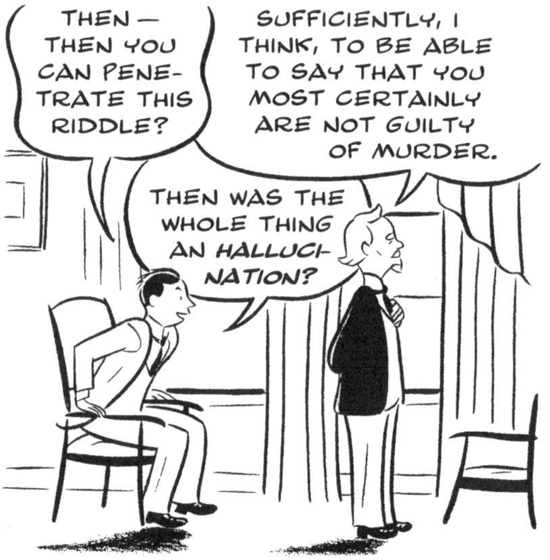
THEN — THEN YOU CAN PENETRATE THIS RIDDLE?
SUFFICIENTLY, I THINK, TO BE ABLE TO SAY THAT YOU MOST CERTAINLY ARE NOT GUILTY OF MURDER.
THEN WAS THE WHOLE THING AN *HALLUCINATION?*

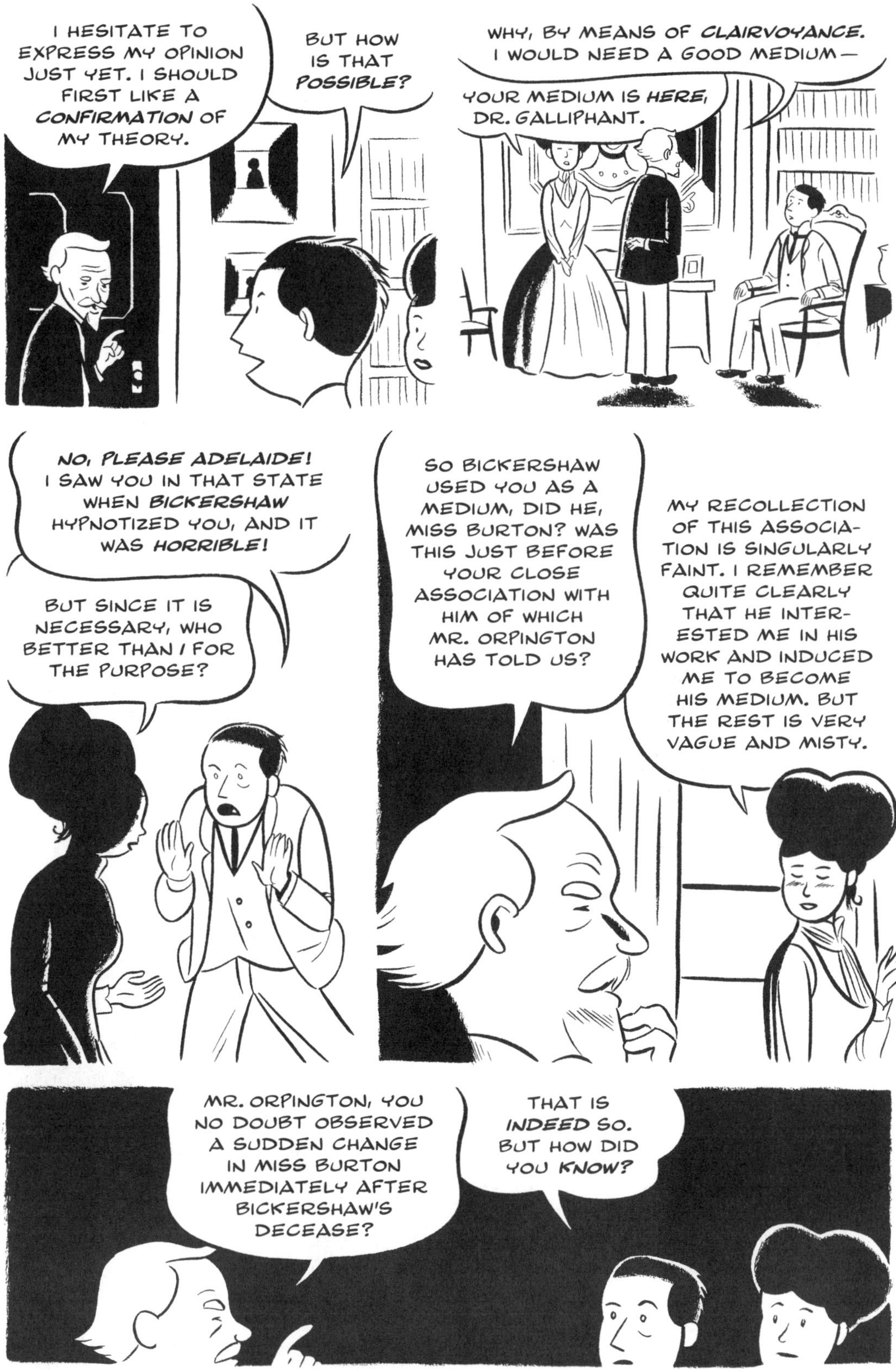
I HESITATE TO EXPRESS MY OPINION JUST YET. I SHOULD FIRST LIKE A CONFIRMATION OF MY THEORY.
BUT HOW IS THAT POSSIBLE?
WHY, BY MEANS OF CLAIRVOYANCE. I WOULD NEED A GOOD MEDIUM—
YOUR MEDIUM IS HERE, DR. GALLIPHANT.
NO, PLEASE ADELAIDE! I SAW YOU IN THAT STATE WHEN BICKERSHAW HYPNOTIZED YOU, AND IT WAS HORRIBLE!
BUT SINCE IT IS NECESSARY, WHO BETTER THAN I FOR THE PURPOSE?
SO BICKERSHAW USED YOU AS A MEDIUM, DID HE, MISS BURTON? WAS THIS JUST BEFORE YOUR CLOSE ASSOCIATION WITH HIM OF WHICH MR. ORPINGTON HAS TOLD US?
MY RECOLLECTION OF THIS ASSOCIATION IS SINGULARLY FAINT. I REMEMBER QUITE CLEARLY THAT HE INTERESTED ME IN HIS WORK AND INDUCED ME TO BECOME HIS MEDIUM. BUT THE REST IS VERY VAGUE AND MISTY.
MR. ORPINGTON, YOU NO DOUBT OBSERVED A SUDDEN CHANGE IN MISS BURTON IMMEDIATELY AFTER BICKERSHAW'S DECEASE?
THAT IS INDEED SO. BUT HOW DID YOU KNOW?

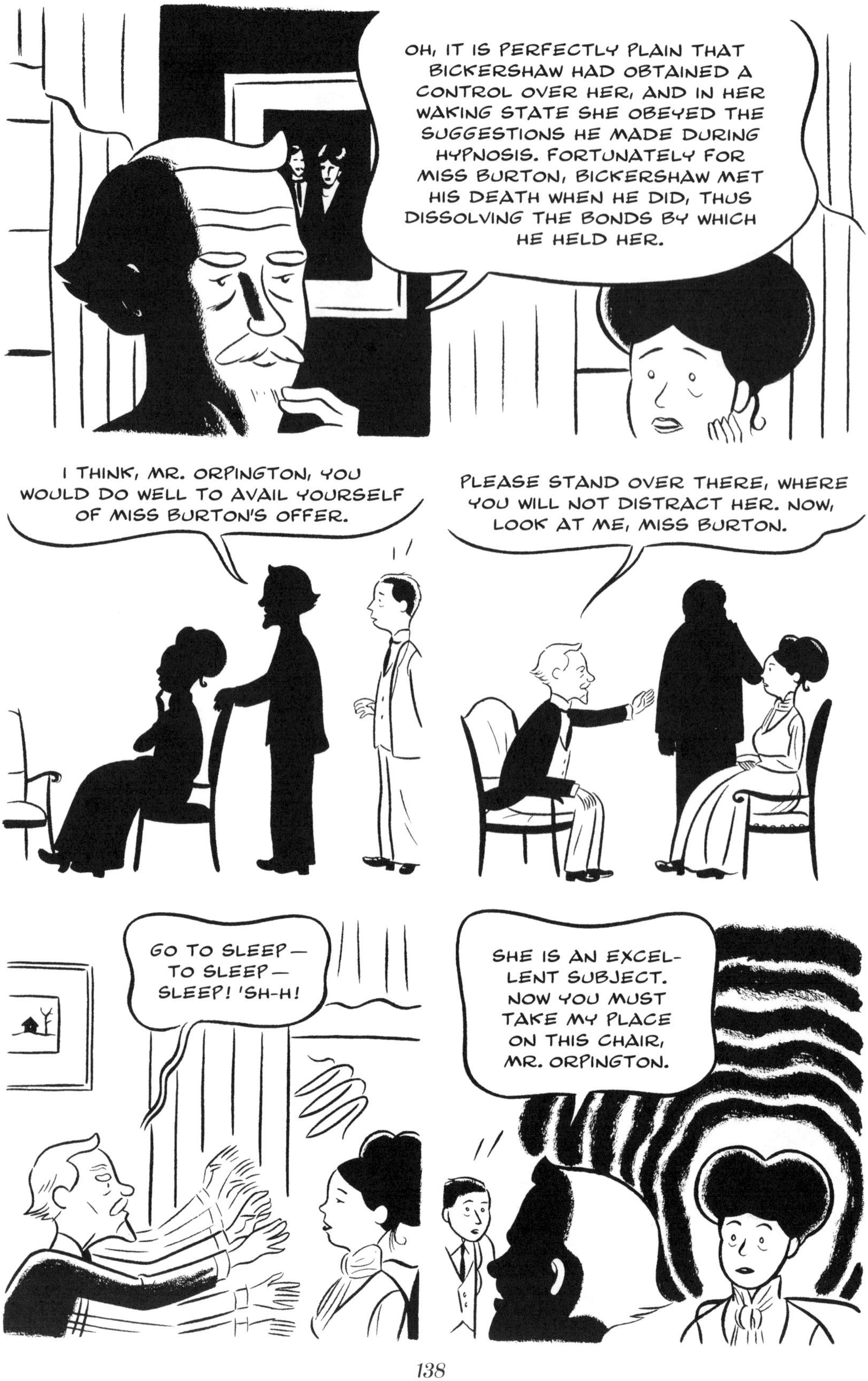
OH, IT IS PERFECTLY PLAIN THAT BICKERSHAW HAD OBTAINED A CONTROL OVER HER, AND IN HER WAKING STATE SHE OBEYED THE SUGGESTIONS HE MADE DURING HYPNOSIS. FORTUNATELY FOR MISS BURTON, BICKERSHAW MET HIS DEATH WHEN HE DID, THUS DISSOLVING THE BONDS BY WHICH HE HELD HER.
I THINK, MR. ORPINGTON, YOU WOULD DO WELL TO AVAIL YOURSELF OF MISS BURTON'S OFFER.
PLEASE STAND OVER THERE, WHERE YOU WILL NOT DISTRACT HER. NOW, LOOK AT ME, MISS BURTON.
GO TO SLEEP— TO SLEEP— SLEEP! 'SH-H!
SHE IS AN EXCEL-LENT SUBJECT. NOW YOU MUST TAKE MY PLACE ON THIS CHAIR, MR. ORPINGTON.

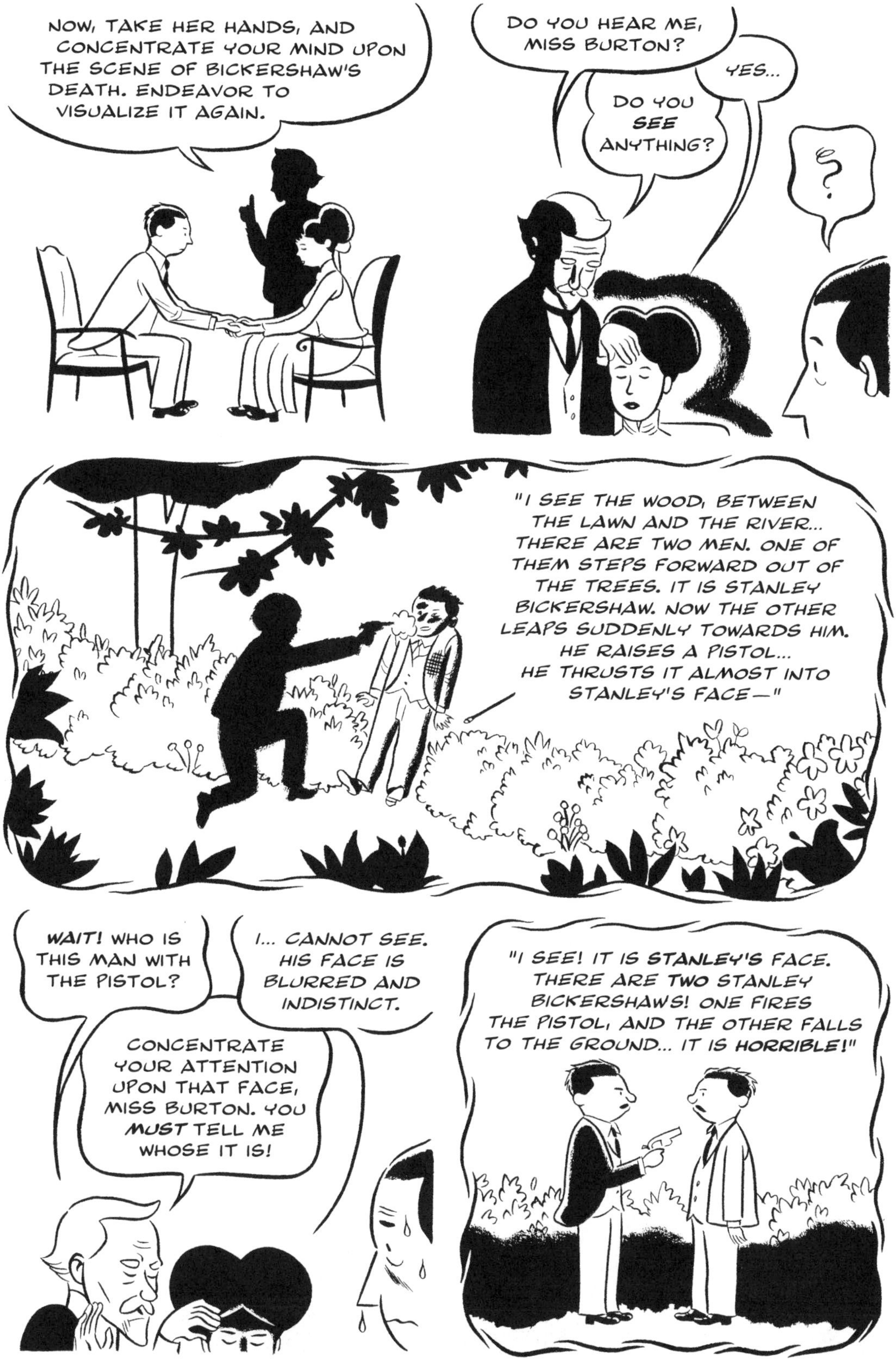
NOW, TAKE HER HANDS, AND CONCENTRATE YOUR MIND UPON THE SCENE OF BICKERSHAW'S DEATH. ENDEAVOR TO VISUALIZE IT AGAIN.
DO YOU HEAR ME, MISS BURTON?
YES...
DO YOU SEE ANYTHING?
?
"I SEE THE WOOD, BETWEEN THE LAWN AND THE RIVER... THERE ARE TWO MEN. ONE OF THEM STEPS FORWARD OUT OF THE TREES. IT IS STANLEY BICKERSHAW. NOW THE OTHER LEAPS SUDDENLY TOWARDS HIM. HE RAISES A PISTOL... HE THRUSTS IT ALMOST INTO STANLEY'S FACE—"
WAIT! WHO IS THIS MAN WITH THE PISTOL?
I... CANNOT SEE. HIS FACE IS BLURRED AND INDISTINCT.
CONCENTRATE YOUR ATTENTION UPON THAT FACE, MISS BURTON. YOU MUST TELL ME WHOSE IT IS!
"I SEE! IT IS STANLEY'S FACE. THERE ARE TWO STANLEY BICKERSHAWS! ONE FIRES THE PISTOL, AND THE OTHER FALLS TO THE GROUND... IT IS HORRIBLE!"

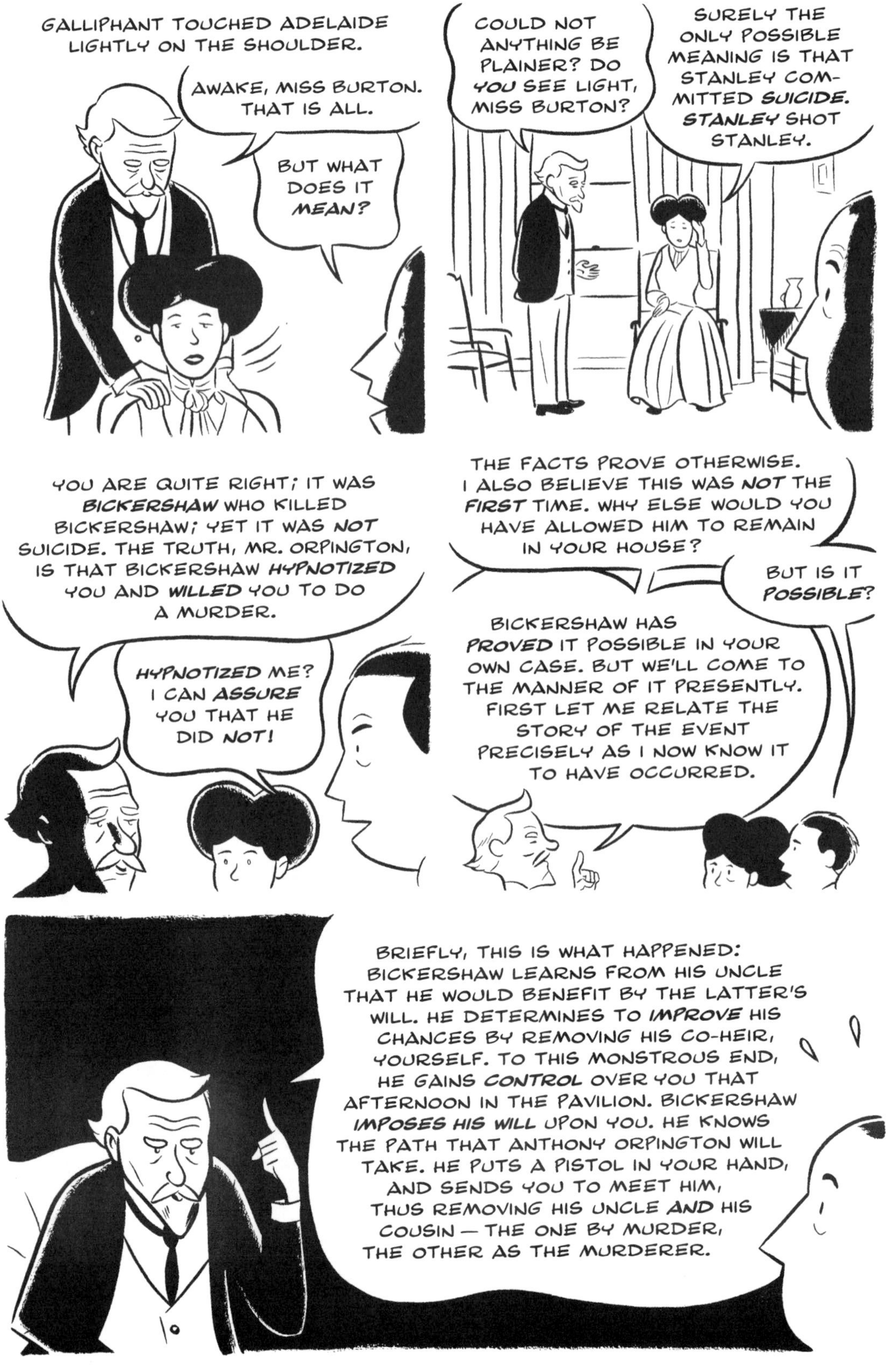
GALLIPHANT TOUCHED ADELAIDE LIGHTLY ON THE SHOULDER.
AWAKE, MISS BURTON. THAT IS ALL.
BUT WHAT DOES IT *MEAN?*
COULD NOT ANYTHING BE PLAINER? DO *YOU* SEE LIGHT, MISS BURTON?
SURELY THE ONLY POSSIBLE MEANING IS THAT STANLEY COM-MITTED *SUICIDE. STANLEY* SHOT STANLEY.
YOU ARE QUITE RIGHT; IT WAS *BICKERSHAW* WHO KILLED BICKERSHAW; YET IT WAS *NOT* SUICIDE. THE TRUTH, MR. ORPINGTON, IS THAT BICKERSHAW *HYPNOTIZED* YOU AND *WILLED* YOU TO DO A MURDER.
HYPNOTIZED ME? I CAN *ASSURE* YOU THAT HE DID *NOT!*
THE FACTS PROVE OTHERWISE. I ALSO BELIEVE THIS WAS *NOT* THE *FIRST* TIME. WHY ELSE WOULD YOU HAVE ALLOWED HIM TO REMAIN IN YOUR HOUSE?
BUT IS IT *POSSIBLE?*
BICKERSHAW HAS *PROVED* IT POSSIBLE IN YOUR OWN CASE. BUT WE'LL COME TO THE MANNER OF IT PRESENTLY. FIRST LET ME RELATE THE STORY OF THE EVENT PRECISELY AS I NOW KNOW IT TO HAVE OCCURRED.
BRIEFLY, THIS IS WHAT HAPPENED: BICKERSHAW LEARNS FROM HIS UNCLE THAT HE WOULD BENEFIT BY THE LATTER'S WILL. HE DETERMINES TO *IMPROVE* HIS CHANCES BY REMOVING HIS CO-HEIR, YOURSELF. TO THIS MONSTROUS END, HE GAINS *CONTROL* OVER YOU THAT AFTERNOON IN THE PAVILION. BICKERSHAW *IMPOSES HIS WILL* UPON YOU. HE KNOWS THE PATH THAT ANTHONY ORPINGTON WILL TAKE. HE PUTS A PISTOL IN YOUR HAND, AND SENDS YOU TO MEET HIM, THUS REMOVING HIS UNCLE *AND* HIS COUSIN — THE ONE BY MURDER, THE OTHER AS THE MURDERER.

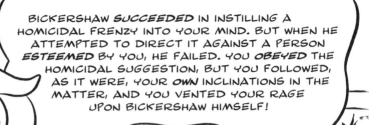

BICKERSHAW *SUCCEEDED* IN INSTILLING A HOMICIDAL FRENZY INTO YOUR MIND. BUT WHEN HE ATTEMPTED TO DIRECT IT AGAINST A PERSON *ESTEEMED* BY YOU, HE FAILED. YOU *OBEYED* THE HOMICIDAL SUGGESTION, BUT YOU FOLLOWED, AS IT WERE, YOUR *OWN* INCLINATIONS IN THE MATTER, AND YOU VENTED YOUR RAGE UPON BICKERSHAW HIMSELF!

BUT WHY DID ADELAIDE SEE *BICKERSHAW*, WHEN THE SHOOTER WAS I?

IT WAS *NOT* YOU. YOU MUST REMEMBER THAT A MEDIUM DOES NOT SEE THINGS WITH PHYSICAL EYES. THE *WILL* AT THE BACK OF YOUR DEED WAS BICKERSHAW'S; THEREFORE IT WAS *BICKERSHAW* THAT MISS BURTON SAW COMMIT THE CRIME.

I DON'T KNOW *HOW* TO THANK YOU! YOU HAVE SHOWN ME THAT THE FINDING OF THE JURY WAS, AFTER ALL, SUBSTANTIALLY CORRECT.

IT HAS BEEN PROFOUNDLY INTERESTING. AND I NEED HARDLY SAY I SHALL OBSERVE THE SECRECY OF THE CONFESSIONAL.

WHEN THE EMINENT OCCULTIST HAD DEPARTED, ADELAIDE SMILED AND ATTEMPTED LIGHTNESS.

WELL? IS IT TO BE SCOTLAND AND THE SALMON?

IF YOU'LL MARRY ME, ADELAIDE, I CARE VERY LITTLE WHERE THE HONEYMOON IS SPENT!

141

RAFAEL SABATINI

Dubbed "the Prince of Storytellers," "the heir to Dumas" and "the Last of the Great Swashbucklers," Rafael Sabatini was, in the 1920s and '30s, one of the most popular authors in the world. Born in Italy in 1875, the son of professional opera singers, Sabatini attended schools in Portugal and Switzerland, and at the age of seventeen moved to England, the birthplace of his mother. His multilingual background landed him a job as translator for an import firm, but his real interest was in writing. Sabatini was fluent in Italian, French, German, Spanish and Portugese, but chose to write stories in English for the British magazines, as he believed "all the best stories are written in English." He wrote contemporary short stories, plays, and nonfiction histories, but his greatest success came with his historical adventures, including *Scaramouche*, *The Sea Hawk* and *Captain Blood*. Captain Blood appears in three books by Sabatini. *Captain Blood: His Odyssey* (1922) is the original novel from which our adaptation is taken. This was followed by two collections of short stories; *Captain Blood Returns* and T*he Fortunes of Captain Blood*. *Blood Money*, a Captain Blood story originally published in 1921, is adapted to comics in *Adventure Classics*.

JOEL F. NAPRSTEK (cover)

Joel has been a freelance illustrator for over 25 years. His clients include NBC, CBS, Time Inc., McGraw-Hill, *Business Week*, *Financial World*, *Fortune*, and numerous ad agencies. He has painted covers for DC Comics, Marvel, Dark Horse, Pulp Adventures and other publishers. A graduate of New York's School of Visual Arts, Joel taught painting and illustration there for nine years, and currently teaches at the Joe Kubert School of Cartoon and Graphic Art in Dover, New Jersey. A car racing enthusiast, Joel paints classic auto racing scenes, as well as comics and pulp heroes like Batman, Zorro and The Spider. You can see more examples of his paintings at www.JFNStudios.net.

HUNT EMERSON (page 2)

Hunt Emerson describes himself as "a cartoonist and occasional musician." Others consider him the dean of British comics artists. He has drawn comics since the early 1970s, and has published around 30 books, including *Lady Chatterley's Lover*, *The Rime of the Ancient Mariner*, and *Casanova's Last Stand*, and his comics have been translated into ten languages. His work also appears in *Graphic Classics: Jack London*, *Graphic Classics: Bram Stoker*, *Graphic Classics: Robert Louis Stevenson* and *Adventure Classics*. Hunt says he "likes sleep, beer, and Laurel & Hardy, and dislikes artichokes, both singly and in gangs." You can see more of Hunt's cartoons, comics, fun and laffs at www.largecow.demon.co.uk.

ROD LOTT (page 4)

Based in Oklahoma City, Rod Lott is a freelance writer and graphic designer in advertising and journalism. For twelve years, he has published and edited the more-or-less quarterly magazine *Hitch: The Journal of Pop Culture Absurdity* (www.hitchmagazine.com), and recently started *Bookgasm*, a daily book review and news site at www.bookgasm.com. Rod's humorous essays have been published in several anthologies, including *May Contain Nuts* and *101 Damnations*. He has scripted comics adaptations of stories by Edgar Allan Poe, Clark Ashton Smith, Sax Rohmer, H.G. Wells and O. Henry for *Graphic Classics*, and is now scripting a new comics adaptation of *To Kill a Man* for the revised edition of *Graphic Classics: Jack London*. You can learn more about Rod's work online at www.rodlott.com.

CARLO VERGARA (pages 1, 4)

Carlo Vergara is a comics creator living in the Philippines. His gay superhero graphic novel *Ang Kagila-gilalas na Pakikipagsapalaran ni Zsazsa Zaturnnah* won a National Book Award from the Manila Critics Circle, while its musical adaptation is scheduled to run onstage in February 2006. Carlo started writing his own comics professionally in 2001 with the drama *One Night In Purgatory*, though he has been drawing comics since 1993. Primarily a graphic designer by profession, he has spent most of his career in public relations and marketing communications, and has also dabbled in acting for theater and teaching in the university classroom. His comics adaptation of *Captain Blood* marks Carlo's *Graphic Classics* debut, and his first work to be published in the U.S.

ROGER LANGRIDGE (pages 3, 58)

New Zealand-born artist Roger Langridge is the creator of Fred the Clown, whose online comics appear every Monday at www.hotel-fred.com. Fred also shows up in print three times a year in *Fred the Clown* comics. With his brother Andrew, Roger's first comics series was *Zoot!* published in 1988 and recently reissued as *Zoot Suite*. Other titles followed, including *Knuckles, The Malevolent Nun* and *Art d'Ecco*. Roger's work has also appeared in numerous magazines in Britain, the U.S., France and Japan, including *Deadline, Judge Dredd, Heavy Metal, Comic Afternoon, Gross Point* and *Batman: Legends of the Dark Knight*. For *Graphic Classics* he has adapted poems by Edgar Allan Poe and Arthur Conan Doyle, a fable by Robert Louis Stevenson, and collaborated with Mort Castle on a comics bio of Jack London. Roger now lives in London, where he divides his time between comics, children's books and commercial illustration.

MORT CASTLE (page 44)

A writing teacher and author specializing in the horror genre, Mort Castle has written and edited fourteen books and around 500 short stories and articles. His novels and collections include *Cursed Be the Child, The Strangers, Moon on the Water* and *Nations of the Living, Nations of the Dead*. He has produced an audio CD of one of his stories, *Buckeye Jim in Egypt*, and is the author of the essential reference work for aspiring horror writers, *Writing Horror*. Mort has won numerous writing awards, and he has had several dozen stories cited in "year's best" compilations in the horror, suspense, fantasy, and literary fields. He has been a writer and editor for several comics publishers, and is a frequent keynote speaker at writing conferences. Mort's comics biographies appear in *Graphic Classics: Jack London, Graphic Classics: Ambrose Bierce,* and *Graphic Classics: Robert Louis Stevenson*. He created the unique introduction to *Graphic Classics: Bram Stoker*, and co-authored an O. Henry "sequel" in *Graphic Classics: O. Henry*.

KEVIN ATKINSON (page 44)

"I've lived in Texas my whole life with the exception of 1985–1988, when I went to New Jersey to study with [famed comics artist and teacher] Joe Kubert," says Kevin. Since then he has created short stories and full-length comics for various publishers. He wrote and drew two series, *Snarl* and *Planet 29*, and collaborated on another, *Rogue Satellite Comics*. Lately he's inked *The Tick* comics, and illustrated Drew Edward's *Halloween Man, The Celebrated Jumping Frog* for *Graphic Classics: Mark Twain* and *Some Words with a Mummy* for *Horror Classics*. Kevin also illustrated *Blood Money*, a later tale of Captain Blood, for *Adventure Classics*. Visit www.meobeco.com/pulptoons/index.htm to see more of his art.

STANLEY SHAW (page 50)

Stan Shaw has been illustrating for over twenty years. His clients include *The Village Voice, Esquire, Slate,* Starbucks, Nintendo, Rhino Records, Microsoft, DC Comics, Dark Horse, ABCNEWS.com, Wizards of The Coast, *Vibe,* Hasbro, Washington Mutual, Lucas Film Licensing, *Mad, Premiere,* Penguin Books, Harcourt Brace, and *Washington Post Sunday Magazine*. His work has appeared in *How, CA, Print,* and *Covers and Jackets* by Steven Heller. Additional *Graphic Classics* stories are in the *Edgar Allan Poe, Ambrose Bierce* and *O. Henry* volumes. In addition to practicing illustration Shaw also teaches it. He has taught at Cornish School of the Arts, School of Visual Concepts, Tacoma Art Museum, Charles Wright Academy, Seattle Public Library, AIGA Design Camp, local elementary schools and several LINKS workshops, sponsored by the Seattle AIGA. He currently teaches at Pacific Lutheran University, and was part of a group of artists advising "Exploring Illustration," an in-depth guide to the art and techniques of contemporary illustration. Stan hosts an illustration blog at drawstanley.blogspot.com.

GERRY ALANGUILAN (page 68)

Gerry Alanguilan is a licensed architect who chooses to write and draw comic books. In his native Philippines he has created comics including *Timawa, Crest Hut Butt Shop, Dead Heart* and *Wasted. Wasted* has received acclaim abroad, and has been filmed in the Philippines. In America, he has contributed inks on such titles as *X-Men, Fantastic Four, Wolverine, X-Force, High Roads, Superman: Birthright,* and *Batman/Danger Girl*, working with pencillers Leinil Francis Yu and Whilce Portacio. He is currently inking *Silent Dragon* for Wildstorm Comics and is writing and illustrating *Humanis Rex!* and *Johnny Balbona*, two continuing series for magazines in the Philippines. Gerry's comics and illustrations also appear in *Graphic Classics: H.P. Lovecraft*, *Graphic Classics: Jack London*, *Graphic Classics: Bram Stoker* and *Graphic Classics: O. Henry*.

MILTON KNIGHT (*page 79, back cover*)

Milton Knight claims he started drawing, painting and creating his own attempts at comic books and animation at age two. "I've never formed a barrier between fine art and cartooning," says Milt. "Growing up, I treasured Chinese watercolors, Breughel, Charlie Brown and Terrytoons equally." His work has appeared in magazines including *Heavy Metal*, *High Times*, *National Lampoon* and *Nickelodeon Magazine*, and he has illustrated record covers, posters, candy packaging and T-shirts, and occasionally exhibited his paintings. Labor on *Ninja Turtles* comics allowed him to get up a grubstake to move to the West Coast in 1991, where he became an animator and director on *Felix the Cat* cartoons. His comics titles include *Midnite the Rebel Skunk* and *Slug and Ginger*. His adaptation of *The Fool's Love Story* features characters from his long-running series *Hugo*. Milt has contributed to the *Graphic Classics* volumes *Edgar Allan Poe*, *H.G. Wells*, *Jack London*, *Ambrose Bierce*, *Mark Twain*, *O. Henry*, *Horror Classics* and *Adventure Classics*. Check the latest news at www.miltonknight.net.

ANTONELLA CAPUTO (*page 96*)

Antonella Caputo was born and educated in Rome, and is now living in England. She has been an architect, archaeologist, art restorer, photographer, calligrapher, interior designer, theater designer, actress and theater director. Antonella's first published work was *Casa Montesi*, a weekly comic strip that appeared in *Il Journalino*. She has since written comedies for children and scripts for comics in Europe and the U.S., before joining Nick Miller as a partner in Sputnik Studios. Antonella has collaborated with Nick, as well as with artists Rick Geary, Mark A. Nelson and Francesca Ghermandi in *Graphic Classics: H.G. Wells*, *Graphic Classics: Jack London*, *Graphic Classics: Ambrose Bierce*, *Graphic Classics: O. Henry*, *Graphic Classics: Mark Twain*, *Horror Classics* and *Adventure Classics*.

JACKIE SMITH (*page 96*)

Jackie Smith comes from Sheffield, in northern England. She originally trained as an animator and has drawn comics since the late 1970s. She has been a T-shirt designer, graphic artist, Youth Arts Worker and a freelance cartoonist, writer and illustrator since 1980. Her work has appeared in *Knockabout Comics*, as well as *Graphic Classics: Ambrose Bierce*, *Graphic Classics: Mark Twain* and *Horror Classics*. Other long-term contracts have been with *Big Mags* and *Myatt McFarlane*. She also takes comics and illustration into schools and has used *Graphic Classics* in her work with excluded teenagers. Jackie enjoys drawing caricatures and portraits at fairs and occasionally sneaks off to the wild peaks to paint landscapes. Present projects include a graphic novel and a series of portraits of scary teenagers.

RICH TOMMASO (*page 110*)

Currently residing in Vermont, Rich Tomasso grew up in what he calls "one of the dullest parts of the New Jersey suburban-lands." He became a student at The Joe Kubert Art School, but quit after his first year, never being interested in a career drawing superheroes, and instead spent many years making pizza while trying to find more personal things to write and draw about. He says he has been "struggling to do a decent comic for over ten years, and after eight years at it, my recent works, *Perverso* and *8 ½ Ghosts*, make me *sometimes* think I just may accomplish this feat some day." His work (much more "decent" than Rich admits) has appeared in collections from Fantagraphics, Dark Horse, Top Shelf, Alternative Comics and Chronicle Books as well as *Graphic Classics: H.G. Wells*. He is currently working on a graphic novel about Satchel Paige with James Sturm for Hyperion Books.

TOM POMPLUN

The designer, editor and publisher of the *Graphic Classics* series, Tom previously designed and produced *Rosebud*, a journal of poetry, fiction and illustration, from 1993 to 2003. He is now working on a third revised edition of *Graphic Classics: Edgar Allan Poe*, scheduled for release in June 2006. You can find previews, sample art, and much more at www.graphicclassics.com.